Mastering QGIS

Go beyond the basics and unleash the full power of QGIS with practical, step-by-step examples

Kurt Menke, GISP

Dr. Richard Smith Jr., GISP

Dr. Luigi Pirelli

Dr. John Van Hoesen, GISP

BIRMINGHAM - MUMBAI

Mastering QGIS

First published: March 2015

Production reference: 1240315

Published by Packt Publishing Ltd.
Livery Place
35 Livery Street
Birmingham B3 2PB, UK.

ISBN 978-1-78439-868-2

www.packtpub.com

Cover image by NASA Earth Observatory

Credits

Authors
Kurt Menke, GISP
Dr. Richard Smith Jr., GISP
Dr. Luigi Pirelli
Dr. John Van Hoesen, GISP

Reviewers
Paolo Corti
Abdelghaffar Khorchani
Gergely Padányi-Gulyás

Commissioning Editor
Dipika Gaonkar

Acquisition Editors
Richard Harvey
Rebecca Youé

Content Development Editor
Samantha Gonsalves

Technical Editors
Ruchi Desai
Manal Pednekar

Copy Editors
Sonia Michelle Cheema
Jasmine Nadar

Project Coordinator
Kinjal Bari

Proofreaders
Martin Diver
Maria Gould
Elinor Perry-Smith

Indexer
Rekha Nair

Graphics
Valentina D'silva

Production Coordinator
Alwin Roy

Cover Work
Alwin Roy

Foreword

It has been my pleasure to witness the development of both this book, *Mastering QGIS*, and the QGIS software in the past 12 months. Who could have predicted the rapid development and adoption of QGIS in such a short time? QGIS is now on a par, in terms of its functionality and features, with the best of commercial GIS application software. With an aggressive code development schedule of quarterly updates, the QGIS project is adding new features faster than most GIS professionals can keep pace. To help with the dire need for professional training, this book has been created to provide you with the concise technical expertise that will serve you well, both now and in future versions of this powerful GIS software. I have enjoyed the privilege of working closely with the contributing authors of this book for the past 2 years. We have been engaged in an intense curriculum development process to create the first-ever national GIS curriculum that is based around a national standard—the U.S. Department of Labor's Geospatial Technology Competency Model (GTCM). This effort has resulted in a series of GIS courses, all based around QGIS, that provide a solid foundation upon which this book can be used to enhance your technical skills. Each of the contributing authors is a very experienced GIS professional and many of them serve as instructors for highly respected academic GIS programs. Dr. Richard (Rick) Smith, a certified GIS Professional (GISP), serves as an assistant professor for the Geographic Information Science program at Texas A&M University—Corpus Christi, Texas, USA. Rick has been onboard the curriculum effort since day one, where his expertise in GIS and cartography is highlighted. Kurt Menke is a certified GIS Professional (GISP) and operates his own GIS consulting business (Bird's Eye View GIS) in New Mexico, USA, where he teaches open source GIS software at the local college and universities. Kurt is well respected in both conservation and healthcare GIS and has completed numerous GIS projects in these disciplines. Dr. John Van Hoesen (GISP) serves as an associate professor of geology and is the Environmental Studies Community Mapping Lab Director at Green Mountain College in Vermont, USA. His passions include open source software, environmental science, and the great outdoors, where he leads students in the discovery of our natural world. Luigi Pirelli, from Spain, is a core contributor to QGIS and a contributing author of this book.

He provided us with the chapters on programming for QGIS. A huge thanks to our most capable editor, Samantha Gonsalves, for her management during the creation of this book. A former systems engineer at Infosys in Mumbai, India, and now an editor for Packt Publishing, her leadership kept the team on a tight deadline to complete *Mastering QGIS* while maintaining the highest editorial standards. For all of us, it has been a fascinating and rewarding experience and now you hold the results of our effort in your hands. Best wishes for success on *Mastering QGIS*, now and in the future!

Phillip Davis
Director, National Information Security & Geospatial Technology Consortium,
Del Mar College,
Texas, USA

About the Authors

Kurt Menke, a certified GIS Professional (GISP), has been working in the GIS field since 1997. Prior to this, he worked as a professional archaeologist for 10 years in the American Southwest. He earned a master's degree (MA) in geography from the University of New Mexico in 2000. That same year, he founded Bird's Eye View (`www.BirdsEyeViewGIS.com`) to apply his expertise with the GIS technology to the world's mounting ecological and social problems. Toward this end, Mr. Menke's work focuses largely on wildlife conservation and public health. His specialties are spatial analysis, modeling, and cartography.

He is a longtime advocate of FOSS4G. He began writing MapServer applications in 2001 and has been using QGIS since 2007. He is one of the coauthors of the curriculum at the FOSS4G Academy (`http://foss4geo.org/`) and has been teaching FOSS4G college courses since 2009. In 2014, Kurt began authoring an award-winning blog on FOSS4G technologies and their use in community health mapping (`http://communityhealthmaps.nlm.nih.gov/`).

A special thanks goes to Phil Davis for his leadership in the development of the FOSS4G Academy and for his continuing efforts to promote FOSS4G in the U.S. educational system. I would like to thank Rick Smith for being such a joy to work with. I'd also like to acknowledge Karl Benedict for introducing me to the world of FOSS4G and Jeffery Cavner for his ongoing camaraderie. Finally, I'd like to thank my beautiful wife, Sarah, for her steady support and encouragement.

Dr. Richard Smith Jr., is an assistant professor of geographic information science at the School of Engineering and Computing Sciences at Texas A&M University Corpus Christi. He has a PhD in geography from the University of Georgia and holds a master of science in computer science and a bachelor of science in geographic information science degree from Texas A&M University Corpus Christi. Richard actively does research in cartography, systems integration, and the use of geospatial technology for disaster response. Richard is an advocate of FOSS4G and building FOSS4G curriculum. He is one of the coauthors of the FOSS4G Academy (`http://foss4geo.org`).

Richard has collaborated with other writers in his field, but *Mastering QGIS* is his first book.

I would like to thank my wife and daughter for putting up with my late-night and weekend writing sessions. I would also like to thank my coauthor Kurt Menke for being patient with my edits. I would especially like to thank the editorial team; you have made my first book-writing experience an excellent one.

Outside those directly involved or affected by the writing of this book, I'd like to thank my academic and life mentors, Dr. Stacey Lyle, Dr. Thomas Hodler, Dr. Gary Jeffress, and Dr. Robin Murphy, for providing their support and good wishes as I begin my career. In addition to teaching me, you have inspired me to have the confidence to teach and write. To those of you reading this, I hope I do my mentors justice by providing a clear and useful text to assist you in mastering QGIS.

Dr. Luigi Pirelli is a freelance software analyst and developer with an honors degree in computer science from the University of Bari. He worked for 15 years in Satellite Ground Segment and Direct Ingestion for the European Space Agency. Since 2006, he has been involved with the GFOSS world, contributing to QGIS, GRASS, and MapServer core and developing and maintaining many QGIS plugins. He actively participates in QGIS Hackmeetings. He is the founder of the OSGEO Italian Local Chapter (`http://gfoss.it/drupal/`) and now lives in Spain and contributes to this GFOSS community. During the last few years, he started teaching PyQGIS by organizing trainings from basic to advanced levels and supporting companies to develop their specific QGIS plugins.

He is the founder of the local hackerspace group Bricolabs.cc that is focused on Open Hardware. He likes cycling, repairing everything, and trainings groups on conflict resolution. Besides this book, he has also contributed to *Lonely Planet Cycling Italy*.

A special thanks to the QGIS developer community and core developers as the project is managed in a really open way by allowing contributions from everyone.

I want to thank everyone with whom I have worked. I learned from each of them, and without them, I wouldn't be here giving my contribution to free software and to this book.

A special thanks to my friends and neighbors who helped me with my son during the writing of this book.

I would like to dedicate this book to my partner and especially to my son for his patience when he used to see me sitting in front of a computer for hours instead of playing with him.

Dr. John Van Hoesen is an associate professor of geology and environmental studies at Green Mountain College in rural west-central Vermont. He earned an MS in 2000 and a PhD in geology from the University of Nevada, Las Vegas, in 2003. He is a certified GIS Professional (GISP) with a broad background in geosciences and has been using some flavor of GIS to evaluate and explore geologic processes and environmental issues since 1997. He has used and taught some variant of FOSS GIS since 2003, and over the last 3 years, he has taught graduate, undergraduate, and continuing education courses using only FOSS GIS software.

About the Reviewers

Paolo Corti is an environmental engineer based in Rome, Italy. He has more than 15 years of experience in the GIS field; after working with proprietary solutions for some years, he proudly switched to open source technologies and Python almost a decade ago.

He has been working as a software architect, developer, and analyst for organizations such as the United Nations World Food Programme, the European Commission Joint Research Centre, and the Italian Government.

Currently, he is working within the GeoNode project, for which he is the core developer, in the context of emergency preparedness and response.

He is an OSGeo charter member and a member of the pyCSW and GeoNode Project Steering committees. He is the coauthor of *PostGIS Cookbook* by *Packt Publishing*, and he writes a popular blog on open source geospatial technologies at `http://www.paolocorti.net`.

Abdelghaffar Khorchani has a license degree in geographic information systems, a fundamental license in natural science applied in biology and geology, and a master's degree in geomatics and planning. He is also a computer engineer. Currently, he is pursuing his master's degree in planning and regional development (University of Laval—Canada) and his PhD in marine sciences (University of Milano-Biccoca - Italy).

He has prepared courses in Japan on fishery resource management approaches for young leaders and in Spain in the field use of geographic information systems for scheduling and management. He has also prepared other training modules in Tunisia on urban administration.

He has 8 years of experience in the geomatics field and has worked on several projects in the agriculture sector, environment, transport, and mapping.

Currently, he is in the Ministry of Agriculture in Tunisia and is responsible for the mapping service for project VMS (short for Vessel Monitoring System).

He is also a trainer in the mapping field of Geographic Information System, GPS, and CAD. He is particularly interested in the development of decision support tools.

A special thanks to Packt Publishing for this opportunity to participate in the review of this book. I thank my family, especially my parents, for their physical and moral support. Finally, I want to thank Cheima Ayachi, who helped me a lot when I was reviewing this book.

Gergely Padányi-Gulyás is a GIS and web developer and remote sensing analyst with over 7 years of experience. He specializes in designing and developing web mapping applications and Geographic Information Systems (GIS). He is a dedicated user/developer of open source software, and he is also an active member of the OSGeo local chapter. He is familiar both with client- and server-side programming.

For more than 4 years, he worked for archaeologists as a GIS engineer and remote sensing analyst where he contributed to laying the foundation of the Hungarian Archaeological predictive modelling. After that, he became a Java web developer for a private company. Since then, he has been working at a state nonprofit corporation as a GIS and web developer where he uses the skills he learned from his previous jobs: combining GIS with development. During the past few years, he has been involved with plugin development in different programming languages such as Java for GeoServer and Python for QGIS.

He has a website (`www.gpadanyig.com`).

www.PacktPub.com

Support files, eBooks, discount offers, and more

For support files and downloads related to your book, please visit www.PacktPub.com.

Did you know that Packt offers eBook versions of every book published, with PDF and ePub files available? You can upgrade to the eBook version at www.PacktPub.com and as a print book customer, you are entitled to a discount on the eBook copy. Get in touch with us at service@packtpub.com for more details.

At www.PacktPub.com, you can also read a collection of free technical articles, sign up for a range of free newsletters and receive exclusive discounts and offers on Packt books and eBooks.

https://www2.packtpub.com/books/subscription/packtlib

Do you need instant solutions to your IT questions? PacktLib is Packt's online digital book library. Here, you can search, access, and read Packt's entire library of books.

Why subscribe?

- Fully searchable across every book published by Packt
- Copy and paste, print, and bookmark content
- On demand and accessible via a web browser

Free access for Packt account holders

If you have an account with Packt at www.PacktPub.com, you can use this to access PacktLib today and view nine entirely free books. Simply use your login credentials for immediate access.

Table of Contents

Preface

Welcome to *Mastering QGIS*. The goal of this book is to help intermediate and advanced users of GIS develop a deep understanding of the capabilities of QGIS while building the technical skills that would facilitate in making the shift from a proprietary GIS software package to QGIS.

QGIS embodies the open source community's spirit. It seamlessly works with other free and open source geospatial software, such as SAGA, GDAL, GRASS, and fTools, and supports standards and formats that are published by myriad organizations. QGIS is about freedom in the geospatial world: freedom to choose your operating system, freedom from licensing fees, freedom to customize, freedom to look under the hood, and freedom to contribute to the development of QGIS. As you work through this book, we believe that you will be amazed at how much capability and freedom QGIS provides.

QGIS has rapidly risen from the initial version written by Gary Sherman in 2002 to become a globally used and developed volunteer-led project. In 2009, QGIS version 1.0 was released as an Open Source Geospatial Foundation (OSGeo) project and continues to be rapidly adopted worldwide. The enduring support of the open source community has really delivered QGIS to a point where it is now a top-shelf product that should be in all GIS users' toolboxes, and we want this book to be your tour guide and reference as you learn, use, and contribute to QGIS.

What this book covers

Chapter 1, A Refreshing Look at QGIS, reviews the installation and basic functionality of QGIS that will be the assumed knowledge for the remainder of the book.

Chapter 2, Creating Spatial Databases, covers how to create and edit spatial databases using QGIS. While QGIS supports many spatial databases, SpatiaLite will be used in this chapter. First, core database concepts will be covered, followed by the creation of a spatial database. Next, importing, exporting, and editing data will be covered. The chapter will conclude with queries and view creation.

Chapter 3, Styling Raster and Vector Data, covers styling raster and vector data for display. First, color selection and color ramp management are covered. Next, singleband and multiband raster data are styled using custom color ramps and blending modes. Next, complex vector styles and vector layer rendering are covered. Rounding out the chapter is the use of diagrams to display thematic map data.

Chapter 4, Preparing Vector Data for Processing, covers techniques useful for turning raw vector data into a more usable form. The chapter will start with data massaging and modification techniques such as merging, creating indices, checking for geometry errors, and basic geoprocessing tools. Next, advanced field calculations will be covered, followed by complex spatial and aspatial queries. The chapter will end by defining new or editing existing coordinate reference systems.

Chapter 5, Preparing Raster Data for Processing, covers the preparation of raster data for further processing using the GDAL menu tools and the Processing Toolbox algorithms. Specifically, these include reclassification, resampling, rescaling, mosaics, generating pyramids, and interpolation. The chapter will conclude by converting raster to vector.

Chapter 6, Advanced Data Creation and Editing, provides advanced ways to create vector data. As there is a great deal of data in tabular format, this chapter will cover mapping coordinates and addresses from tables. Next, georeferencing of imagery into a target coordinate reference system will be covered. The final portion of the chapter will cover testing topological relationships in vector data and correcting any errors via topological editing.

Chapter 7, The Processing Toolbox, begins with an explanation and exploration of the QGIS Processing Toolbox. Various algorithms and tools, available in the toolbox, will be used to complete common spatial analyses and geoprocessing tasks for both raster and vector formats. To illustrate how these processing tools might be applied to real-world questions, two hypothetical scenarios are illustrated by relying heavily on GRASS and SAGA tools.

Chapter 8, Automating Workflows with the Graphical Modeler, covers the purpose and use of the graphical modeler to automate analysis workflows. In the chapter, you will develop an automated tool/model that can be added to the Processing Toolbox.

Chapter 9, Creating QGIS Plugins with PyQGIS and Problem Solving, covers the foundational information to create a Python plugin for QGIS. Information about the API and PyQGIS help will be covered first, followed by an introduction to the iface and QGis classes. Next, the steps required to create and structure a plugin will be covered. The chapter will be wrapped up after providing you with information on creating graphical user interfaces and setting up debugging environments to debug code easily.

Chapter 10, PyQGIS Scripting, provides topics for integrating Python analysis scripts with QGIS outside of the Processing Toolbox. Layer loading and management are first covered, followed by an exploration of the vector data structure. Next, programmatic launching of other tools and external programs are covered. Lastly, the QGIS map canvas is covered with respect to how a script can interact with the map canvas and layers within.

What you need for this book

To get the most from this book, it is recommended that you install QGIS and follow the explanations. If you choose to do so, you will need a reasonably modern computer with access to the Internet to download and install QGIS, read documentation, and install plugins. QGIS can run on Windows, Mac OS X, and many Linux distributions.

Who this book is for

This book is for intermediate to advanced GIS users, developers, and consultants who are familiar with QGIS but want to look deeper into the software to unleash its full potential. The reader is expected to be comfortable with common GIS functions and concepts, as possession of this knowledge is assumed throughout the book. This book focuses on how to use QGIS and its functions beyond the basics.

Conventions

In this book, you will find a number of styles of text that distinguish between different kinds of information. Here are some examples of these styles, and an explanation of their meaning.

Code words in text, database table names, folder names, filenames, file extensions, pathnames, dummy URLs, and user input are shown as follows: "Type a comma after `$now`, and enter `'dd/MM/yyyy'` followed by a close parenthesis."

A block of code is set as follows:

```
CASE
WHEN "POP1996" > 5000000 THEN
  Result
ELSE
  "STATE_NAME"
END
```

When we wish to draw your attention to a particular part of a code block, the relevant lines or items are set in bold:

```
CASE
WHEN "POP1996" > 5000000 THEN
  Result
ELSE
  "STATE_NAME"
END
```

Any command-line input or output is written as follows:

```
sudo apt-get install qgis-plugin-grass
```

New terms and **important words** are shown in bold. Words that you see on the screen, in menus or dialog boxes for example, appear in the text like this: "You can explore the QGIS plugin ecosystem by navigating to **Plugins** | **Manage and Install Plugins**."

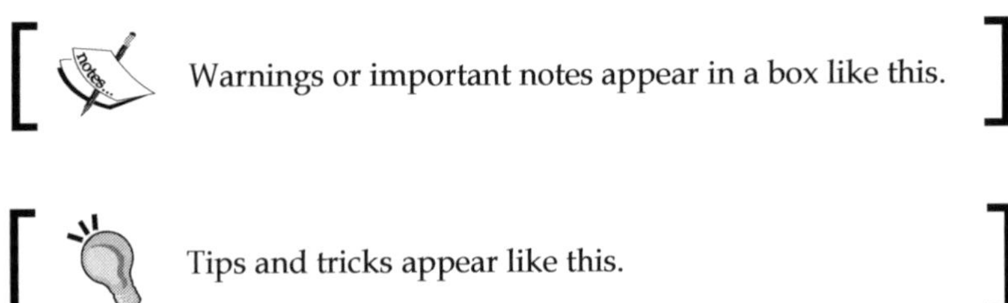

Warnings or important notes appear in a box like this.

Tips and tricks appear like this.

Reader feedback

Feedback from our readers is always welcome. Let us know what you think about this book—what you liked or disliked. Reader feedback is important for us as it helps us develop titles that you will really get the most out of.

To send us general feedback, simply e-mail `feedback@packtpub.com`, and mention the book's title in the subject of your message.

If there is a topic that you have expertise in and you are interested in either writing or contributing to a book, see our author guide at `www.packtpub.com/authors`.

Customer support

Now that you are the proud owner of a Packt book, we have a number of things to help you to get the most from your purchase.

Downloading the example code

You can download the example code files from your account at `http://www.packtpub.com` for all the Packt Publishing books you have purchased. If you purchased this book elsewhere, you can visit `http://www.packtpub.com/support` and register to have the files e-mailed directly to you.

Downloading the color images of this book

We also provide you with a PDF file that has color images of the screenshots/diagrams used in this book. The color images will help you better understand the changes in the output. You can download this file from `https://www.packtpub.com/sites/default/files/downloads/8682OS_ImageBundle.pdf`.

Errata

Although we have taken every care to ensure the accuracy of our content, mistakes do happen. If you find a mistake in one of our books—maybe a mistake in the text or the code—we would be grateful if you could report this to us. By doing so, you can save other readers from frustration and help us improve subsequent versions of this book. If you find any errata, please report them by visiting `http://www.packtpub.com/submit-errata`, selecting your book, clicking on the **Errata Submission Form** link, and entering the details of your errata. Once your errata are verified, your submission will be accepted and the errata will be uploaded to our website or added to any list of existing errata under the Errata section of that title.

To view the previously submitted errata, go to `https://www.packtpub.com/books/content/support` and enter the name of the book in the search field. The required information will appear under the **Errata** section.

Piracy

Piracy of copyrighted material on the Internet is an ongoing problem across all media. At Packt, we take the protection of our copyright and licenses very seriously. If you come across any illegal copies of our works in any form on the Internet, please provide us with the location address or website name immediately so that we can pursue a remedy.

Please contact us at `copyright@packtpub.com` with a link to the suspected pirated material.

We appreciate your help in protecting our authors and our ability to bring you valuable content.

Questions

If you have a problem with any aspect of this book, you can contact us at `questions@packtpub.com`, and we will do our best to address the problem.

1
A Refreshing Look at QGIS

QGIS is a volunteer-led development project licensed under the GNU General Public License. It was started by Gary Sherman in 2002. The project was incubated with the **Open Source Geospatial Foundation (OSGeo)** in 2007. Version 1.0 was released in 2009. At the time of writing this book, QGIS 2.6 was the stable version and new versions are released every four months.

In this chapter we will review the basic functionality of QGIS, which will be assumed knowledge for the remaining chapters in this book. If you need a refresher on QGIS or a quick-start guide to QGIS, you should read this chapter. The topics we will cover in this chapter are as follows:

- Downloading QGIS and its installation
- The QGIS graphical user interface
- Loading data
- Working with coordinate reference systems
- Working with tables
- Editing data
- Styling data
- Composing a map
- Finding and installing plugins

QGIS download and installation

QGIS can be installed on Windows, Mac OS X, Unix, Linux, and Android operating systems, making it a very flexible software package. Both the binary installers and source code can be downloaded from `download.qgis.org`. In this section, we will briefly cover how to install QGIS on Windows, Mac OS X, and Ubuntu Linux. For the most up-to-date installation instructions, refer to the QGIS website.

Installing QGIS on Windows

For Windows, there are two installation options, which are as follows:

- **QGIS Standalone Installer**: The standalone installer installs the binary version of QGIS and the **Geographic Resource Analysis Support System (GRASS)** using a standard Windows installation tool. You should choose this option if you want an easy installation experience of QGIS.
- **OSGeo4W Network Installer**: This provides you with the opportunity to download either the binary or source code version of QGIS, as well as experimental releases of QGIS. Additionally, the OSGeo4W installer allows you to install other open source tools and their dependencies.

Installing QGIS on Mac OS X

To install QGIS on Mac OS X, the **Geospatial Data Abstraction Library (GDAL)** framework and matplotlib Python module must be installed first, followed by the QGIS installation. The installation files for GDAL, matplotlib, and QGIS are available at `http://www.kyngchaos.com/software/qgis`.

Installing QGIS on Ubuntu Linux

There are two options when installing QGIS on Ubuntu: installing QGIS only, or installing QGIS as well as other FOSSGIS packages. Either of these methods requires the use of the command line, sudo rights, and the apt-get package manager.

Installing QGIS only

Depending on whether you want to install a stable release or an experimental release, you will need to add the appropriate repository to the `/etc/apt/sources.list` file.

With sudo access, edit `/etc/apt/sources.list` and add the following line to install the current stable release or current release's source code respectively:

```
deb         http://qgis.org/debian trusty main
deb-src     http://qgis.org.debian trusty main
```

Depending on the release version of Ubuntu you are using, you will need to specify the release name as `trusty`, `saucy`, or `precise`. For the latest list of QGIS releases for Ubuntu versions, visit `download.qgis.org`.

With the appropriate repository added, you can proceed with the QGIS installation by running the following commands:

```
sudo apt-get update
sudo apt-get install qgis python-qgis
```

To install the GRASS plugin (recommended), install the optional package by running this command:

```
sudo apt-get install qgis-plugin-grass
```

Installing QGIS and other FOSSGIS Packages

The `ubuntugis` project installs QGIS and other FOSSGIS packages, such as GRASS on Ubuntu. To install the `ubuntugis` package, remove the `http://qgis.org/debian` lines from the `/etc/apt/sources.list` file, and run the following commands:

```
sudo apt-get install python-software-properties
sudo add-apt-repository ppa:ubuntugis/ubuntugis-unstable
sudo apt-get update
sudo apt-get install qgis python-qgis qgis-plugin-grass
```

> QGIS is also available for Android. We have not provided detailed installation instructions because it is in alpha testing at the moment. However, there are plans to have a normalized installation process in a future release. You can find more information about this at `http://hub.qgis.org/projects/android-qgis`.
>
> The download page is available at `http://qgis.org/downloads/android/`.
>
> A related app has recently been announced and it is named QField for QGIS. For a short time, it was named QGIS Mobile. It is described as a field data capture and management app that is compatible with QGIS. At the time of writing this, it was in invite-only alpha testing. It is eventually expected to be available in the Android Play Store. You can find more information on this app at `http://www.opengis.ch/tech-blog/`.

Tour of QGIS

QGIS is composed of two programs: QGIS Desktop and QGIS Browser. Desktop is used for managing, displaying, analyzing, and styling data. Browser is used to manage and preview data. This section will give you a brief tour of the graphical user interface components of both QGIS Desktop and QGIS Browser.

QGIS Desktop

The QGIS interface is divided into four interface types: **menu bar**, **toolbars**, **panels**, and **map display**. The following screenshot shows QGIS Desktop with all four interface types displayed:

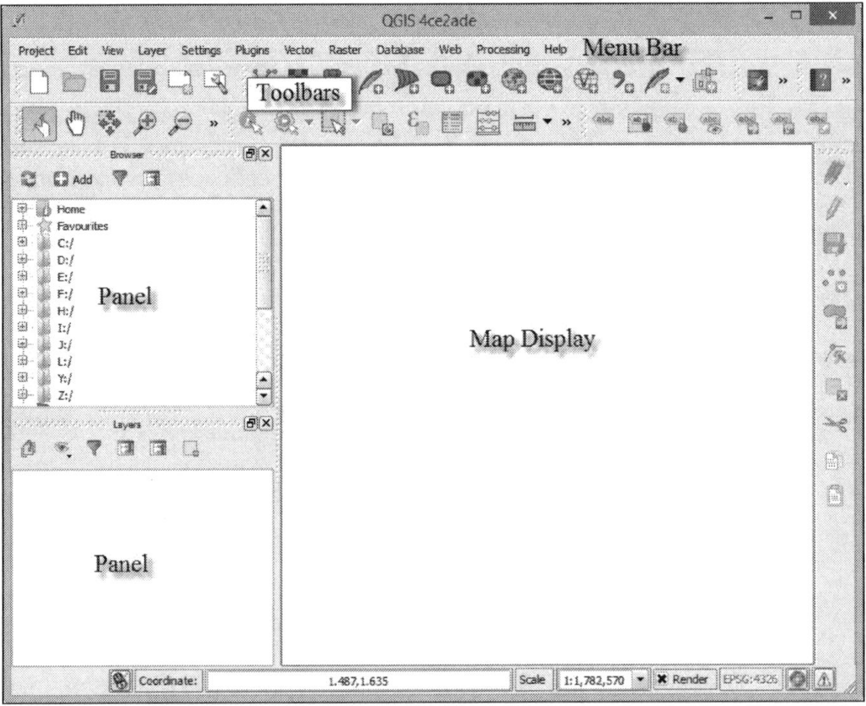

The map display shows the styled data added to the QGIS project and, by default, takes up the majority of the space in QGIS Desktop. The menu bar, displayed across the top, provides access to most of QGIS Desktop's functionality. The toolbars provide quick access to QGIS Desktop functionality. The toolbars can be arranged to either float independently or dock at the top, bottom, left, or right sides of the application. The panels, such as **Browser** and **Layers**, provide a variety of functionality and can be arranged to either float independently or dock above, below, right, or left of the map display.

There are four toolbars that are particularly useful, and it is recommended that you enable them:

- The File toolbar provides quick access to create, open, and save QGIS projects and create and manage print composers
- The Manage Layers toolbar contains tools to add vector, raster, database, web service, text layers, and create new layers
- The Map Navigation toolbar contains tools that are useful for panning, zooming, and refreshing the map display
- The Attributes toolbar provides access to information, selection, field calculator, measuring, bookmarking, and annotation tools

QGIS Desktop offers a number of customization options. You can toggle the visibility of toolbars by navigating to **View** | **Toolbars**, or by right-clicking on the menu bar or the enabled toolbar button, which will open a context menu allowing you to toggle the toolbar and panel visibility. You can assign shortcut keys to operations by navigating to **Settings** | **Configure shortcuts**. You can also change application options, such as interface language and rendering options by navigating to **Settings** | **Options**.

QGIS Browser

The QGIS Browser interface (shown in the following screenshot) is composed of three parts: toolbar, data tree view, and information panel.

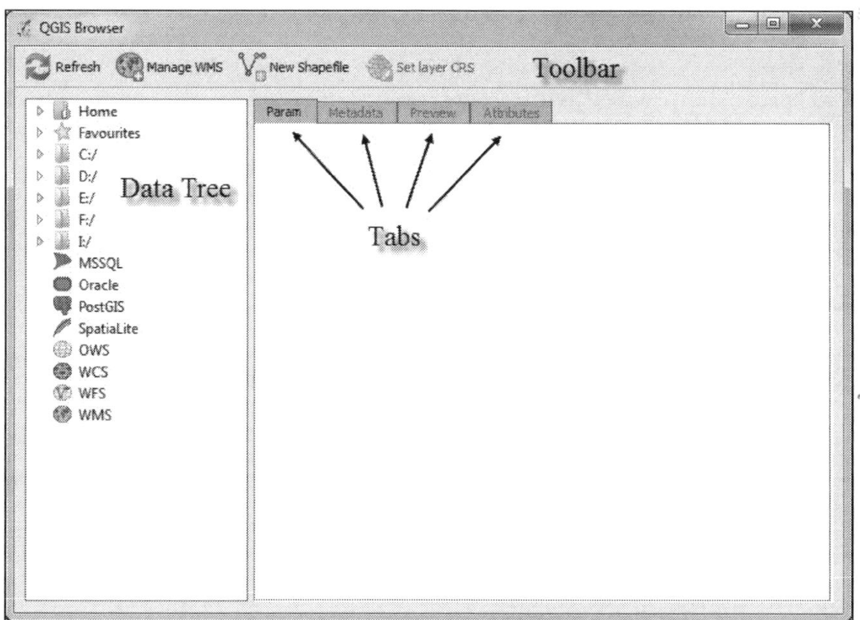

The data tree view is an expandable tree listing of all geospatial data files on your computer and through connections. The information display, which takes most of the space on the application, contains four tabs that provide different views of the selected data in the data tree listing, and they are as follows:

- **Param**: This tab displays details of data that is accessed through connections, such as a database or WMS.
- **Metadata**: This tab displays the metadata (if any) of the selected data.
- **Preview**: This tab renders the selected data. You can zoom into the data using your mouse wheel and pan using the arrow keys on your keyboard.
- **Attribute**: This tab displays the attribute table associated with the selected data. You can sort the columns by clicking on the column headings.

The toolbar provides access to four functions. The **Refresh** function reloads the data tree view while the **Manage WMS** function opens the WMS management screen allowing you to manage the WMS connections. The **New Shapefile** function opens the new vector layer dialog allowing new shapefiles to be created. Finally, the **Set layer CRS** function allows you to define the coordinate reference system of the geospatial data file that is selected in the data tree view.

Loading data

One strength of QGIS is its ability to load a large number of data types. In this section, we will cover loading various types of data into QGIS Desktop.

In general, data can be loaded in four ways. The first way, which will be covered in detail in this section, is to use the **Add Layer** menu under **Layer** and select the appropriate type of data that you wish to load. The second way is to open the **Browser** panel, navigate to the data you wish to load, and then drag the data onto the map display or onto the **Layers** panel. The third way to load data is to enable the **Manage Layers** toolbar and click on the button representing the data type that you wish to load. The fourth way is to locate the data in QGIS Browser, drag the data, and drop it onto the QGIS Desktop map display or the **Layers** panel.

Loading vector data

To load vector files, click on **Add Vector Layer** by navigating to **Layer** | **Add Layer**. This will open the **Add Vector Layer** dialog that will allow us to choose the source type and source of the dataset that we wish to load.

The source type contains four options: **File**, **Directory**, **Database**, and **Protocol**. When you choose a source type, the source interface will change to display the appropriate options. Let's take a moment to discuss what type of data these four source types can load:

- **File**: This can load flat files that are stored on disk. The commonly used flat file types are as follows:
    - ESRI shapefile (`.shp`)
    - AutoCAD DXF (`.dxf`)
    - Comma separated values (`.csv`)
    - GPS eXchange Format (`.gpx`)
    - Keyhole Markup Language (`.kml`)
    - SQLite/SpatiaLite (`.sqlite`/`.db`)
- **Directory**: This can load data stored on disk that is encased in a directory. The commonly used directory types are as follows:
    - U.S. Census TIGER/Line
    - Arc/Info Binary Coverage
- **Database**: This can load databases that are stored on disk or those available through service connections. The commonly used database types are as follows:
    - ODBC
    - ESRI Personal GeoDatabase
    - MSSQL
    - MySQL
    - PostgreSQL
- **Protocol**: This can load protocols that are available at a specific URI. QGIS currently supports loading the GeoJSON protocol.

Loading raster data

To load raster data into QGIS, click on **Add Raster Layer** by navigating to **Layer | Add Layer**. This will open a file browser window and allow you to choose a GDAL-supported raster file. The commonly used raster types supported by GDAL are as follows:

- ArcInfo ASCII Grid (`.asc`)
- Erdas Imagine (`.img`)

- GeoTIFF (`.tif`/`.tiff`)
- JPEG/JPEG-2000 (`.jpg` or `.jpeg`/`.jp2` or `.j2k`)
- Portable Network Graphics (`.png`)
- Rasterlite (`.sqlite`)
- USGS Optional ASCII DEM (`.dem`)

To add an Oracle GeoRaster, click on **Add Oracle GeoRaster Layer** by navigating to **Layer** | **Add Layer**, then connect to an Oracle database to load the raster. More information about loading database layers is in the following section.

The **Geospatial Data Abstraction Library** (**GDAL**) is a free and open source library that translates and processes vector and raster geospatial data formats. QGIS, as well as many other programs, use GDAL to handle many geospatial data processing tasks.

You may see references to OGR or GDAL/OGR as you work with QGIS and GDAL. OGR is short for OGR Simple Features Library and references the vector processing parts of GDAL. OGR is not really a standalone project, as it is part of the GDAL code now; however, for historical reasons, OGR is still used.

More information about GDAL and OGR can be found at `http://gdal.org`. GDAL is an Open Source Geospatial Foundation (`http://osgeo.org`) project.

Loading databases

QGIS supports PostGIS, SpatiaLite, MSSQL, and Oracle databases. Regardless of the type of database you wish to load, the loading sequence is very similar. Therefore, instead of covering specific examples, the general sequence will be covered.

First, click on **Add Layer** under **Layer** and then choose the database type you wish to load. This will open a window with options for adding the data stored in a database. As an example, the following screenshot shows the window that opens when you navigate to **Layer** | **Add Layer** | **Add SpatiaLite Layer**:

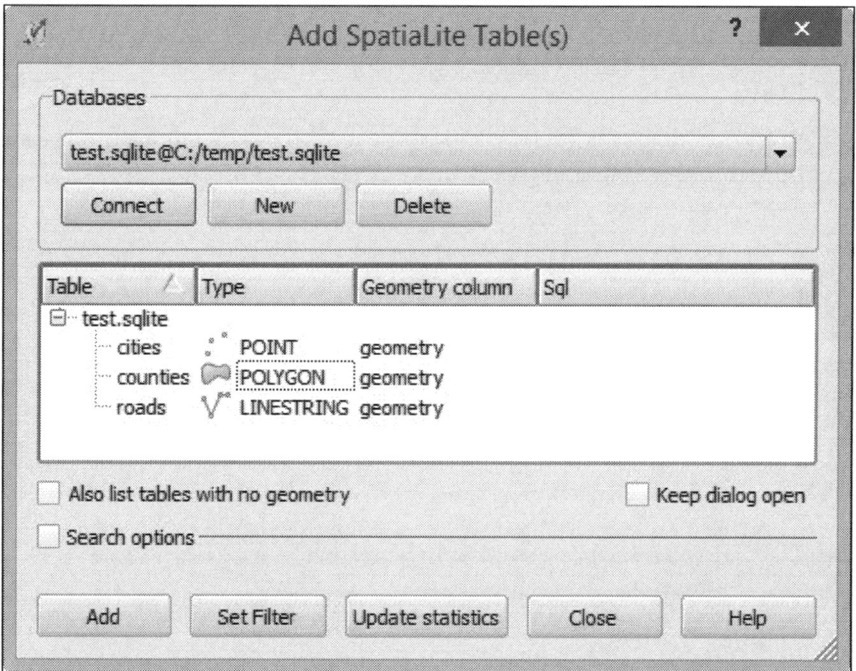

Note that the window will look the same for any database you choose, except for the window name.

To load data from a database, we must first create a connection to the database. To create a new connection, click on the **New** button to open a connection information window. Depending on the database type you are connecting to, different connection options will be shown. Once you have created a database connection, select it from the drop-down list and click on **Connect**; you will see a list of all layers contained within the database display. If there are a large number of tables, you can select **Search options** and perform a search on the database. To load a layer, select it in the list and click on **Add**. If you only wish to load a portion of the layer, select the layer and then click on **Set Filter** to open the query builder. If you set a query and then add the layer, only the filtered features will be added.

Web services

QGIS supports the loading of OGC-compliant web services such as WMS/WMTS, WCS, and WFS. Loading a web service is similar to loading a database service. In general, you will create a new server connection, connect to the server to list the available services, and add the service to the QGIS project.

Working with coordinate reference systems

When working with spatial data, it is important that a **coordinate reference system** (**CRS**) is assigned to the data and the QGIS project. To view the CRS for the QGIS project, click on **Project Properties** under **Project** and choose the **CRS** tab.

It is recommended that all data added to a QGIS project be projected into the same CRS as the QGIS project. However, if this is not possible or convenient, QGIS can project layers "on the fly" to the project's CRS.

If you want to quickly search for a CRS, you can enter the EPSG code to quickly filter through the CRS list. An EPSG code refers to a specific CRS stored in the EPSG Geodetic Parameter Dataset online registry that contains numerous global, regional, and local CRS. An example of a commonly used EPSG code is `4326` that refers to WGS 84. The EPSG online registry is available at `http://www.epsg-registry.org/`.

To enable the "on the fly" projection, perform the following steps:

1. Click on **Project Properties** under **Project**.
2. Choose the **CRS** tab and **Enable 'on the fly' CRS transformation**.
3. Set the CRS that you wish to apply to the project and make all layers that are not set to the project's CRS transform "on the fly".

To view the CRS for a layer, perform the following steps:

1. Open the layer's properties by either navigating to **Layer** | **Properties** or by right-clicking on the layer in the **Layers** panel.
2. Choose **Properties** from the context menu and then choose the **General** tab.
3. If the layer's CRS is not set or is incorrect, click on **Specify** to open the CRS selector window and select the correct CRS.

To project a layer to a different CRS, perform the following steps:

1. Right-click on the layer in the **Layers** panel and then choose **Save As** from the context menu.
2. In the **Save vector layer as** dialog, set the file format and filename, then set **CRS** to **Selected CRS** and click on **Change** to set the target CRS, and save the file.

To create a new CRS or modify an existing CRS, perform the following steps:

1. Click on **Custom CRS** under **Settings** to open the **Custom Coordinate Reference System Definition** window.
2. Click on the **Add new CRS** button to add a new entry to the CRS list.
3. With the new CRS selected, we can set the name and parameters of the CRS. The CRS properties are set using the Proj.4 format. To modify an existing CRS, click on **Copy existing CRS** and select the CRS from which you wish to copy parameters; otherwise, enter the parameters manually.

Proj.4 is another Open Source Geospatial Foundation (`http://osgeo.org`) project used by QGIS, and it is similar to OGR and GDAL. This project is for managing coordinate systems and projections. For a detailed user manual for the Proj.4 format used to specify the CRS parameters in QGIS, download it from `ftp://ftp.remotesensing.org/proj/OF90-284.pdf`.

Working with tables

There are two types of tables you can work with in QGIS: attribute tables and standalone tables. Whether they are from a database or associated with a shapefile or a flat file, they are all treated the same. Standalone tables can be added by clicking on the **Add Vector Layer** menu by navigating to **Layer | Add Layer**. QGIS supports the table formats supported by OGR along with database tables. Tables are treated like any other GIS layer; they simply have no geometry. Both types of tables can be opened within Desktop by selecting the layer/table in the **Layers** panel, and then by either clicking on **Open Attribute Table** under **Layer** or by right-clicking on the data layer, and choosing **Open Attribute Table** from the context menu. They can also be previewed in Browser by choosing the **Attribute** tab.

The table opens in a new window that displays the number of table rows and selected records in the title bar. Below the title bar are a series of buttons that allow you to toggle between editing, managing selections, and adding and deleting columns. Most of the window is filled with the table body. The table can be sorted by clicking on the column names. An arrow will appear in the column header, indicating either an ascending or a descending sort. Rows can be selected by clicking on the row number on the left-hand side. In the lower-left corner is a **Tables** menu that allows you to manage what portions of the table should be displayed. You can choose **Show All Features** (default setting), **Show Selected Features**, **Show Features Visible on Map** (only available when you view an attribute table), **Show Edited and New Features**, create column filters, and advanced filters (expression). The lower-right corner has a toggle between the default table view and a forms view of the table.

Attribute tables are associated with the features of a GIS layer. Typically, one record in the attribute table corresponds to one feature in the GIS layer. The exception to this is multipart features, which have multiple geometries linked to a single record in the attribute table. Standalone tables are not associated with GIS data layers. However, they may have data of a spatial nature from which a spatial data layer can be generated (for more information, see *Chapter 6, Advanced Data Creation and Editing*. They may also contain data that you wish to join to an existing attribute table with a table join.

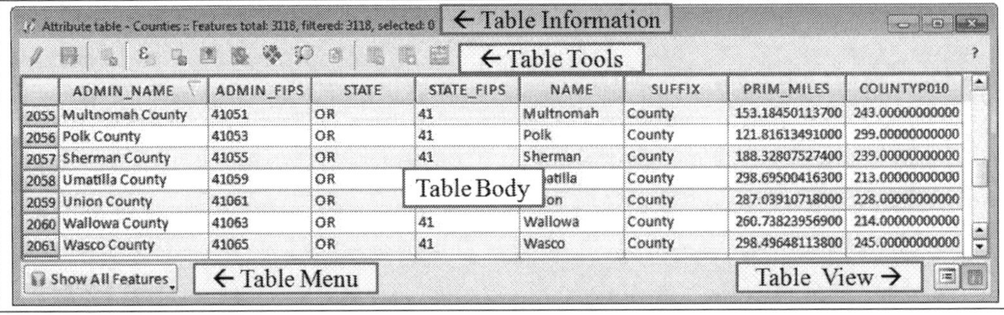

Table joins

Let's say that you need to make a map of the total population by county. However, the counties' GIS layer does not have population as an attribute. Instead, this data is contained in an Excel spreadsheet. It is possible to join additional tabular data to an existing attribute table.

There are two requirements, which are as follows:

- The two tables need to share fields with attributes to match for joining
- There needs to be a cardinality of one-to-one or many-to-one between the attribute table and the standalone table

To create a join, load both the GIS layer and the standalone table into QGIS Desktop. QGIS will accept a variety of standalone table file formats including Excel spreadsheets, `.dbf` files, and comma delimited text files. You can load this tabular data using the **Add Vector Layer** menu by navigating to **Layer** | **Add Layer** and setting the file type filter to All files (*) (*.*) as shown in the following screenshot:

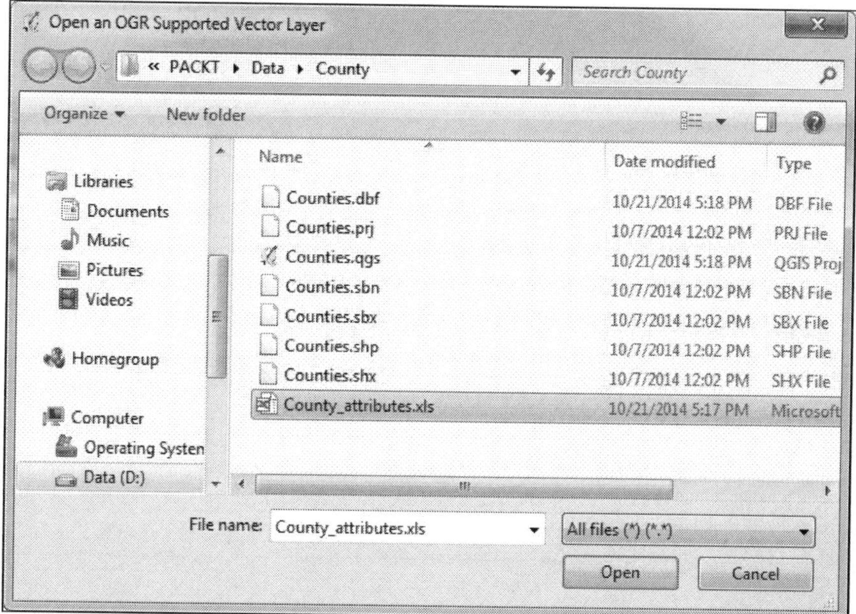

Once the data is loaded, a join can be completed by following these steps:

1. Select the GIS layer in the **Layers** panel that will receive the new data from the join.
2. Navigate to **Layer** | **Properties** and choose the **Joins** menu.
3. Click on the add join button (the one with green plus sign).
4. Choose the **Join Layer**, **Join Field**, and **Target Field** values. The **Join Layer** and **Join Field** values represent the standalone table. The **Target Field** value is the column in the attribute table on which the join will be based.

> Although in this example the join field and the target field have the same name, this is not a requirement. The two fields merely need to hold the same unique ID.

5. At this point, you can choose **Cache the join in virtual memory**, **Create attribute index on the join field**, and **Choose which fields are joined**. The last option lets you to choose which fields from the join layer to append to the attribute table. At this point, the **Add vector join** window will look like the following screenshot.
6. Once created, the join will be listed on the **Joins** tab. The extra attribute columns from the join layer will be appended to the attribute table, where the value in the join field matched the value in the target field.

7. Joins can be removed by clicking on the remove join button (the one with red minus sign).

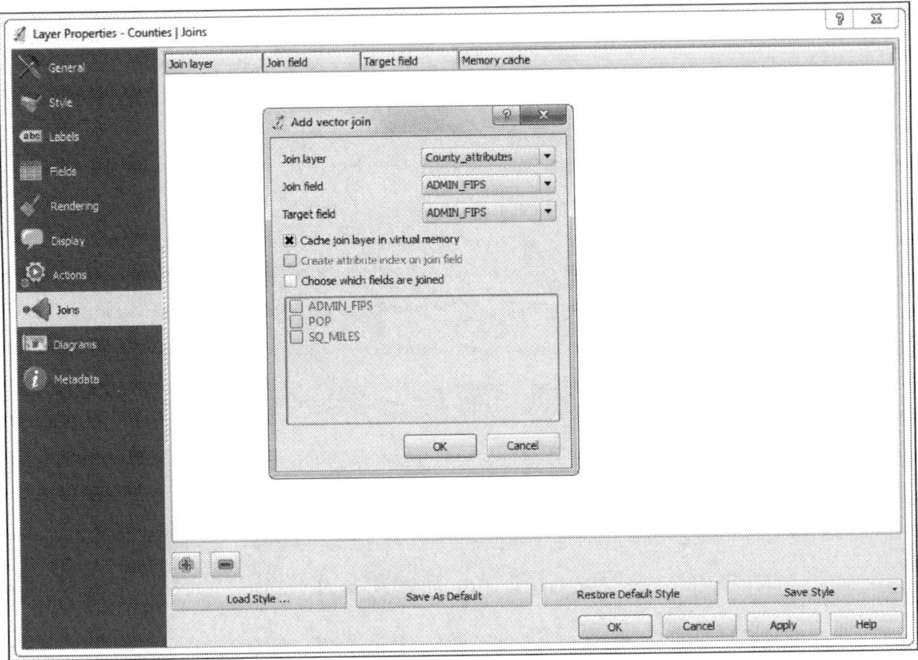

Joins only exist in virtual memory within the QGIS Desktop document. To preserve the join outside the map document click on **Save as...** under **Layer** and save a new copy of the layer. The new layer will include the attributes appended via the join.

Editing data

Vector data layers can be edited within QGIS Desktop. Editing allows you to add, delete, and modify features in vector datasets. The first step is to put the dataset into edit mode. Select the layer in the **Layers** panel and click on **Toggle Editing** under **Layer**. Alternatively, you can right-click on a layer in the **Layers** panel and choose **Toggle Editing** from the context menu. Multiple layers can be edited at a time. The layer currently being edited is the one selected in the **Layers** panel. Once you are in the edit mode, the digitizing toolbar (shown in the following screenshot) can be used to add, delete, and modify features.

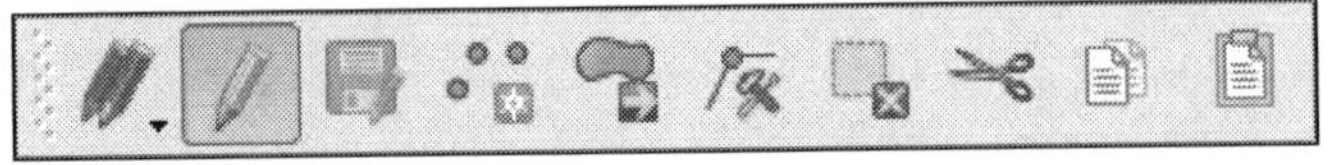

From left to right, the tools in the digitizing toolbar are as follows:

- The Current Edits tool allows you to manage your editing session. Here, you can save and rollback edits for one or more selected layers.
- The Toggle Editing tool provides an additional means to begin or end an editing session for a selected layer.
- The Save Layer Edits tool allows you to save edits for the selected layer(s) during an editing session.
- The Add Features tool will change to the appropriate geometry depending on whether a point, line, or polygon layer is selected. Points and vertices of lines and polygons are created by clicking. To complete a line or polygon feature, right-click. After adding a feature, you will be prompted to enter the attributes.
- Features can be moved with the Move tool by clicking on them and dragging them to the new position.
- Individual feature vertices can be moved with the Node tool. Click on a feature once with the tool to select it and the vertices will change into red boxes. Click again on an individual vertex to select it. The selected vertex will turn into a dark-blue box. Now, the vertex can be moved to the desired location. Additionally, edges between vertices can be selected and moved. To add vertices to a feature, simply double-click on the edge where you want the vertex to be added. Selected vertices can be deleted by pressing the *Delete* key on the keyboard.
- Features can be deleted, cut, copied, and pasted using the Delete Selected, Cut Features, Copy Features, and Paste Features tools.

Snapping

Snapping is an important editing consideration. It is a specified distance (tolerance) within which vertices of one feature will automatically align with vertices of another feature. The specific snapping tolerance can be set for the whole project or per layer. The method for setting the snapping tolerance for a project varies according to the operating system, which is as follows:

- **For Windows,** navigate to **Settings** | **Options** | **Digitizing**
- **For Mac,** navigate to **QGIS** | **Preferences** | **Digitizing**
- **For Linux,** navigate to **Edit** | **Options** | **Digitizing**

In addition to setting the snapping tolerance, here the snapping mode can also be set to vertex, segment, or vertex and segment. Snapping can be set for individual layers by navigating to **Settings** | **Snapping Options**. Individual layer snapping settings will override those of the project. The following screenshot shows examples of multiple snapping option choices.

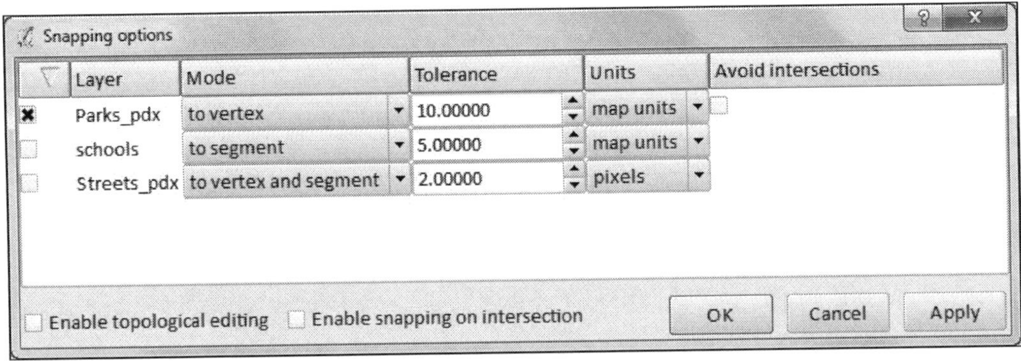

> There are many digitizing options that can be set by navigating to **Settings** | **Options** | **Digitizing**. These include settings for **Feature Creation**, **Rubberband**, **Snapping**, **Vertex markers**, and **Curve Offset Tool**. There is also an Advanced Digitizing toolbar which is covered in *Chapter 6, Advanced Data Creation and Editing*.

Styling vector data

When you load spatial data layers into QGIS Desktop, they are styled with a random single symbol rendering. To change this, navigate to **Layer** | **Properties** | **Style**.

There are several rendering choices available from the menu in the top-left corner, which are as follows:

- **Single Symbol**: This is the default rendering in which one symbol is applied to all the features in a layer.
- **Categorized**: This allows you to choose a categorical attribute field to style the layer. Choose the field and click on **Classify** and QGIS will apply a different symbol to each unique value in the field. You can also use the **Set column expression** button to enhance the styling with a SQL expression.
- **Graduated**: This allows you to classify the data by a numeric field attribute into discrete categories. You can specify the parameters of the classification (classification type and number of classes) and use the **Set column expression** button to enhance the styling with a SQL expression.

- **Rule-based**: This is used to create custom rule-based styling. Rules will be based on SQL expressions.
- **Point displacement**: If you have a point layer with stacked points, this option can be used to displace the points so that they are all visible.
- **Inverted polygons**: This is a new renderer that allows a feature polygon to be converted into a mask. For example, a city boundary polygon that is used with this renderer would become a mask around the city. It also allows the use of **Categorized**, **Graduated**, and **Rule-based** renderers and SQL expressions.

The following screenshot shows the Style properties available for a vector data layer:

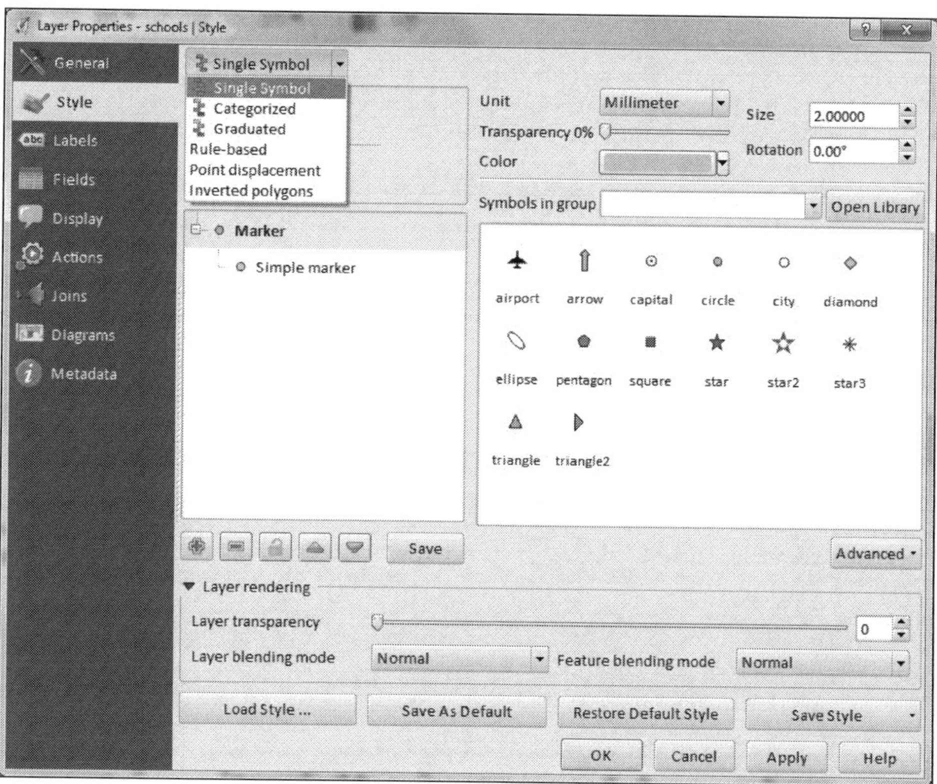

In the preceding screenshot, the renderer is the layer symbol. For a given symbol, you can work with the first level, which gives you the ability to change the transparency and color. You can also click on the second level, which gives you control over parameters such as fill, border, fill style, border style, join style, border width, and X/Y offsets. These parameters change depending on the geometry of your layer. You can also use this hierarchy to build symbol layers, which are styles built from several symbols that are combined vertically.

Styling raster data

You also have many choices when styling raster data in QGIS Desktop. There is a different choice of renderers for raster datasets, which are as follows:

- **Singleband gray**: This allows a singleband raster or a single band of a multiband raster to be styled with either a black-to-white or white-to-black color ramp. You can control contrast enhancement and how minimum and maximum values are determined.
- **Multiband color**: This is for rasters with multiple bands. It allows you to choose the band combination that you prefer.
- **Paletted**: This is for singleband rasters with an included color table. It is likely that it will be chosen by QGIS automatically, if this is the case.
- **Singleband pseudocolor**: This allows a singleband raster to be styled with a variety of color ramps and classification schemes.

The following is a screenshot of the **Style** tab of a raster file's **Layer Properties** showing where the aforementioned style choices are located:

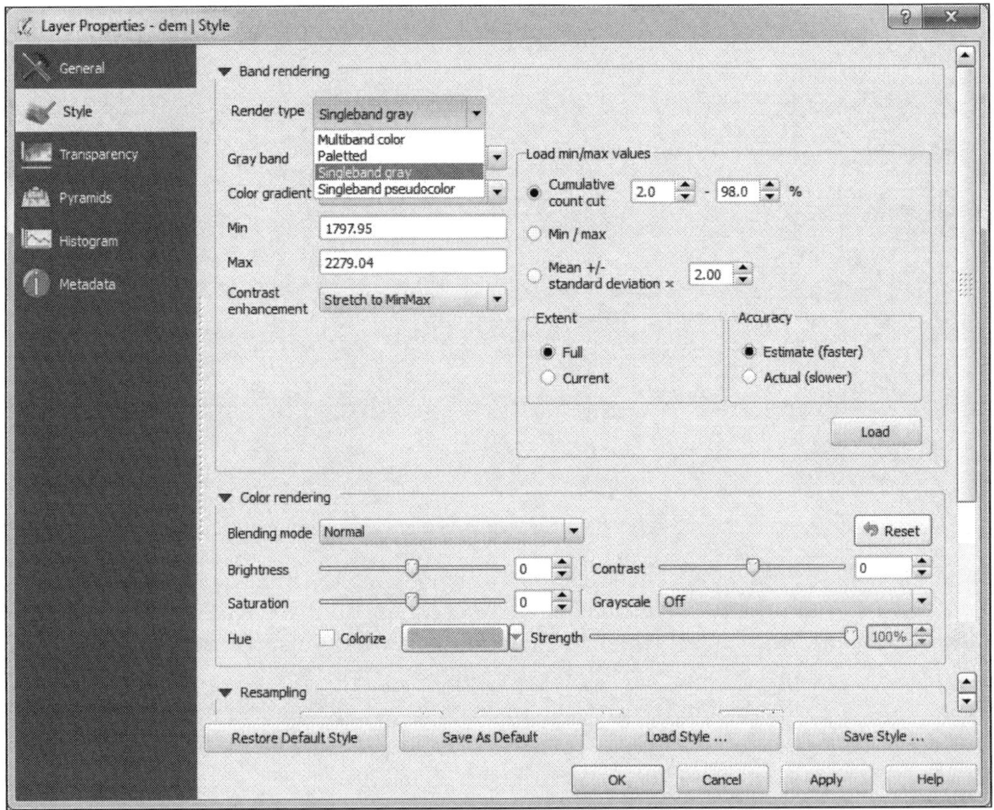

Contrast enhancement

Another important consideration with raster styling is the settings that are used for contrast enhancement when rendering the data. Let's start by loading the `Jemez_dem.img` image and opening the **Style** menu under **Layer Properties** (shown in the figure below). This is an elevation layer and the data is being stretched on a black-to-white color ramp from the **Min** and **Max** values listed under **Band rendering**. By default, these values only include those that are from 2 percent to 98 percent of the estimation of the full range of values in the dataset, and cut out the outlying values. This makes rendering faster, but it is not necessarily the most accurate.

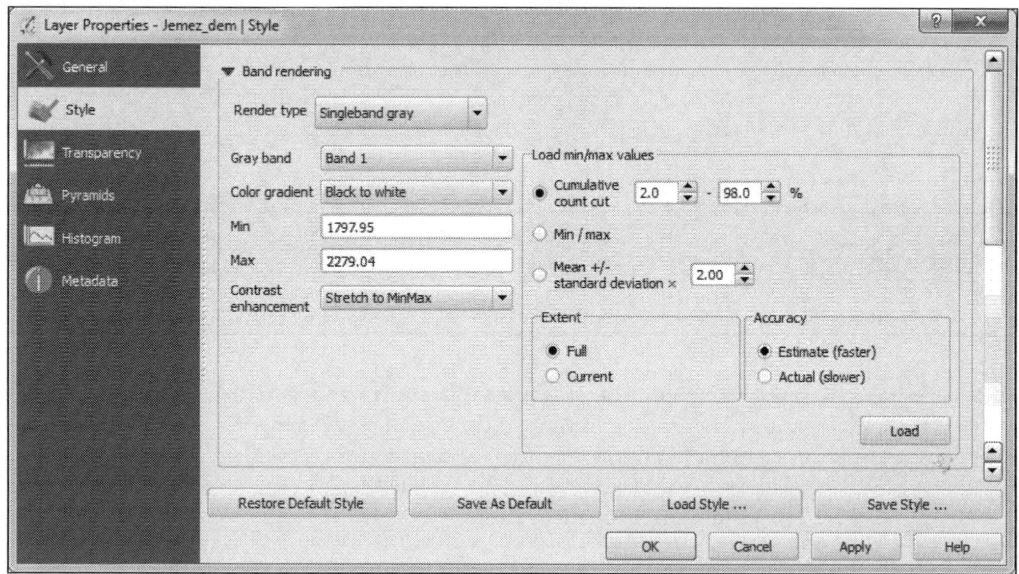

Next, we will change these settings to get a full stretch across all the data values in the raster. To do this, perform the following steps:

1. Under the **Load min/max** section, choose **Min / max** and under **Accuracy**, choose **Actual (slower)**.
2. Click on **Load**.

3. You will notice that the minimum and maximum values change. Click on **Apply**.

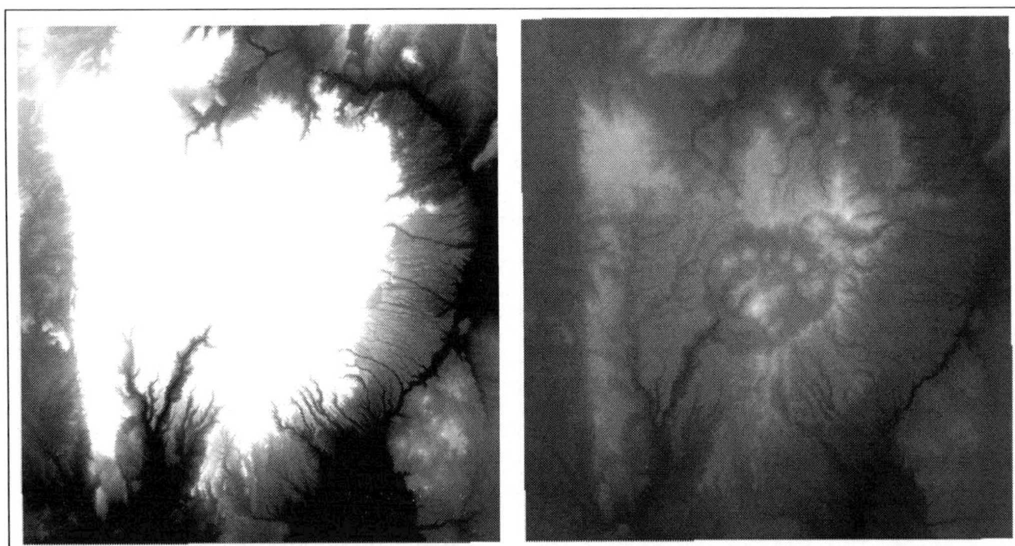

Default singleband contrast enhancement (left) and more accurate contrast enhancement (right)

> You can specify the default settings for rendering rasters by navigating to **Settings** | **Options** | **Rendering**. Here, the defaults for the **Contrast enhancement**, **Load min/max values**, **Cumulative count cut** thresholds, and the standard deviation multiplier can be set.

Blending modes

The blending modes allow for more sophisticated rendering between GIS layers. Historically, these tools have only been available in graphics programs and they are a fairly new addition to QGIS. Previously, only layer transparency could be controlled. There are now 13 different blending modes that are available: Normal, Lighten, Screen, Dodge, Addition, Darken, Multiply, Burn, Overlay, Soft light, Hard light, Difference, and Subtract. These are much more powerful than simple layer transparency, which can be effective but typically results in the underneath layer being washed out or dulled. With blending modes, you can create effects where the full intensity of the underlying layer is still visible. Blending mode settings can be found at the bottom of the **Style** menu under **Layer Properties** in the **Layer Rendering** section along with the **Layer** transparency slider. They are available for both vector and raster datasets.

In this example of using blending modes, we want to show vegetation data (`Jemez_vegetation.tif`) in combination with a hillshade image (`Jemez_hillshade.img`). Both data sets are loaded and the vegetation data is dragged to the top of the layer list. Vegetation is then styled with a Singleband pseudocolor renderer; you can do this by performing the following steps:

1. Choose **Random colors**.
2. Set **Mode** to **Equal interval**.
3. Set the number of **Classes** to **13**.
4. Click on **Classify**.
5. Click on **Apply**.

The following screenshot shows what the Style properties should look like after following the preceding steps.

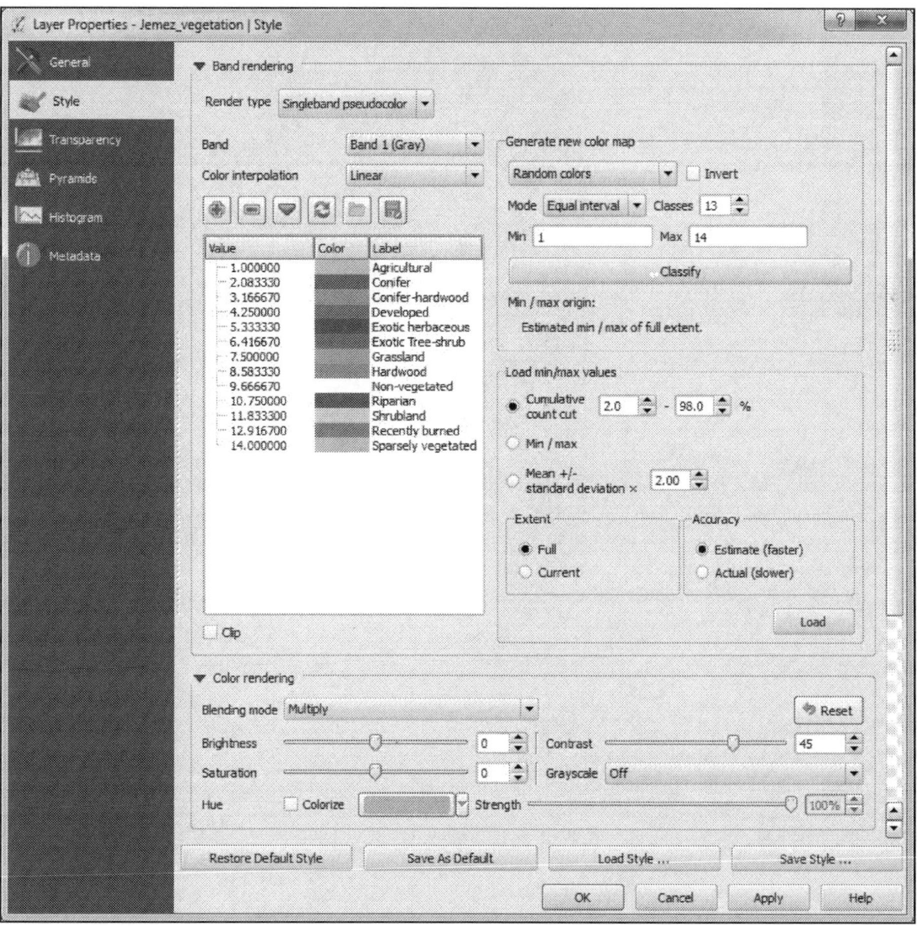

At the bottom of the **Style** menu under **Layer Properties**, set the **Blending mode** to **Multiply** and the **Contrast** to **45** and click on **Apply**. The blending mode allows all the details of both the datasets to be seen. Experiment with different blending modes to see how they change the appearance of the image. The following screenshot shows an example of how blending and contrast settings can work together to make a raster 'pop' off the screen:

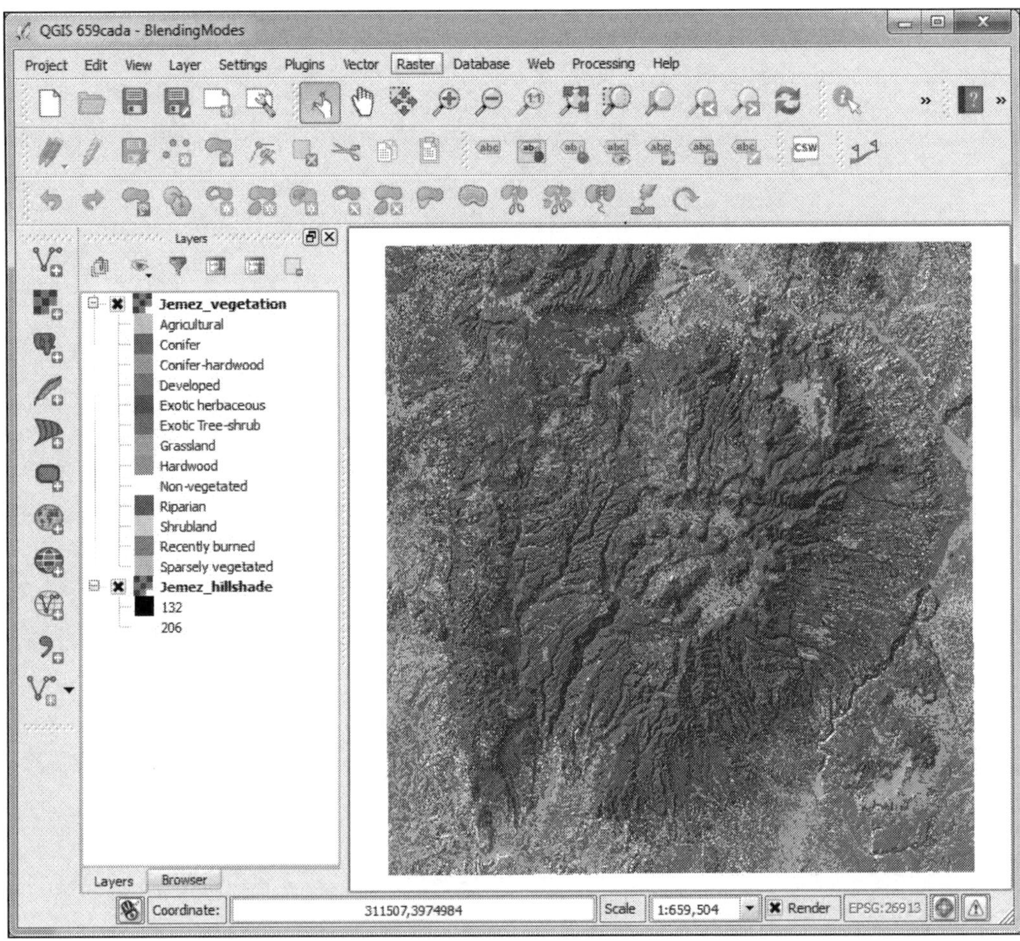

Composing maps

With QGIS, you can compose maps that can be printed or exported to image and graphic files. To get started, click on **New Print Composer** under **Project**. Give the new composition a name, click on **OK**, and the composer window will open.

The composer presents you with a blank sheet of paper upon which you can craft your map. Along the left-hand side, there are a series of tools on the Composer Items toolbar. The lower portion of the toolbar contains buttons for adding map elements to your map. These include the map body, images, text, a legend, a scale bar, graphic shapes, arrows, attribute tables, and HTML frames. Map elements become graphics on the composition canvas. By selecting a map element, graphic handles will appear around the perimeter. These can be used to move and resize the element. The upper portion of the Composer Items toolbar contains tools for panning the map data, moving other graphic content, and zooming and panning on the map composition.

The majority of the map customization options can be found in the composer tabs. To specify the sheet size and orientation, use the **Composition** tab. Once map elements have been added to the map, they can be customized with the **Item properties** tab. The options available on the **Item properties** tab change according to the type of map element that is selected. The **Atlas generation** tab allows you to generate a map book. For example, a municipality could generate an atlas by using a map sheet GIS layer and specifying which attribute column contains the map sheet number for each polygon. The **Items** tab allows you to toggle individual map elements on and off.

The toolbars across the top contain tools for aligning graphics (the Composer Item Actions toolbar), navigating around the map composition (the Paper Navigation toolbar), and tools for managing, saving, and exporting compositions (the Composer toolbar). Maps can be exported as images, PDFs, and SVG graphic files. To export the map, click on the **Composer** menu and select one from among **Export as image...**, **Export as SVG...**, or **Export as PDF...** depending on your needs. The following is a screenshot showing parts of the composer window.

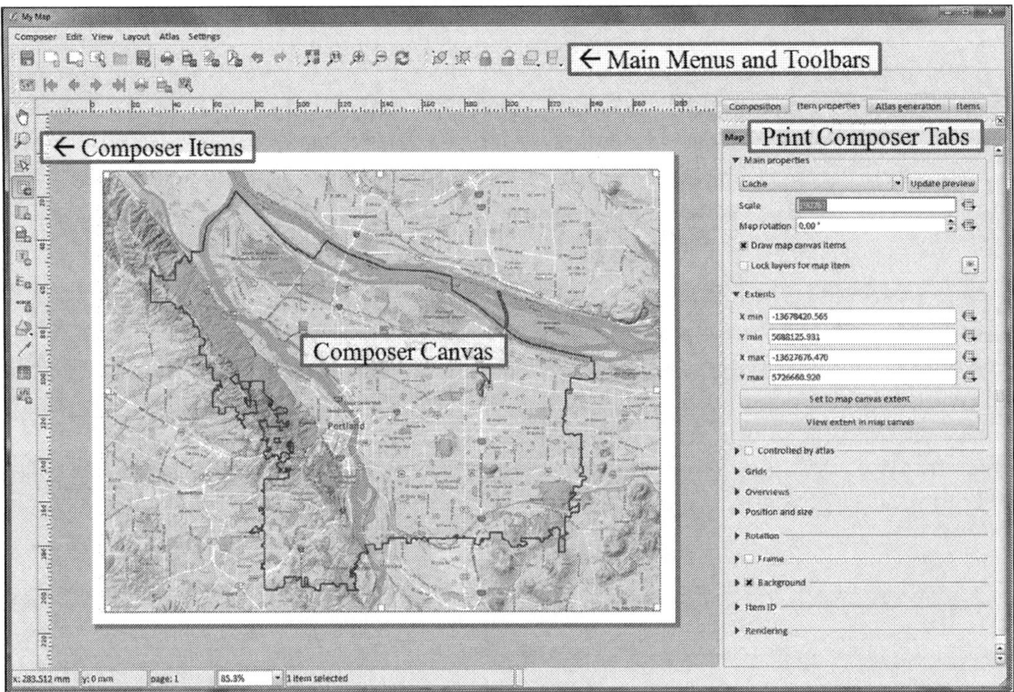

Adding functionality with plugins

There are so many potential workflows, analysis settings, and datasets within the broad field of GIS that no out-of-the-box software could contain the tools for every scenario. Fortunately, QGIS has been developed with a plugin architecture. Plugins are add-ons to QGIS that provide additional functionality. Some are written by the core QGIS development team and others are written by QGIS users.

You can explore the QGIS plugin ecosystem by navigating to **Plugins | Manage and Install Plugins**. This opens the **Plugins Manager** window (shown in figure below) that will allow you to browse all plugins, those that are installed, and those that are not installed, and adjust the settings. If there are installed plugins with available upgrades, there will also be an **Upgradable** option. The search bar can be used to enter search terms and find available plugins related to the topic. This is the first place to look if there's a tool or extra type of functionality that you need! To install a plugin, simply select it and click on the **Install Plugin** button. Installed plugins can be toggled on and off by checking the box next to each.

You will be notified by a link at the bottom of the QGIS Desktop application if there are updates available for your installed plugins. Clicking on the link will open the **Plugins Manager** window, where the **Upgrades** tab will allow you to install all or some of the available updates. Plugins themselves may show up as individual buttons, toolbars, or as items under the appropriate menu, such as **Plugins**, **Vector**, **Raster**, **Database**, **Web**, or **Processing**.

> To add a base map to QGIS, enable the OpenLayer plugin. It appears under the **Web** menu and allows you to add base maps from OpenStreetMap, Google Maps, Bing Maps, Map Quest, OSM/Stamen, and Apple Maps. This plugin requires an Internet connection.

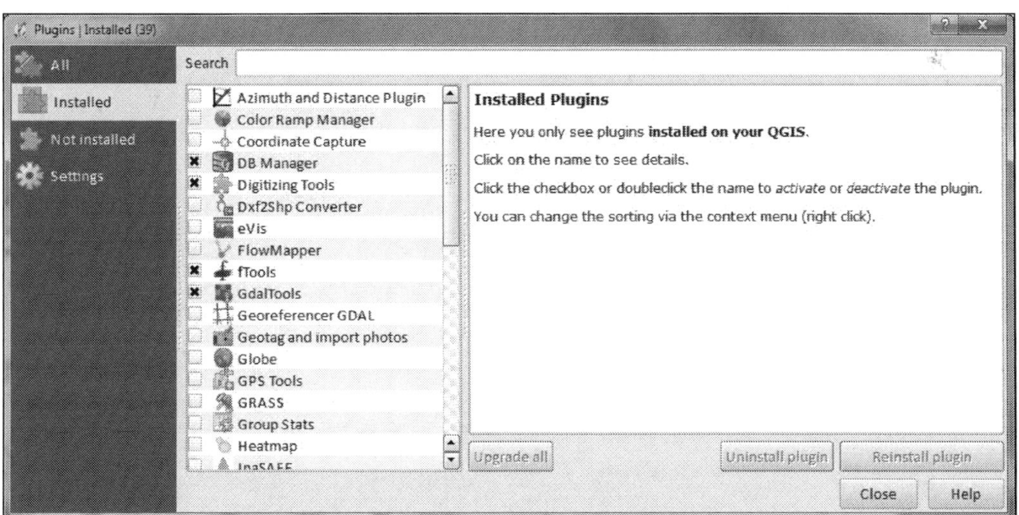

> You can also browse the QGIS Python Plugins Repository at `https://plugins.qgis.org/plugins/`.

Summary

This chapter provided a refresher in the basics of Desktop and QGIS Browser. We covered how to install the software on several platforms and described the layout of both QGIS Desktop and QGIS Browser. We then covered how to load vector, raster, and database data layers. Next, you were shown how to work with coordinate reference systems and style data. We covered the basics of working with tables, including how to perform a table join. The chapter concluded with a refresher on composing maps and how to find, install, and manage plugins.

The next chapter will cover creating spatial databases. Data is the foundation of any GIS. Now that you have had a refresher on the basics of QGIS, it is time to learn how to expand your work to include spatial databases. In *Chapter 2, Creating Spatial Databases*, you will learn how to create and manage spatial databases within QGIS.

2

Creating Spatial Databases

This chapter covers the creation and editing of spatial databases using QGIS. The core concepts of databases will be briefly reviewed; however, we have assumed that you are generally familiar with database concepts and SQL for most of the content covered in this chapter. The topics that we will cover in this chapter are as follows:

- Core concepts of database construction
- Creating spatial databases
- Importing and exporting data
- Editing databases
- Creating queries
- Creating views

Fundamental database concepts

A database is a structured collection of data. Databases provide multiple benefits over data stored in a flat file format, such as shapefile or KML. The benefits include complex queries, complex relationships, scalability, security, data integrity, and transactions, to name a few. Using databases to store geospatial data is relatively easy, considering the aforementioned benefits.

There are multiple types of databases; however, the most common type of database, and the type of database that this chapter will cover, is the relational database.

Database tables

A relational database stores data in tables. A table is composed of rows and columns, where each row is a single data record and each column stores a field value associated with each record. A table can have any number of records; however, each field is uniquely named and stores a specific type of data.

A data type restricts the information that can be stored in a field, and it is very important that an appropriate data type, and its associated parameters, be selected for each field in a table. The common data types are as follows:

- Integer
- Float/Real/Decimal
- Text
- Date

Each of these data types can have additional constraints set, such as setting a default value, restricting the field size, or prohibiting null values.

In addition to the common data types mentioned previously, some databases support the geometry field type, allowing the following geometry types to be stored:

- Point
- Multi-point
- Line
- Multi-line
- Polygon
- Multi-polygon

The multi-point/line/polygon types store multi-part geometries so that one record has multiple geometry parts associated with it.

ESRI shapefiles store geospatial data in multi- type geometry, so using multi- type geometry is a good practice if you plan on converting between formats.

Table relationships

A table relationship connects records between tables. The benefit of relating tables is reducing data redundancy and increasing data integrity. In order to relate two tables together, each table must contain an indexed key field.

> The process of organizing tables to reduce redundancy is called normalization. Normalization typically involves splitting larger tables into smaller, less redundant tables, followed by defining the relationship between the tables.

A field can be defined as an index. A field set as an index must only contain values that are unique for each record, and therefore, it can be used to identify each record in a table uniquely. An index is useful for two reasons. Firstly, it allows records to be quickly found during a query if the indexed field is part of the query. Secondly, an index can be set to be a primary key for a table, allowing for table relationships to be built.

A primary key is one or more fields that uniquely identify a record in its own table. A foreign key is one or more fields that uniquely identify a record in another table. When a relationship is created, a record(s) from one table is linked to a record(s) of another table. With related tables, more complex queries can be executed and redundancy in the database can be reduced.

Structured Query Language

Structured Query Language (**SQL**) is a language designed to manage databases and the data contained within them. Covering SQL is a large undertaking and is outside the scope of this book, so we will only cover a quick refresher that is relevant to this chapter.

SQL provides functions to select, insert, delete, and update data. Four commonly used SQL data functions are discussed as follows:

- `SELECT`: This retrieves a temporary set of data from one or more tables based on an expression. A basic query is `SELECT <field(s)> FROM <table> WHERE <field> <operator> <value>;` where `<field>` is the name of the field from which values must be retrieved and `<table>` is the table on which the query must be executed. The `<operator>` part checks for equality (such as `=`, `>=`, `LIKE`) and `<value>` is the value to compare against the field.

- `INSERT`: This inserts new records into a table. The `INSERT INTO <table> (<field1>, <field2>, <field3>) VALUES (<value1>, <value2>, <value3>);` statement inserts three values into their three respective fields, where `<value1>`, `<value2>`, and `<value3>` are stored in `<field1>`, `<field2>`, and `<field3>` of `<table>`.
- `UPDATE`: This modifies an existing record in a table. The `UPDATE <table> SET <field> = <value>;` statement updates one field's value, where `<value>` is stored in `<field>` of `<table>`.
- `DELETE`: This deletes record(s) from a table. The following statements deletes all records matching the `WHERE` clause: `DELETE FROM <table> WHERE <field> <operator> <value>;` where `<table>` is the table to delete records from, `<field>` is the name of the field, `<operator>` checks for equality, and `<value>` is the value to check against the field.

Another SQL function of interest is view. A view is a stored query that is presented as a table but is actually built dynamically when the view is accessed. To create a view, simply preface a `SELECT` statement with `CREATE VIEW <view_name> AS` and a view named `<view_name>` will be created. You can then treat the new view as if it were a table.

Creating a spatial database

Creating a spatial database in QGIS is a simple operation. QGIS supports PostGIS, SpatiaLite, MSSQL, SQL Anywhere, and Oracle Spatial databases. We will cover SpatiaLite, an open source project that is cross-platform, simple, and lightweight, and provides quite a bit of functionality. SpatiaLite is a spatial **database management system (DBMS)** built on top of SQLite, a lightweight personal DBMS.

> SpatiaLite (and thus, SQLite) is built on a personal architecture, which makes installation and management virtually nonexistent. The trade-off, however, is that it neither does a good job of supporting multiple concurrent connections nor does it support a client-server architecture. For a more complex DBMS, PostGIS is an excellent open source option.

We will create a new SpatiaLite database that we will use for the remaining exercises in this chapter; to do this, perform the following steps:

1. Open QGIS Desktop and open the **Browser** panel. If the **Browser** panel is missing, click on **Browser** by navigating to **View** | **Panels**. In the **Browser** panel, you will find the SpatiaLite entry below your hard drive folders.

2. Create a new SpatiaLite database by right-clicking on **SpatiaLite** and then choose **Create database...** (as shown in the following screenshot).
3. Create a new folder on disk and save the new database as `GiffordPinchot.sqlite`. The newly created database will appear under the SpatiaLite database entry.

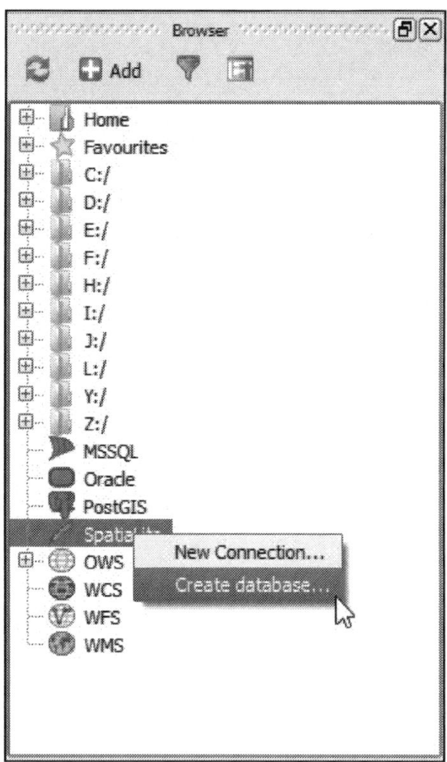

Now that we have a new SpatiaLite database, let's look at its initial structure and contents. To do this, we will use DB Manager, a built-in QGIS plugin. DB Manager provides a simple graphical interface to manage PostGIS and SpatiaLite databases. Using **DB Manager**, we will be able to view and manage our SpatiaLite database. Let's start by getting familiar with the **DB Manager** interface.

1. Click on **DB Manager** under **Database** to open the DB Manager. The DB Manager interface (as shown in the following screenshot) is composed of four parts: menu bar, toolbar, tree view, and information panel.

2. Navigate to **SpatiaLite | GiffordPinochet.sqlite** to see a tree listing of all tables, views, and general information about the database, as shown in in the following screenshot:

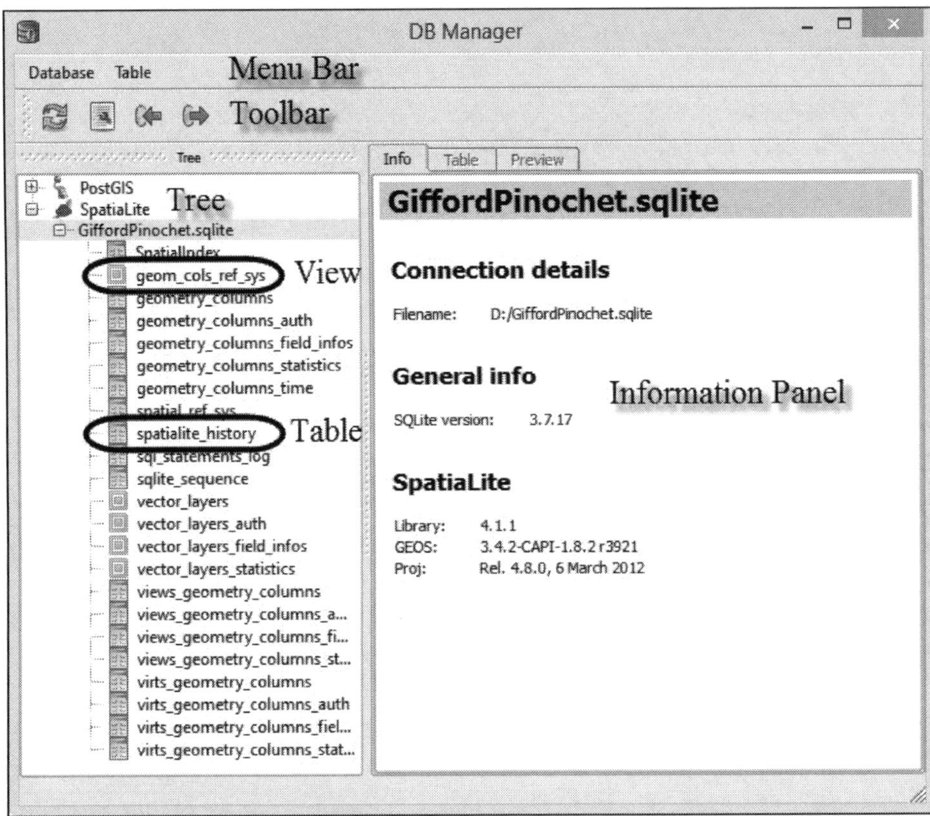

When a new SpatiaLite database is created, it is automatically populated with multiple tables and views. These tables and views hold records used by the DBMS to manage the structure and operation of the database. You should not modify or delete these tables or views unless you are absolutely sure of what you are doing.

Importing data into a SpatiaLite database

Importing data into a SpatiaLite database is easy using the DB Manager. SpatiaLite supports the following formats for importing files:

- Shapefile (`.shp`)
- Dbase (`.dbf`)
- Text (`.txt`), Commas Separate Values (`.csv`), and Excel spreadsheets (`.xls`)
- Well-known Text (`.wkt`) and Well-known Binary (`.wkb`)
- PostGIS (`.ewkt / .ewkb`)
- Geography Markup Language (`.gml`)
- Keyhole Markup Language (`.kml`)
- Geometry JavaScript Object Notation (`.geojson`)
- Scalable Vector Graphics (`.svg`)

Let's use DB Manager to import data in a few different formats into our `GiffordPinochet.sqlite` database.

Importing KML into SpatiaLite

To import a KML file into a SpatiaLite database, complete the following steps:

1. Open DB Manager by clicking on **DB Manager** under **Database**. Expand **SpatiaLite** and select **GiffordPinochet.sqlite** on the **Tree** panel.
2. Navigate to **Table | Import layer/file** to open the **Import vector layer** dialog.
3. Click on the ellipsis button at the right-hand side of the **Input** drop-down box and select and open `streams.kml` from the sample dataset that is available for download on the Packt Publishing website.
4. Click on the **Update options** button to load the remainder of the dialog box. The output table name will populate as `streams`, and it will match the base name of the input file.
5. Set the following options as shown in the next screenshot:
    - Select **Source SRID** and enter `4326`. This is the EPSG code for all KML datasets.
    - Select **Target SRID** and enter `26910`. This is the EPSG code for NAD 83/UTM Zone 10 North.
    - Select **Create spatial index**.

6. Refer the following screenshot to make sure your settings match. If so, click on the **OK** button to import the file.

> By setting the target SRID to a different value than the source SRID, the data will be projected to the new coordinate system during the import process, saving you a step.

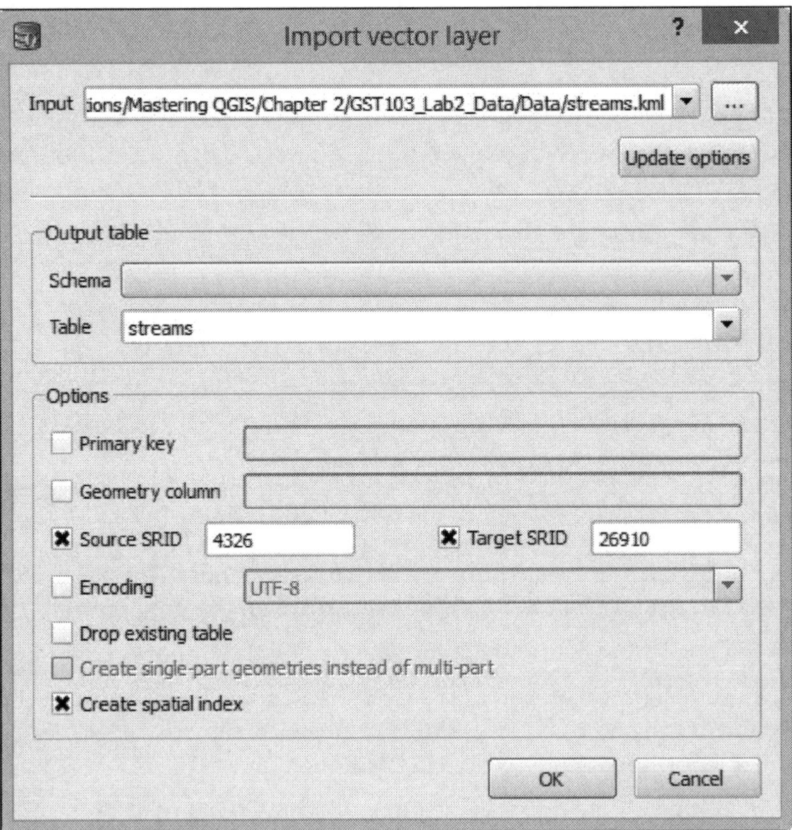

7. After a few moments, you will be notified that the import is complete. To view the newly created table, you'll need to refresh the **Tree** panel by selecting **GiffordPinochet.sqlite** in the tree and then click on **Refresh** under **Database**, or press the *F5* key on your keyboard. The `streams` table should now appear and have the polyline icon next to it.
8. To preview the attribute table, click on the **Table** tab on the information panel. To preview the geometry, click on the **Preview** tab on the information panel. To view the newly created SpatiaLite layer in QGIS Desktop, right-click on **streams** on the **Tree** panel, and then choose **Add to canvas**.

Importing a shapefile into SpatiaLite

1. Open DB Manager by clicking on **DB Manager** under **Database**. Expand **SpatiaLite** and select **GiffordPinochet.sqlite** on the **Tree** panel.
2. Navigate to **Table | Import layer/file** to open the **Import vector layer** dialog, as shown in the following screenshot.
3. Click on the ellipsis button at the right-hand side of the **Input** drop-down box and select and open `NF_roads.shp` from the sample dataset that is available for download on the Packt Publishing website.
4. Click on the **Update options** button to load the remainder of the dialog box. The output table name will populate as `NF_roads`, and it will match the base name of the input file.
5. Set the following options:
    - Select **Source SRID** and enter `26910`. This is the EPSG code for NAD 83/UTM Zone 10 North. Since we don't want to change the coordinate system during import, we do not need to set **Target SRID**.
    - Select **Create spatial index**.
6. Click on the **OK** button to import the file.

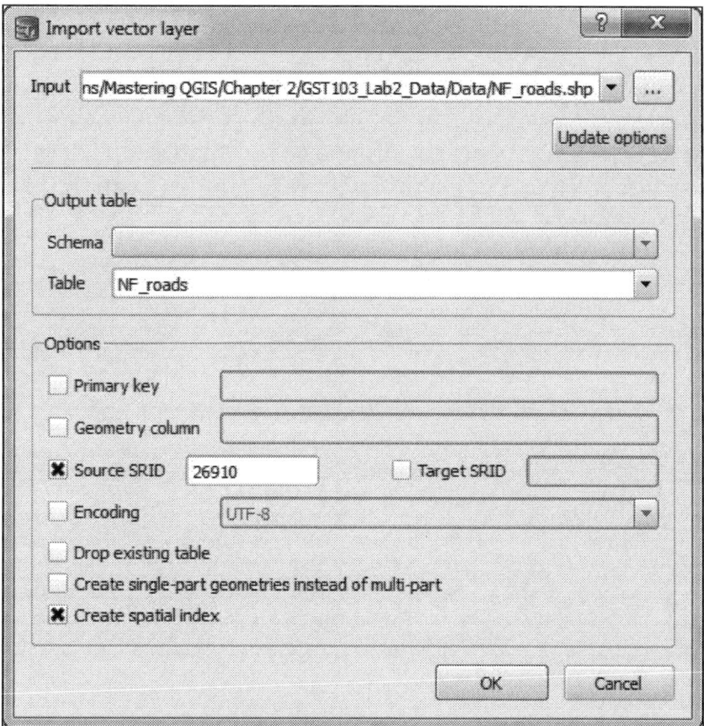

7. After a few moments, you will be notified that the import is complete. To view the newly created table, you'll need to refresh the **Tree** panel by selecting **GiffordPinochet.sqlite** in the tree, and then click on **Refresh** under **Database**, or press the *F5* key on your keyboard. The `NF_roads` table should now appear and have the polyline icon next to it.
8. To preview the attribute table, click on the **Table** tab on the information panel. To preview the geometry, click on the **Preview** tab on the information panel. To view the newly created SpatiaLite layer in QGIS Desktop, right-click on **NF_roads** in the tree, and then choose **Add to canvas**.

Importing tables into SpatiaLite

To import a table file into a SpatiaLite database, complete the following steps:

1. Open DB Manager by clicking on **DB Manager** under **Database**. Expand **SpatiaLite** and select **GiffordPinochet.sqlite** on the **Tree** panel.
2. Navigate to **Table** | **Import layer/file** to open the **Import vector layer** dialog.
3. Click on the ellipsis button to the right-hand side of the **Input** drop-down box and select and open **Waterfalls.xls** from the sample dataset that is available for download on the Packt Publishing website.
4. Click on the **Update options** button to load the remainder of the dialog box. The output table name will populate as `Waterfalls`, and it match the base name of the input file. Note that all options related to spatial datasets are not modifiable and are grayed out (as shown in in the following screenshot). This is because SpatiaLite treats the input as a nonspatial table, even though it has coordinates stored in the table. We will add the spatial component to the table in a later step.

5. Click on the **OK** button to import the file.

6. After a few moments, you will be notified that the import is complete. To view the newly created table, you'll need to refresh the **Tree** panel by selecting **GiffordPinochet.sqlite** in the tree and then click on **Refresh** under **Database,** or press the *F5* key on your keyboard. The `Waterfalls` table should now appear and have the table icon next to it.
7. Select the `Waterfalls` table. Click on the **Info** tab on the information panel. Note the **Northing** and **Easting** fields. These fields contain the coordinates of the waterfalls in NAD 83/UTM Zone 10 North (EPSG 26910). Click on the **Table** tab on the information panel to view the entries in the table. Note that the **Preview** tab is not selectable, because the selected table does not have any geometry field.

At this point, the table import is complete. However, since the `Waterfalls` table has coordinate pairs, a point geometry column can be added to the table that would essentially convert the table to a point layer. Let's do this now:

1. With the **Waterfalls** table selected in the **Tree** panel, navigate to **Table** | **Edit Table** to open the **Table properties** window.

2. Click on the **Add geometry column** button. In the new window, set the following options to match the following screenshot and then click on **OK** to create the geometry field:
    - **Name**: `geom` (the name of the field that will contain the geometry information)
    - **Type**: **POINT** (the type of geometry the field will hold)
    - **Dimensions**: **2** (the number of dimensions (values) the geometry field will hold for each record)
    - **SRID**: `26910` (the coordinate system of the geometry field)

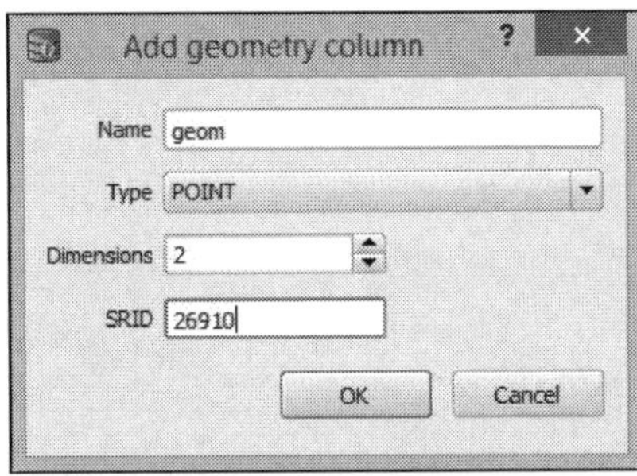

3. Close the table properties. To view the newly edited table, you'll need to refresh the **Tree** panel by selecting **GiffordPinochet.sqlite** in the tree and then clicking on **Refresh** under **Database**, or press the *F5* key on your keyboard. The `Waterfalls` table should now appear and have the point icon next to it.

Now that the `Waterfalls` table has a geometry field, we need to populate it with the coordinates. We will accomplish this by writing a SQL update query and using the SpatiaLite `MakePoint` function. To do this, perform the following steps:

1. In the SQL window, click on the **Clear** button to clear the **SQL query** text area.
2. Enter the following query in the **SQL query** text area:

```
UPDATE Waterfalls
SET geom = MakePoint(Easting,Northing,26910);
```

> Let's discuss the `MakePoint` function.
>
> `MakePoint(Easting,Northing,26910)` is a SpatiaLite function that creates a new point geometry object. `Easting` and `Northing` are the columns in the same row that hold the values for the *x* and *y* coordinates respectively. `26910` is the SRID of the *x* and *y* coordinates.

3. Click on the **Execute (F5)** button to execute the query. The query will return no result but will indicate that 100 rows were affected. This indicates that the geometry field of 100 rows have been populated with point geometry. The following screenshot shows the query and the indication that 100 rows were affected:

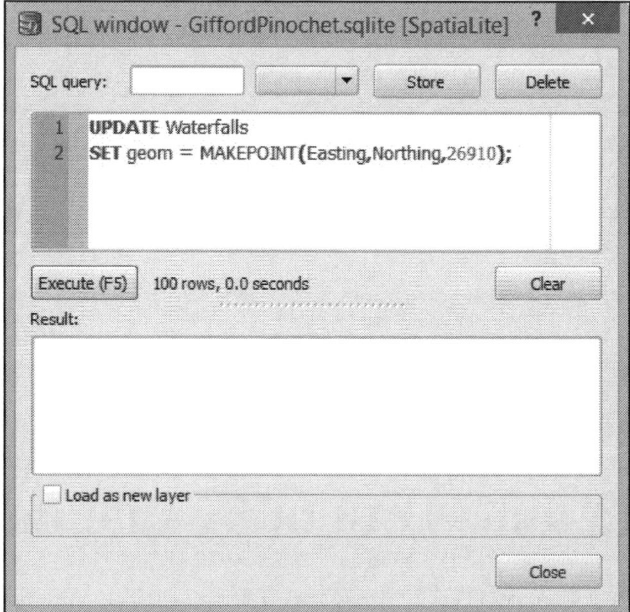

4. On the SQL window, click on the **Close** button to close the window.
5. To view the changes made to the `Waterfalls` table, you'll need to refresh the **Tree** panel by selecting **GiffordPinochet.sqlite** in the tree and then clicking on **Refresh** under **Database**, or press the *F5* key on your keyboard.

6. Note that the **Waterfalls** table now has the point icon next to it. Click on the **Info** tab on the information panel. Under the **SpatiaLite** section of the information printout, note that a warning is displayed stating that no spatial index has been defined (shown in following figure). To improve access speed, it is best that a spatial index be set. Click on **create it** and then click on the **Yes** button on the pop up.

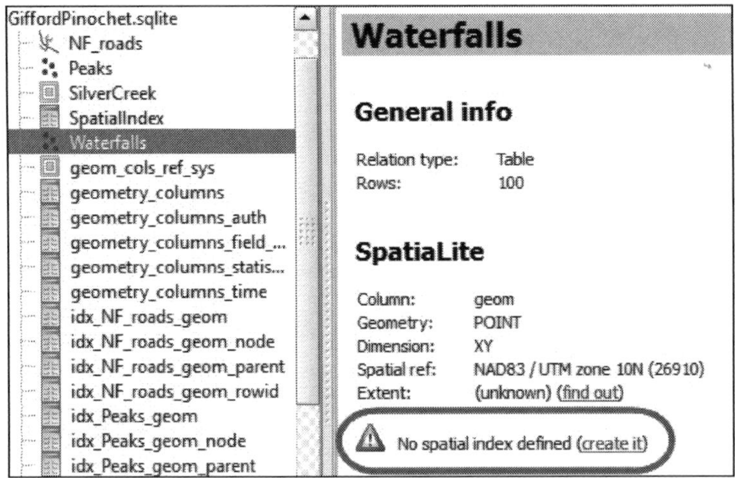

7. To preview the attribute table, click on the **Table** tab on the information panel. To preview the geometry, click on the **Preview** tab on the information panel. To view the newly created SpatiaLite layer in QGIS Desktop, right-click on **NF_roads** in the tree and then choose **Add to canvas**.

Exporting tables out of SpatiaLite as a shapefile

To export a table as a shapefile, perform the following steps:

1. Open DB Manager by clicking on **DB Manager** under **Database**. Expand **SpatiaLite** and select the database from which you wish to export a table in the **Tree** panel.
2. In the **Tree** panel, select the table that you wish to export.
3. Navigate to **Table** | **Export to file** to open the **Export vector file** dialog.
4. Click on the ellipsis button at the right-hand side of the **Output file** text box and name the output file. Note that you can only export to the shapefile format using this tool.

5. Set the **Source SRID**, **Target SRID**, and **Encoding** options or leave them unselected to use the default values. Select **Drop existing one** if you wish to overwrite an existing shapefile.

The following screenshot shows the **Export to vector file** dialog ready to export to `waterfalls.shp`.

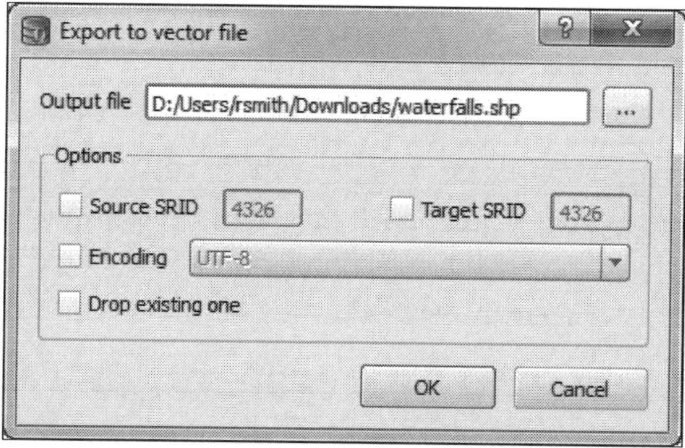

Managing tables

DB Manager provides functions to create, rename, edit, delete, and empty tables using tools found under the **Table** menu. In this section, we will discuss each tool.

Creating a new table

Creating new tables using DB Manager is fairly straightforward. When creating a new table, you can specify whether it will be a spatial table or a nonspatial table. In this section, we will create a new spatial table in SpatiaLite to hold data about mountain peaks in a park; to do this, perform the following steps:

> To quickly create a new SpatiaLite layer (and optionally a database) in one dialog box in QGIS Desktop, navigate to **Layer** | **Create Layer** | **New SpatiaLite Layer...**.

1. Open DB Manager by clicking on **DB Manager** under **Database**. Expand **SpatiaLite** and select **GiffordPinochet.sqlite** in the **Tree** panel.
2. Navigate to **Table** | **Create Table** to open the **Create Table** window.
3. Enter `Peaks` as the table name.
4. Click on the **Add field** button to add a new table field. A new row will appear in the field list. Set the **Name** field to `Name` and the **Type** field to `character(20)` from the list of field type options.

5. Click on the **Add field** button to add a second field, with the **Name** field set to `Elevation` and the **Type** field set to `integer`.
6. Set the **Primary key** field to **Name**. This will require the peak names to be unique.
7. Select **Create geometry column** and choose the following options:
    - **Create geometry column**: **POINT**
    - **Name**: `geom`
    - **Dimensions**: **2**
    - **SRID**: `26910`
8. Select **Create spatial index** to create a spatial index for the table.
9. Your dialog should look like the following screenshot. If it does, click on the **Create** button to create the new table.

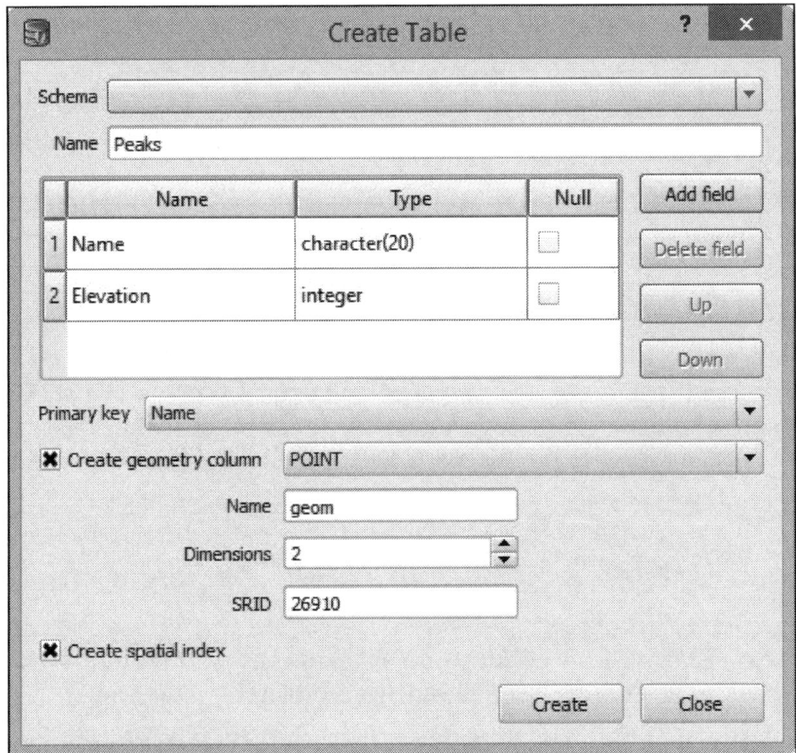

10. If the table is created successfully, a prompt will confirm that everything went fine. Dismiss the dialog, then click on the **Close** button to close the **Create Table** window.

11. To view the new `Peaks` table, you'll need to refresh the **Tree** panel by selecting **GiffordPinochet.sqlite** in the tree and then click on **Refresh** under **Database**, or press the *F5* key on your keyboard. Note that the `Peaks` table has the point icon, indicating that it is a geometry table.

Renaming a table

To rename a table, perform the following steps:

1. Open DB Manager by clicking on **DB Manager** under **Database**. In the **Tree** panel, expand the tree and select the database that contains the table that you wish to rename.
2. In the **Tree** panel, select the table you wish to edit. Right-click on the table and choose **Rename** from the contextual menu to rename it.

Editing table properties

To edit table properties, perform the following steps:

1. Open DB Manager by clicking on **DB Manager** under **Database**. In the **Tree** panel, expand the tree and select the database that contains the table that you wish to edit.
2. In the **Tree** panel, select the table that you wish to edit. Navigate to **Table | Edit table** to open the **Table properties** window.
3. The **Table properties** window (shown in the following screenshot) has three tabs—**Columns**, **Constraints**, and **Indexes**—that allow the editing of their respective table properties.

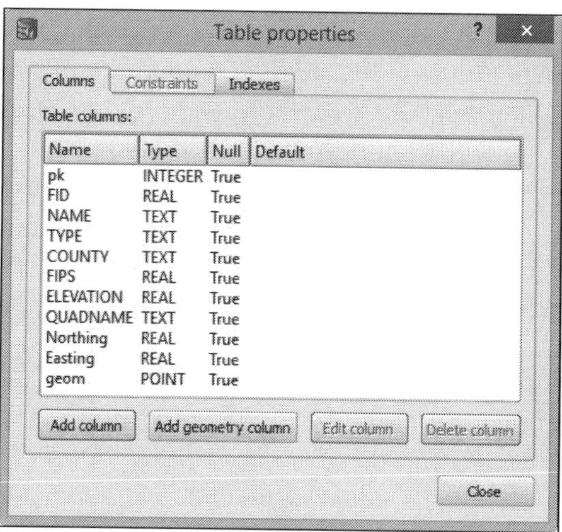

The **Columns** tab lists all the fields, their type, whether they allow null values, and their default values. Below the field list, there are four buttons. The **Add column** button opens a window and allows you to create a new field and specify its properties. The **Add geometry column** button opens a window and allows you to create a new geometry field and specify its properties. The **Edit column** button opens a window and lets you change the selected field's properties. The **Delete column** button deletes the selected field.

SpatiaLite does not support table-altering commands, such as editing and deleting existing fields; therefore, these options will be disabled.

The **Constraints** tab lists all the constraints on the table; their name, their type, and the column(s) that are affected by the constraints. The **Add primary key/unique** button opens a window and allows you to create a new primary key constraint. The **Delete constraint** button deletes the selected constraint.

SpatiaLite does not support adding or removing a constraint from an existing table: therefore, these options will be disabled. The constraints can be managed using other SQLite clients.

The **Indexes** tab lists all the indexes on the table, their name, and the column(s) that are a part of the index. The **Add index** button opens a window that allows you to create a new index by selecting the field to index and provides an index name. The **Add spatial index** button adds a spatial index to the table. This option is only available if the table is a geometry field. The **Delete index** button deletes the currently selected index.

Deleting a table

There are two ways to delete a table from a database within QGIS: by using the **Browser** panel in QGIS Desktop or by using the DB Manager.

To delete a table using the **Browser** panel in QGIS Desktop, expand the database from which you wish to delete a table, then right-click on the table and choose **Delete layer**.

To delete a table using DB Manager, open DB Manager by clicking on **DB Manager** under **Database**. In the **Tree** panel, expand the tree and select the database that contains the table that you wish to delete. In the **Tree** panel, select the table that you wish to delete. Then, click on **Delete table/view** under **Table**. You can also right-click on the table in the **Tree** panel and choose **Delete** from the contextual menu.

Emptying a table

To remove every record from a table without deleting the table, open DB Manager by clicking on **DB Manager** under **Database**. In the **Tree** panel, expand the tree and select the database that contains the table that you wish to empty. In the **Tree** panel, select the table you wish to empty. Then, click on **Empty table** under **Table**.

Creating queries and views

DB Manager has a SQL window that allows SQL queries to be executed against the database. This section will explain how to use the SQL window to query a table and create a spatial view in SpatiaLite.

Different databases support different SQL commands. SQLite supports much of, but not all, the standard SQL. For a complete listing of supported SQL operations, visit `http://www.sqlite.org/sessions/lang.html`.

Creating a SQL query

To create a SQL query, perform the following steps:

1. Open DB Manager by clicking on **DB Manager** under **Database**.
2. In the **Tree** panel, navigate to and select the database on which you wish to perform a SQL query.
3. Navigate to **Database** | **SQL window**, or press *F2* on your keyboard, to open the SQL window.

4. Enter a SQL query in the textbox at the top. Click on the **Execute** button or *F5* on your keyboard to execute the SQL query against the database. The results of the query will be displayed in the results box at the bottom, and the number of affected rows and execution time will appear next to the **Execute** button. An example of a successfully run query is shown in the following screenshot:

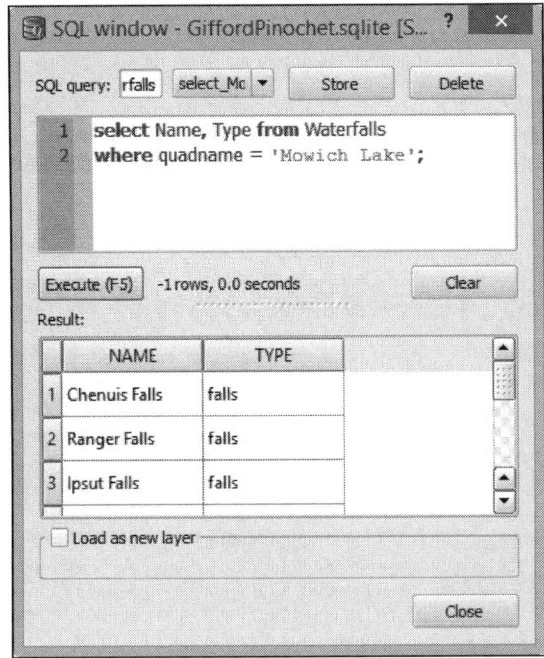

You can store any query by entering a name in the textbox at the top and then click on the **Store** button. To load and run the stored query, select the query name in the drop-down box at the top. To delete a stored query, select the query in the drop-down box and then click on the **Delete** button.

Creating a spatial view

Creating a spatial view on a SpatiaLite database using the SQL window in DB Manager is a two-step process. The first step is to create a view that includes a field with unique identifiers and the geometry column. The second step is to insert a new record in the `views_geometry_columns` table to register the view as a spatial view. In this section, we will create a spatial view on the `Waterfalls` table to show all the waterfalls in the Mowich Lake quad; to do this, perform the following steps:

1. Open DB Manager by clicking on **DB Manager** under **Database**.
2. In the **Tree** panel, navigate to and select the **GiffordPinochet.sqlite** database.

3. Navigate to **Database** | **SQL window**, or press *F2* on your keyboard, to open the SQL window.
4. Enter the following query:

    ```
    CREATE VIEW mowich_lake_waterfalls AS
    SELECT w.pk as ROWID, w.NAME, w.TYPE, w.geom from Waterfalls as w
    WHERE w.quadname = 'Mowich Lake';
    ```

    In the `CREATE VIEW` query, two fields are required to be included in the `SELECT` statement: the unique identifier field should be renamed to `ROWID` and the geometry field. You must rename the unique identifier to `ROWID` or the view cannot be registered as a spatial view.

5. Click on the **Execute** button to create the view. The following screenshot displays a successfully written and executed view of the `Waterfalls` table:

    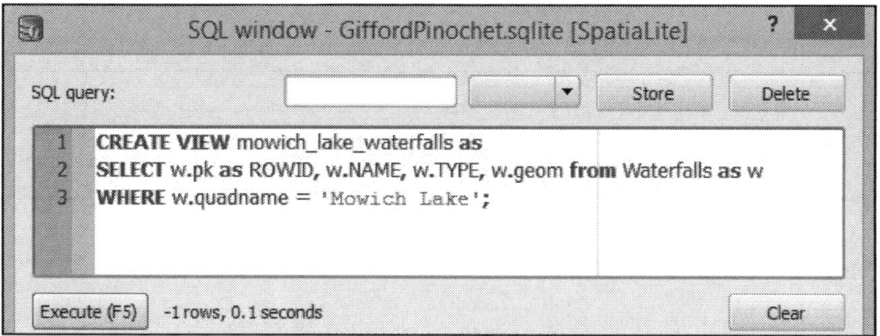

    Now that the view is created, we need to register it as a spatial view by inserting a new row in the `views_geometry_columns` table. This table links the view's geometry to the geometry of the table it selects from.

6. In the SQL window, click on the **Clear** button to clear the SQL query textbox.
7. Enter the following query:

    ```
    INSERT INTO views_geometry_columns (view_name, view_geometry,
    view_rowid, f_table_name, f_geometry_column, read_only)
    VALUES('mowich_lake_waterfalls', 'geom', 'rowid', 'waterfalls',
    'geom', 1);
    ```

    In this `INSERT` query, six fields have values inserted in them.

    - `view_name`: This contains the name of the view that we wish to register as spatial.
    - `view_geometry`: This contains the name of the geometry field in the view.

- `view_rowid`: This contains the name of the `rowid` field. Note that it *must* be `rowid`. If the `rowid` field is named something else, you will need to recreate the view with a `rowid` field.
- `f_table_name`: The name of the table the view is selecting from.
- `f_geometry_column`: The name of the geometry field in the table the view is selecting from.
- `read_only`: In this field, enter `1` for the spatial view to be read-only and enter `0` for the spatial view to be read/write. Note that as of version 2.6.0 of QGIS, views set as read/write cannot be edited in QGIS Desktop. However, views may be editable in some plugins or with SQL queries.

8. Click on the **Execute** button to create the view. The following screenshot displays a successfully written and executed view of the `Waterfalls` table:

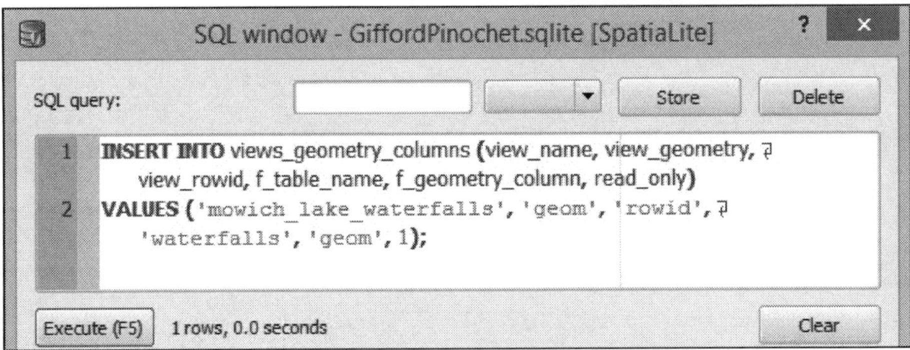

The view is now registered as spatial and can be added to the QGIS Desktop canvas like any other SpatiaLite spatial table.

Dropping a spatial view

Dropping a spatial view requires that you drop the spatial view table and delete the relating entry in the `view_geometry_columns` table.

To drop the spatial view table, use the SQL `DROP VIEW` command. For example, to drop the `mowich_lake_waterfalls` view, you will need to execute the following SQL command:

```
DROP VIEW mowich_lake_waterfalls
```

With the view dropped, the final step is to delete the related entry in the `view_geometry_columns` table by using the SQL `DELETE` command. For example, to drop the entry related to the `mowich_lake_waterfalls` view, you will need to execute the following SQL command:

```
DELETE FROM views_geometry_columns
WHERE view_name = 'mowich_lake_waterfalls';
```

Downloading the example code

You can download the example code files from your account at `http://www.packtpub.com` for all the Packt Publishing books you have purchased. If you purchased this book elsewhere, you can visit `http://www.packtpub.com/support` and register to have the files e-mailed directly to you.

Summary

This chapter provided you with the steps to handle databases in QGIS. While QGIS can handle multiple databases, we used SpatiaLite as it provides a good amount of functionality with little overhead or administration.

Using the DB Manager you can perform a number of operations on databases. Operations of note are: creating indices, spatial and aspatial views, importing and exporting, and performing queries. From the introduction to DB Manager and SpatiaLite in this chapter, you are now well-equipped to write more complex queries that take full advantage of the SQL commands and SpatiaLite SQL extension commands. A full listing of SQLite SQL commands are available at `http://www.sqlite.org/lang.html`. A full listing of the SpatialLite SQL extension commands are available at `http://www.gaia-gis.it/gaia-sins/spatialite-sql-4.2.0.html`.

The next chapter moves us from the storage of geospatial data to the display of geospatial data. The styling capabilities of QGIS will be covered for both vector and raster files. Additionally, the rendering options that were first introduced in QGIS 2.6 will be covered.

3
Styling Raster and Vector Data

In this chapter, we will cover advanced styling and labeling of raster and vector data in QGIS. It is assumed that you are familiar with basic styling in QGIS and are looking to improve your styling techniques. The topics that we will cover in this chapter are as follows:

- Choosing and managing colors
- Managing color ramps
- Styling single band rasters
- Styling multiband rasters
- Creating a raster composite
- Raster color rendering
- Raster resampling
- Styling vectors
- Vector layer rendering
- Using diagrams to display thematic data
- Saving, loading, and setting default styles

Choosing and managing colors

As colors are used throughout the styling process, we will first review the ways in which you can select and manage color collections in QGIS. The **color picker** is accessible in any window that allows a color selection to take place. For example, when choosing a color in the **Style** window under **Layer Properties**, click on the down arrow next to the color display and then select **Choose color...** as shown in the following screenshot:

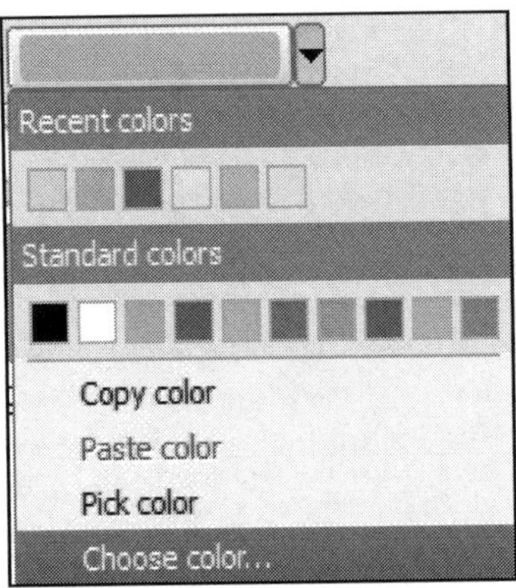

This will open the color picker tool, as shown in the following screenshot:

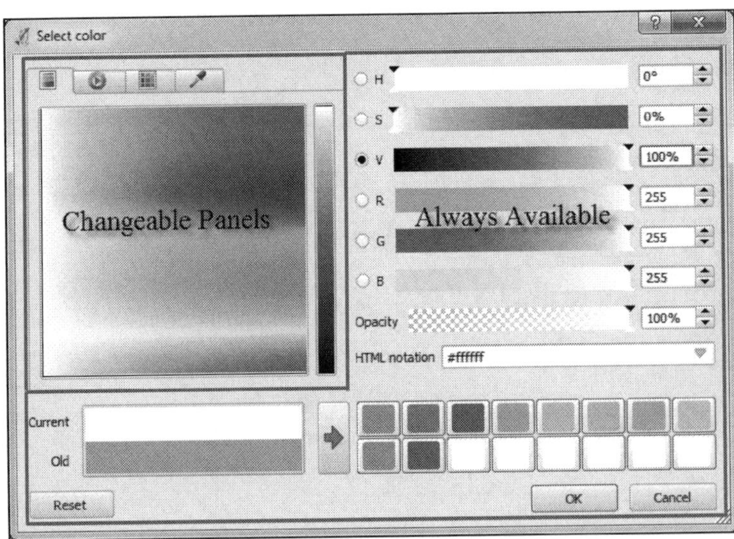

Let's take a tour of the color picker tool by starting with the components that are always available, and conclude our tour by looking at the four changeable panels.

Always available color picker components

The current and previous colors are displayed in the bottom-left corner of the color picker tool. In the preceding screenshot, the **Old** field depicts the color that is currently chosen, and the color mentioned in the **Current** field will replace the one in the **Old** field if the **OK** button is clicked. The current color can be saved into a quick-access color collection (the 16 colored squares in the bottom-right corner) using either of the following two ways:

- By clicking on the button with the blue arrow ( ). This will save the current color in the first column of the top row of the color collection, overwriting any existing color. Subsequent clicks on the blue arrow button will store the current color in the next column until all 16 boxes are full and then will loop back to the beginning.
- By Dragging and dropping the current color on top of a quick-access color box. The old color can also be saved using the drag and drop method.

The color picker displays and allows manipulation of the value in the **Current** field in two color models: HSV and RGB. On the right half of the color picker, the hue (**H**), saturation (**S**), value (**V**), red (**R**), green (**G**), and blue (**B**) values for the currently selected color are displayed. Each of these color parameters can be individually modified by either using the slider controls or by changing the numeric values.

Red, green, and blue values must be specified between `0` and `255` where `0` represents no color and `255` represents full color.

Hue is specified in degrees ranging from `0°` to `359°` where each degree represents a different location (and color) on the color wheel. Saturation and value are specified using percentages and range between `0%`, representing no saturation or value, and `100%` , representing full saturation or value.

Below the color parameters is the **Opacity** setting. The right half of the **Current** and **Old** fields display the color with the applied opacity level. For example, in the following screenshot, the current color is shown with no opacity (`100%`) on the left and with the currently selected opacity of `50%` on the right. The old color is shown with no opacity on the left and with the previously selected opacity of `100%` on the right (in this case, both sides are the same).

The **HTML notation** textbox displays the HTML color notation of the current color. The color notation can be changed to one of the four different formats by clicking on the down arrow ( ) in the **HTML notation** textbox.

Lastly, the **Reset** button resets the current color to match the old color.

Changeable panels in the color picker

The color picker has four changeable panels: Color ramp ( ), Color wheel ( ), Color swatches ( ), and Color sampler ( ). Each of these panels provide convenient ways to select and manage colors. This section will provide details of each of the four panels.

Color ramp

The color ramp panel is an interactive selection tool that sets the currently selected HSV or RGB parameter values based on the location of a mouse click. To select the color-model parameters that the color ramp will display, click on one of the radio selection buttons next to the **H**, **S**, **V**, **R**, **G**, or **B** values on the right half of the color picker. The selected parameter can be individually modified using the thin vertical slider control on the right-hand side of the color ramp panel. The other two color model parameters can be set simultaneously by clicking on the large color display on the left side of the color ramp panel. In the following screenshot, the **V** (Value) value in the HSV color model is selected and is represented in the thin vertical slider control; the **H** (Hue) and **S** (Saturation) values are combined and are represented in the large color display:

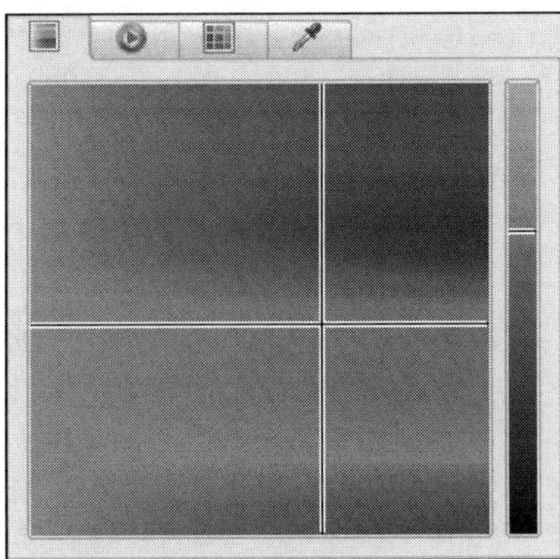

Color wheel

The color wheel panel, shown in the following screenshot, is an interactive selection tool that sets the color value based on mouse clicks. The ring contains the hue, while the triangle contains the saturation and value. To set the hue, click on the ring. To set the saturation and value (while not changing the hue), click on the triangle.

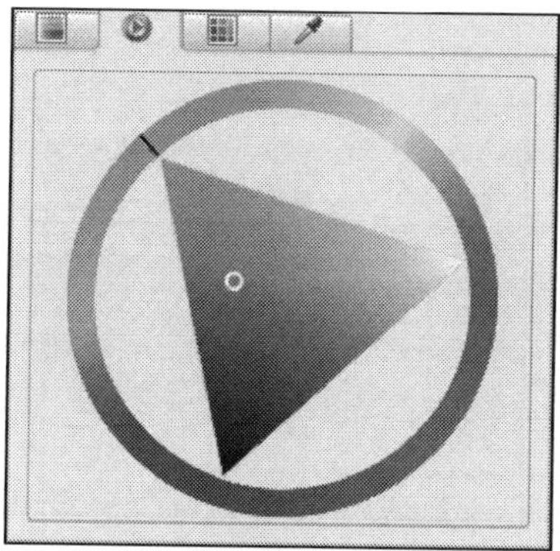

Color swatches

The color swatches panel, shown in the following screenshot, provides an interface to manage color palettes and select colors from the palettes:

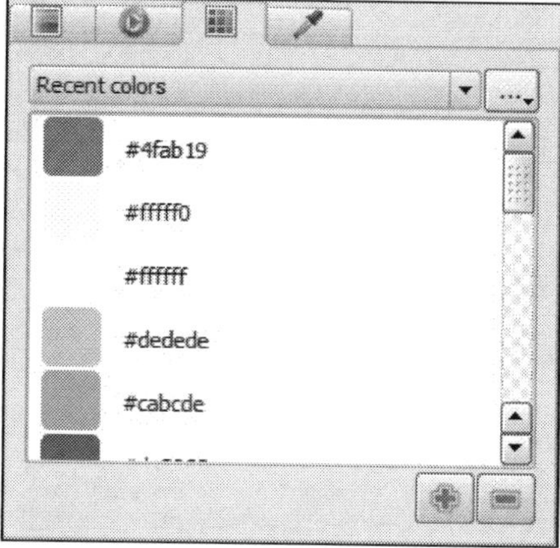

To switch between color palettes, select the desired color palette from the drop-down box at the top. The following three default color palettes are listed in the drop-down box:

- **Recent colors**: This contains the most recent colors selected in the color picker. This palette cannot be modified.

- **Standard colors**: This contains the colors that are always available as quick selections in QGIS.
- **Project colors**: This contains the colors that are stored within the QGIS project file.

The three default color palettes can be quickly accessed by clicking on the down arrow next to a color display, as shown in the following screenshot:

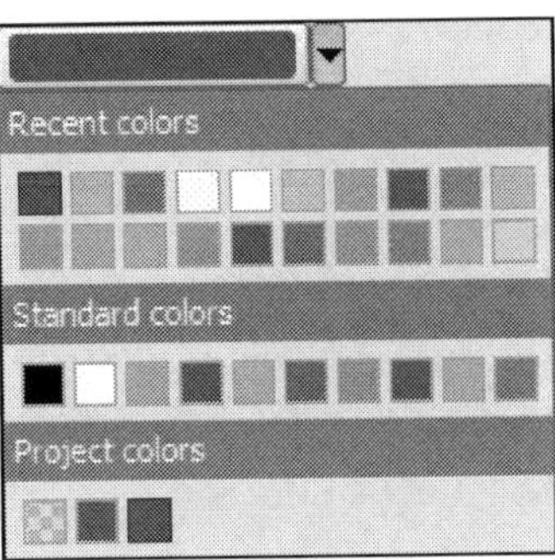

The current color can be added to a color palette by clicking on the plus sign button ( ). The color(s) selected in the palette can be removed by clicking on the minus sign button ( ). To apply a label to a color in a palette, double-click on the space to the right of the color swatch, enter the label, and press *Enter* on the keyboard. The label will be displayed as a tooltip when hovering the mouse over the color in the palette quick-access menu that was shown in the preceding screenshot.

The ellipsis drop-down button to the right of the palette select box provides seven handy functions to manage palettes. Let's review each one:

- **Copy Colors**: This copies the selected color(s) in the current palette to the clipboard.
- **Paste Colors**: This pastes color(s) stored in the clipboard to the current palette.
- **Import Colors**: This imports colors from a GPL palette file and places them into the current palette.
- **Export Colors**: This exports the current palette to a GPL palette file.
- **New Palette**: This create a new, empty palette that you can name. The palette will persist in the color picker until it is removed.
- **Import Palette**: This imports a GPL palette file into the list of palettes. The palette will persist in the color picker until it is removed.
- **Remove Palette**: This removes the current palette from the list. Note that the three default palettes cannot be removed.

Color sampler

The color sampler sets the current color to a color sample collected from the screen using the mouse pointer. The color sample is based on the average of all colors under the mouse pointer within the specified **Sample average radius** value. To collect a sample color, click on the **Sample color** button, then move the mouse cursor to a location where you want to sample a color, and then either press the spacebar or click to collect the sample. As you move the mouse cursor around, a preview of the sample color will appear under the **Sample color** button. The following screenshot shows the color sampler with **Sample average radius** of `5 px` (pixels) and a preview of the green color currently under the mouse cursor:

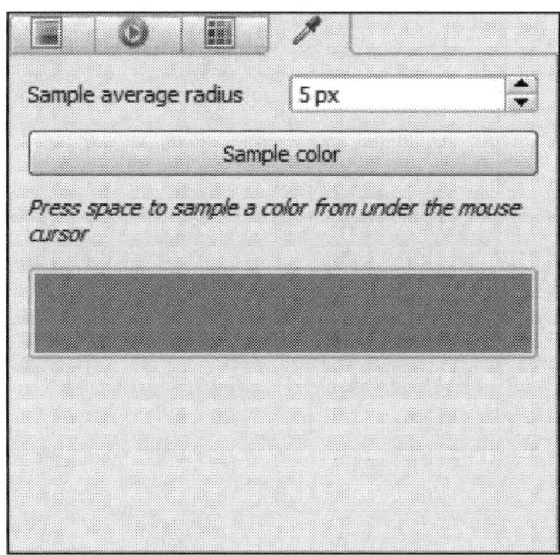

Now that the color picker dialog has been toured, and you know how to select colors and manage them in palettes, we will look at how to create and manage color ramps.

Managing color ramps

Color ramps are used in multiple applications when styling data. A color ramp is a series of continuous or discrete colors that can be applied to raster or vector data values. QGIS contains a number of color ramps that are ready to use and also allows you to add new color ramps. In this section, we will first demonstrate how to manage the QGIS color ramp collection and then how to add new color ramps.

Managing the QGIS color ramp collection

Color ramps can be managed and created using the **Style Manager** window. The **Style Manager** window provides an interface to manage the marker, line, fill, and color ramps that are available in the **Style** tab of the layer property window. To open the Style Manager, navigate to **Settings** | **Style Manager** and then click on the **Color ramp** tab. The **Style Manager** window is shown in the following screenshot:

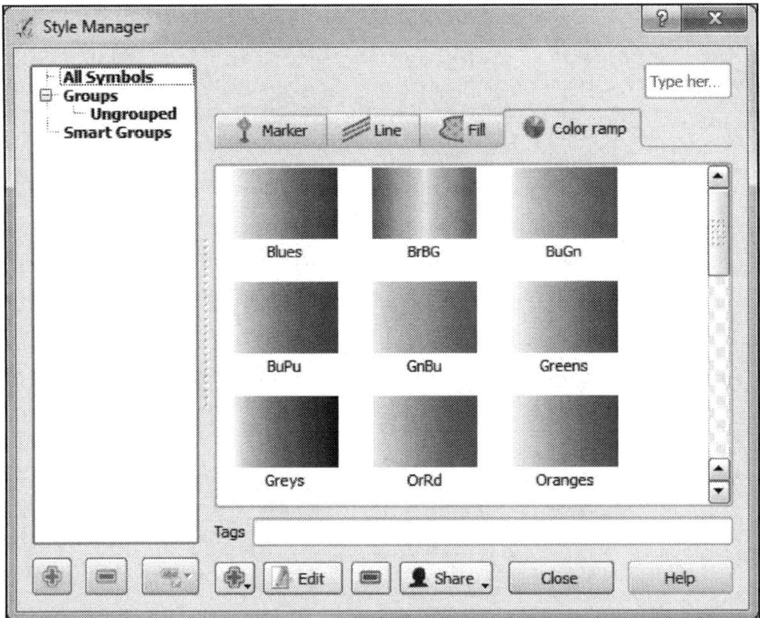

The color ramps displayed in the **Color ramp** tab are available for quick access from drop-down selection boxes when you style the data. For example, the following screenshot shows the quick-access color ramps in a drop-down box when we specify a color ramp to apply a pseudocolor to a single band raster:

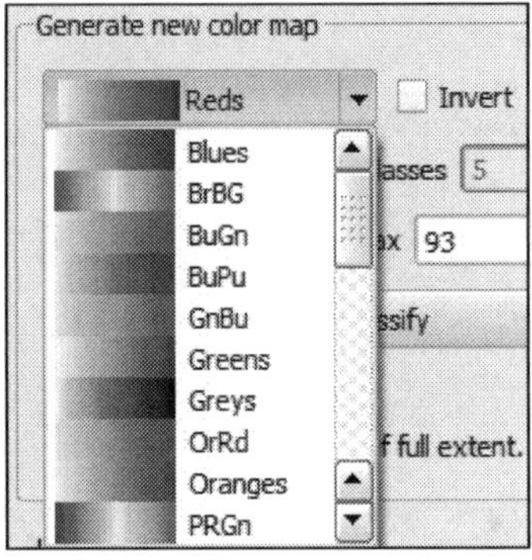

Six operations are available to manage color ramps in the Style Manager: rename, remove, export, import, add, and edit. Each of these operations will be explained now.

Renaming a color ramp

To rename a color ramp, click once on the color ramp to select it, *pause*, and then click on it a second time (this is a slow double-click) to make the name editable. Type in the new color ramp name, then press *Enter* to save it.

Removing a color ramp

To remove a color ramp, select the color ramp, then click on the Remove item button ( ). The color ramp will no longer be available.

Exporting a color ramp

To export a color ramp, navigate to **Share** | **Export** to open the **Export style(s)** window (shown in the following screenshot):

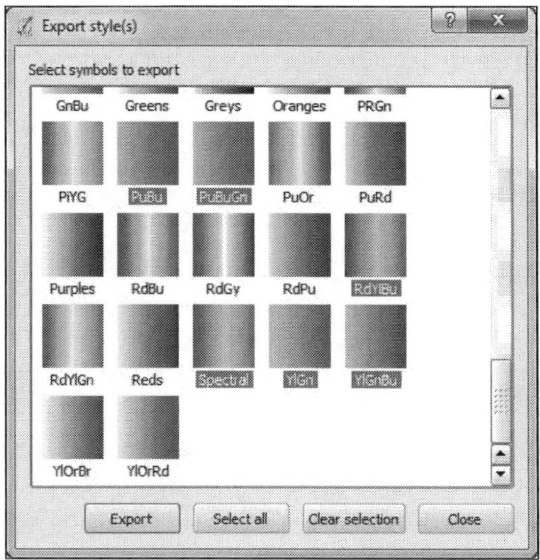

Select the symbols that you wish to export and then click on **Export** to export the selected symbols to an XML file. The exported symbols can later be imported to the Style Manager using the Import function.

Importing a color ramp

To import color ramps from an XML file, navigate to **Share** | **Import** to open the **Import style(s)** window (shown in the following figure):

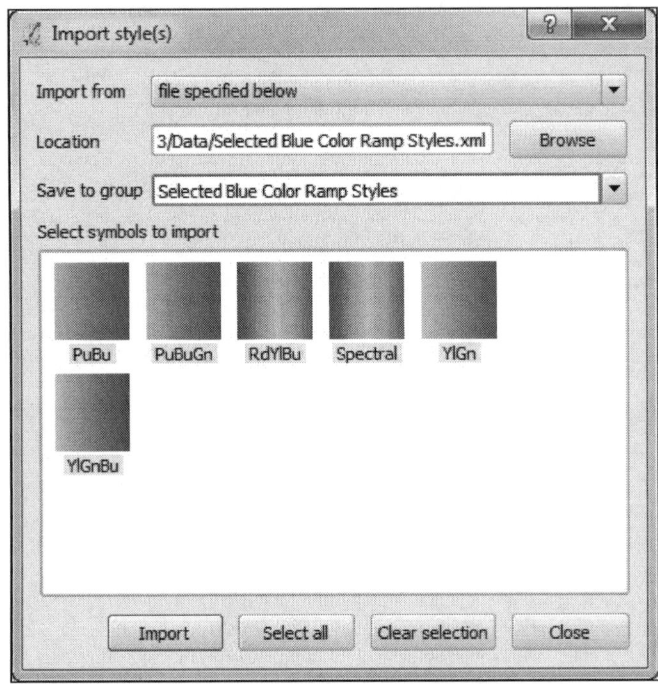

Exported color ramp styles can be imported from an XML file or a URL that is pointing to an XML file. To import from a file, select **file specified below** for the **Import from** parameter, then click on **Browse** to select the XML file. Once the **Location** value is specified, the color ramps will be displayed. Select the color ramps that you wish to import, select the group into which you wish to import the color ramps, and then click on **Import**. The imported color ramps (and other symbol types, if selected) will be added to the color ramp list in the Style Manager.

Adding a color ramp

Using the Add item button ( ), three types of color ramps—*Gradient*, *Random*, and *ColorBrewer*—can be added to the color ramp list in the Style Manager. These color ramp types can be created from scratch, or they can be selected from a large collection of existing color ramps from the cpt-city archive of color gradients.

Let's add one color ramp of each type and then add a cpt-city color ramp.

Adding a Gradient color ramp

To add a Gradient color ramp, click on the Add item button ( ) and then choose **Gradient**. This will open the **Gradient color ramp** window. A Gradient color ramp uses two colors, which are specified as **Color 1** and **Color 2**, to set the start and end colors. QGIS applies an algorithm to create a gradation between the two colors. Additional colors can be added to the gradient by clicking first on **Multiple stops** and then on **Add stop**; this will open the color picker. Once a color is chosen, you can enter the percentage along the gradient to apply the stop's color. Additional stops can be added by again clicking on **Add stop**. As an example, in the following screenshot, a gradient is created between red and green with a yellow stop at the 50 percent location:

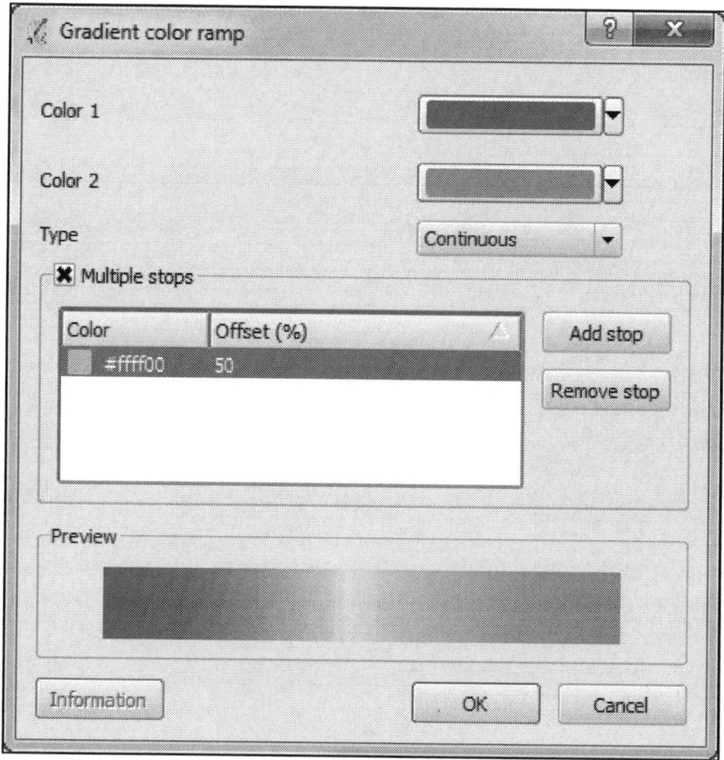

When all the gradient parameters have been set, click on **OK** to save the gradient. QGIS will prompt you to name the gradient. Once it is named, the gradient will appear in the Style Manager's list of color ramps after the default color ramps.

Adding a Random color ramp

To add a Random color ramp, click on the Add item button ( ) and then choose **Random**. This opens the **Random color ramp** window (shown in the following screenshot). A Random color ramp generates a number of randomly generated colors that fall within specified **Hue**, **Saturation**, and **Value** ranges. The **Classes** parameter determines how many colors to generate. Colors are randomly generated each time any one of the parameters are changed. As an example, in the following screenshot, five random colors are generated with different hues (between `100` and `320`) but with the same saturation and value:

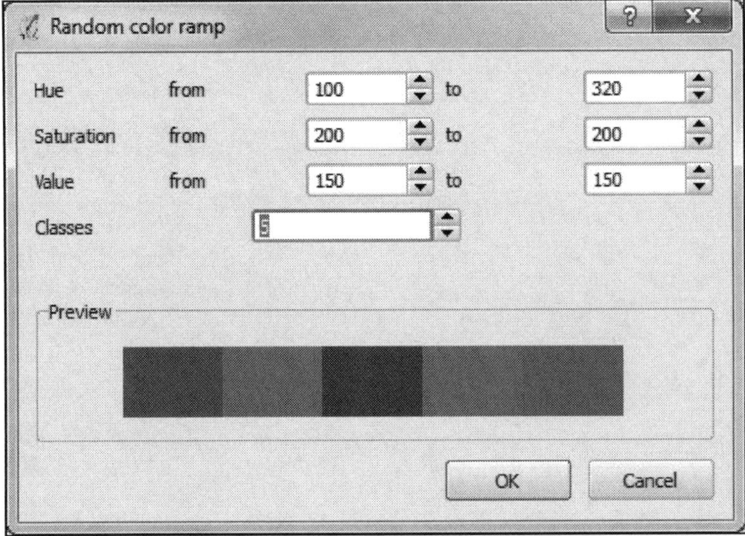

When all the parameters have been set, click on **OK** to save the Random color ramp. QGIS will prompt you to name the color ramp. Once it is named, the Random color ramp will appear in the Style Manager's list of color ramps.

Add a ColorBrewer color ramp

To add a ColorBrewer color ramp, click on the Add item button ( ) and then choose **ColorBrewer**. This opens the **ColorBrewer ramp** window (shown in the following figure). A ColorBrewer color ramp generates three to eleven colors using one of the available schemes. The **Colors** parameter determines how many colors to generate and the **Scheme name** parameter sets the color scheme that will be used. As an example, in the following screenshot, five colors are generated using the **RdGy** (Red to Grey) color scheme:

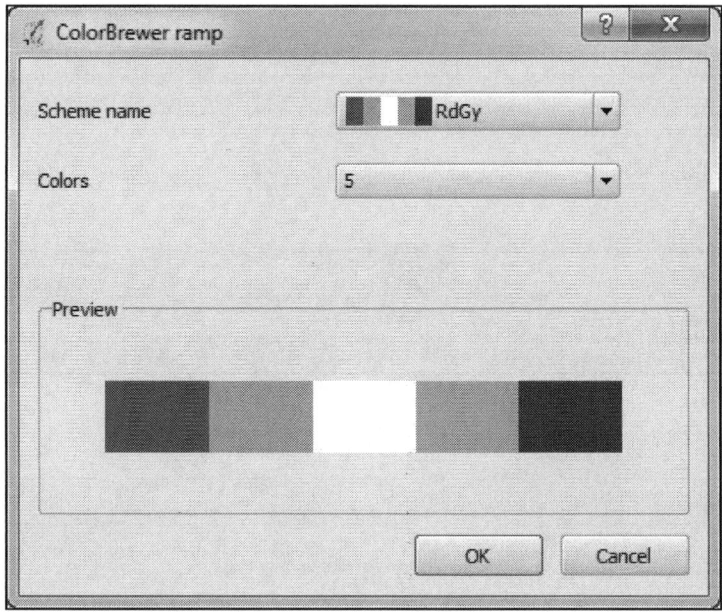

When all the parameters have been set, click on **OK** to save the ColorBrewer color ramp. QGIS will prompt you to name the color ramp. Once it is named, the ColorBrewer color ramp will appear in the Style Manager's list of color ramps.

[The ColorBrewer color ramps are based on the work of Cynthia Brewer. For more information and an interactive color selector, visit the ColorBrewer website at `http://colorbrewer2.org/`.]

Adding a cpt-city color ramp

If you do not want to add a color ramp from scratch, a large collection of existing color ramps from the cpt-city archive of color gradients is available for use in QGIS. To add a cpt-city color ramp, click on the Add item button ( ) and then choose **cpt-city**. This opens the **cpt-city color ramp** window (shown in the following screenshot):

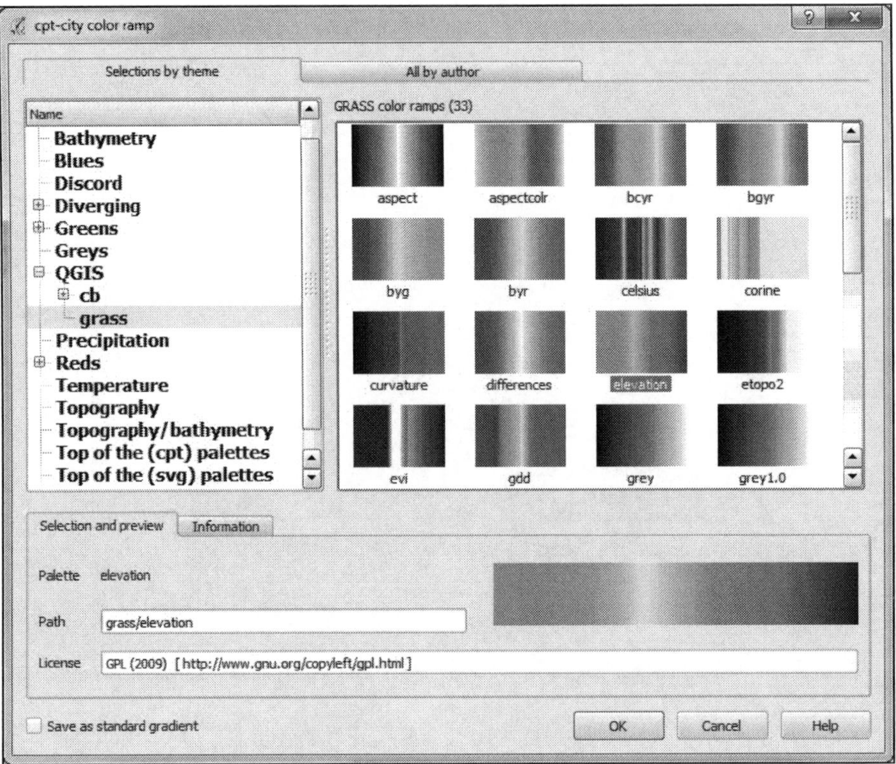

Color ramps can be selected by theme or by author by choosing the appropriate tab at the top of the window. In either case, the color ramps are presented in an expandable tree on the left with a listing of color ramps in each tree element on the right. When a color ramp is selected, the **Selection and preview** and **Information** tabs are populated.

There are two ways to add a cpt-city color ramp to the list in the Style Manager: as a cpt-city or as a standard gradient color ramp.

To save the color ramp as a cpt-city color ramp, click on **OK** with a color ramp selected. This will keep the link between the added color ramp and the cpt-city color ramp list. The color ramp cannot be modified if it is added as a cpt-city color ramp.

To save the color ramp as a standard gradient color ramp, check **Save as standard gradient** and then click on **OK**. This will save the color ramp as a gradient color ramp and the color ramp will not link back to the cpt-city color ramp collection. The color ramp can be modified later as it has been converted to a standard gradient color ramp.

Be sure to review the license information for the cpt-city color ramps in the **Information** tab's **License** field. Many different licenses are used and some require attribution before they can be used.

The cpt-city archive of gradients is available at `http://soliton.vm.bytemark.co.uk/pub/cpt-city/`. The archive contains thousands of gradients. The gradients that are most applicable to style geographic data have been included in the QGIS cpt-city collection.

Editing a color ramp

To edit a color ramp, select the color ramp and then click on the **Edit** button. This will open one of the four types of windows depending on which type of color ramp was selected: Gradient, Random, ColorBrewer, or cpt-city. Using the opened window, the properties of the color ramp can be modified.

Now that color ramps have been discussed, we will put the color ramps to work by styling raster data with color ramps and later, we will use color ramps to style vector data.

Styling single band rasters

In this section, the three different band render types that are appropriate for single band rasters will be covered. Single band rasters can be styled using three different band render types: paletted, singleband gray, and singleband pseudocolor.

Note that even though raster color rendering and resampling are part of raster style properties, they will be discussed separately in later sections as they are common to all single band and multiband raster renderers.

The raster band render type should be chosen to best match the type of data. For instance, a palette renderer is best used on rasters that represent discrete data, such as land use classes. The singleband gray would be a good choice for a hillshade, while a singleband pseudocolor would work well on a raster containing global temperature data.

Paletted raster band rendering

The paletted raster band renderer applies a single color to a single raster value. QGIS supports the loading of rasters with paletted colors stored within and the changing the color assigned to the raster value. QGIS does not currently support the creation of color palettes for single band rendering. However, existing QGIS layer style files (`.qml`) that contain palettes can be applied by clicking on the **Load Style** button in the layer properties.

As an example of a raster with a color palette stored within it, add `NA_LC_1km.tif` from the sample data to the QGIS canvas and open the **Style** tab under **Layer Properties**. The following figure shows the **Paletted band** renderer being applied to **Band 1** of the raster:

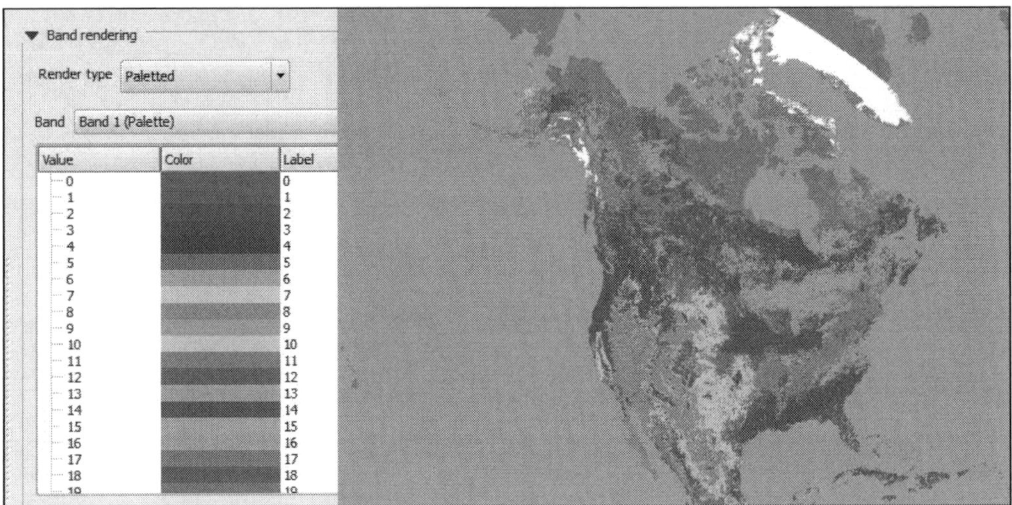

To change a color, double-click on a color in the **Color** column to open the color picker.

Singleband gray raster band rendering

The singleband gray band renderer stretches a gradient between black and white to a single raster band. Additionally, contrast enhancements are available to adjust the way the gradient is stretched across the raster band's values. Let's apply a singleband gray renderer and a contrast enhancement to the sample `GRAY_50M_SR_W.tif` raster file that represents shaded relief, hypsography, and flat water for Earth.

Add `GRAY_50M_SR_W.tif` to the QGIS canvas and open its **Style** tab from **Layer Properties**. As this is a singleband raster, QGIS defaults the **Render type** value to **Singleband gray** with the following parameters (as shown in the following screenshot):

- **Gray band**: **Band 1 (Gray)** (The raster band that is being styled. If a multiband raster is being used, then the combobox will be populated with all raster bands.)
- **Color gradient**: **Black to white** (The gradient to apply to the selected gray band. The choices are **Black to white** and **White to black**.)
- **Min**: `105` (The minimum cell value found in the gray band.)
- **Max**: `207` (The maximum cell value found in the gray band.)
- **Contrast enhancement**: **Stretch to MinMax** (The method used to stretch the color gradient to the gray band with respect to the **Min** and **Max** values.)

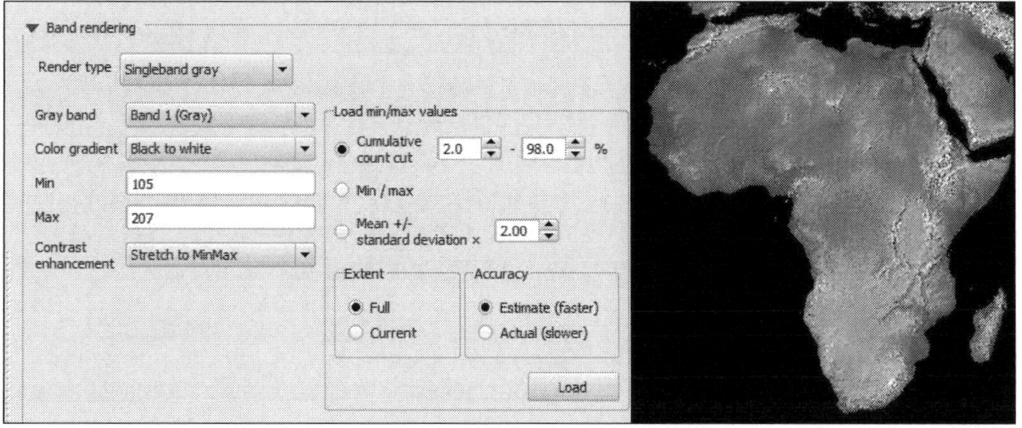

The **Min**, **Max**, and **Contrast enhancement** parameters work together to determine how to stretch the color gradient to the gray band. To understand how these parameters work together, we need to first discuss how the **Min** and **Max** values are derived, which draws our attention to the **Load min/max values** section of the **Band rendering** options. The **Load min/max values** section contains parameters that are used to calculate which **Min** and **Max** values should be set. Three sets of parameters must be set before you click on the **Load** button; they are as follows:

- **Cell value selection**: Selects cell values to include in the **Min** and **Max** value determination. Rasters may have cell values that are outliers, which may affect the rendering of the image. For instance, if only a few cells have an abnormally high value, then the gradient will stretch all the way to these high values, which will cause the raster to look overly gray and bland. To combat this grayness, some cell values can be excluded so that the gradient is not skewed by these outliers. Three methods are available to select cell values, and it is recommended that you experiment with these values to achieve the most desirable selection of cell values:
    - **Cumulative count cut**: This includes all values between the two parameters. In the preceding screenshot, all values between `2%` and `98%` of the cell data range were included. In general, this will remove the few very high and very low values that may skew the gradient.
    - **Min / max**: This includes all values.
    - **Mean +/- standard deviation**: This includes all values within the specified number of standard deviations about the mean of all values.
- **Extent**: The extent of the raster to sample for cell values. Either the **Full** extent of the raster or the **Current** canvas extent can be used.
- **Accuracy**: This determines the accuracy of the min/max calculation. The calculation can either be an **Estimate (faster)** or an **Actual (slower)** option. In general, **Actual (slower)** is the preferred option; however, for very large rasters, **Estimate (faster)** may be preferred to save time.

With the **Load min/max values** set, click on the **Load** button to calculate the **Min** and **Max** values. With the **Min** and **Max** values set, we can turn our attention to the **Contrast enhancement** parameter. The **Contrast enhancement** parameter sets how to stretch the color gradient across the cell values of the gray band. The following four methods are available for **Contrast enhancement**:

- **No enhancement**: No enhancement is applied. The color gradient is stretched across all values in the entire gray band. While this may be desired sometimes, it may tend to make the raster look overly gray.

- **Stretch to MinMax**: This method stretches the color gradient across the gray band between the **Min** and **Max** values. It generally produces a higher contrast, a darker rendering than **No enhancement**. All cell values below the **Min** value are assigned the lowest gradient color and all cell values above the **Max** value are assigned the highest gradient color.
- **Stretch and clip to MinMax**: This method stretches the color gradient across the gray band between the **Min** and **Max** values. It produces the same rendering as the **Stretch to MinMax** method, except that all cell values below the **Min** value and all values above the **Max** value are assigned no color (and they are transparent).
- **Clip to MinMax**: This method stretches the color gradient across all values in the gray band, which is the same result as **No enhancement**, except that all cell values below the **Min** value and all values above the **Max** value are assigned no color (and they are transparent).

The following figure shows the effects of the four different **Contrast enhancement** methods on the `Gray_50M_SR_W.tif` sample file when the **Color gradient** field is set to **Black to white, Min** is set to `107`, and **Max** is set to `207`. A **Min** value of `107` is selected to exclude the cell value of `106` that is associated with the oceans.

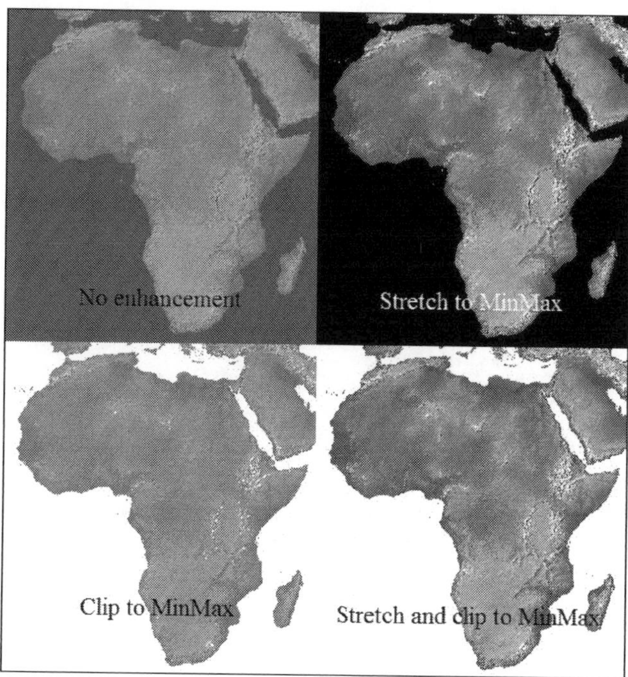

Singleband pseudocolor raster band rendering

The singleband pseudocolor band renderer stretches a color ramp to a single raster band. Additionally, three **Color interpolation** methods are available to adjust the way the color ramp is stretched across the raster band's values with respect to the min and max cell values (for a discussion on determining min and max values, see the preceding section).

Let's apply a singleband pseudocolor renderer to the `GRAY_50M_SR_W.tif` sample data raster file that represents shaded relief, hypsography, and flat water for Earth. Add `GRAY_50M_SR_W.tif` to the QGIS canvas and open its **Style** tab from **Layer Properties**. For the **Render type** field, choose **Singleband pseudocolor**.

The singleband pseudocolor render type has many interworking parameters that are best explained as a whole through the lens of a workflow, instead of explaining them as separate parts. The example shown in the following screenshot will be the basis for explaining the parameters:

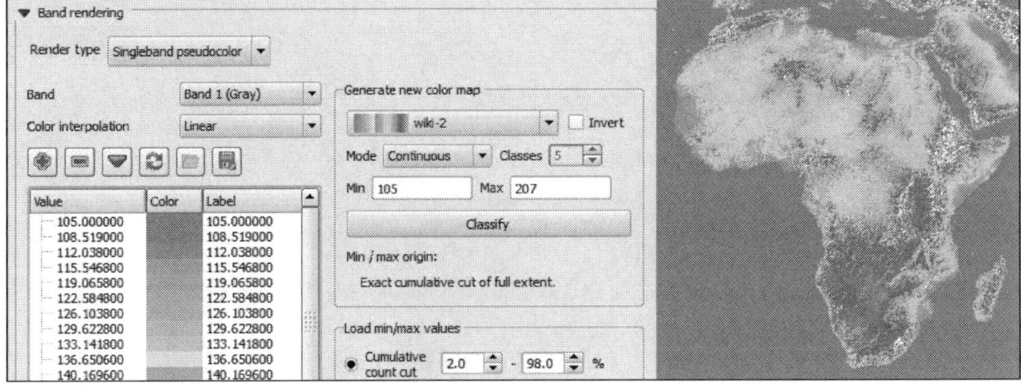

1. First, the band should be selected. For the **Band** field, choose **Band 1 (Gray)**. If this were a multiband raster, more bands would be available for selection.
2. Next, we should choose the color ramp to apply to the raster. As none of the default color ramps are suitable for our example, click on the color ramp combobox to open it, scroll to the bottom, and choose **New color ramp** (as shown in following screenshot):

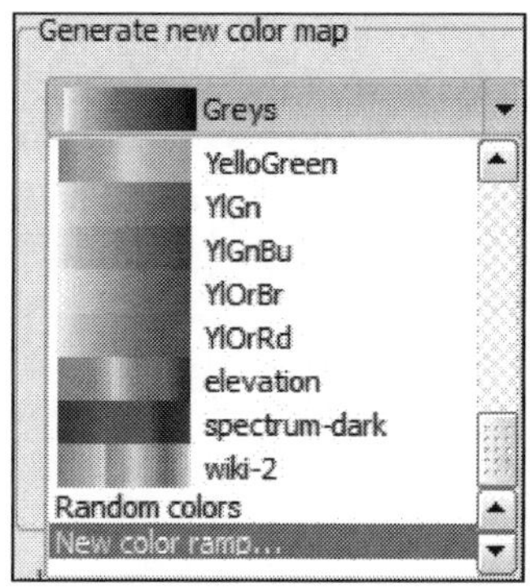

3. When prompted, choose **cpt-city** as the color ramp type, then click on **OK**. This will open the **cpt-city color ramp** window. In the **Topography/bathymetry** group, select the **wiki-2.0** color ramp and add it. Optionally, the color ramp can be inverted by checking the **Invert** parameter.

   The color ramp can be applied to the raster cell values in a **Continuous** or **Equal interval** classification mode terminating at the **Min** and **Max** values:

   - **Continuous**: This stretches the color ramp between the **Min** and **Max** values with each unique value being assigned a unique color.
   - **Equal interval**: This assigns a number of colors, designated by the **Classes** parameter, across groups of values. For instance, if five classes are specified, then no matter how many unique values exist in the raster, five colors will be applied to the raster where each color will be applied to groups of values with group value ranges of *(Max – Min)/Classes*.

4. Set the mode to **Continuous**, the **Min** value to `105`, and **Max** value to `207`.
5. Click on the **Classify** button to apply the color ramp to the values. The classification list on the left will populate with values, colors, and labels.

   The last step is to choose the **Color interpolation** method. The following three methods are available and they have a significant effect on how the raster will be rendered:

   - **Discrete**: Assigns only, and exactly, the colors chosen in the classification list. Values between values listed in the **Value** column are assigned the color assigned to the next highest listed value. In other words, if there are, say, 164 unique values in the raster and 15 colors listed in the classification list, the raster will be rendered with exactly the 15 listed colors. This method is best for cases where you want to reduce the number of colors that will be used to render the raster.

- **Linear**: This assigns a unique color to each unique raster value. Values between values listed in the **Value** column are assigned a unique color that is calculated linearly and is based on its location between the surrounding listed values. In other words, if there are, say, 164 unique values in the raster and 15 colors listed in the classification list, the raster will be rendered with the 164 unique colors that appear as a nice, linear progression through the 15 listed colors. This method is best for raster data that represents continuous information (for example, elevation or temperature data) where you want a smooth progression of color that is stretched across the raster values.
- **Exact**: This assigns a unique color to only the values listed in the **Value** column of the classification list. In other words, if there are, say, 164 unique values in the raster and 15 colors (and 15 associated values) listed in the classification list, only the 15 raster values that are listed will be rendered with their associated colors. No other values will be assigned a color. This method is best for raster data that represents discrete data classes where you do not want non-listed values to be assigned any color.

  The following figure shows the effects of the three **Color interpolation** methods on our sample data as configured so far:

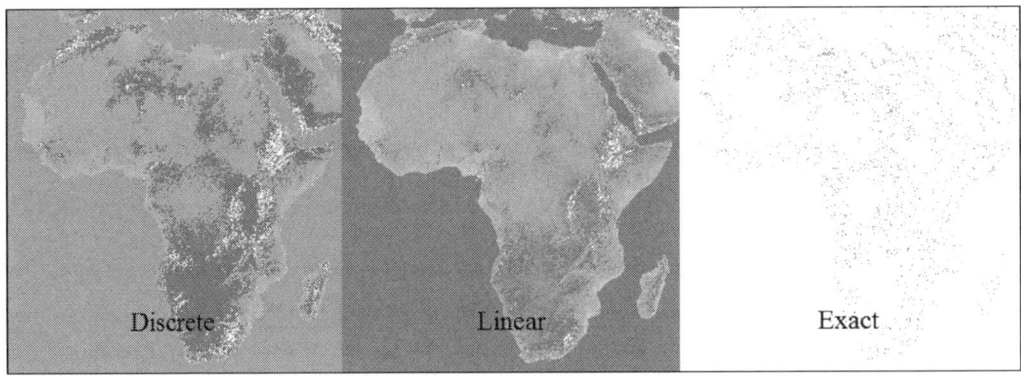

6. Set the **Color interpolation** field to **Linear** to assign all unique values a unique color.

   Optionally, you could check **Clip** (below classification list); this would not assign colors to values outside the maximum and minimum values listed in the classification list.

7. Click on **Apply** or **OK** to render the raster.

These three single band render types (paletted, singleband gray, and singleband pseudocolor) provide a large amount of flexibility and customization to fit your styling needs. The next section covers the remaining band render type that is best applied to multiband rasters: multiband color.

Styling multiband rasters

The multiband color band renderer stretches three gradients (red, green, and blue) to three separate raster bands. The basic idea is that the computer will display natively used combinations of red, green, and blue lights to create the desired image. By matching individual raster bands to the red, green, and blue lights used by the display, the three bands' colors will mix so that they are perceived as other colors, thereby creating a red, green, and blue image composite that is suitable for display.

Contrast enhancements are available to adjust the way the gradients are stretched across the raster bands' values. Contrast enhancements have already been covered in the *Singleband gray raster band rendering* section, so refer to this section for an in-depth coverage of the topic.

Let's see how multiband rasters are rendered in QGIS. Add `TL_ASTER.jpg` from the sample data to the QGIS canvas. This sample image is a TerraLook image derived from an ASTER image. Open the **Style** tab from **Layer Properties**. As this is a multiband raster, QGIS defaults the **Render type** field to **Multiband color** with the parameters shown in the following screenshot:

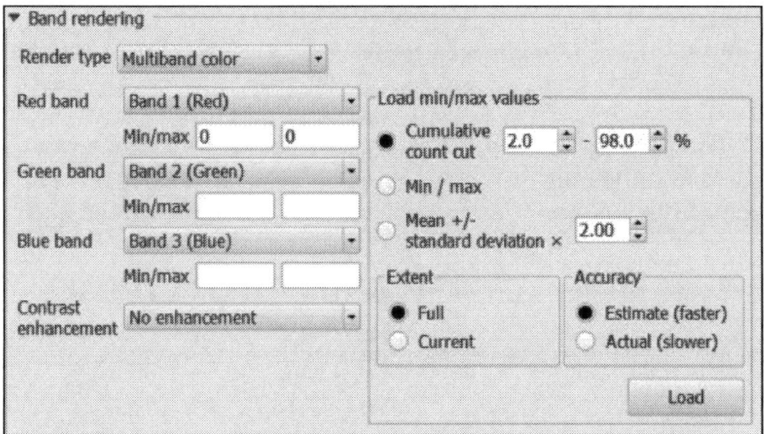

The multiband color renderer allows you to designate which raster band will be applied to each of the three color bands (which you can think of as color ramps). In the preceding screenshot, the raster has three bands with **Band 1 (Red)** applied to **Red band**, **Band 2 (Green)** applied to **Green band**, and **Band 3 (Blue)** applied to **Blue band**.

To change which raster band is applied to the color bands, select the band from the drop-down boxes. The drop-down boxes will list all the bands stored in the raster as well as **Not set** (that is shown in the following screenshot). Choosing **Not set** does not apply a raster band to a color band.

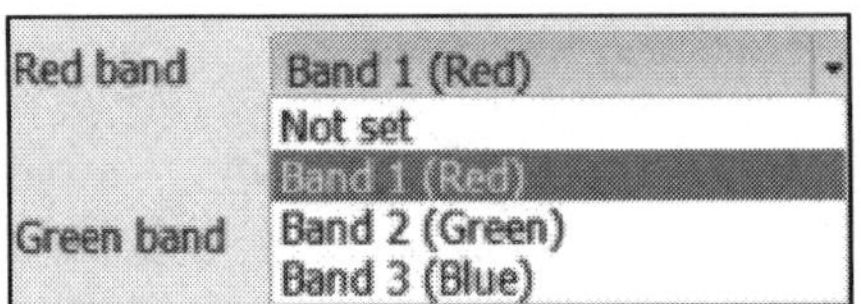

After exploring all the four band-rendering options, it is time to shift our focus to the bottom two sections of the raster style window: color rendering and resampling.

Creating a raster composite

To combine many separate raster files (each representing one raster band) into a raster composite, we can use the r.composite tool in the Processing Toolbox. The processing toolbox (which is covered in detail in *Chapter 7, The Processing Toolbox*) allows us to access tools from GRASS GIS, which contains the r.composite tool. The r.composite tool assigns three singleband rasters to a red, green, and blue raster band and produces one multiband raster.

To open the r.composite tool, open the processing toolbox first by navigating to **Processing | Toolbox**. In the search box at the top of the processing toolbox, type `r.composite` to find the tool and then double-click on the tool to open it. This will open the r.composite tool window, as shown in the following screenshot:

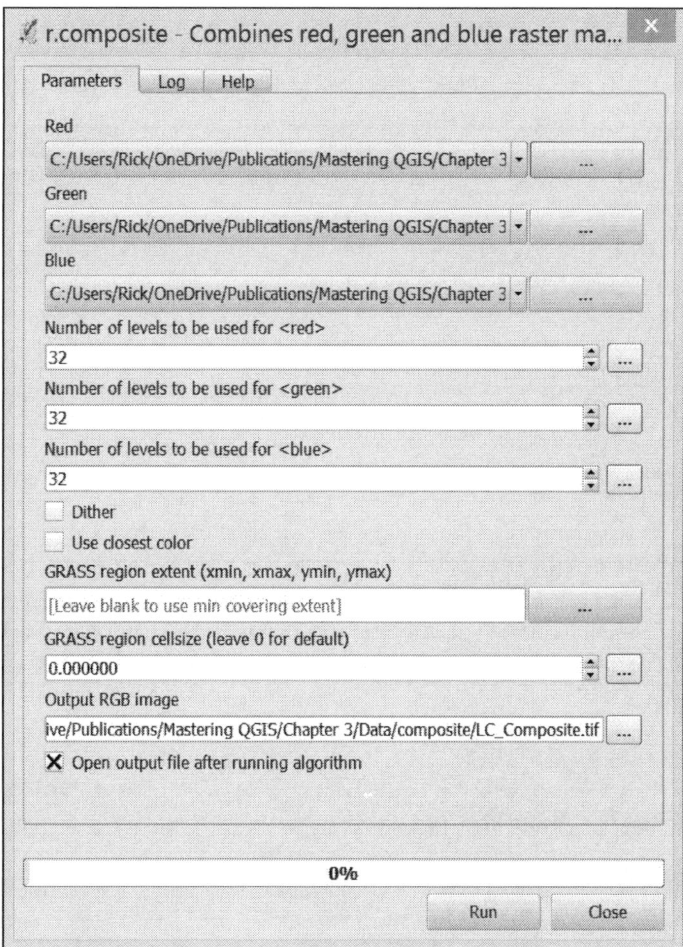

The r.composite tool has a number of parameters that can be set and these are as follows:

- **Red**: This includes the raster that will be assigned to the red band.
- **Green**: This include the raster that will be assigned to the green band.
- **Blue**: This includes the raster that will be assigned to the blue band.
- **Number of levels to be used for <band>**: This includes the number of levels that the input raster values will be mapped to.
- **Dither**: If this is checked, will dither the image to reduce banding and loss of detail.
- **Use closest color**: If this is checked, the original pixel colors will be translated into the closest palette color. No dithering will occur if this is enabled.

- **GRASS region extent**: This sets the region extent of the output composite raster. Uses the minimum of inputs by default; otherwise, the extent can be set from the current canvas extent or by a layer in the **Layers** panel.
- **GRASS region cell size**: This sets the cell size of the output composite raster.
- **Output RGB image**: This includes the name and location of the output composite raster.
- **Open output file after running algorithm**: If this is checked, the output composite raster will be added to the map canvas.

The output raster composite will contain three bands and it will be automatically styled as a multiband raster in QGIS.

Raster color rendering

Raster color rendering modifies the properties of the raster to change the way it displays and interacts with the layer below it in the **Layers** panel. Color rendering is a part of the raster style properties for all band renderer types and works in the same way, regardless of the selected band renderer. In this section, we will discuss the parameters available for change in the **Color rendering** section of the raster style properties.

When a raster is first loaded, the **Color rendering** parameters are set to their default values, as shown in the following screenshot. At any time, the default values can be reloaded by clicking on the **Reset** button.

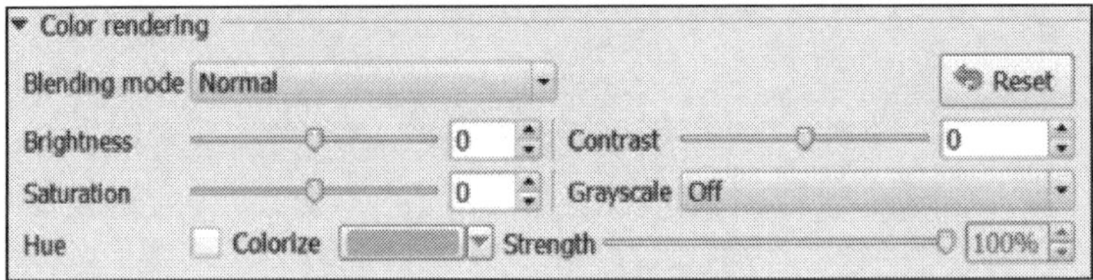

There are six parameters that can be set in the **Color rendering** section and these are as follows.

- **Blending mode**: This applies a blending method to the raster that mixes with layers below it in the **Layers** panel. A number of blending modes are available to choose from and these are commonly found in graphics editing programs. There are 13 blending modes and these are as follows:
    - **Normal**: This is the default blending node. If the raster has any transparent cells, the colors from the layer below the raster will show through, otherwise no colors will be mixed.

- **Lighten**: In this mode, for each raster cell in the or the raster below, the maximum value for each color component that is found in either raster is used.
- **Screen**: In this mode, lighter cells from the raster below are displayed transparently over the raster while darker pixels are not.
- **Dodge**: This mode increases the brightness and saturation of the raster cells below based on the brightness of the raster's cells.
- **Addition**: This mode adds the color components of each cell of this raster and the raster below together. If the color component value exceeds the maximum allowed value, then the maximum value is used.
- **Darken**: In this mode, for each raster cell in the raster, or the raster below, the minimum value of each color component found in either raster is used.
- **Multiply**: This mode multiplies the color components of each cell of the raster and the raster below together. This will darken the raster.
- **Burn**: In this mode, the raster below is darkened using the darker colors from this raster. Burn works well when you want to apply the colors of this raster subtly to the raster below.
- **Overlay**: This mode combines the multiply and screen methods. When this is used for the raster below, lighter areas become lighter and darker areas become darker.
- **Soft light**: This mode combines the burn and dodge methods.
- **Hard light**: This mode is the same as the overlay method; however, this raster and the raster below are swapped for inputs.
- **Difference**: This mode subtracts this raster's cell values from the cell values of the raster below. If a negative value is obtained, then the cell value from the raster below is subtracted from this raster's cell value.
- **Subtract**: This mode subtracts this raster's cell values from the cell values of the raster below. If a negative value is obtained, a black color is displayed.

• **Brightness**: This changes the brightness of the raster. Brightness affects how bright or dark the raster appears. Brightness affects all cells in the raster in the same way.

- **Contrast**: This changes the contrast value of the raster. **Contrast** separates the lightest and darkest areas of the raster. An increase in contrast increases the separation and makes darker areas darker and brighter areas brighter. For example, a large negative contrast of `-75`, would produce a mostly gray or monotone image, since the bright and dark colors are not separated very much at all.
- **Saturation**: This changes the saturation value of the raster. Saturation increases the separation between colors. An increase in saturation makes the colors look more vibrant and distinct, while a decrease in saturation makes the colors look duller and more neutral.
- **Grayscale**: This renders the raster using a grayscale color ramp. The following three rendering methods are available:
    - **By lightness**: In this method, an average of the lightness value of multiple raster band values will be applied to the gray color ramp with the saturation set as `0`. If the raster only has one band, then each cell's lightness value will be used. The lightness value is calculated using the formula *0.5 * (max(R,G,B) + min(R,G,B))*.
    - **By luminosity**: In this method, a weighted average of multiple raster band values will be applied to the gray color ramp. Luminosity approximates how you perceive brightness from colors. The weighted average is calculated using the formula *0.21 * red + 0.72 * green + 0.07 * blue*.
    - **By average**: In this method, the average of the raster band values for each cell will be applied to the color ramp. If the raster only has one band, this selection will have no effect. For example, if the raster had three bands with cell values of `25`, `50`, and `75`, then `50` would be applied as the cell value for the gray color ramp. The average is calculated using the formula *(R+G+B)/3*.
- **Hue**: This parameter adds a hue to each cell of the raster. To apply a hue, check the **Colorize** box and then select a color using the color picker. The **Strength** parameter linearly scales the application of the selected **Colorize** color to the existing raster colors.

Raster resampling

Raster resampling prepares the raster for display when not every raster cell can be mapped to its own pixel on the display. If each raster cell is mapped to its own display pixel, the raster renders at full resolution (also known as 1:1). However, since screen sizes are limited and we may wish to enlarge or reduce the size of the raster as we work at different map scales, the raster cells must be mapped to more than one pixel or a number of raster cells must be combined, or dropped, to map to a single pixel. As some raster cells cannot be shown at different resolutions, QGIS must determine how to render the raster and still maintain the character of the full-resolution raster. This section will discuss the parameters available for determining how the raster will be resampled for display.

The **Resampling** section of the raster **Style** tab has three parameters: **Zoomed: in**, **Zoomed: out**, and **Oversampling**. The **Resampling** section with its default parameters is shown in the following screenshot:

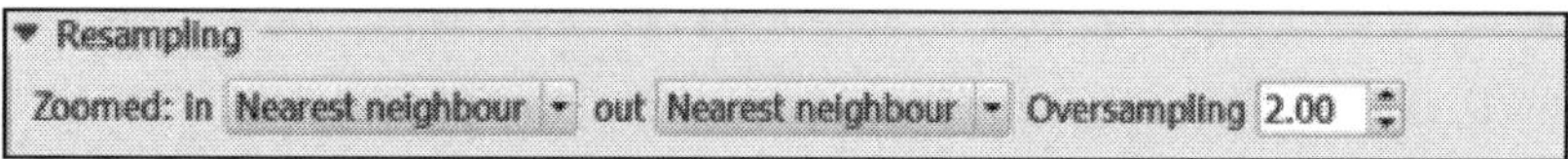

The **Zoomed: in** parameter sets the resampling method when zoomed in on the raster. Three resampling methods are available for selection: **Nearest neighbour**, **Bilinear**, and **Cubic**.

The **Zoomed: out** parameter sets the resampling method when zoomed out from the raster. Two resampling methods are available for selection: **Nearest neighbour** and **Average**.

The **Oversampling** parameter determines how many subpixels will be used to compute the value when zoomed out.

The four resampling methods that can be selected for use are as follows:

- **Nearest neighbour**: In this method, each raster cell is assigned the value of the nearest cell (measure between cell centers). This is a great method to choose when the raster represents discrete, categorical data as no new values are created.
- **Bilinear**: In this method, each raster cell is assigned an average value based on the four closest cells with original values. This method will smooth the data and may flatten peaks and fill valleys.
- **Average**: In this method, each raster cell is assigned an average value based on surrounding cells with original values. This method will smooth the data and may flatten peaks and fill valleys.

- **Cubic**: In this method, each raster cell is assigned an interpolated value based on the surrounding cells with original values. Unlike the bilinear method, this method will not smooth the peaks or valleys as much and it tends to maintain local averages and variability. This is the most computationally intensive method.

Styling vectors

In this section, the six different vector styling types will be covered. The six types are single symbol, categorized, graduated, rule-based, point-displacement, and inverted polygons.

Note that even though layer rendering is part of vector style properties, it will be discussed separately in the next section as it is common to all vector styling types.

Single-symbol vector styling

The single-symbol vector style applies the same symbol to every record in the vector dataset. This vector style is best when you want a uniform look for a map layer, such as when you style lake polygons or airport points.

The following screenshot shows the **Single Symbol** style type with default parameters for point vector data. Its properties will be very similar to line and polygon vector data.

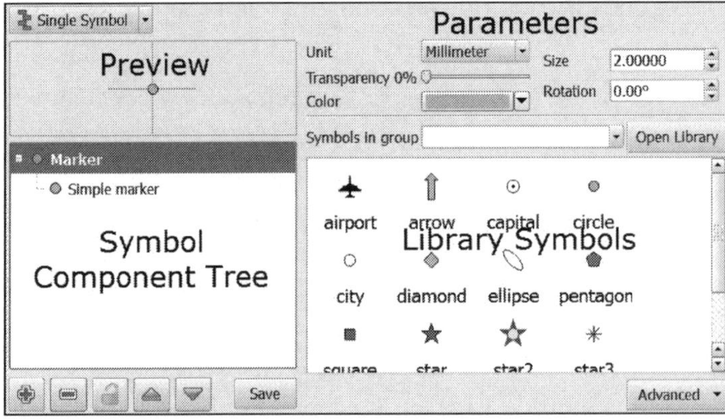

Let's take a quick tour of the four parts of the properties window for the **Single Symbol** style type that is shown in the previous screenshot:

- Symbol preview, in the upper-left corner, shows a preview of a symbol with the current parameters.

- Symbol parameters, in the upper-right corner, has the parameters for the symbol selected in the symbol component tree (these will change slightly depending on geometry type of the vector data).
- Library symbols, in the bottom-right corner, lists a group of symbols from the library (which is also known as **Style Manager**). Clicking on a symbol sets it as the current symbol design. If symbol groups exist, they can be selected for viewing in the **Symbols in group** drop-down menu. To open the Style Manager, click on **Open Library**.
- Symbol component tree, in the bottom-left corner, lists the layers of symbol components. Clicking on each layer changes the symbol parameters so that the symbol can be changed.

As an example of how to use the **Single Symbol** style properties to create a circle around a gas pump ( ), a second layer with the **SVG marker** symbol layer type was added by clicking on the Add symbol layer button ( ), and was then moved on top of the circle by clicking on the Move up button ( ). The following figure shows the parameters used to create the symbol:

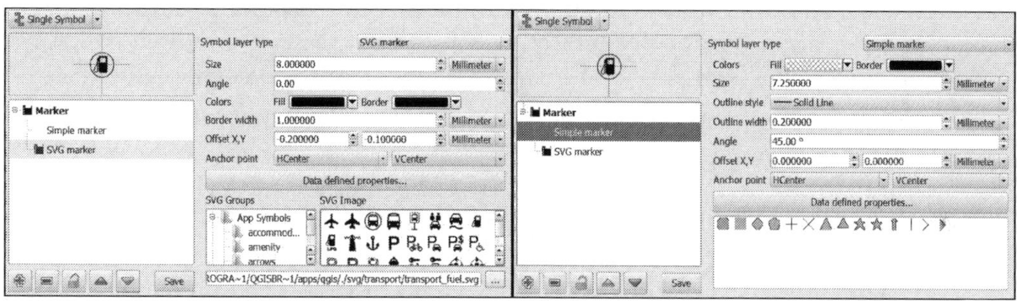

To save your custom symbol to the Style Manager, click on the **Save** button to name and save the style. The saved style will appear in the Style Manager and the list of library symbols.

Categorized vector styling

The categorized vector style applies one symbol per category of the attribute value(s). This vector style is the best when you want a different symbol that is based on attribute values, such as when styling country polygons or classes of roads lines. The categorized vector style works best with nominal or ordinal attribute data.

The following screenshot shows the **Categorized** style type with parameters for point vector data of schools. Its properties will be very similar to those for line and polygon vector data.

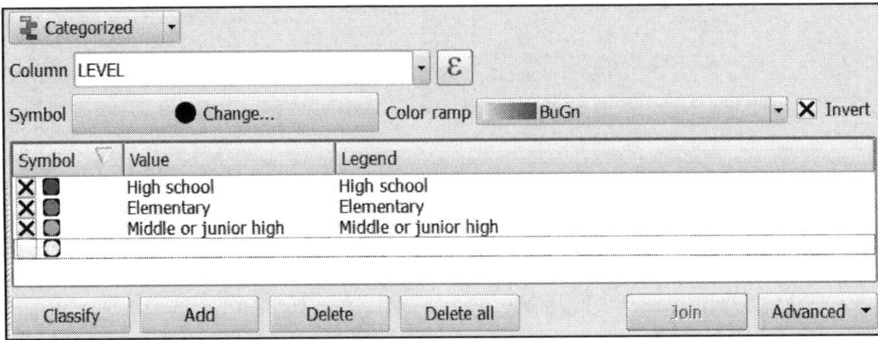

Styling vector data with the **Categorized** style type is a four-step process, which is as follows:

1. Select an appropriate value for the **Column** field to use the attributes for categorization. Optionally, an expression can be created for categorization by clicking on the Expression button (ε) to open the **Expression** dialog.
2. Create the classes to list by either clicking on the **Classify** button to add a class for each unique attribute that is found; otherwise, click on the **Add** button to add an empty class and then double-click in the **Value** column to set the attribute value to be used to create the class. Classes can be removed with the **Delete** or **Delete all** buttons. They can be reordered by clicking and dragging them up and down the list. Classes can also be modified by double-clicking in the **Value** and **Label** columns.
3. Set the symbol for all classes by clicking on the **Symbol** button to open the **Symbol selector** window. Individual class symbols can be changed by double-clicking on the **Symbol** column of the class list.
4. Choose the color ramp to apply to the classes. Individual class colors can be changed by double-clicking on the **Symbol** column of the class list.

Other symbol options (which will change availability based on vector layer type), such as transparency, color, size, and output unit, are available by right-clicking on a category row. Additionally, advanced settings are available by clicking on the **Advanced** button.

Graduated vector styling

The graduated vector style applies one symbol per range of numeric attribute values. This vector style is the best when you want a different symbol that is based on a range of numeric attribute values, such as when styling gross domestic product polygons or city population points. The graduated vector style works best with ordinal, interval, and ratio numeric attribute data.

The following screenshot shows the **Categorized** style type with parameters for polygon vector data of the populations of the countries. Its properties will be very similar to that of point and line vector data.

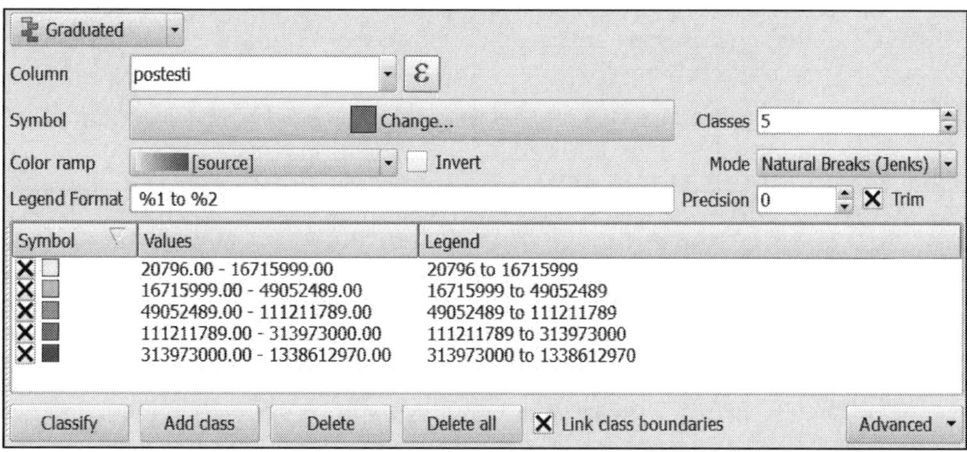

Styling vector data with the **Categorized** style type is a five-step process, which is as follows:

1. Select an appropriate value for the **Column** field to use the attributes for classification. Optionally, an expression can be created for classification by clicking on the Expression button (ε) to open the **Expression** dialog.
2. Choose the number of classes and the classification mode. The following five modes are available for use:
    - **Equal Interval**: In this mode, the width of each class is set to be the same. For example, if input values ranged between 1 and 100 and four classes were desired, then the class ranges would be 1-25, 26-50, 51-75, and 76-100 so that there are 25 values in each class.

- **Quantile (Equal Count)**: In this mode, the number of records in each class is distributed as equally as possible, with lower classes being overloaded with the remaining records if a perfectly equal distribution is not possible. For example, if there are fourteen records and three classes, then the lowest two classes would contain five records each and the highest class would contain four classes.
- **Natural Breaks (Jenks)**: The Jenks Breaks method maximizes homogeneity within classes and creates class breaks that are based on natural data trends.
- **Standard Deviation**: In this mode, classes represent standard deviations above and below the mean record values. Based on how many classes are selected, the number of standard deviations in each class will change.
- **Pretty Breaks**: This creates class boundaries that are round numbers to make it easier for humans to delineate classes.

3. Create the classes to list by either clicking on the **Classify** button to add a class for each unique attribute that is found; otherwise, click on the **Add Class** button to add an empty class and then double-click in the **Value** column to set the attribute value range to be used to create the class. Classes can be removed with the **Delete** or **Delete All** buttons. They can be reordered by clicking and dragging them up and down the list. Classes can also be modified by double-clicking in the **Value** and **Label** columns.
4. Set the symbol for all classes by clicking on the **Symbol** button to open the **Symbol selector** window. Individual class symbols can be changed by double-clicking on the **Symbol** column of the class list.
5. Choose the color ramp to apply to the classes. Individual class colors can be changed by double-clicking on the **Symbol** column of the class list.

The **Legend Format** field sets the format for all labels. Anything can be typed in the textbox. The lower boundary of the class will be inserted where `%1` is typed in the textbox, and the upper boundary of the class will be inserted where `%2` is typed.

If **Link class boundaries** is checked, then the adjacent class boundary values will be automatically changed to be adjacent if any of the class boundaries are manually changed.

Other symbol options, such as transparency, color, and output unit, are available by right-clicking on a category row. Advanced settings are available by clicking on the **Advanced** button.

Rule-based vector styling

The rule-based vector style applies one symbol per created rule and can apply maximum and minimum scales to toggle symbol visibility. This vector style is the best when you want a different symbol that is based on different expressions or when you want to display different symbols for the same layer at different map scales. For example, if you are styling roads, a rule could be set to make roads appear as thin lines when zoomed out, but when zoomed in, the thin lines will disappear and will be replaced by thicker lines that are more scale appropriate.

There are no default values for rule-based styling; however, if a style was previously set using a different styling type, the style will be converted to be rule-based when this style type is selected. The following screenshot shows the **Categorized** style type from the previous section that is converted to the **Rule-based** style type parameters for polygon vector data of the populations of the countries. Its properties will be very similar to that of point and line vector data.

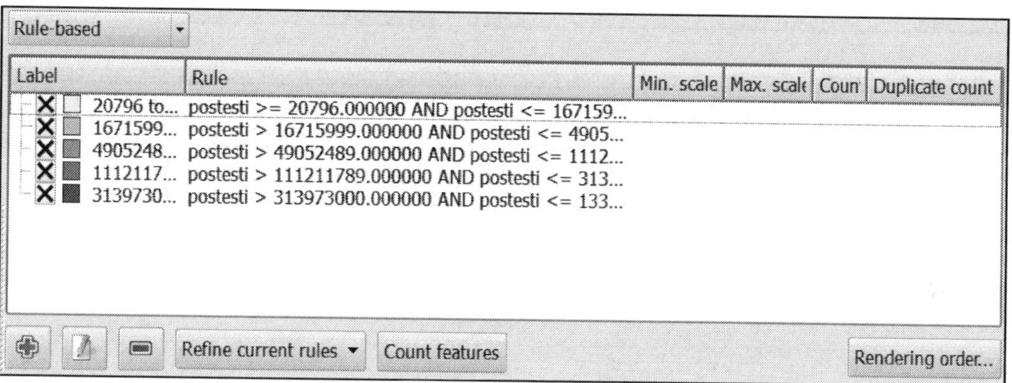

The **Rule-based** style properties window shows a list of current rules with the following columns:

- **Label**: The symbol and label that will be visible in the **Layers** panel are displayed here. The checkbox toggles rule activation; unchecked rules will not be displayed.
- **Rule**: This displays the filter applied to the vector dataset to select a subset of records.
- **Min. Scale**: This displays the smallest (zoomed-out) scale at which the rule will be visible.

- **Max. Scale**: This displays the largest (zoomed-in) scale at which the rule will be visible.
- **Count**: This displays the number of features that are included in this rule. This is calculated when the **Count features** button is clicked.
- **Duplicate count**: This displays the number of features that are included in the current and other rules. This is helpful when you are trying to achieve mutually exclusive rules and need to determine where duplicates exist. This is calculated when the **Count features** button is clicked.

To add a new rule, click on the Add rule button ( ) to open the **Rule properties** window. To edit a rule, select the rule and then click on the Edit rule button ( ) to open the **Rule properties** window. To remove a rule, select the rule and then click on the Remove rule button ( ).

Additional scales, categories, and ranges can be added to each rule by clicking on the **Refine current rules** button. To calculate the number of features included in each rule and to calculate the duplicate feature count, click on the **Count features** button.

When a rule is added or edited, the **Rule properties** window (which is shown in the following screenshot) displays five rule parameters, which are as follows:

- **Label**: This should have the rule label that will be displayed in the **Layers** panel.
- **Filter**: This will have the expression that will select a subset of features to include in the rule. Click on the ellipsis button to open the **Expression string builder** window. Then, click on the **Test** button to check the validity of the expression.
- **Description**: This has a user-friendly description of the rule.
- **Scale range**: This has the **Minimum (exclusive)** and **Maximum (inclusive)** scales between which the rule will be visible.
- **Symbol**: This has the symbol that will be used to symbolize features included in the rule.

None of the parameters are required (**Label**, **Filter**, and **Description** could be left blank); to exclude **Scale range** and **Symbol** from the rule, uncheck the boxes next to these parameters.

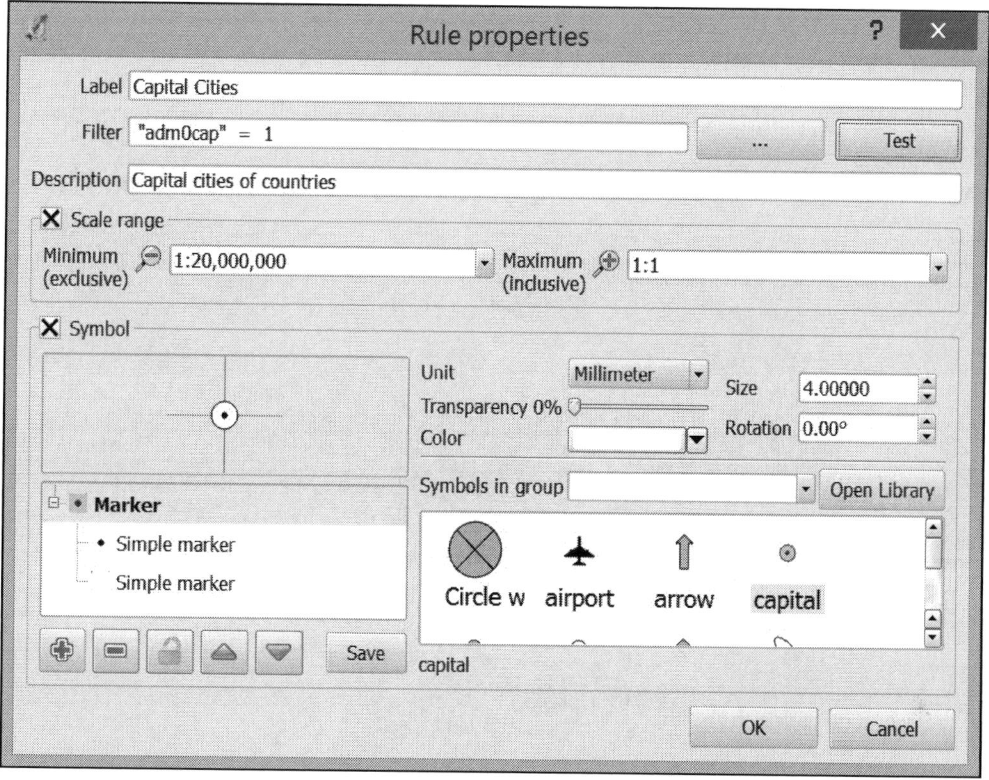

As an example of use, using the `Populated Places.shp` sample data, capital cities, megacities, and all other places can be styled differently by using rule-based styling. Additionally, each rule is visible to the minimum scale of 1:1, although they become invisible at different maximum scales. The following screenshot shows the rules created and a sample map of selected populated places in the country of Nigeria:

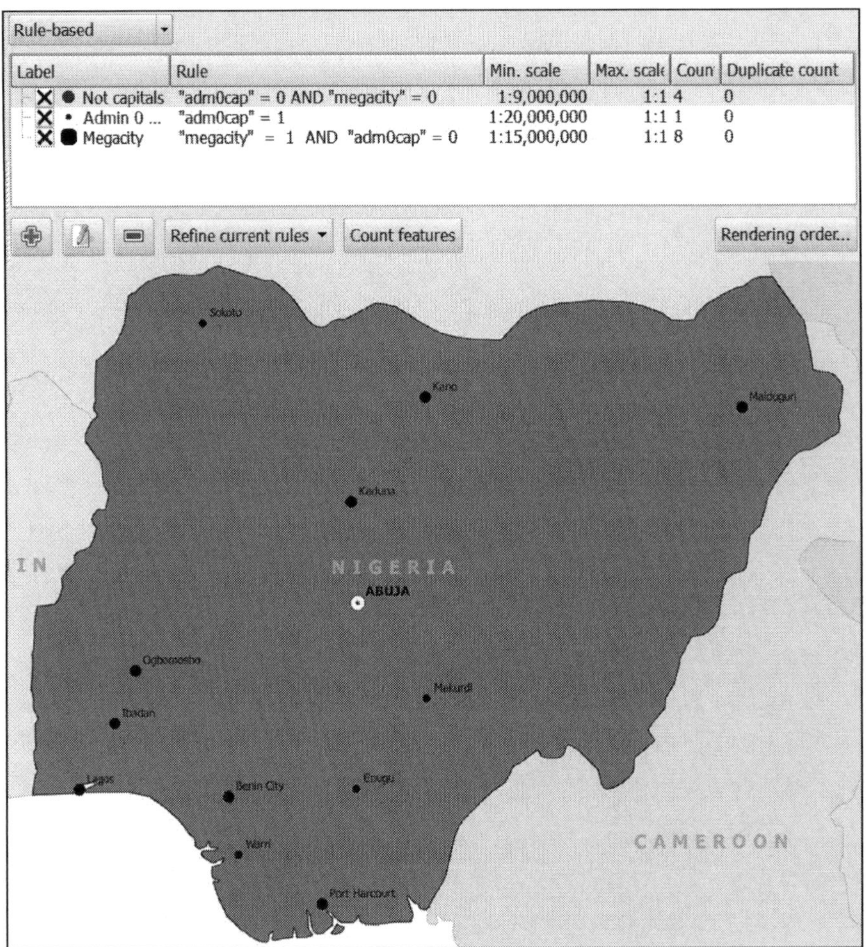

Point-displacement vector styling

The point-displacement vector style radially displaces points that lie within a set distance from each other so that they can be individually visualized. This vector style works best on data where points may be stacked on top of each other, thereby making it hard to see each point individually. This vector style only works with the point vector geometry type.

The following screenshot shows how the **Point displacement** style works by using the **Single Symbol** renderer, which is applied to the `Stacked Points.shp` sample data. Each point within the **Point distance tolerance** value of at least one other point is displaced at a distance of the **Circle radius modification** value around a newly-created center symbol. In this example, three groups of circles have been displaced around a center symbol.

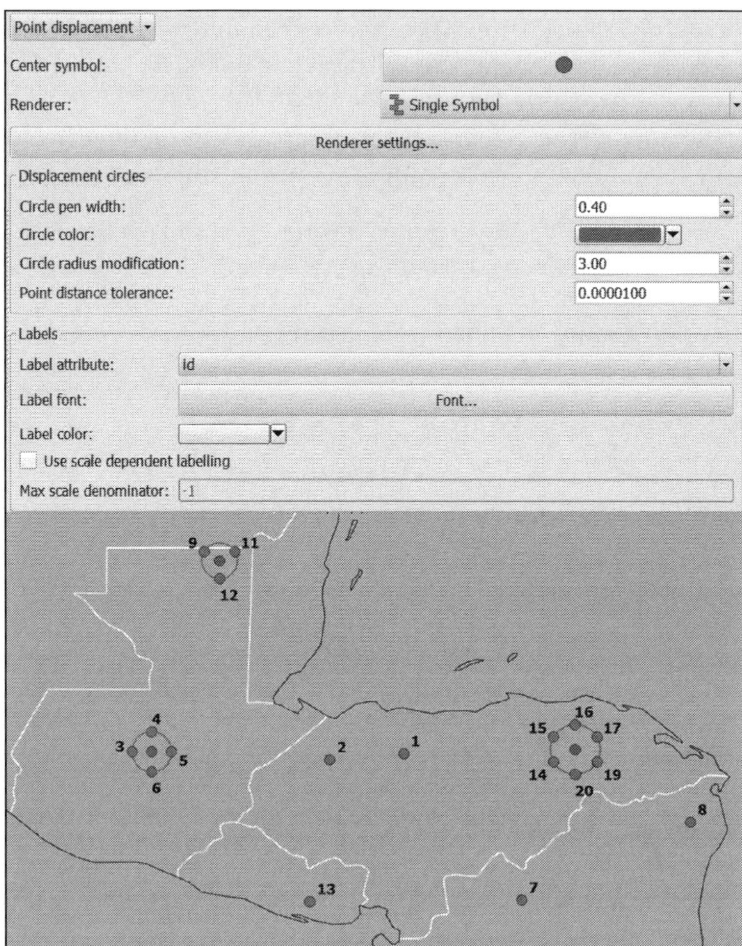

The **Point displacement** style parameters, shown in the preceding figure, provide multiple parameters to displace the points, set the sub-renderer, style the center symbol, and label the displaced points. Let's review parameters that are unique to the point-displacement style:

- **Center symbol**: This contains the style for the center symbol that is created at the location from where the point symbols are being displaced.

- **Renderer**: This contains the renderer that styles the displaced points. Click on the **Renderer settings** button to access renderer settings.
- **Circle pen width**: This sets the outline pen width in millimeters that visualizes the **Circle radius modification** value.
- **Circle color**: This contains the outline pen color for the **Circle radius modification** circle.
- **Circle radius modification**: The number of millimeters that the points are displaced from the center symbol. This circle can be displayed on the map if the **Circle pen width** value is greater than 0.
- **Point distance tolerance**: For each point, if another point(s) is within this distance tolerance (defined in millimeters), then all points will be displaced.

The **Labels** parameters applies to all points (displaced or not) in the vector data. It is important to use these label parameters, rather than the label parameters on the **Labels** tab of the **Layer Properties** window, because the labels set in the **Labels** tab will label the center symbol and not the displaced points.

Inverted polygons vector styling

The inverted polygons vector style inverts the area that a polygon covers. This vector style only works with the polygon vector geometry type.

The following figure shows the **Inverted polygons** style for a polygon of the country of Nigeria on the left and all countries underneath the transparent inverted polygon of Nigeria on the right. Notice that the entire canvas is covered by the inverted polygon, which has the effect of cutting out Nigeria from the map.

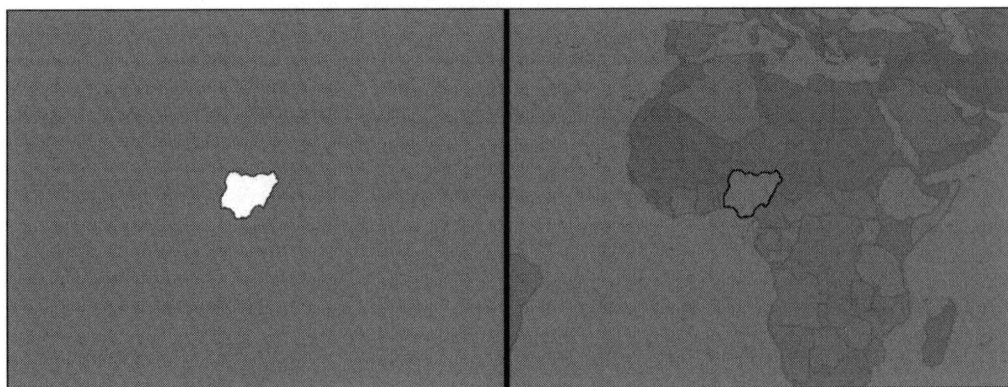

The **Inverted polygons** style parameters rely on a sub-renderer to determine the symbol used for the inverted polygons. By choosing the sub-renderer, the polygon rendering is inverted to cover the entire map canvas. The following screenshot shows the **Inverted polygons** style parameters that created the inverted polygon of Nigeria:

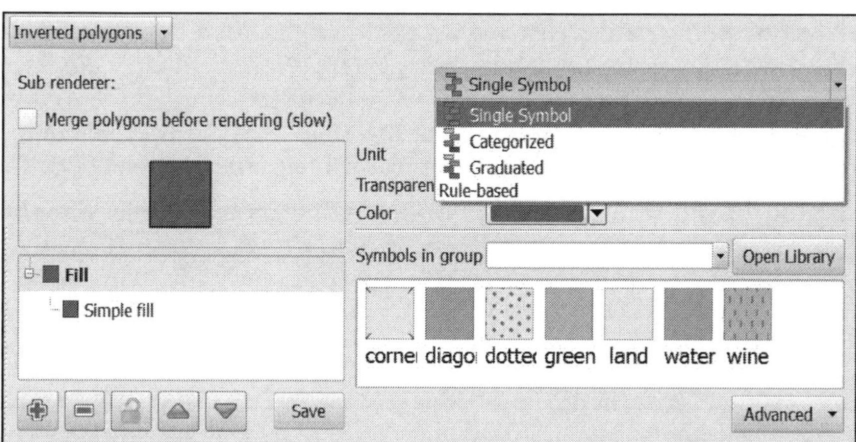

If multiple polygons are going to be inverted and the polygons overlap, **Merge polygons before rendering (slow)** can be checked so that the inverted polygons do not cover the area of overlap.

Vector layer rendering

Layer rendering modifies the properties of the vector to change the way it displays and interacts with the layer below and the features within the vector. Layer rendering is a part of vector style properties for all style types and works in the same way, regardless of the selected style type. In this section, we will discuss the parameters that are available for change in the **Layer rendering** section of vector style properties.

When a vector is first loaded, the **Layer rendering** parameters are set to their default values, as shown in the following screenshot:

The **Layer rendering** section has three parameters, which are as follows:

- **Layer transparency**: This contains the percentage of transparency for the layer. The higher the transparency value, the more the layers below will be visible through this layer.
- **Layer blending mode**: This applies a blending method to the vector that mixes with layers below in the **Layers** panel. A number of blending modes are available to choose from and are commonly found in graphics editing programs. In fact, there are 13 blending modes. Each of these blending modes is discussed in more detail in the *Raster color rendering* section of this chapter.
- **Feature blending mode**: This applies a blending method to the vector that mixes with other features in the same vector layer. A number of blending modes are available to choose from and are commonly found in graphics editing programs. There are 13 blending modes. Each of these blending modes is discussed in more detail in the *Raster color rendering* section of this chapter.

The new blending modes should be explored before you use transparency for overlays. Let's consider an example where we want to add a hillshade to our map to give it some depth. In the following figure, the top-left map shows Africa's countries by using polygons and **Normal Layer** blending. A common way to place a hillshade behind polygons is to make the polygons semi-transparent so that the hillshade can give depth to the polygons. However, this tends to wash out the colors in the polygons and the hillshade is muted, which is illustrated at the top-right corner of the following figure. Instead, the **Hard Light** or **Multiply Layer** blending methods (illustrated at the bottom-left and bottom-right corners respectively in the following figure) can be used to maintain strong color and include the hillshade.

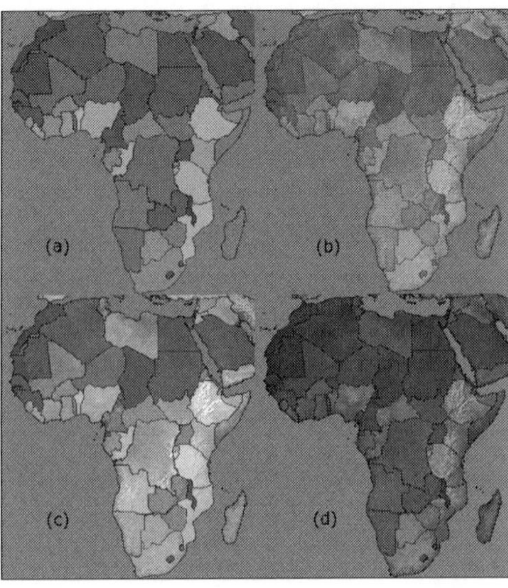

Layer rendering can really improve the look of your map. So, experiment with the layer-rendering methods to find the ones that work best for your overlays.

Using diagrams to display thematic data

QGIS supports the addition of three diagram types as overlays on top of vector data. The three diagram types are pie chart, text diagram, and histogram. The underlying vector data can still be styled to provide a nice base map.

To add a diagram, open the vector's **Layer Properties** window and then click on the **Diagrams** tab. The **Diagrams** tab, shown in the following screenshot, is split into two sections. The top section contains the **Appearance** and **Options** tabs, which contain parameters that are unique to each selectable **Diagram type** value. It also contains the **Size** and **Position** tabs, which contain parameters shared by all the **Diagram types** value. The bottom section, **Attributes**, is common to all diagram types and provides the mechanism for adding attributes to diagrams.

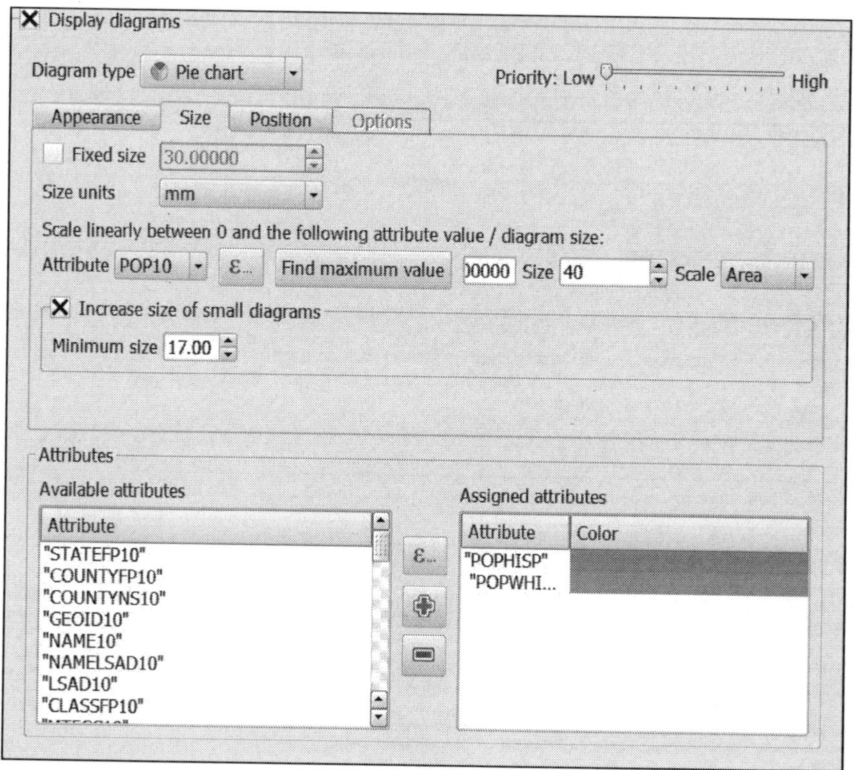

Parameters common to all diagram types

Since the **Size**, **Position**, and **Attributes** sections are common to all diagrams, the next section will first cover these parameters. The following three sections will cover the parameters that are unique to each type of diagram.

Diagram size parameters

The **Size** tab, shown in the following screenshot, provides the following parameters:

- **Fixed size**: If this is checked, all charts will have the specified area or diameter (for a pie and text chart) or length (for a bar chart).
- **Size units**: This contains the unit of the **Fixed size** parameter.
- **Scale linearly between 0 and and the following attribute value / diagram size**: If **Fixed size** is *not* checked, then the length (for a bar chart), area, or diameter (for a pie and text chart) set by the **Scale** parameter of the charts will be scaled down linearly from the selected **Size** value. The selected **Size** value represents the maximum or set **Attribute** value. To enable QGIS to determine the maximum attribute value, click on the **Find maximum value** button.
- **Increase size of small diagrams**: If checked, this parameter sets the **Minimum size** value to which the charts will be scaled.

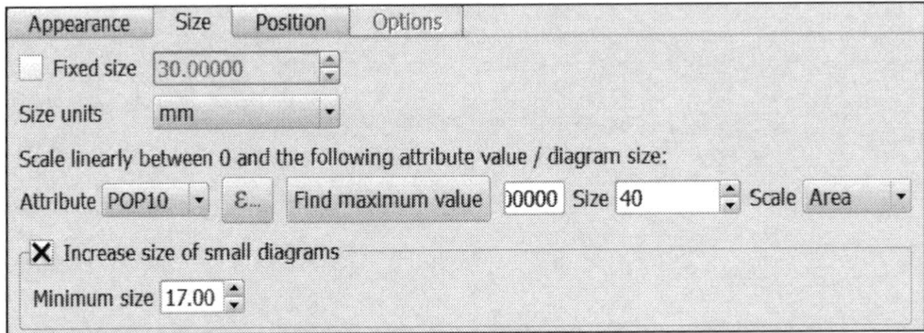

Diagram position parameters

The **Position** tab, shown in the following screenshot, provides the following parameters:

- **Placement**: This sets the placement of the chart. The available options are **Around point**, **Over point**, **Line**, **Horizontal**, and **Free**.

- **Data defined position**: If this is checked, the **x** and **y** positions of the chart can be set by attributes.
- **Automated placement settings**: This provides more parameters to fine-tune the placement of charts, such as showing all charts and showing partial labels.

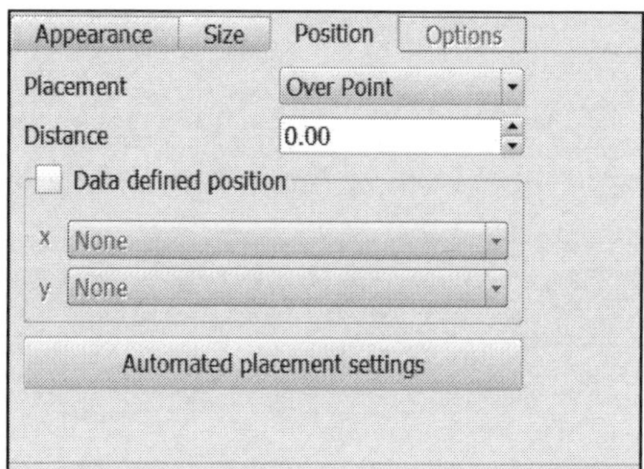

Adding attributes to diagrams

Each of these diagram types supports the display of multiple attributes. To add or remove attributes, you must move (or build) an expression from the **Available attributes** list to the **Assigned attributes** list. Attributes in the **Assigned attributes** list will be used in the diagram.

There are two ways to add an attribute to the **Assigned attributes** list, which are as follows:

- Select the attribute(s) from the **Assigned attributes** list, then click on the Add attribute button ( )
- Click on the Add expression button ( ) and then create an expression that will be added as a single entry

Once an attribute has been added, the **Assigned attributes** colors can be changed by double-clicking on the color patches in the **Color** column.

The following figure shows two examples. The top example shows a single attribute that has been added to the **Assigned attributes** list, and the bottom one is an example of a single attribute and an attribute that was calculated with an expressions.

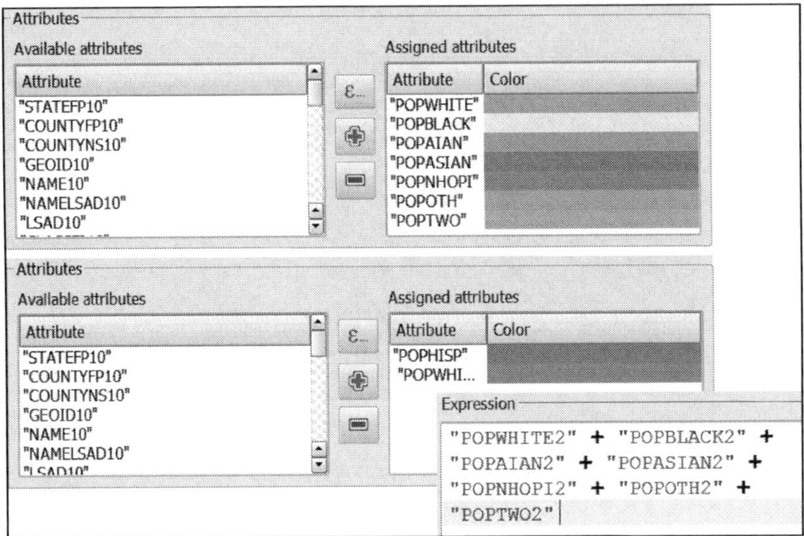

Creating a pie chart diagram

A pie chart diagram displays attribute(s) in a round pie chart where each attribute occupies a pie slice proportional to the percentage that the attribute represents from the total of all attributes added to the pie chart. As an example, the following figure shows a portion of a state with pie charts showing the proportion of different racial population in each county:

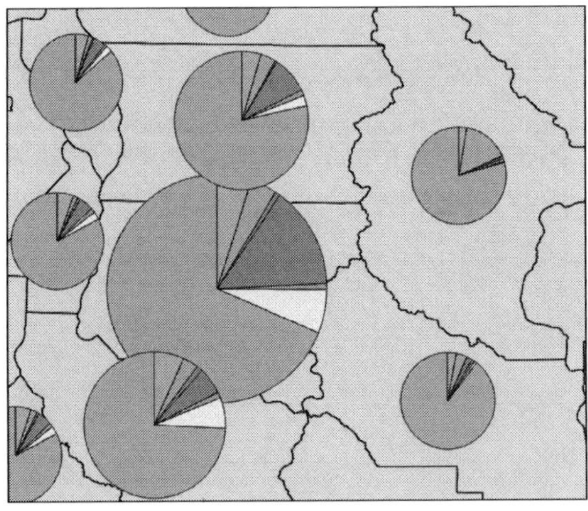

By reviewing the pie charts in the preceding figure, let's note down a few things:

- The pie slices differ for each county's race attributes and are colored based on each attribute's selected color
- The size of the pie charts vary based on the total population in each county
- The pie slice outlines are black and thin
- The pie charts are displayed above the centroid of each polygon

These four noted items, among others that are not noted, are all customizable using parameters available in the **Diagrams** tab of the **Layer Properties** window. The **Diagrams** tab for pie charts has three tabs with parameters: **Appearance**, **Size**, and **Position**.

The **Appearance** tab, shown in the following screenshot, provides the following parameters:

- **Transparency**: This is used to specify the transparency percentage for the pie chart.
- **Line color**: This contains the color of the lines surrounding the pie and in-between pie slices.
- **Line width**: This contain the width of the lines surrounding the pie and in-between pie slices.
- **Start angle**: This is used to specify the angle from which the pie slices will begin to rotate in a clockwise manner. The available options are **Top**, **Right**, **Bottom**, and **Left**.
- **Scale dependent visibility**: If this is checked, the **Minimum** and **Maximum** visibility scales can be set.

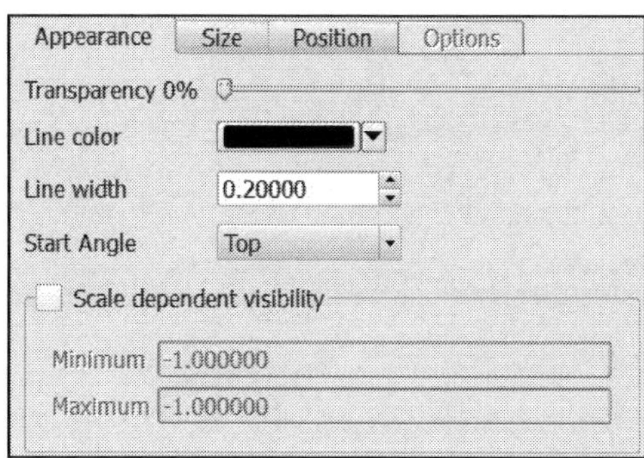

Creating a text chart diagram

The text chart diagram displays attributes in a round circle where each attribute occupies a horizontal slice of the circle and the attribute value is labeled inside the slice. As an example, the following figure shows a portion of a state's counties with text charts showing the Hispanic population in the top half and non-Hispanic population in the bottom half of the circle:

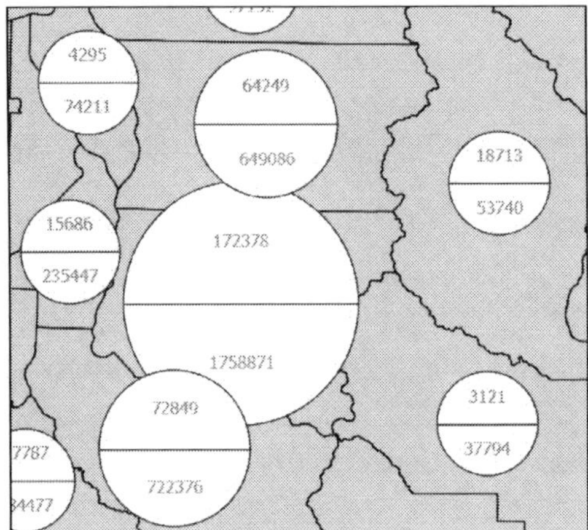

By reviewing the text charts in the preceding figure, let's note down a few things:

- The labels report each race's attribute and are colored based on the selected attribute colors
- The size of the chart varies according to the total population of each county
- The horizontal slice outlines are black and thin
- The text charts are displayed above the centroid of each polygon

These four noted items, among others that are not noted, are all customizable using parameters available in the **Diagrams** tab of the **Layer Properties** window. The **Diagrams** tab for text charts has four tabs with parameters: **Appearance**, **Size**, **Position**, and **Options**.

The **Appearance** tab, shown in the following screenshot, provides the following parameters:

- **Transparency**: This is used to specify the transparency percentage for the text chart.
- **Background color**: This contains the background/fill color for the circle.

- **Line color**: This contains the color of the lines surrounding the circle and in-between slices.
- **Line width**: This contains the width of the lines surrounding the circle and in-between slices.
- **Font**: This can be used to set the font. Open the **Select Font** dialog to set the font parameters for the attribute labels that appear inside the circle slices.
- **Scale dependent visibility**: If this is checked, the **Minimum** and **Maximum** visibility scales can be set.

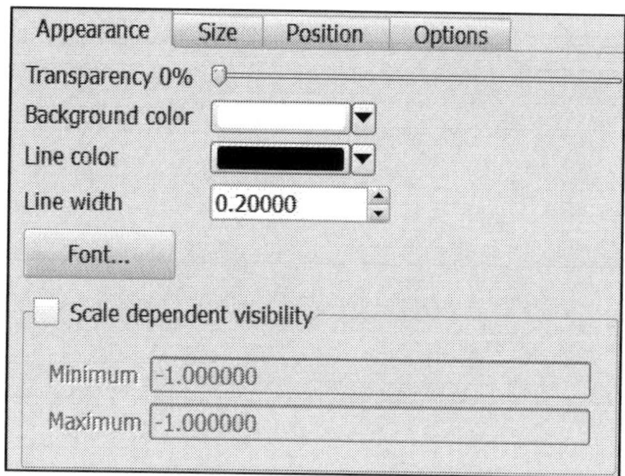

The **Options** tab, shown in the following screenshot, provides the **Label placement** parameter This parameter sets the baseline position for the vertical placement of the text. The available options are **x-height**, which sets the text at the x-height position of the text, and **Height**, which sets the text at the bottom position of the text height.

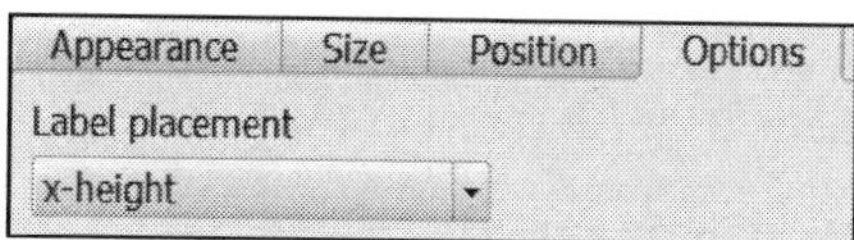

Creating a histogram chart diagram

The histogram chart diagram displays attributes in a histogram/bar chart where each attribute can be visualized as a bar that varies in length in proportion to the attributes' values. As an example, the following figure shows a portion of a state's counties with histogram charts showing the Hispanic population as one bar and non-Hispanic population as the other bar:

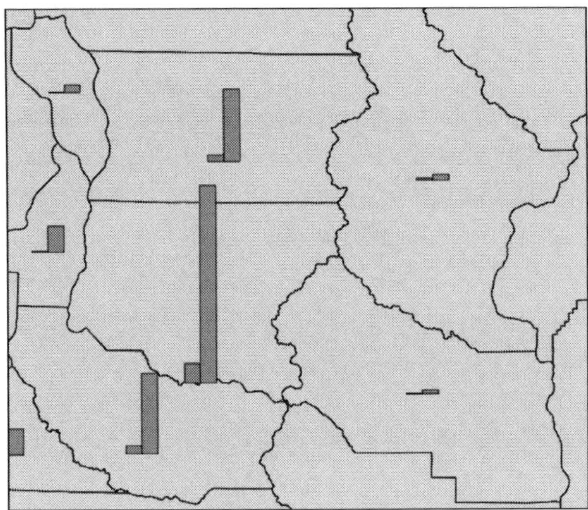

By reviewing the histogram charts in the preceding figure, let's note down a few things:

- The bars report each race's attribute and are colored according to the selected attribute colors
- The bar outlines are black and thin
- The histogram charts are displayed above the centroid of each polygon

These three noted items, among others that are not noted, are all customizable using parameters available in the **Diagrams** tab of the **Layer Properties** window. The **Diagrams** tab for text charts has four tabs with parameters: **Appearance**, **Size**, **Position**, and **Options**.

The **Appearance** tab, shown in the following screenshot, provides the following parameters:

- **Bar width**: This contain the width, in millimeters, of each bar in the histogram
- **Transparency**: This is used to specify the transparency percentage for the histogram chart

- **Line color**: This contains the color for the lines surrounding the bars
- **Line width**: This contains the width of the lines surrounding the bars
- **Scale dependent visibility**: If this is checked, the **Minimum** and **Maximum** visibility scales can be set:

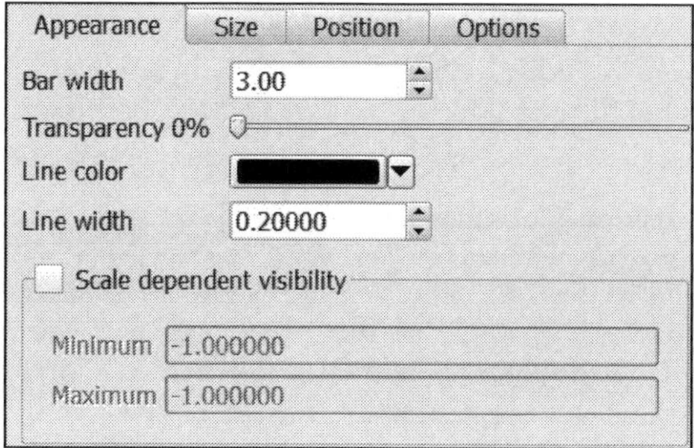

The **Options** tab, shown in the following screen, provides the **Bar Orientation** parameter. This parameter sets the orientation of the bars. The options available are **Up**, **Down**, **Right**, and **Left**.

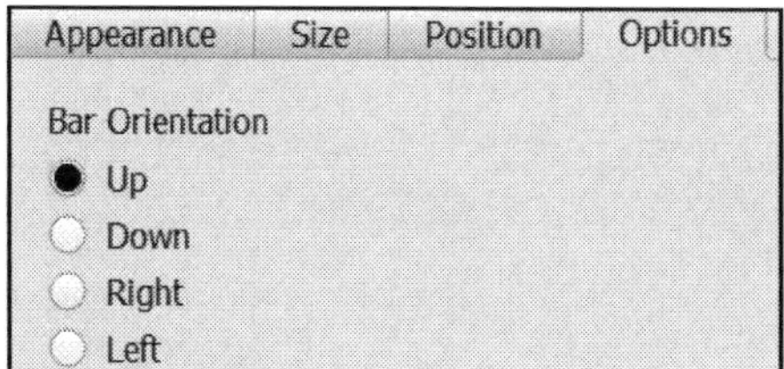

Saving, loading, and setting default styles

Now that you have set the styles that you want for raster and vector layers, you will likely want to save the styles so that they can be used again later or applied to other layers. There are four buttons that are used to manage styles. These four buttons, shown in the following screenshot, are always displayed near the bottom of the **Layer Properties** window:

In this section, we will use these four buttons to save a style to a style file, load a saved style file, and set and restore a default style.

Saving a style

QGIS can save styles in two file formats: `.qml` and `.sld`. The `.qml` style file is specific to QGIS, while the `.sld` style file is useable by other programs to style files. In general, you should plan on saving styles using the `.qml` file type as it does the best job of saving your styles; however, if portability is a priority, then the `.sld` file is the better choice. To save a style, open the **Layer Properties** window, set the style that you wish to save, then click on the **Save Style** button and save the style as either a `.qml` or a `.sld` file. The saved style file can later be loaded and applied to other data files.

> To have a style always apply to the layer you are saving the style from, save the style file as a `.qml` and name it the same name as the source file. For example, if the shapefile name was `Coastlines.shp`, then you should save the style file as `Coastlines.qml`. Creating a style file with the same name has the same effect as setting the default style.

Loading a style

QGIS can load styles from two formats: `.qml` and `.sld`. To load a style, open the **Layer Properties** window, click on the **Load Style** button, and open the style file that you wish to load. This will apply the style to the layer. QGIS will try and apply the styles even if the geometry of the style is not applicable to the geometry of the current layer; this can create unexpected output, so it is usually best to load styles that match the geometry type.

Setting and restoring a default style

To set a layer's current style as the default style for use in other QGIS projects, click on the **Save As Default** button in the **Layer Properties** window. This will save a `.qml` file with the same name as the layer on disk. When the layer is added to the map canvas (in this or another QGIS project) the saved default style will be automatically applied.

If you have made changes to the style of a layer that had a default style and wish to revert back to the default style, click on the **Restore Default Style** button.

Lastly, to remove a default style for a layer, delete the `.qml` file of the same name as the layer on disk.

Summary

In this chapter, we provided you with steps on how to style vector and raster data in QGIS. We first covered how to pick colors using the new color picker, then we covered how to create and manage color ramps using the style manager. Next, we reviewed the different ways to style single band and multiband rasters, create a raster composite, as well as how to overlay rasters using renderers. Vector styling was reviewed next and we covered the six different style types. We also looked at how to use vector renderers for layer overlays. Next, we toured the three diagram types that can be visualized on top of vector datasets. We finished the chapter with instructions on how to save and load the styles for use in other QGIS projects.

In the next chapter, we will move from viewing data to preparing data for processing. Preparation topics will range from spatial and aspatial queries and converted geometry types to defining new coordinate reference systems.

4
Preparing Vector Data for Processing

Typically, raw data obtained for a GIS project needs to be massaged for use in the specific application. It may need to be merged, converted to a different geometry type, saved to the coordinate reference system of the project, subset to the extent of the study area, or subset by attribute values. While QGIS provides a powerful set of tools that can handle many types of vector preparation and transformation tasks, this chapter will cover what we consider to be commonly used vector-preparation tasks. Many of the tools covered in this chapter are found on the **Vector** menu in QGIS; however, others are available in the processing toolbox. Additional vector processing tasks will be covered in *Chapter 7, The Processing Toolbox* and *Chapter 8, Automating Workflows with the Graphical Modeler*. The topics that we will cover in this chapter are as follows:

- Merging shapefiles
- Creating spatial indices
- Checking for geometry errors
- Converting vector geometries
- Adding geometry columns
- Using basic vector geoprocessing tools
- Advanced field calculations
- Complex spatial and aspatial queries
- Defining new coordinate reference systems
- Raster to vector format conversions

Merging shapefiles

The Merge Shapefiles to One tool merges (that is, combines) multiple input shapefiles to a new shapefile. The input shapefiles must be in a common coordinate reference system and should contain common attributes. For example, vector data is often provided in tiles or by political jurisdiction such as counties or states. In these cases, the data may need to be merged to form a seamless layer covering the study area. The **Merge Shapefiles to One** tool that can be found by navigating to **Vector | Data Management Tools** will combine them.

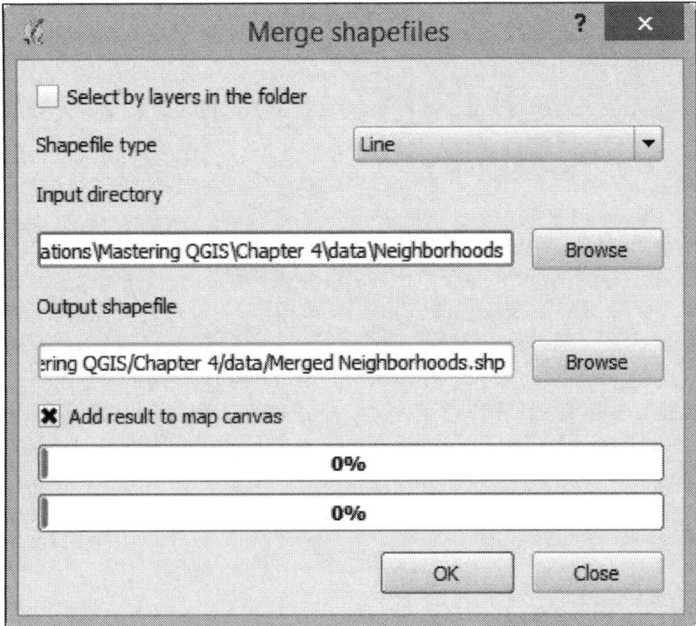

In the **Merge shapefiles** dialog, you have the option to choose whether you wish to merge all shapefiles in a folder or pick individual shapefiles to merge.

1. Depending on how your shapefiles are stored, you can do either of the following:
   - Keep **Select by layers in the folder** unchecked to merge all shapefiles in a directory
   - Check **Select by layers in the folder** to select individual files to merge

2. If the previous option is enabled, choose the shapefile type (**Point**, **Line**, or **Polygon**).
3. Set the input directory/files by clicking on **Browse**.
4. Name the output shapefile by clicking on **Browse**.
5. Choose whether you wish to select **Add result to map canvas**.
6. Click on **OK** to merge the shapefiles.

Creating spatial indices

Large data layers with hundreds or thousands of features will render much more quickly with a spatial index. To create a spatial index, choose the **Create Spatial Index** tool by navigating to **Vector** | **Data Management Tools**. Select the loaded canvas layers or check the **Select files from disk** option and navigate to a folder and select layers on disk. Click on **OK** to create the spatial indexes.

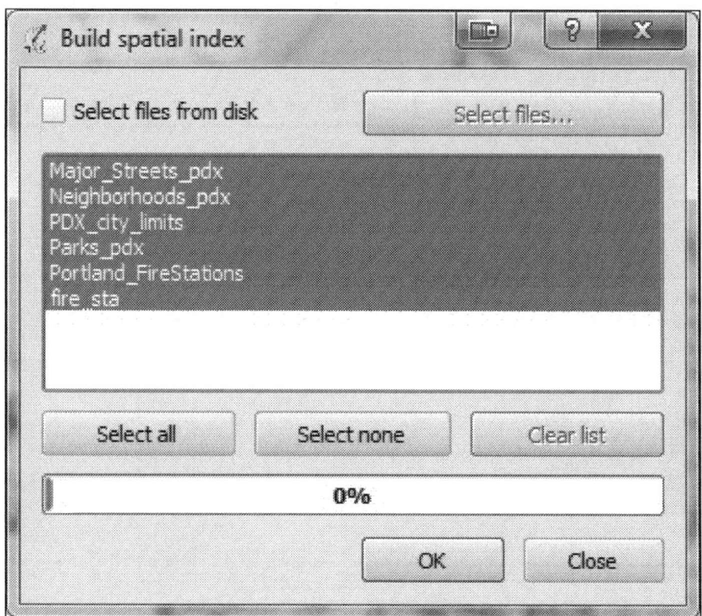

Checking for geometry errors

Data (even from reputable sources) can contain geometry errors. These can often be tiny geometry errors that are not obvious but that prevent geoprocessing tools from running or producing valid results.

The Check Geometry Validity tool (which can be found by navigating to **Vector | Geometry Tools | Check Geometry Validity**) takes an input vector layer that is loaded in the canvas and scans the data for errors, such as geometric intersections. The errors can be displayed in a window on the tool or can be output to a point layer. The resulting point layer will have an attribute describing the error. In the following screenshot, you can see that the tool has been run using the `DRECP_Alternative1_Integrated.shp` sample dataset. This data is portion one of five alternatives for the Desert Renewable Energy Conservation Plan for Southern California. The tool found 267 errors. The errors still need to be repaired, but at least you now know where they are!

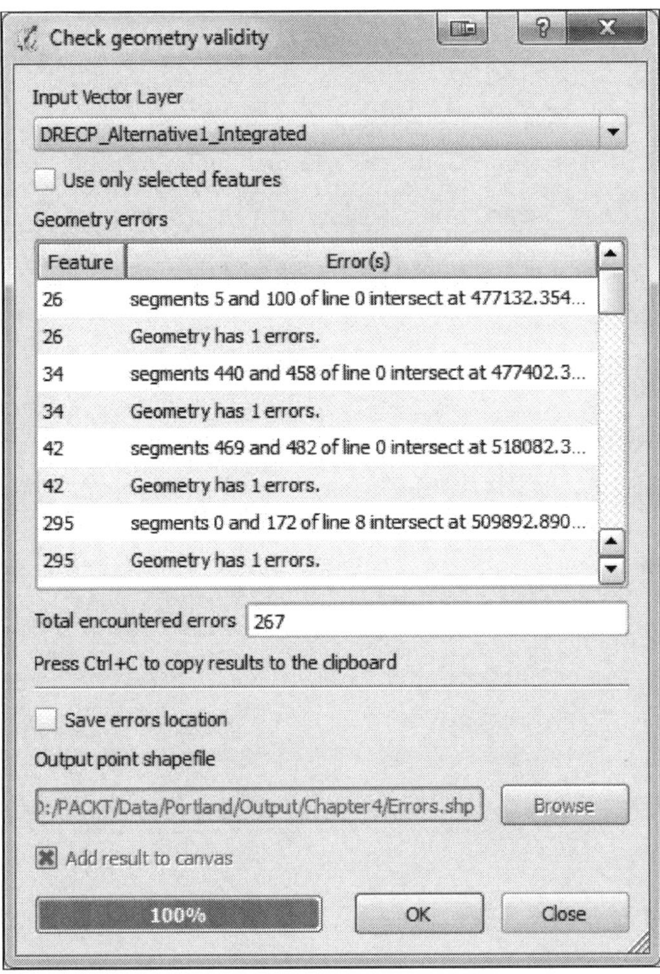

If you have a layer with hundreds or thousands of errors, the most elegant way to repair them is to use the GRASS GIS plugin to import them into a GRASS database. GRASS uses a topological vector data model. When importing, you can set a snapping tolerance below which vertices will be snapped together. This will likely clean up the majority of the errors. For the remainder, you can use the v.clean GRASS tool. Once the errors have been cleaned up, the data can be exported out of GRASS into the vector format that you require.

Converting vector geometries

Sometimes, it is necessary to make conversions among point, line, and polygon vector geometries. For example, you may need to generate point centroids from zip code polygons or a town boundary polygon from a line layer. Such conversions may be necessary to put the data into the most appropriate geometry for analysis. For example, if you need to determine the acreage of parcels, but they are provided in a line format, you will need to convert them to polygons to calculate their areas. Sometimes, you may want to convert geometries for cartographic reasons, such as converting polygons to points to create label points. The following tools can be found on the **Geometry Tools** menu under **Vector**:

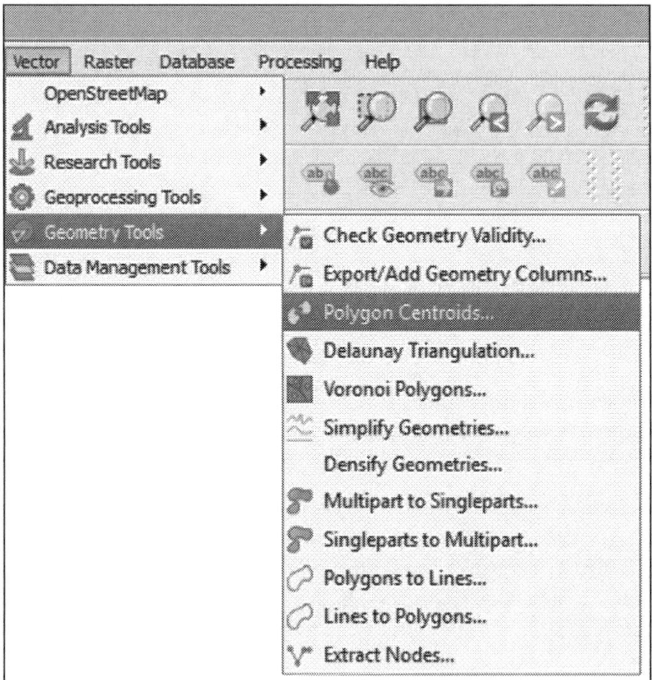

Creating polygon centroids

With the **Polygon Centroids** tool that can be found by navigating to **Vector | Geometry Tools**, you can generate points that will be located at the center of polygons. Simply provide the input polygon layer and name the output. In the following example, centroids of the `Neighborhoods_pdx.shp` shapefile have been generated. This tool preserves all the attributes during the conversion. With the data in point form, you can generate a heat map, compute densities, or measure distances.

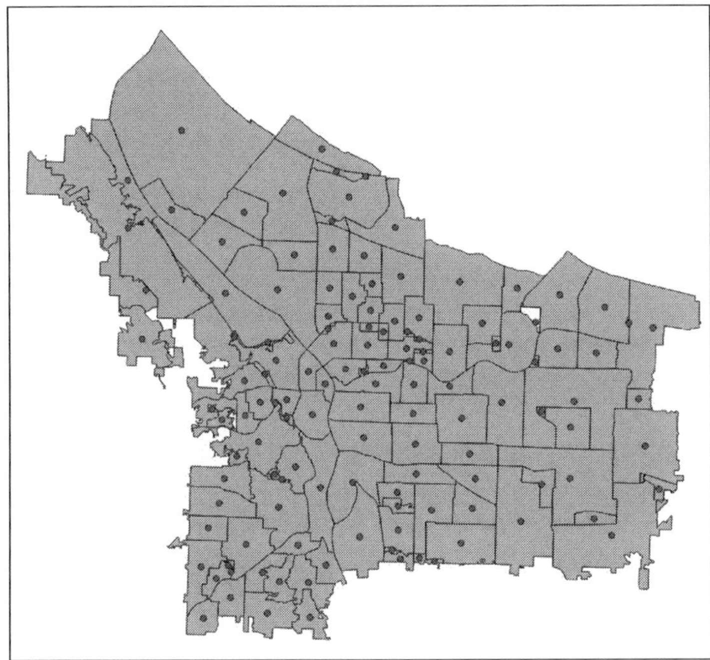

Converting polygons to lines and lines to polygons

With the Polygons to Lines and Lines to Polygon tools that can be found by navigating to **Vector | Geometry Tools**, you can convert between these two geometry types. There are many reasons why this conversion may be desirable. In the following example, we are provided with a slope layer in a polygon format. Here, we will convert it to a line geometry so that it can be styled as contour lines. All the attributes will be maintained during either conversion. Conversions from line to polygon are necessary if the area needs to be calculated. An example of this is parcel data from a CAD program that is provided to you as a line layer. In a GIS environment, parcel data is better represented as a polygon layer than as a line layer.

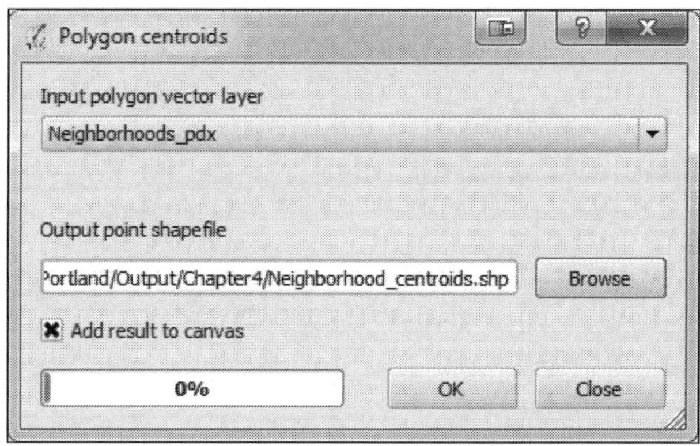

Creating polygons surrounding individual points

There are two tools for generating polygons around individual points in a layer: Voronoi and Delaunay triangulation. Voronoi polygons represent the area of influence around each point. These are named after the Russian mathematician Georgy Voronoy who invented the algorithm. They are also referred to as Thiessen polygons and are named after Alfred Thiessen who independently created the same algorithm. You can use the Voronoi polygon in QGIS by navigating to **Vector | Geometry Tools | Voronoi Polygons**. The resulting polygon represents the areas closer to the point used as the input than any other points in the layer. The Delaunay triangulation tool can be found by navigating to **Vector | Geometry Tools | Delaunay Triangulation**.

Delaunay triangulation creates a series of triangular polygons. The method creates a triangle in such a way that a circle drawn through the three nodes of the triangle will contain no other nodes. This is the same technique that is used to generate **triangulated irregular networks** (**TINs**).

Here, we'll use the `High_schools_pdx.shp` data to compare these two methods. The two tools are intuitive. You need to provide the input point vector layer and specify the output polygon shapefile name. The Voronoi polygons tool has an option to set a buffer region. This is the amount by which the resulting polygons will extend beyond the perimeter points. In the following example, the **Buffer region** field has been set to **10%**:

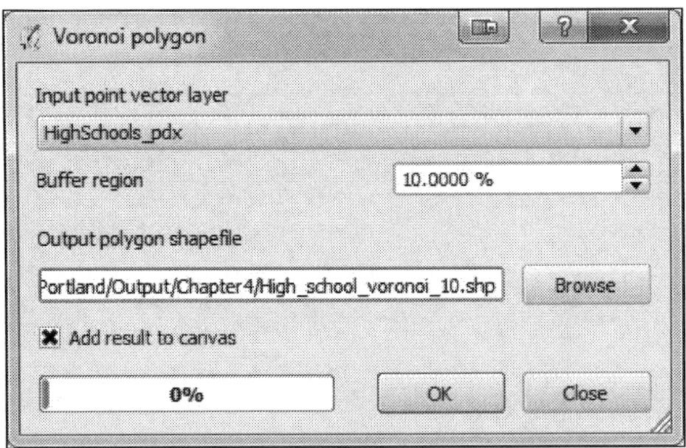

The following figure shows the output differences between Voronoi polygons and Delaunay polygons:

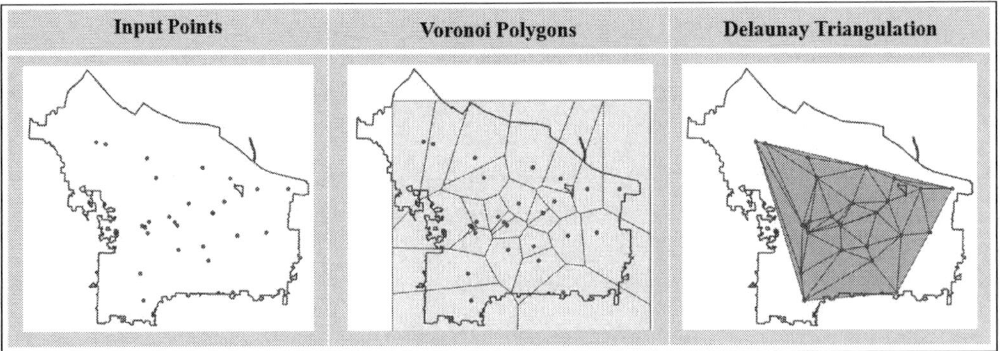

Extracting nodes from lines and polygons

The Extract Nodes tool (which can found by navigating to **Vector** | **Geometry Tools** | **Extract Nodes**) can be used to convert either line or polygon layers into a point layer. Each individual vertex from the input layer will be extracted and output to a new layer. In the following example, we are interested in identifying street intersections. By extracting the nodes from the `Selected_streets.shp` layer, a point for each intersection is generated, as shown in the following screenshot:

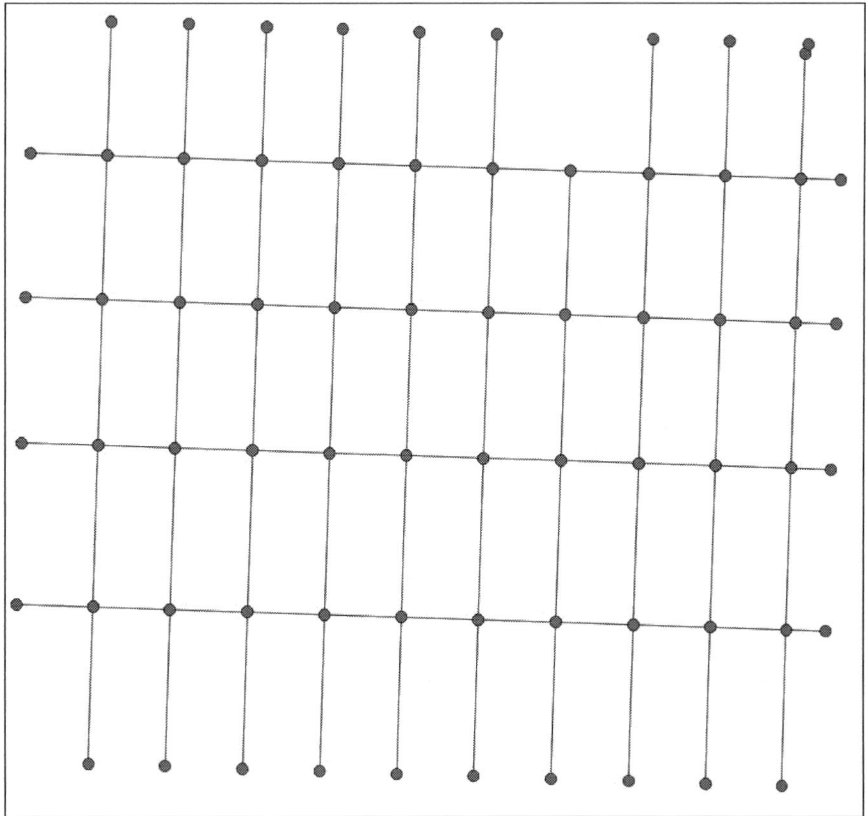

Street lines and extracted nodes representing intersections

Simplifying and densifying features

The Simplify Geometries and Densify Geometries tools (which can found by navigating to **Vector | Geometry Tools**) remove and add vertices, respectively. They are only suitable for line and polygon data.

Simplifying data may be desirable to make it more suitable for use at a smaller scale. It may also be helpful if the data is to be used in an online interactive mapping scenario. The simplify tool uses a modified Douglas-Peucker algorithm that reduces the number of vertices while attempting to maintain the shape of the features. In the following example, the polygons of the `Neighborhoods_pdx.shp` data are simplified with a simplify tolerance of 20. The tolerance is specified in map units.

Here, the data is in a State Plane coordinate reference system with units in feet. With the **Simplify tolerance** field set to **20**, the algorithm will try to eliminate vertices within 20 feet of one another. With this setting, the number of vertices is reduced from 31,637 to 6,189 with almost no change in the shapes of the polygons! This reduced the size of the data on disk from 1.05 MB to 208 KB.

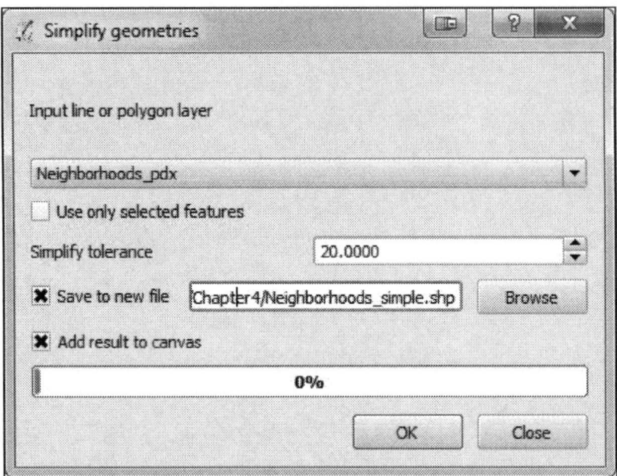

The following figure shows the result of the simplification operation. When zoomed in to 1:1,000, the difference between the input and output geometries can be seen. The black lines are the original neighborhood boundaries and the red lines are the boundaries after being simplified. The largest shift in position represents 15 feet in real-world units.

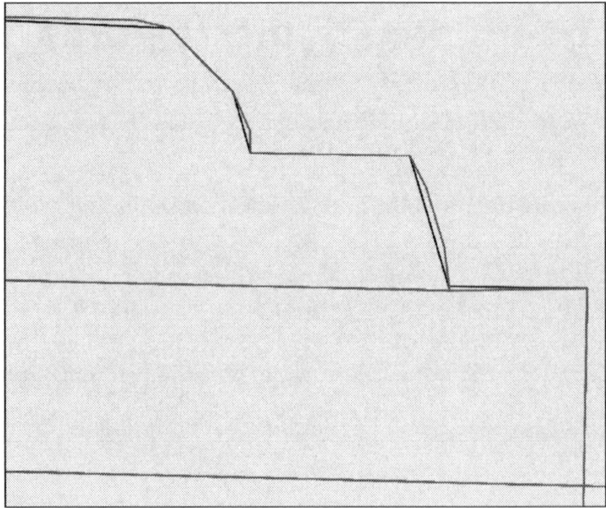

The Densify Geometries tool adds vertices to a line or polygon layer. The operation is run per polygon or line segment. The tool asks for vertices to be added. The default is one per segment but can be set to the desired number. This might be the first step before the Extract Nodes tool is used or there may be other reasons for densifying the geometries.

Converting between multipart and singlepart features

In a typical vector layer, one feature corresponds to one record in the attribute table. In a multipart layer, there are multiple features that are tied to one record in the attribute table. This is often the case with data representing islands. For example, we have some sample data of county boundaries for Hawaii. Hawaii has five counties and the GIS data has five records in the attribute table. However, several of these counties include multiple islands.

To illustrate this point, the following figure shows a single record selected in the attribute table that selects multiple polygons that are tied to the single record:

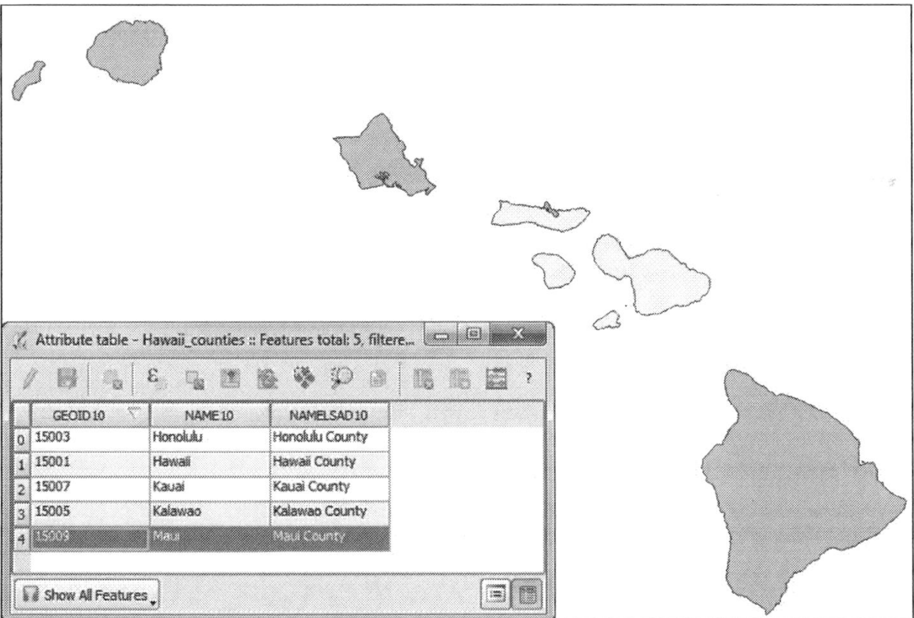

Using the **Multipart to Singleparts** tool, which can be found by navigating to **Vector | Geometry Tools**, with `Hawaii_counties.shp` as the input, we generate a singlepart shapefile with 32 features. The following figure shows that a single polygon is now tied to a single record in the attribute table:

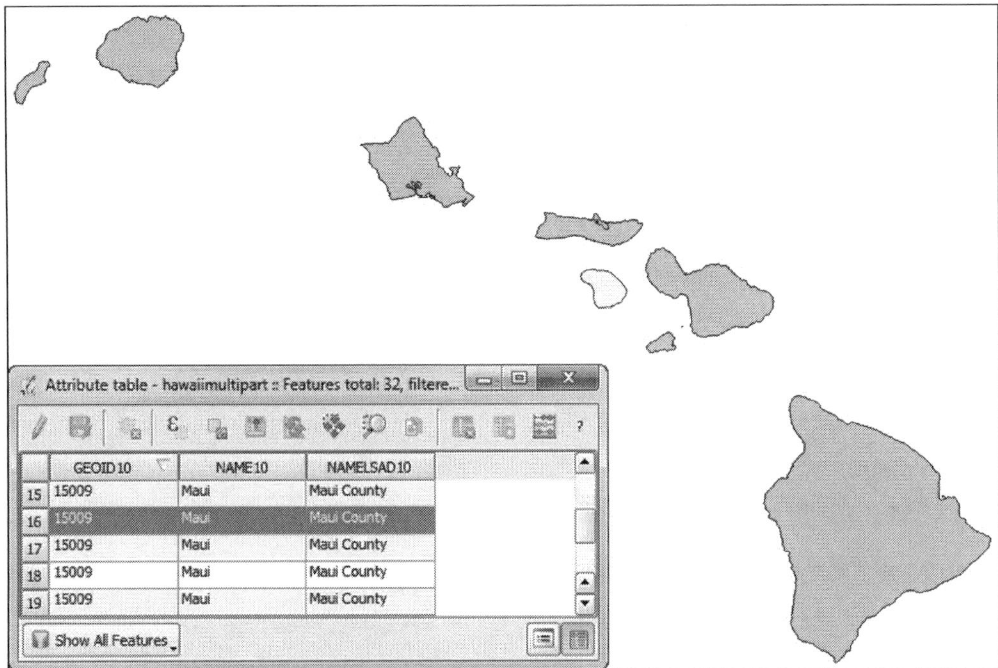

The **Singleparts to Multipart** tool, which can be found by navigating to **Vector | Geometry Tools**, generates a multipart layer based on an attribute you specify in the **Unique ID field** input. The options of the Singleparts to Multipart tool are shown in the following screenshot:

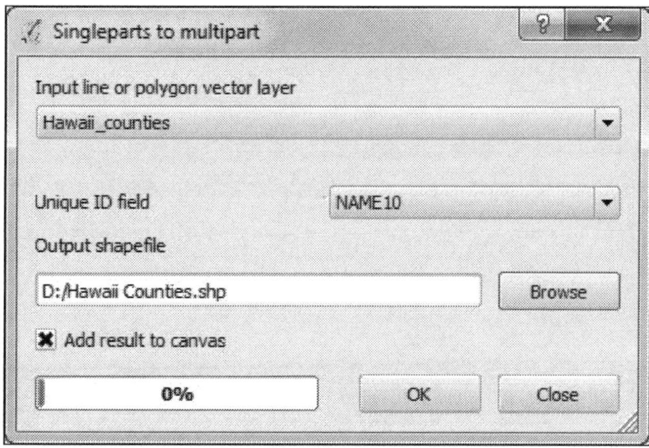

Adding geometry columns to an attribute table

To add geometry values to new attribute columns in a vector layer's attribute table, click on **Export/Add Geometry Columns** by navigating to **Vector | Geometry Tools**. As shown in the following screenshot, the tool requires an input vector layer, a determination of which CRS will be used for the calculations (**Calculate using**), and a choice of whether you wish to create the columns in the existing file or **Save to new shapefile** with the added geometry columns:

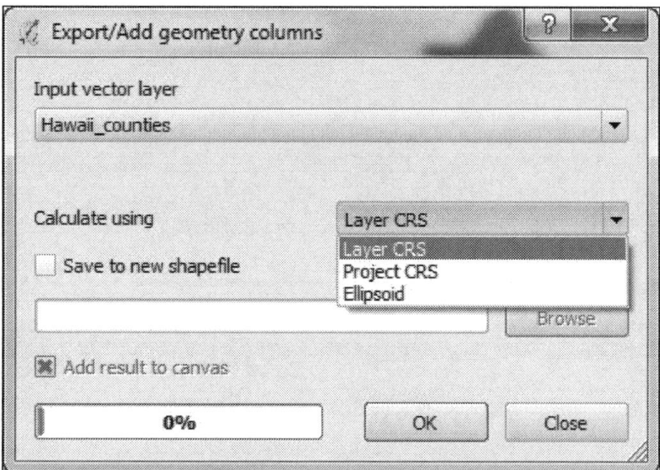

Depending on the geometry type of the input vector layer, different geometry columns will be created as follows:

- **Point**: The `XCOORD` and `YCOORD` columns will contain the *x* and *y* coordinates of the point
- Line: The `SHAPE_LEN` column will contain the length of the record's line(s)
- Polygon: The `AREA` and `PERIMETER` columns will contain the area and perimeter of the record's polygon(s)

Using basic vector geoprocessing tools

This section will focus on geoprocessing tools that use vector data layers as inputs to produce derived outputs. Geoprocessing tools are part of the fTools plugin that is automatically installed with QGIS and enabled by default. The tools can be found in the **Geoprocessing Tools** menu under **Vector**. The icons next to each tool in the menu give a good indication of what each tool does.

We will look at some commonly used spatial overlay tools such as clip, buffer, and dissolve. In the case of a simple analysis, these tools may serve to gather all the information that you need. In more complex scenarios, they may be part of a larger workflow.

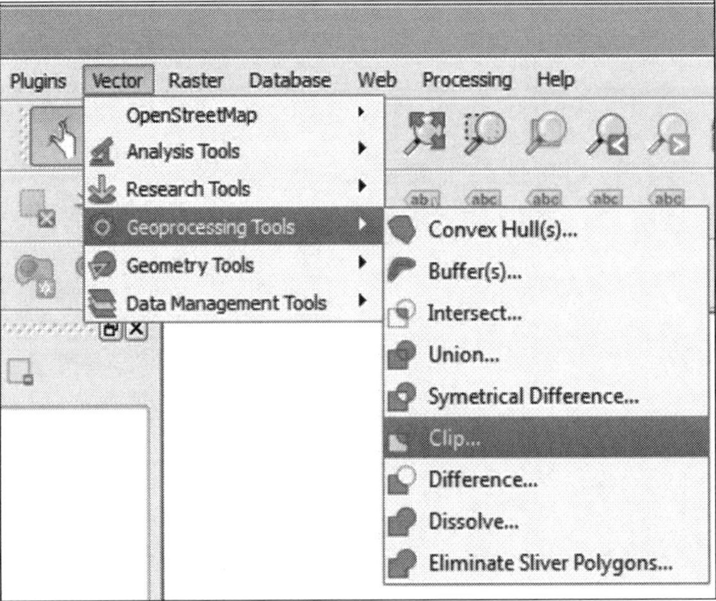

The tools covered in this chapter are also available via the Processing plugin, which is installed by default with QGIS Desktop. When enabled, this plugin turns on the **Processing** menu from which you can open the **Processing Toolbox**. The toolbox is a panel that docks to the right side of QGIS Desktop. The tools are organized in a hierarchical fashion. The toolbox contains tools from different software components of QGIS such as GRASS, the Orfeo toolbox, SAGA, and GDAL/OGR, as well as the core QGIS tools covered in this chapter. Some tools are duplicated. For example, the GRASS commands, SAGA tools, and QGIS geoalgorithms all include a buffer tool. At the bottom of the **Processing Toolbox**, there is a toggle between the default simplified interface and the advanced interface. The advanced interface organizes the tools by the source software package. With the default installation of QGIS 2.6, the toolbox contains almost 400 tools; so, the search box is a convenient way to locate tools within the toolbox. For a more detailed look at the **Processing Toolbox**, refer to *Chapter 7, The Processing Toolbox*.

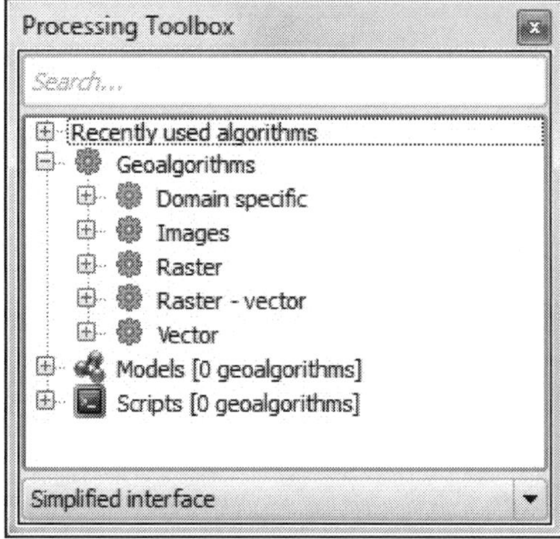

Spatial overlay tools

Spatially overlaying two data layers is one of the most fundamental types of GIS analysis. It allows you to answer spatial questions and produce information from data. For instance, how many fire stations are located in Portland, Oregon? What is the area covered by parks in a neighborhood?

This series of spatial overlay tools compute the geometric intersection of two or more vector layers to produce different outputs. Some tools identify overlaps between layers and others identify areas of no overlap. The spatial overlay tools include Clip, Difference, Intersect, Symmetrical Difference, and Union.

When using a tool that requires multiple vector input data layers, the layers must be in the same coordinate reference system.

Using the Clip and Difference tools

These two tools are related in that they are the inverse of each other. Data often extends beyond the bounds of your study area. In this situation, you can use the Clip tool to limit the data to the extent of your study area. It is often described as a "cookie cutter". It takes an input vector layer and uses a second layer as the clip layer to produce a new dataset that is clipped to the extent of the clip layer. The Difference tool takes the same inputs but outputs the input features that do not intersect with the clip layer.

In this example, we will clip fire stations to the boundary of the city of Portland. Load the `fire_sta.shp` and `PDX_city_limits.shp` files from the sample data. Select `fire_sta` in the **Input vector layer** field and `PDX_city_limits` in the **Clip layer** field. The output shapefile will be loaded into QGIS automatically since **Add result to canvas** is checked. This is the default setting for most tools. If you have any selected features, you can choose to just use them as inputs. The operation creates a fire stations' layer consisting of the 31 features that lie within the Portland city limits.

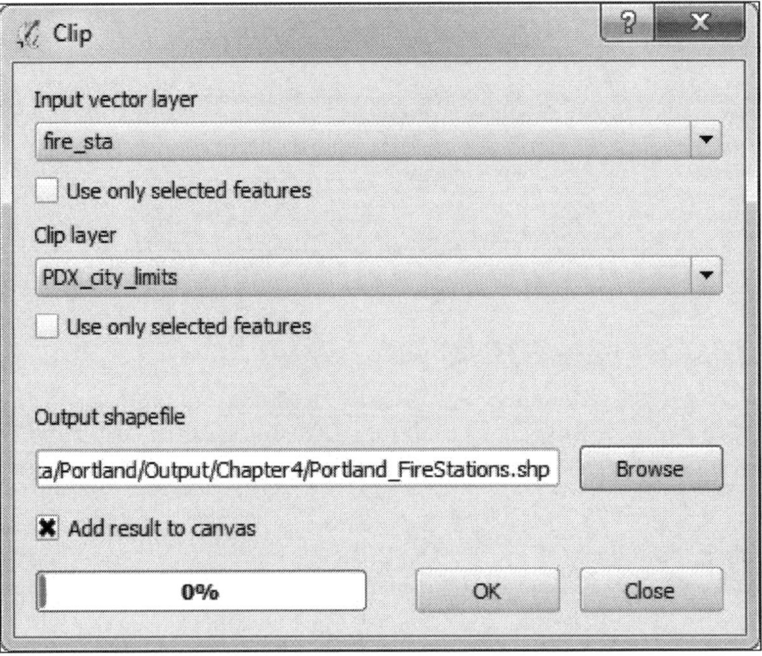

Using the Difference tool with the same inputs that were used with Clip results in the output fire stations that lie beyond the limits of the clip layer. The outputs from these two tools contain only attributes from the input vector layer.

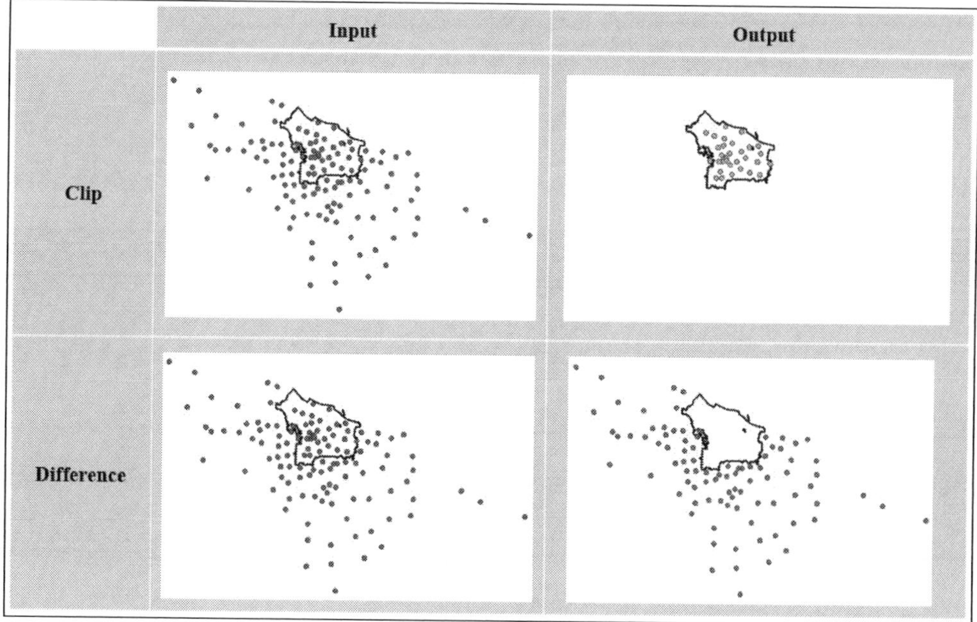

Inputs and outputs from the Clip and Difference tools

Using the Intersect and Symmetrical Difference tools

The Intersect tool preserves only the areas common to both datasets in the output. Symmetrical Difference is the opposite; only the areas that do not intersect are preserved in the output. Unlike Clip and Difference, the output from these two tools contains attributes from both input layers. The output will have the geometry type of the minimum geometry of the inputs. For example, if a line and polygon layer are intersected, the output will be a line layer. The following is an example of running the Intersect tool. After that, you will see a figure that demonstrates the output from each tool.

The following examples uses the `North_PDX_parks.shp` and `Kenton.shp` shapefiles from the sample data:

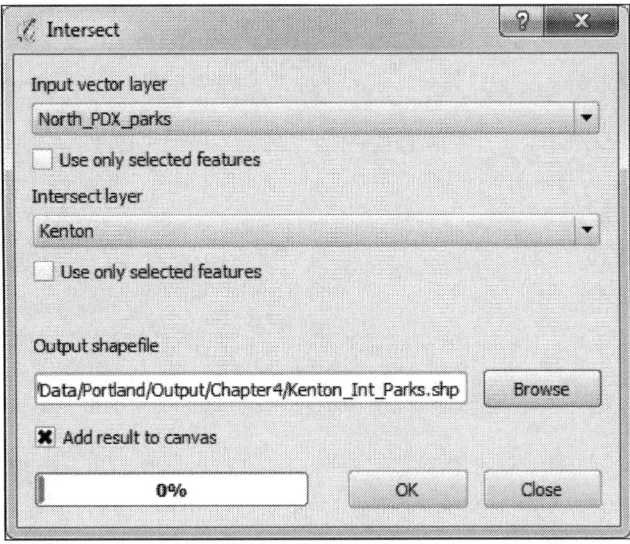

The following figure compares the Intersect and Symmetrical Difference tools by showing example inputs and outputs for each:

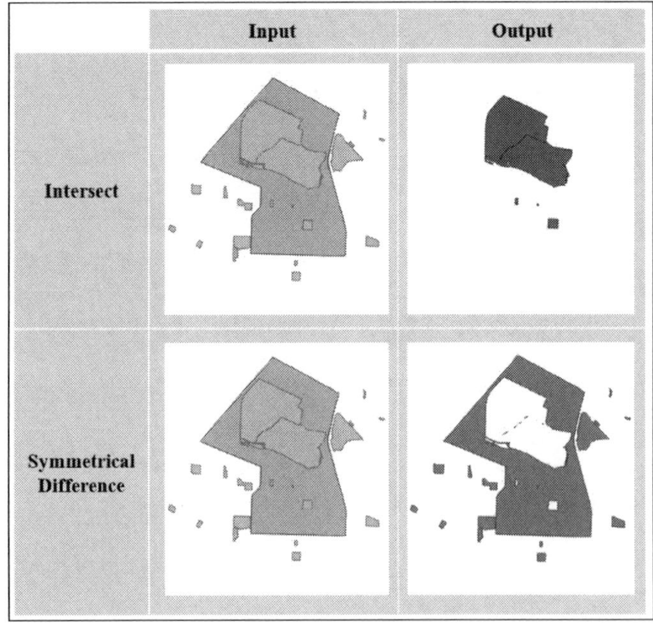

Overlaying polygon layers with Union

The Union tool overlays two polygon layers and preserves all the features of both datasets, whether or not they intersect. The following figure displays an example union using the `North_PDX_parks.shp` and `Kenton.shp` shapefiles from the sample data. Attributes from both datasets are contained in the output attribute table.

Output of the Union tool

Creating buffers

The Buffer tool is a commonly used tool that produces a new vector polygon layer that represents a specific distance from the input features. It can be used to identify proximity to a feature. Here, we will buffer the Portland fire departments by one mile; this will identify all the areas within the one-mile buffer distance. To buffer, we will perform the following steps:

1. The **Input vector layer** field will be set to `Portland_FireStations`.

2. Next, we'll specify the buffer distance. The tool will use the units of the coordinate reference system of the input vector layer as the distance units. This data is in State Plane Oregon North with the unit as feet. Enter `5280` to produce a one-mile buffer. You also have the option of specifying an attribute column containing buffer distances. This allows you to specify different buffer distances for different features.

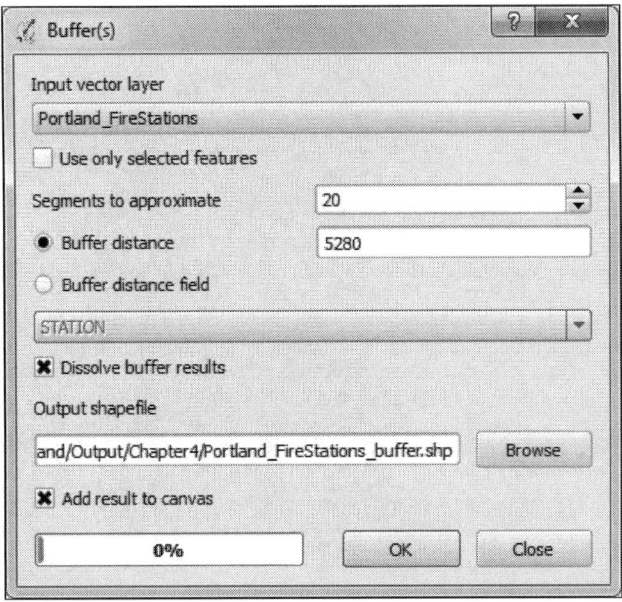

> The **Buffer distance** field will accept both positive and negative values. If a negative value is entered, the buffer will be extended inside the polygon boundary. If a positive value is entered, the buffer will be extended outside the polygon boundary.

3. QGIS cannot create true curves, but it provides an option to set **Segments to approximate**. The higher the number the smoother the output will be because QGIS will use more segments to approximate the curve. In this example, it has been set to `20` instead of the default of `5`.
4. Checking **Dissolve buffer results** will merge buffer polygons if they overlap.

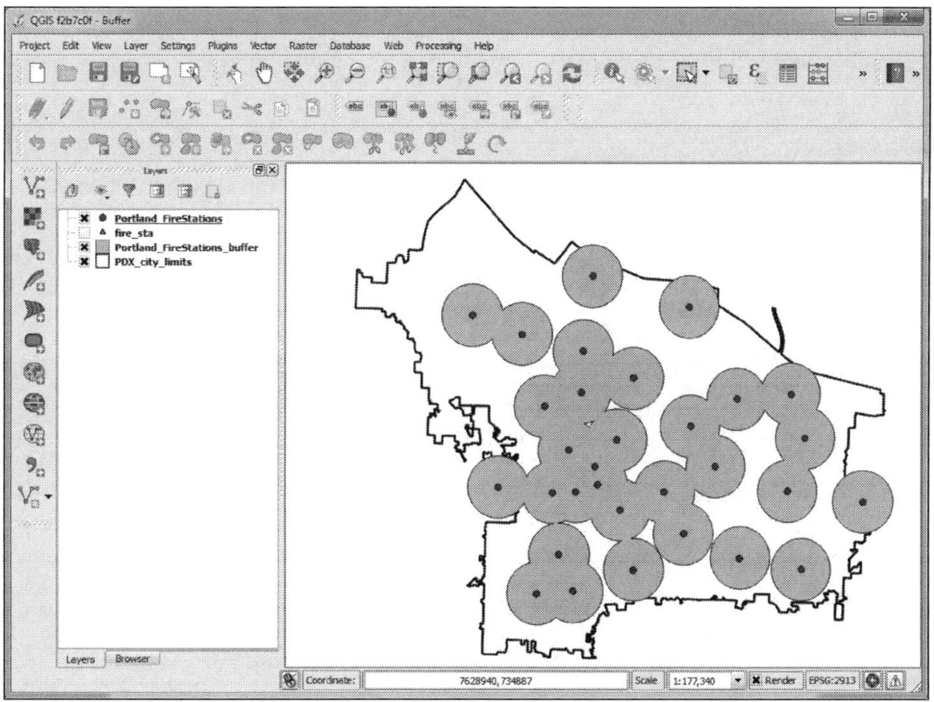

When you navigate to **Processing Toolbox** | **Geoalgorithms** | **Vector** | **Geometry Operations**, you will find the **Variable distance buffer** tool. This tool creates a multiple-ring buffer where the radius of the rings are determined by a distance value stored in an attribute column.

Generating convex hulls

The Convex Hull tool will take a vector layer (point, line, or polygon) and generate the smallest possible convex bounding polygon around the features. It will generate a single minimum convex hull around the features or allow you to specify an attribute column as input. In the latter case, it will generate convex hulls around features with the same attribute value in the specified field.

The result will be the bounding area for a set of points, and it will work well if there are no outlying data points. Here, a convex hull has been generated around `Portland_FireStations.shp`:

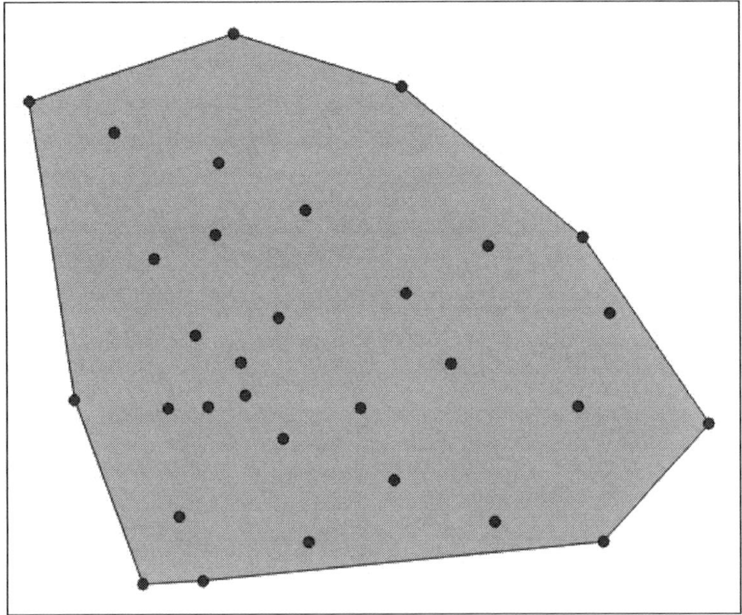

Dissolving features

The Dissolve tool merges the features of a GIS layer. It will merge all the features in a layer into one feature. This can be done via the values of an attribute field or with the **Dissolve all** option. In the following example, the neighborhoods of Portland (`Neighborhoods_pdx.shp`) are dissolved, which creates the city boundary:

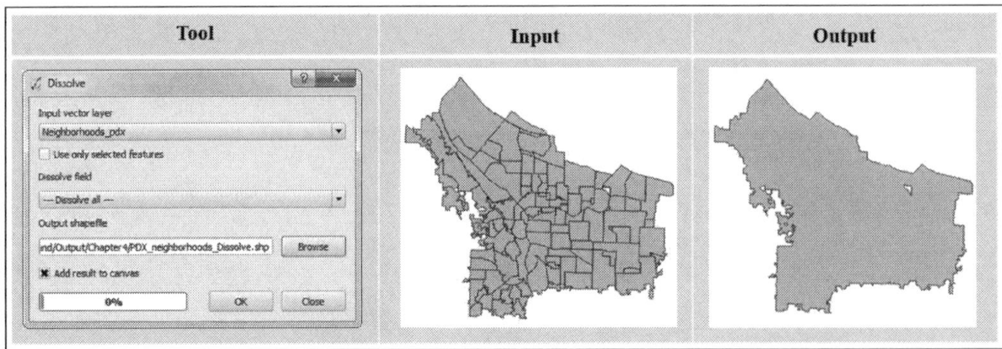

Most tools have a checkbox for using only selected features.

Defining coordinate reference systems

QGIS supports hundreds of coordinate reference systems for data display and analysis. In some cases, however, the supported CRS may not suit your exact needs. QGIS provides the functionality to create custom CRS using the Custom Coordinate Reference System Definition tool that can be found by navigating to **Settings** | **Custom CRS**.

In QGIS, a CRS is defined using the **Proj.4** definition format. We must understand the Proj.4 definition format before we can define a new or modify an existing CRS; therefore, in the first part of this section, we will discuss the basics of Proj.4, and in the second part, we will walk you through an example to create a custom CRS.

Proj.4 is another Open Source Geospatial Foundation (`http://osgeo.org`) project used by QGIS, similar to OGR and GDAL. This project is for managing coordinate systems and projections. For a detailed user manual for the Proj.4 format used to specify the CRS Parameters in QGIS, visit the project website at `https://trac.osgeo.org/proj`.

Understanding the Proj.4 definition format

The Proj.4 definition format is a line composed of a series of parameters separated by spaces. Each parameter has the general form of `+parameter=value`. The parameter starts with the `+` character, followed by a unique parameter name. If the parameter requires a value to be set, then an equal sign, `=`, character will follow the parameter name and the value will follow the equal sign. If a parameter does not require a value to be set, then it is treated as a flag.

As an example, the following figure displays a Proj.4 definition for the USA Eckert IV CRS. Notice that this CRS has seven parameters; each parameter is prefaced with a `+` character. Also, notice that six of the parameters have associated values and one parameter is a flag. Each value is set after the `=` character.

```
USA_Eckert_IV

+proj=eck4 +lon_0=-96.0 +x_0=0 +y_0=0 +datum=WGS84 +units=m
+no_defs
```

The parameters displayed in the preceding figure show only subset parameters that Proj.4 contains. If a CRS does not use a parameter, it is simply omitted from the parameter line. The following is a list and discussion of common parameters used when defining a CRS:

- **Projection** (`+proj`): This is always required. It is the name of the cartographic projection to use. The value provided is an abbreviated name of a supported projection.
- **Spheroid** (`+ellps`): This is a model of the earth's shape that is used in transforming a projection. The reference spheroid, or ellipsoid, is generated by choosing the lengths of the major and minor axes that best fit those of the real earth. Many such models are appropriate for different locations on earth.
- **Datum** (`+datum`): This is the name of the spheroid to use.
- **Central meridian** (`+lon_0`): This is the longitude on which a map is centered (x-origin).
- **Latitude of origin** (`+lat_0`): This is the latitude on which a map is centered (y-origin).
- **False easting** (`+x_0`): This is the x-coordinate value for the central meridian (x-origin). For example, if the central meridian for your projected map is `-96.00` and the false easting is set to `0.00`, then all locations along that meridian are assigned a value of `0.00`. All locations to the west of the central meridian (x-origin) are assigned a negative value and all locations to the east of the central meridian are assigned a positive value, similar to a typical Cartesian plane.
- **False northing** (`+y_0`): This is the y-coordinate value for the latitude of origin (y-origin). For example, if the reference latitude for a conic projection is `37.00`, then all locations along that parallel are assigned a value of `0.00`. All locations to the south of the reference latitude (y-origin) are assigned a negative value and all locations to the north of the reference latitude are assigned a positive value, similar to a typical Cartesian plane.
- **Standard parallel(s)** (`+lat_1`, `+lat_2`): This is the latitude(s) on which a map is centered (sometimes the y-origin), or for conic projections, the parallels along which the cone touches the earth.
- **No defaults** (`+no_defs`): This is a flag to designate that no default values should be utilized for parameters not specified in the projection definition.
- **Coordinate units** (`+units`): These are used to define distances when setting *x* and *y* coordinates.

For a full list of parameters, visit the Proj.4 project website at `https://trac.osgeo.org/proj`.

Defining a new custom coordinate reference system

There are two methods for creating a custom CRS: write a Proj.4 definition from scratch or copy the Proj.4 definition from an existing CRS and modify it. No matter which creation method you choose, both are completed using the **Custom Coordinate Reference System Definition** window.

The following figure shows the `New England.shp` sample data in its unprojected WGS 1984 form. In this section, we will create a custom CRS to display the New England states using an equal-area map projection.

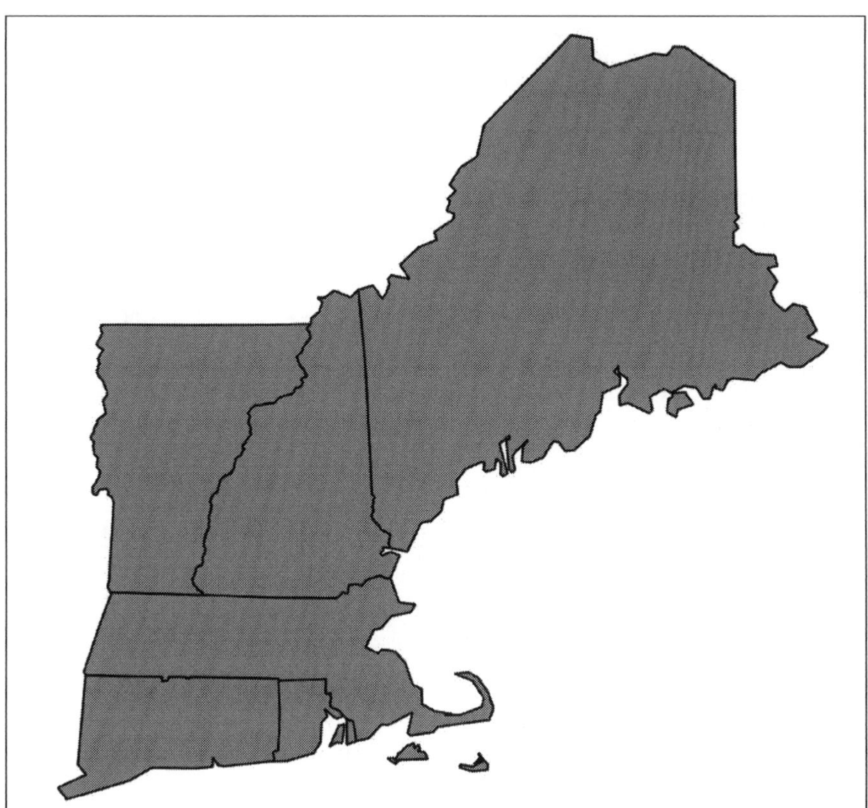

Open the **Custom Coordinate Reference System Definition** window by clicking on **Custom CRS** under **Settings**. This window has two parts: **Define** and **Test**. We will not use/discuss the **Test** part, but instead, we will focus on the **Define** part of the window to create our new CRS. We will modify the `USA_Contiguous_Albers_Equal_Area_Conic EPSG:102003` projection so that it focuses on New England.

1. Click on the **Add new CRS** button to create a blank CRS entry.
2. Set the name of the new CRS to `New England Albers Equal Area Conic`.

   At this point, we have two options; we can write the Proj.4 projection from scratch in the **Parameters** textbox, or we can copy an existing CRS Proj.4 string from a projection that closely matches what we want and then modify it to our needs. Let's elect to copy an existing CRS and modify it.

3. Click on the **Copy existing CRS** button, which will open the **Coordinate Reference System Selector** window.
4. Enter `102003` in the **Filter** text box to find the `USA_Contiguous_Albers_Equal_Area_Conic` projection. Select the found projection and then click on **OK**. This will copy the Proj.4 string back to the **Parameters** text box in the **Custom Coordinate Reference System Definition** window.
5. In the **Parameters** text box, modify the Proj.4 string by changing it to `+proj=aea +lat_1=42.5 +lat_2=45 +lat_0=43.75 +lon_0=-71 +x_0=0 +y_0=0 +datum=NAD83 +units=m +no_defs`. The modified string should look like the one shown in the following figure:

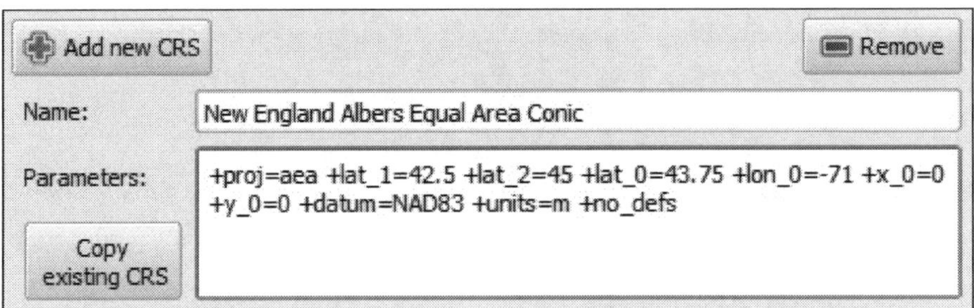

6. Click on **OK** to close the window and store your new custom CRS.

   With the creation of the custom CRS, we can apply it as our project CRS to perform an on-the-fly CRS transformation (by navigating to **Project | Project Properties | CRS**). The new custom CRS can be found at the bottom of the CRS list under **User Defined Coordinate Systems**, as shown in the following screenshot:

The following figure shows the New England states with the custom CRS that we created/defined. Quite a difference!

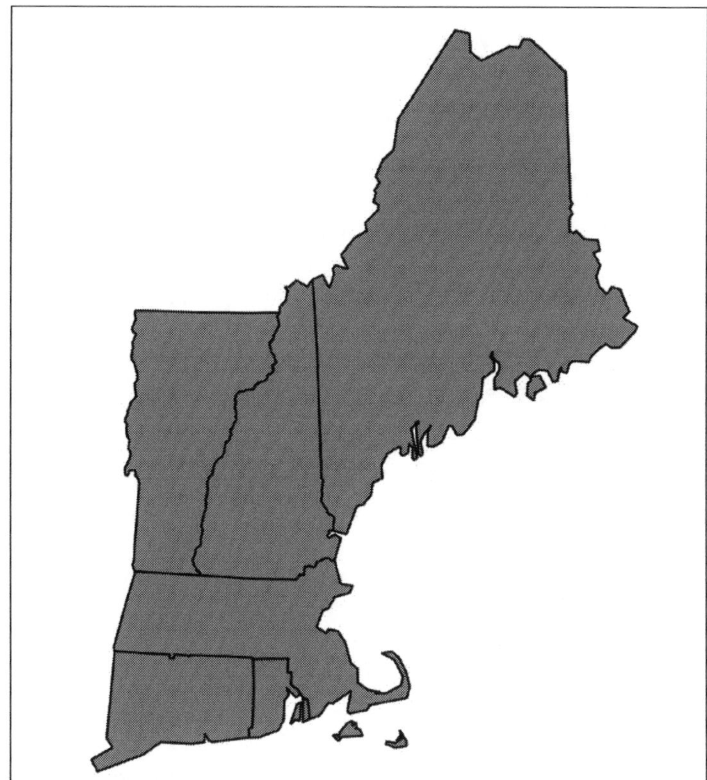

Advanced field calculations

QGIS Desktop provides powerful field-calculation functionality. In the field calculator, advanced mathematical, geometry, string, date and time, type conversion, and conditional functions are available for use. Leveraging these advanced functions along with standard operators allows for some powerful field calculations.

This section will explain the field calculator interface in detail, followed by multiple examples of advanced field calculations from a variety of functional areas. It is assumed that you know the basics of field calculations and common operators.

Exploring the field calculator interface

The field calculator can be opened in three ways, which are as follows:

- Open the attribute table of the layer whose details you wish to calculate and then click on the field calculator button () on the attribute table toolbar
- Open the attribute table of the layer whose details you wish to calculate and then press *Ctrl + I* on your keyboard
- Select the layer whose details you wish to calculate in the **Layers** panel and then click on the field calculator button () on the attributes toolbar

The **Field calculator** window, shown in the following figure, has five sections:

- **Field designation**: This determines which field will hold the output of the expression. You can use **Create a new field** or **Update existing field** by selecting the desired option and setting the relevant option(s). A virtual field can also be created by selecting **Create a new field** and **Create virtual field**. A virtual field is not stored in the dataset; instead, it is stored as an expression in the QGIS project file and will be recalculated every time the field is used.
- **Function list**: This contains a tree of field-calculation functions available for insertion into the expression.
- **Function help**: This displays the help documentation for the selected function in the function list.
- **Operators**: This ensures quick button access to insert commonly used operators into the expression. These operators are also in the function list under the **Operators** branch.
- **Expression**: This is an editable text area that contains the expression that will calculate field values. Underneath the expression is a preview of the output for a sample record. If the expression is invalid, a notice will appear with a link to more information about the expression error.

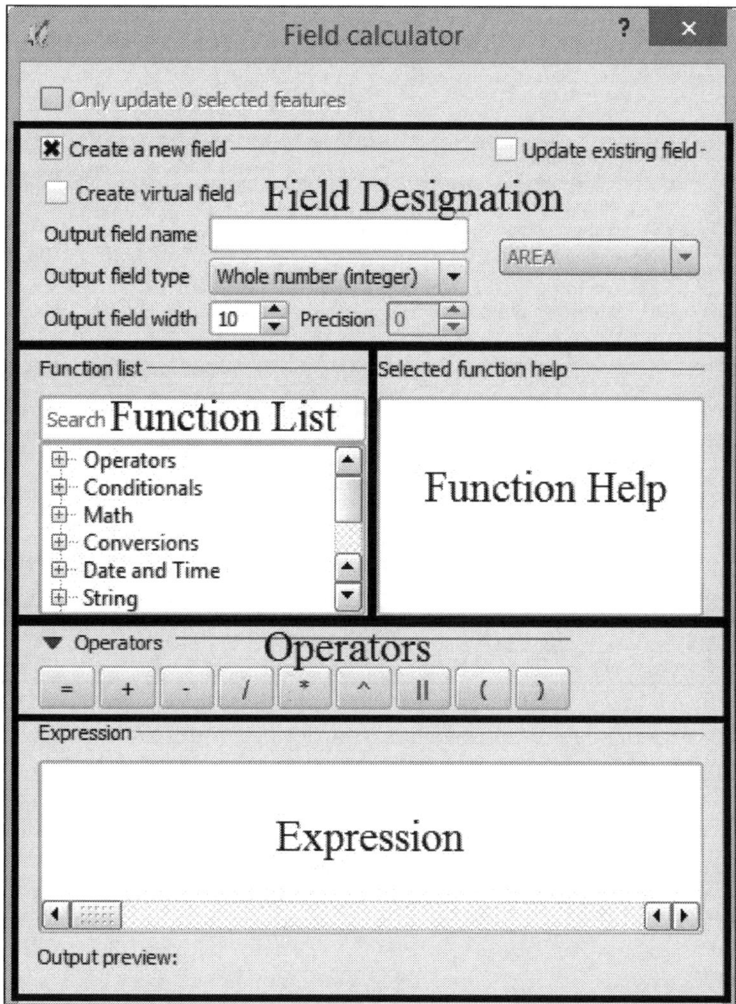

The expression must meet strict syntax guidelines, otherwise the field calculator will report a syntax error instead of an output preview. The following are common syntax rules for expressions:

- Operators should be placed without any special formatting. For example, `+`.
- Fields should be surrounded by double quotes. For example, `"State_Name"`.
- Text (string) values should be surrounded by single quotes. For example, `'Washington'`.

- Whole numbers (integer) and decimal numbers (float) should be entered without any surrounding characters. For example, `153.27`.
- Functions come in two types, as follows:
    - **Functions requiring parameters**: These begin with a function name, followed by a set of parentheses. Inside the parentheses are function parameters separated by commas. For example, `log(base, value)`.
    - **Functions not requiring parameters**: These begin with a dollar sign (`$`) followed by the function name. For example, `$area`.

If this is a little confusing, don't worry, you can rely on the field calculator to enter a portion of the syntax for you correctly. To add an operator, field, or function to the expression, double-click on the desired item in the function list and it will be added to the cursor location in the expression.

In addition to adding functions through the function list, the field calculator can also add to the expression any value that currently exists in any field. To do this, expand the **Fields and Values** branch of the function list tree. A list of the fields in the attribute table will be listed. When you select a field, a **Field values** area will appear to the right underneath the function help (as shown in the following figure). Click on **all unique** to load the **Field values** area with all unique values found in the selected field. Then, click on **10 samples** to load 10 samples that are found in the selected field into the **Field values** area. You can also load values by right-clicking on the field name and selecting it from the contextual menu (contextual menu is shown in following figure). Double-click on a value to add it to the cursor location in the expression.

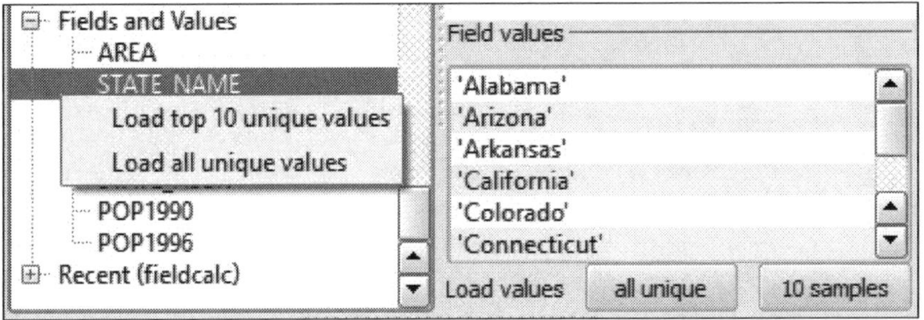

Writing advanced field calculations

Let's put what we learned previously to practice. This section will walk you through creating three advanced field calculations. The first calculation will insert the current date into a field as a formatted string. The second calculation will insert a geometry value. The third calculation will calculate a label string that differs depending on the state's population.

The first example – calculating and formatting the current date

The first example of an advanced field calculation uses two functions to calculate and format the current date. For this example, we will format the current date as dd/mm/yyyy.

1. Open the **Field calculator** window.
2. Select **Create a new field** and set the following options:
    - **Output field name**: `Updated`
    - **Output field type**: `Text (string)`
    - **Output field width**: `10`
3. In the **Function list** field, expand the **String** node and then double-click on **format_date** to add it to the **Expression** area. This function takes two arguments: a time string and a string representing the format to convert the time string to. We will use the current date function for the time and write a format string.
4. In the **Function list** field, expand the **Date and Time** node and then double-click on **$now** to add it to the **Expression** area after the open parenthesis.
5. Type a comma after `$now` and enter `'dd/MM/yyyy'`, followed by a closed parenthesis. The `$now` function returns a string representation of the current time and date. The following figure shows the completed calculation:

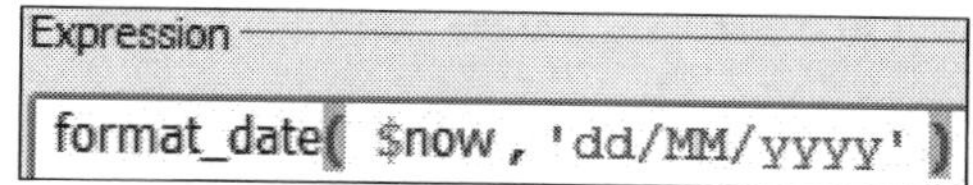

6. Click on **OK** to execute the calculation. This will enable editing on the layer and calculate the field values.
7. Save the edits to the layer and disable the editing mode. The calculated values are now stored in the layer. The following figure shows a sample of the calculated and formatted date:

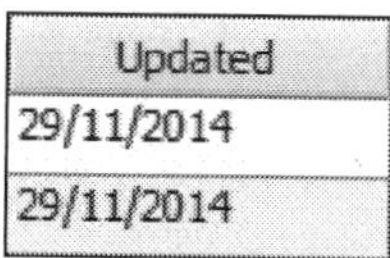

Updated
29/11/2014
29/11/2014

The second example – inserting geometric values

The second example of an advanced field calculation uses two functions to insert the *x* coordinate for a point and the *x* coordinate of a specific vertex for a line or polygon. First, we will calculate the x coordinate of a point. To do this, perform the following steps:

1. Open the **Field calculator** window.
2. Select **Create a new field** and set the following options:
   - **Output field name**: `XCoord`
   - **Output field type**: `Decimal number (real)`
   - **Output field width**: `10`
   - **Output field precision**: `7`
3. In the **Function list** field, expand **Geometry** and then double-click on **$x** to add it to the **Expression** area. This function returns the x coordinate of a point geometry. The following figure shows the completed calculation:

XCoord
7610162.7910105
7630980.8126640

Now let's calculate the first and last x coordinate for a line or polygon:

1. Open the **Field calculator** window.
2. Select **Create a new field** and set the following options:
   - **Output field name**: `XCoord1`
   - **Output field type**: `Decimal number (real)`
   - **Output field width**: `10`
   - **Output field Precision**: `7`
3. In the **Function list** field, expand **Geometry** and then double-click on **xat** to add it to the **Expression** area. This function returns the x coordinate of a vertex specified by a 0-based index number. Inside the parentheses, you will need to specify the index of the vertex whose coordinates you wish to retrieve. For example, to retrieve the x coordinate of the first vertex, the command will be `xat(0)`. You can also specify the vertex using negative numbers. So, to retrieve the x coordinate of the last vertex, the command will be `xat(-1)`.

4. The following figure shows the completed calculations for `xat(0)` and `xat(-1)` for a line geometry type:

XCoord1	XCoord2
7644082.2869363	7644085.7078612
7626380.5004895	7626208.0759656

The third example – calculating a population-dependent label string

This third example populates a new field with a string that is used for labeling states. States that have a population of over five million will have a label with the state name and population. All other states will simply have a label with the state name. The basic logic of our calculation is, "If a state has a population of over five million, then create a label that lists the state name and population; otherwise, create a label that lists the state name".

Since we have two cases of possible labels, we will need to use the `CASE ELSE` conditional function. The purpose of the `CASE ELSE` function is to direct the field calculator to a calculation block when a condition is met. So, we will have one calculation block for states over five million in population and one for all other states.

For this example, the `states48.shp` sample data is being used. The `POP1996` field contains the states' population values as of 1996 and is the field used to determine whether a state's population is over or under five million.

1. Open the **Field calculator** window.
2. Select **Create a new field** and set the following options:
    - **Output field name**: `StateLabel`
    - **Output field type**: `Text (string)`
    - **Output field width**: `35`
3. In the **Function list** field, expand the **Conditionals** node and then double-click on **CASE ELSE** to add it to the **Expression** area.

   This will add `CASE WHEN expression THEN result ELSE result END` to the **Expression** area. We will replace `expression` with the test for populations greater than five million. The `result` after `THEN` will be replaced with the label we wish to create when `expression` is true. The `result` after `ELSE` will be replaced with the label we wish to create when `expression` is false.

4. Let's start by setting the label for states with a population of less than five million. Replace the `result` after `ELSE` with the field name `STATE_NAME`.
5. Now, we will set the condition to check for population greater than five million. Replace `condition` with `"POP1996" > 5000000`. The following figure shows the expression with optional formatting to make it easier to read:

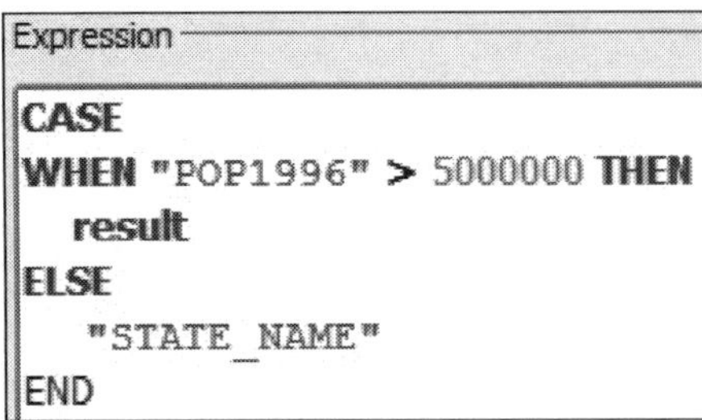

6. The last step is to calculate the string for states with a population greater than five million. The format of the string will be `<state name> Population: <population>`, with the state name on the first line and the population on the second line. As this is a complex string, it will be constructed in three parts, and then concatenated together using the concatenation operator, || (two vertical bars).
7. Replace `result` with the `"STATE_NAME"` field.
8. Add a concatenation operator after `"STATE_NAME"` by either typing two vertical bars (||) or by clicking the concatenation operator button (||). This allows the following text to be concatenated with the contents of the `"STATE_NAME"` field.
9. After the concatenation operator, type `'\nPopulation: '`and keep a space between the colon and closing single quote. The `\n` is interpreted as a new line and starts a new line in the string.

10. Add a concatenation operator to the end of the line.

    The last item to add to the string is the population value stored in the `POP1996` field. However, the population is stored as an integer and an integer (or any other number) cannot be concatenated to a string. Therefore, we need to convert the integer to a string so that we can concatenate. Luckily for us, the `format_number()` function converts a number to a string and adds thousands separators and rounds the number (although rounding is not needed in this case).

To convert a number to a string without formatting, use the `tostring()` function.

11. After the concatenation operator, add the `format_number()` function by expanding **String** in **Function list** and double-click on `format_number`. You can also manually type in the function.
12. Inside the parenthesis of the `format_number()` function, enter `"POP1996", 0` where `"POP1996"` is the first parameter containing the population value, the comma separates the function parameters, and `0` is the number of decimal places to round the number. The following figure shows the completed expression that is formatted across multiple lines for easy reading:

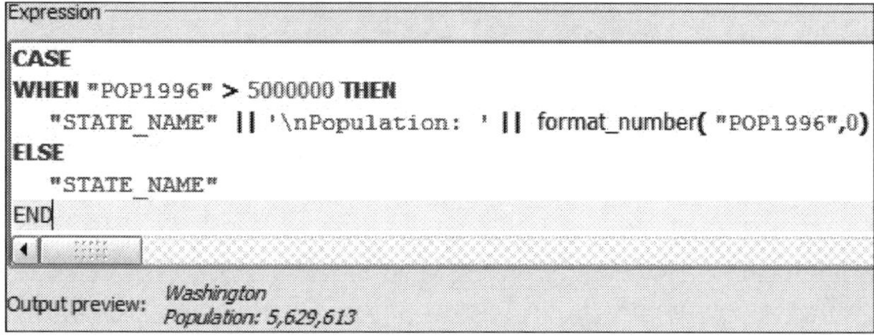

13. Click on **OK** to perform the field calculation. This will enable editing on the layer and calculate the field values.

14. Save the edits to the layer and disable the editing mode. The calculated values are now stored in the layer. The following figure shows a sample of labels calculated for states with populations greater and less than five million:

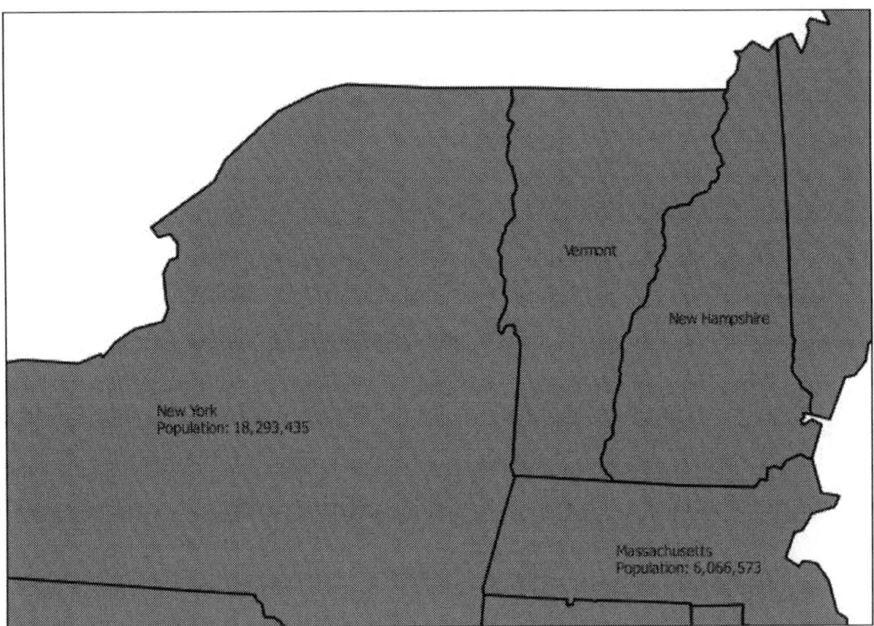

Complex spatial and aspatial queries

QGIS provides powerful spatial and aspatial query tools that allow for the easy creation of data subsets. In this section, a series of spatial and aspatial queries will be used to determine which elementary schools are within the **Southeast Uplift Neighborhood Coalition** (**SEUL**) and **Southwest Neighborhoods Inc.** (**SWNI**) coalitions in Portland, Oregon. This example uses the `Neighborhoods_pdx.shp` and `schools.shp` sample data.

First, we will select the SEUL and SWNI coalition neighborhoods from `Neighborhoods_pdx.shp`. To do this, perform the following steps:

1. Open the attribute table of `Neighborhoods_pdx`. Click on the **Select features using an expression** button (ε) to open the **Select by expression** window. This window is a subset of the **Field calculator** window that was explained in the *Exploring the field calculator interface* section, earlier in this chapter. If you are unfamiliar with the interface, review the aforementioned section.

2. In **Function list**, expand the **Fields and Values** node and double-click on **"COALIT"** to add it to the **Expression** area.
3. In the **Operators** area, click on the Equal operator button (=) or press = on your keyboard to add it to the **Expression** area.
4. With **"COALIT"** still selected in **Function list**, click on the **all unique** button to load a list of all unique values found in the field. Double-click on **'SEUL'** to add it to the **Expression** area after the equal sign.
5. As we want to choose either SEUL or SWNI coalition neighborhoods, we will use the Boolean OR operator to connect the two expressions together. In **Function list**, expand the **Operators** node and double-click on **OR** to add it to the end of the expression.
6. Using what you learned so far, add `"COALIT" = 'SWNI'` to the end of the expression. The completed expression is shown in the following screenshot:

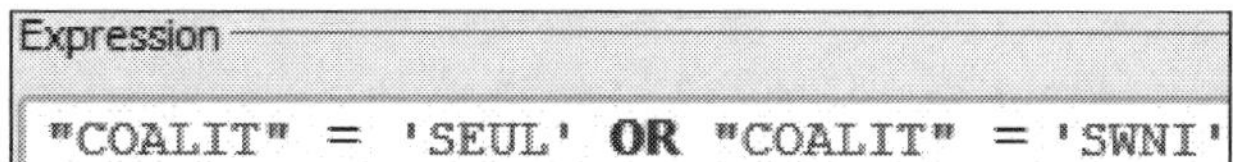

7. Click on **Select** to perform the aspatial selection. Close the **Select by expression** window and the attribute table to view the results on the map. The following figure shows the selected neighborhoods.

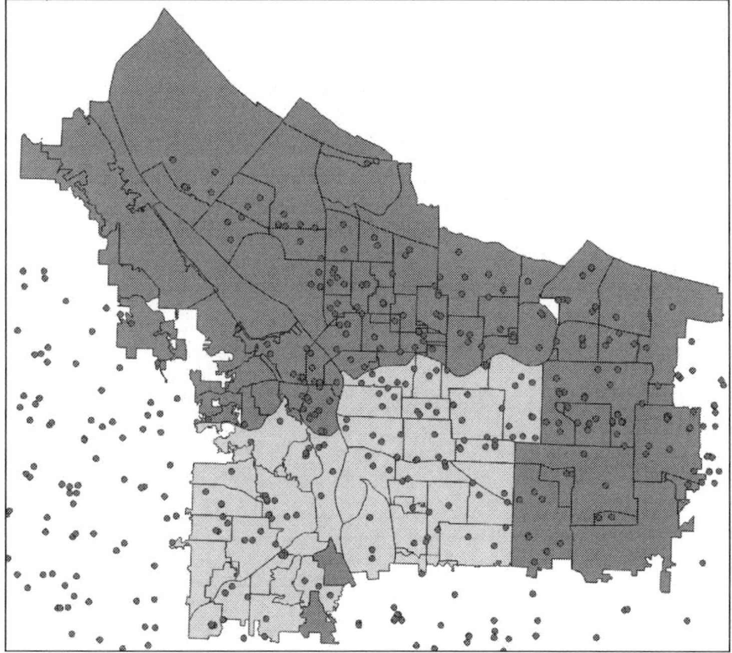

With the two coalitions selected, we will next perform a spatial selection to determine which schools are within the selected neighborhoods. To do this, perform the following steps:

1. Navigate to **Vector | Spatial Query | Spatial Query** from the QGIS menu bar to open the **Spatial Query** window. This window allows features from one layer to be selected based on their spatial relationship with the features in a different layer. Depending on the geometry of the two layers, the spatial relationships will change to match the appropriate selections that are available.
2. In the **Select source features from** section, choose **schools**.
3. Set **Where the feature** to **Within** from the drop down box.
4. In the **Reference features of** section, choose **Neighborhoods_pdx**. Keep **46 selected geometries** selected. With this selected, only the currently selected neighborhoods will be used for the spatial query.
5. For the **And use the result to** field, choose **Create new selection**.
6. Click on **Apply** to execute the query. Once complete, the **Spatial Query** window will expand to display the results.

   The following screenshot shows the expanded **Spatial Query** window. You can select individual result feature IDs and select **Zoom to item** to center the map on the selected item. Note that the window still contains the original spatial query, so it is possible to modify the query and execute it again. In addition, note that you can view log messages of the query. Lastly, you can create a temporary layer to the map from the selected features by clicking on the Create layer with selected button ( ).

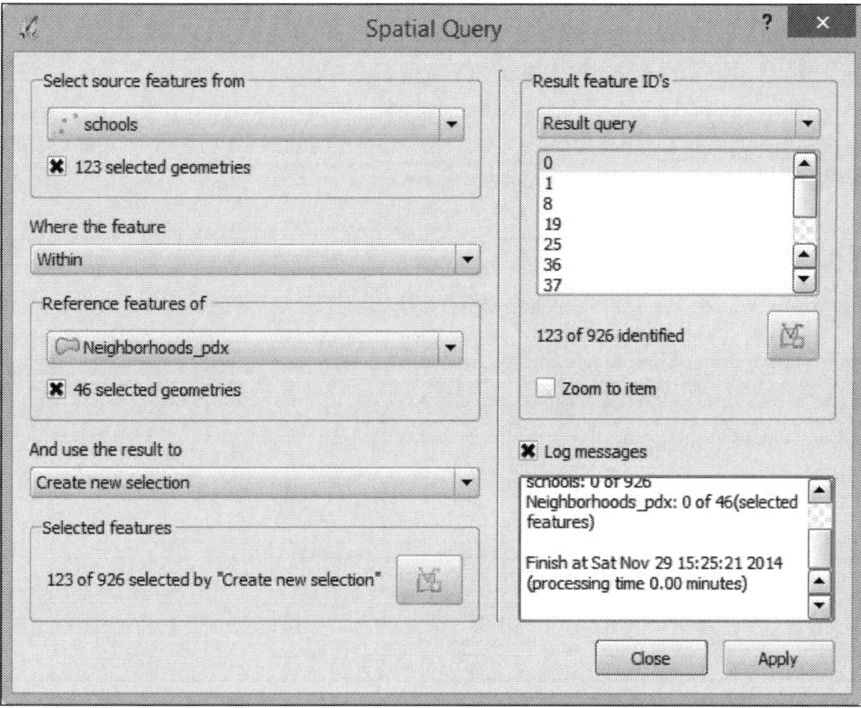

7. Click on **Close** to dismiss the **Spatial Query** window. On the map, the schools layer will have the selected records that fall within the two selected coalition neighborhoods. The last step is to select only the elementary schools from the selection.
8. Open the attribute table of schools. Click on the **Select features using an expression** button to open the **Select by expression** window.
9. Using what you have learned so far, create this expression: **"LEVEL" = 'Elementary'**.
10. Click on the down arrow next to the **Select** button and choose **Select within selection**. This will execute the selection. The remaining 32 selected records are the elementary schools that were previously selected by location. Click on **Close** to close the **Select by expression** window.
11. On the schools attribute table, in the lower-left corner, click on **Show all Features** button and choose **Show Selected Features**. Only the selected records will now display in the attribute table.

Summary

Data is rarely in the form needed to perform processing and analysis. Often, data needs to be merged, checked for validity, converted, calculated, projected, and so on, to make it ready for use. This chapter covered many common preparation tasks to convert raw data into a more useable form.

In the next chapter, this theme of data preparation will continue, but it will be applied to raster data. You will learn how to mosaic, reclassify, resample, interpolate, and convert raster data to make it more meaningful as an input to processing tasks.

5
Preparing Raster Data for Processing

This chapter covers how to prepare raster data for further processing with the GDAL menu tools and Processing Toolbox algorithms. There are specific considerations and tools for managing raster data. The topics that you will cover in this chapter are as follows:

- Reclassification
- Resampling
- Rescaling
- Raster mosaics
- Generating overviews (pyramids)
- Data format conversions
- Interpolation

Reclassifying rasters

Raster data sets often have hundreds or thousands of values. For an analysis, you may need to synthesize the data into meaningful categories. For example, elevation may be an important input in a habitat model for species X. However, you may only be interested in identifying several broad elevation thresholds that help to define the habitat. In the following example, you will use the `elevation.tif` sample data. You will reclassify the elevation data into several categories: less than 2000 meters, 2000 to 2500 meters, and greater than 2500 meters. This will result in a raster with three values: one for each group of elevation values. The following steps outline how to use the r.recode GRASS tool (found in the processing toolbox) to accomplish this:

1. Load `elevation.tif` and set the project's CRS to `EPSG: 26912`.

2. Turn on the Processing plugin (by navigating to **Plugins** | **Manage and Install Plugins**) if it is not enabled.
3. Open the **Processing** panel by clicking on **Toolbox** under **Processing**.

> The Processing Toolbox is covered in more detail in *Chapter 7, The Processing Toolbox.*

4. To help locate the tool, type `recode` into the Processing Toolbox search bar and hit the *Enter* key. Double-click on the tool to open it.
5. Select the input layer by clicking on the down arrow to choose a raster loaded in the canvas or by clicking on the browse button.
6. Next, the tool will ask for a value to be filled in the **File containing recode rules [optional]** field. This file has to be created in a text editor. The syntax for the recode rules file is as follows:

```
input_value_low:input_value_high:output_value_low:output_value_
high
input_value_low:input_value_high:output_value
*:input_value:output_value
input_value:*:output_value
```

7. The following are the recode rules for this example. The first line tells the tool to recode the values less than `2000` meters with a value of `1` in the output raster. The first asterisk is a wildcard for every value less than `2000`. The second line recodes the values greater than and equal to `2000` and less than `2500` as `2` in the output raster. The third line recodes all values greater than `2500` as `3` in the output raster:

```
*:2000:1
2000:2500:2
2500:*:3
```

8. Save the preceding code to a text file named `Elevation_rRecode_Rules.txt`.

9. Select the output raster by clicking on the browse button. You can choose either to **Save to a temporary file** or **Save to file**. The following screenshot shows the completed r.recode tool:

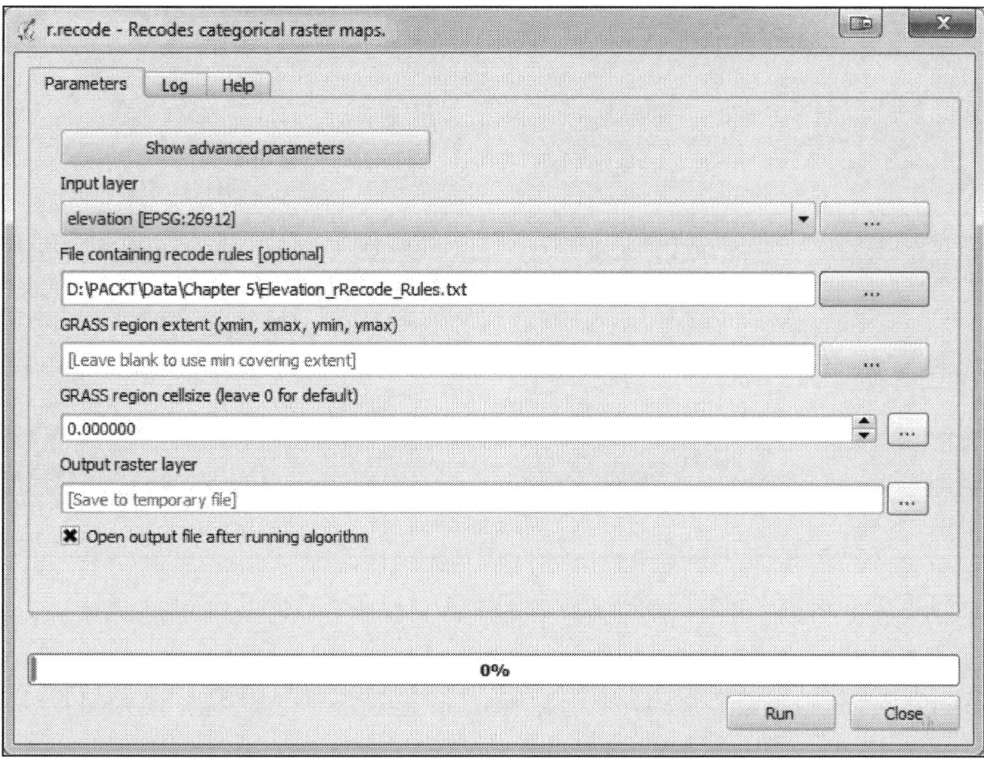

There is a similar GRASS tool in the Processing Toolbox named **r.reclass**. The r.reclass tool is used when reclassifying integer and categorical rasters, while r.recode will reclassify floating-point and decimal value rasters. Both tools use the same format for the rules text file. More complete documentation for these tools can be found on the GRASS GIS help pages at `http://grass.osgeo.org/grass65/manuals/r.reclass.html` and `http://grass.osgeo.org/grass65/manuals/r.recode.html`.

The following figure shows the result of the reclassification. The original elevation raster with the original elevation values is on the left, and the reclassified raster with three values is on the right.

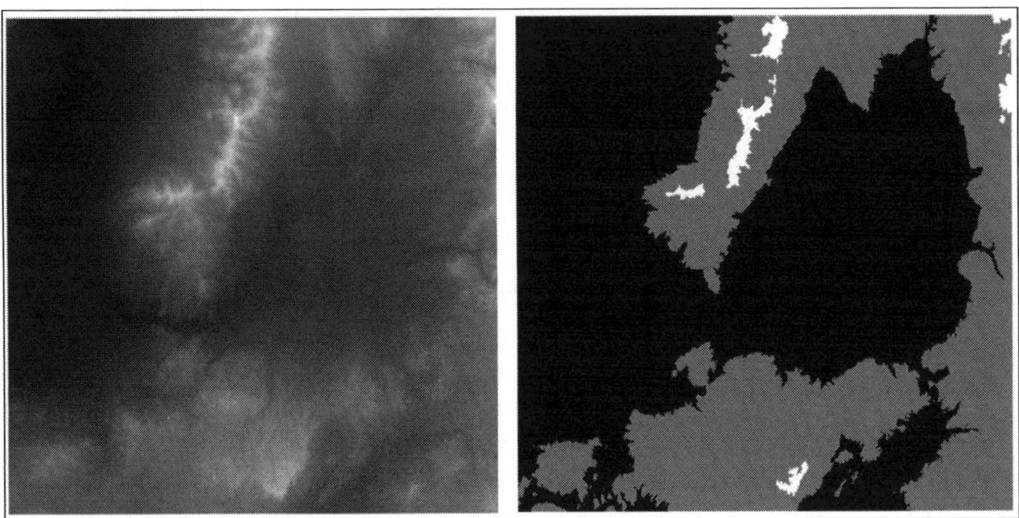

Converting datasets from floating-point to integer rasters

Raster datasets may have integer values or floating-point values with decimal points. The r.recode tool can also be used to convert raster datasets between these formats. The `elevation.tif` sample data is a floating-point raster with values ranging from `1502.1` to `2898.49` meters above sea level.

> To see the full range of values in a raster, navigate to **Layer Properties** | **Style**. Under **Load min/max values**, select the **Min/Max** setting. For **Accuracy**, choose **Actual (slower)**. Then, click on **Apply**.

To convert this raster to an integer raster, you will need to set up a rule text file with the following text:

```
1502.1:2898.49:1502:2898
(input_value_low:input_value_high:output_value_low:
    output_value_high)
```

Conversely, if you have an integer raster with values between `10` and `500` and want to convert it to floating point, you will need to set up a rule text file with this:

```
10:500:0.1:5.0
```

This will result in a raster with cell values ranging from `0.1` to `5.0`.

Resampling rasters

When an analysis requires that multiple raster datasets be combined or overlaid, their pixel resolutions should be equal. The spatial resolution or cell size of a raster can be increased or decreased by a process known as resampling. Although you can increase or decrease the resolution of a raster, it is considered a better practice to decrease the resolution of the finer datasets to match the resolution of the coarsest raster.

As an example, let's say you have two rasters: a 90-meter resolution elevation raster and a 30-meter vegetation raster. In this scenario, it would be best to resample the vegetation data to a 90-meter resolution to match the elevation data. This way all the data will be matched accurately. Conversely, if you resample to match the finest resolution raster, you will introduce false accuracy. The elevation data has a 90-meter resolution because that was the smallest unit that could be differentiated from the neighboring pixels. If you increase the spatial resolution, each elevation pixel is converted to nine 30-meter pixels. You cannot assume that all nine resulting pixels actually have the same elevation value in the real world. It is more likely that only the center pixel would have the same value.

In QGIS, there are several tools that can be used to resample a raster. In this example, the GDAL Translate tool will be used. The resolution of the `elevation.tif` sample data will be changed from 27.3526 meters to 100 meters. While the Translate tool can be found by navigating to **Raster** | **Conversion** | **Translate**, you will use the Processing Toolbox implementation of it here because it has better options for specifying the output pixel size. As you'll see this tool can be used for a variety of raster conversions during the resampling process. As you'll see in the following steps, this tool can be used for a variety of raster conversions during the resampling process:

1. Open the Processing Toolbox.
2. Switch to the advanced view.
3. Locate the tool by navigating to **GDAL/OGR** | **Conversion** | **Translate (convert format)**.
4. Select the **Input layer** raster by clicking on the down arrow to choose a raster loaded in the canvas. or by clicking on the browse button.

5. For a specific output resolution, enter the number in the **Set the size of the output file (In pixels or %)** box. To change the resolution by a percentage, click on the **Output size is a percentage of input size** box.
6. If there are cells to designate as Nodata cells, enter the value in the **Nodata value, leave as none to take the nodata value from input** field. Otherwise, leave this option blank.
7. If there is a one-band raster with a color table, use the **Expand** drop-down menu to choose a setting for converting it to a three-band image.
8. To change the CRS of the raster during the resampling operation, specify the new output CRS by clicking on the browse button for the **Output projection for output file [leave blank to use input projection]** option box.
9. To subset or clip the raster during the resampling operation, enter the coordinates for the desired spatial envelope in the **Subset based on georeferenced coordinates (xmin, xmax, ymin, ymax)** option box.
10. Additional creation parameters can be specified. For a full list of options for the gdal_translate utility, visit the help page at `http://www.gdal.org/gdal_translate.html`.
11. Use the **Output raster type** drop-down menu to choose the radiometric resolution of the output raster. The options are **Byte, Int16, UInt16, UInt32, Int32, Float32, Float64, CInt16, CInt32, CFloat32**, and **CFloat64**.

The **Output raster type** setting in the Translate tool of the Processing Toolbox can also be used to convert from floating-point rasters to integer rasters and vice versa. With a floating-point raster as the input, choose one of the integer settings to convert the raster to an integer.

12. Select the output raster by clicking on the browse button. You can choose to either **Save to a temporary file** or **Save to file**. The following screenshot shows the completed Translate tool:

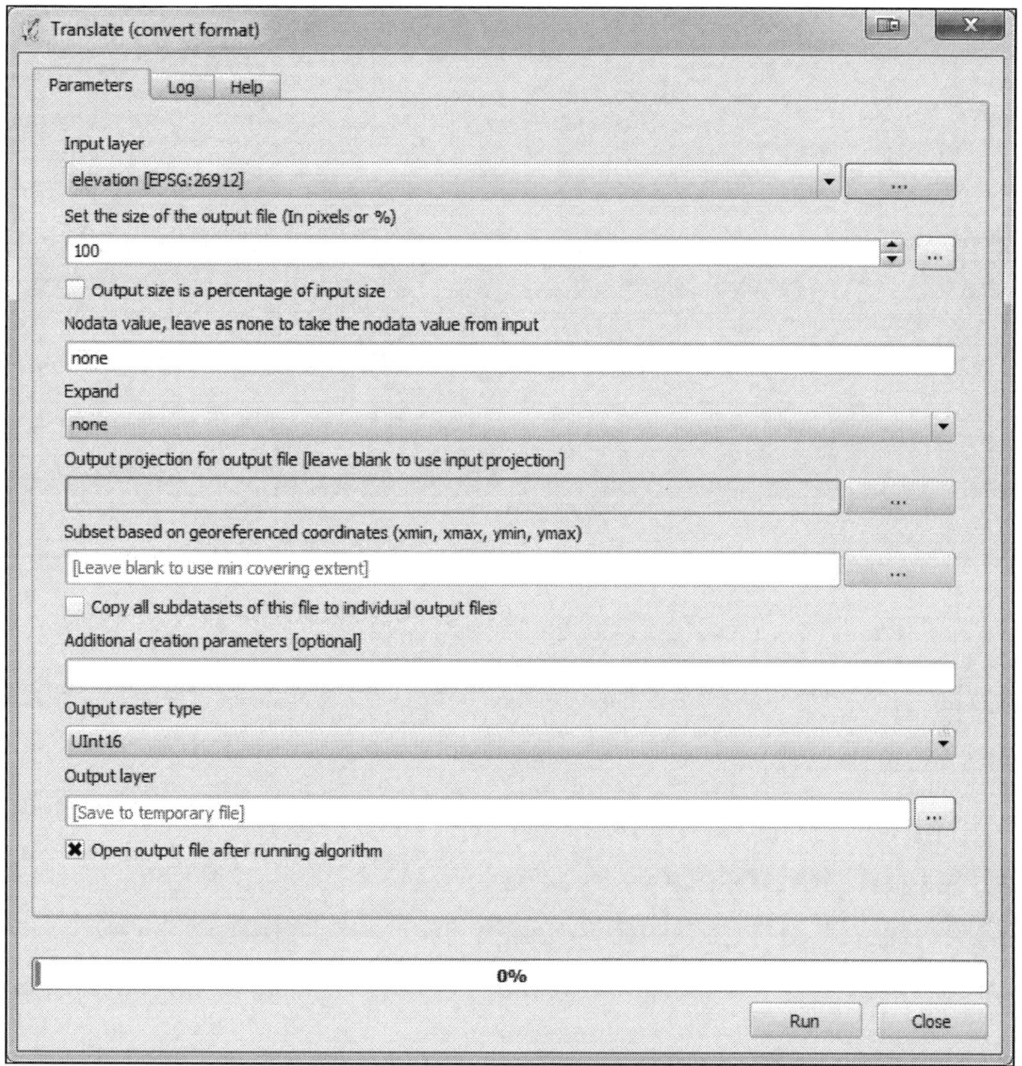

The following figure shows the result of raster resampling. The original elevation raster with 27.3526 meter pixel resolution is on the left and the resampled raster with 100 meter pixel resolution is on the right.

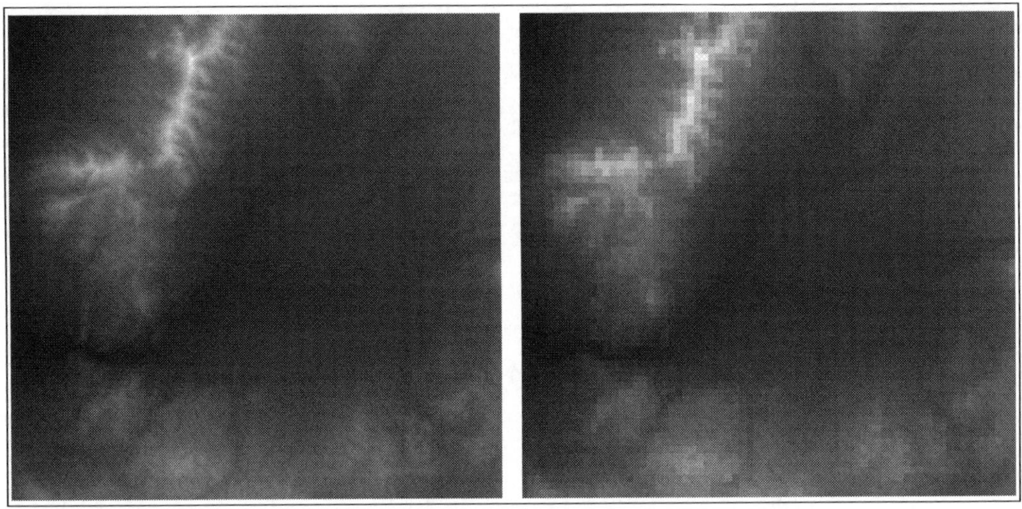

There are two additional tools that can be used to resample raster data, and both are found in the Processing Toolbox. Under **GRASS commands** | **Raster tools** there is the **r.resample** tool. Under **SAGA** | **Grid-Tools** there is the **Resampling** tool. Both these tools have similar options to the GDAL Translate tool and are included with most installations of QGIS.

Installing and troubleshooting SAGA on different platforms

SAGA, like GRASS GIS, is a standalone application whose tools can be accessed from within the QGIS Processing Toolbox. To do this, you need to have both QGIS and SAGA installed. The processing framework must also be configured properly so that QGIS can access the SAGA command-line executable. The following are guides for installing and troubleshooting SAGA on each operating system.

Windows

If you are running Windows and you installed QGIS with either the OSGeo4W or the standalone installer, SAGA will be included (unless SAGA was unchecked during the OSGeo4W installation). More importantly, the path to the SAGA executable is automatically configured. There is nothing you need to do. Just use the SAGA tools!

Mac OS X

When you install QGIS from the Kyngchaos repository at `kyngchaos.com/software/qgis`, SAGA will be included. The main error that you may encounter will state **Missing dependency: This algorithm cannot be run**. If you encounter this error, there are three ways to troubleshoot the problem:

1. There may be a conflict with the GDAL plugins. When they are enabled, the GDAL formats are added to the SAGA file format list and this changes the expected ordering. (This is mentioned in the Kyngchaos QGIS 2.6 README file.) The workaround is to disable the GDAL plugins (GDAL tools and Georeferencer GDAL) when SAGA algorithms are needed. This leaves GDAL unable to use these formats, so remember to re-enable the GDAL plugins when the work with the SAGA tools is complete.
2. There may be multiple versions of the Processing Toolbox plugin installed. Shut down QGIS. Move the `~/.qgis2/python/plugins/processing` folder to your desktop and relaunch QGIS. The folder will be rebuilt and the most recent version of SAGA will be used.
3. Identify the installation path for SAGA. In QGIS, navigate to **Settings** | **Options** | **System** and make sure that the `PATH` variable includes the path to the SAGA binaries. This can be found under **Current environment variables**.

Linux

The SAGA binaries must be installed. They can be found at `http://sourceforge.net/p/saga-gis/wiki/Binary%20Packages/`. There are packages available for Debian, Ubuntu, and FreeBSD. For example, SAGA can be installed on Ubuntu by running the following commands:

```
sudo add-apt-repository ppa:johanvdw/saga-gis
sudo apt-get update
sudo apt-get install saga
```

If you encounter the missing dependencies error, perform the following steps:

1. Open SAGA by navigating to **Processing** | **Options** | **Providers** and uncheck **Use SAGA 2.0.8 syntax**:

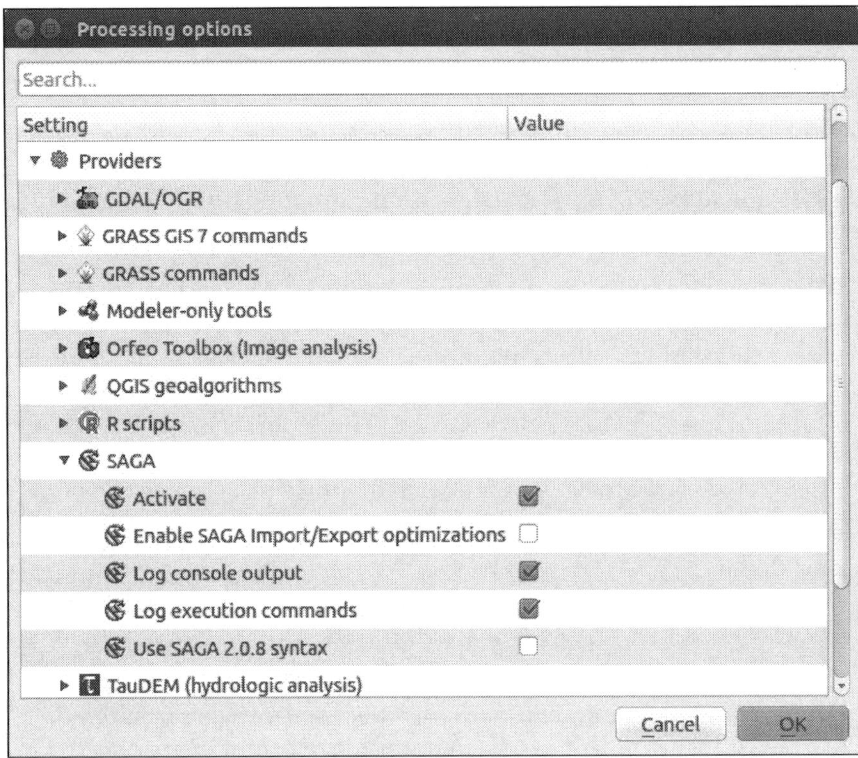

2. If you still get the error, identify the installation path for SAGA. In QGIS, navigate to **Settings** | **Options** | **System** and make sure that the `PATH` variable includes the value for the path to the SAGA binaries. This can be found under **Current environment variables**, as shown in the following screenshot:

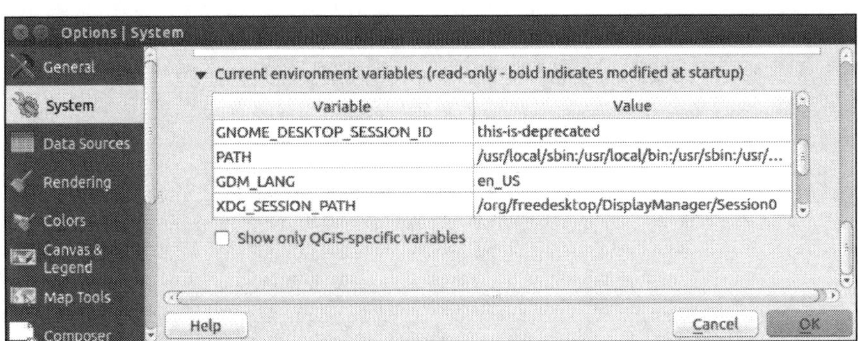

Rescaling rasters

When an analysis calls for multiple rasters to be combined mathematically, it is often desirable to have the values in each raster converted to a common scale. For example, in a site-selection analysis, you need the data values for the input rasters to be scaled from 0 to 100. This can be done with the advanced interface by navigating to **Processing Toolbox** | **GRASS commands** | **Raster** | **r.rescale** tool. In the following example, the `RiparianSurface.img` raster with values ranging from 10 to 95.5 will be rescaled to a raster with values ranging from 0 to 100. To do this, perform the following steps:

1. Select the input raster layer by clicking on the down arrow to choose a raster loaded in the canvas, or by clicking on the browse button.
2. Specify **The input data range to be rescaled**.
3. Specify **The output data range**.
4. Select the output raster layer by clicking on the browse button and choosing **Save to a temporary file** or **Save to file**:

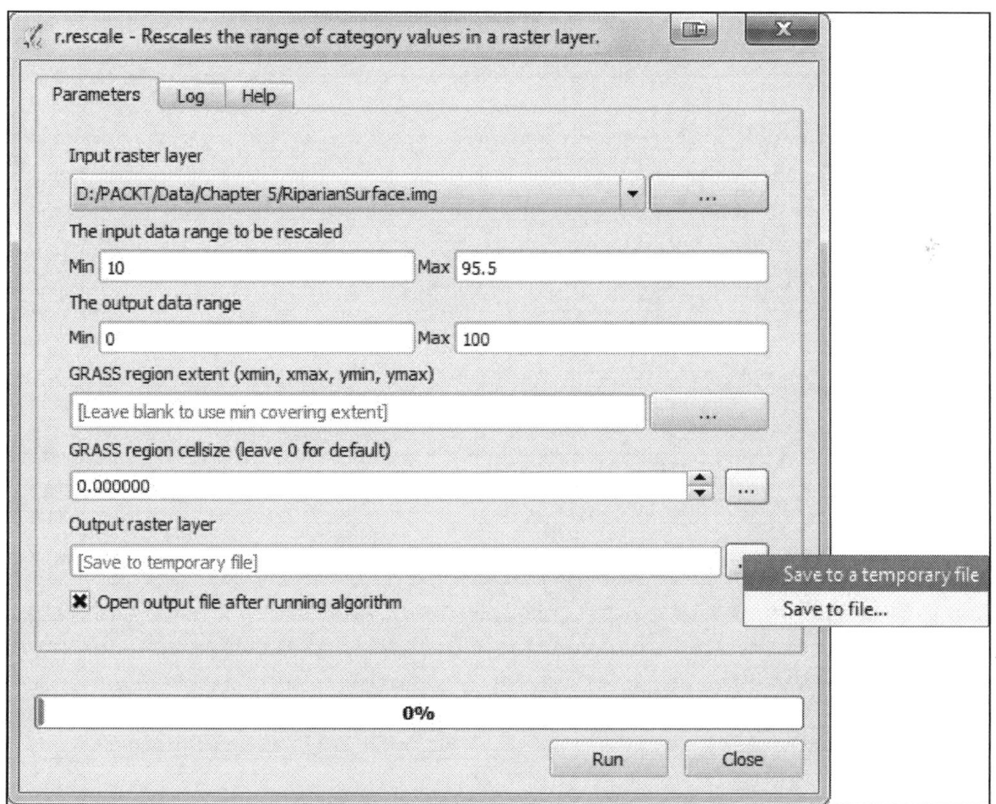

Creating a raster mosaic

Frequently, raster data is made available in tiles. In fact, some consider the *Murphy's Law of GIS* to be that your study area lies at the intersection of four topographic quadrangles. In this situation, the input rasters will need to be combined into a seamless raster that covers the study area. When doing this, the individual input rasters must all be in the same coordinate reference system and have the same number of bands.

Assuming that these two conditions have been met, the **Merge** tool that can be found by navigating to **Raster | Miscellaneous** can be used to merge the individual rasters together. This tool is a GUI version of the `GDAL_merge` command-line tool. Overlap among the input rasters is allowed. If this happens, the data for the last image in the list will be used for the area of overlap. In the **Merge** dialog, you have the option to choose whether you wish to merge all the rasters in a folder or you can pick individual rasters to merge. This provides a nice built-in batch-processing option. The following are the options for running the Merge tool:

1. Depending on how your data is stored, you can choose one of the following options:
    - Select **Choose input directory instead of files**.
    - Click on the **Select...** button and select the individual rasters to merge. In the following example, the sample data `35106-G4.tif`, `35106-G5.tif`, `35106-H4.tif`, and `35106-H5.tif` are being merged. (Note that this data has a CRS of EPSG: 26913, so the project CRS should be set to this.)
2. Name the output file by clicking on **Select...**.
3. If the rasters include a no-data value, you can select **No data value** and specify this value.
4. If the input rasters cover the same geography but contain different bands of information, this tool can be used to create a multiband image. By choosing the **Layer stack** option, each input file becomes a separate band in a stacked image.
5. The **Use intersected extent** option specifies the spatial envelope for the output. It defaults to the extent of the inputs.
6. If the images include a color table that can be passed on to the output by choosing the **Grab pseudocolor table from the first image** option, this option assumes that the same color table is used for all the input rasters.

Notice that the syntax equivalent to the `gdal_merge` command line is displayed as you choose your merge options. If you are familiar with the GDAL command-line syntax, you can use the edit button ( ) to set the tool options by editing the command directly. For example, you could specify the output image format as a 16-bit integer by using the `-ot Int16` parameter. You could also specify the output pixel size with the `-ps` parameter. The GDAL help page for this command can be found at `http://www.gdal.org/gdal_merge.html`.

The **Creation Options** allow you to add your own command-line options and set parameters, such as the compression profile to be used on the output image.

The following screenshot shows the `Merge` command that is configured to mosaic the collection of input rasters. The equivalent command-line syntax is displayed in the window:

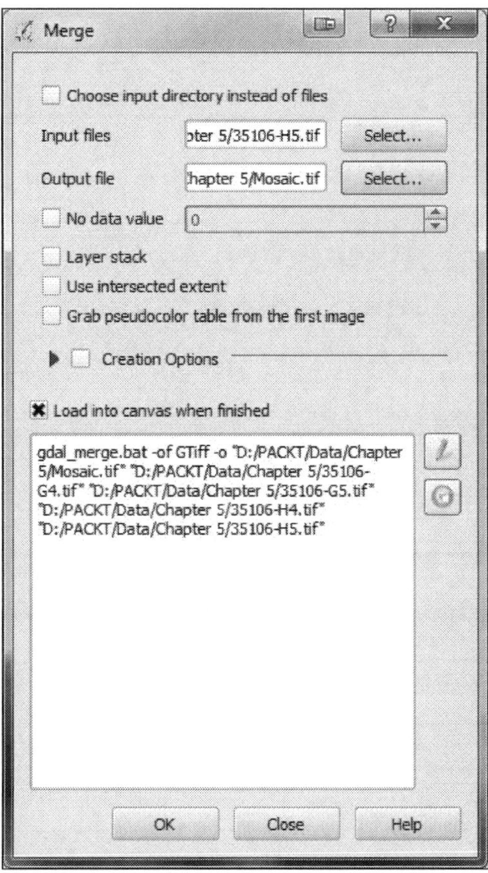

There are two additional tools in QGIS that can be used to create raster mosaics. Both of these require the rasters to be merged and loaded into the QGIS map canvas. The first is the GRASS tool **r.patch**. It can be found by navigating to **Processing Toolbox** | **Grass Commands** | **Raster** | **r.patch**.

The second tool is the SAGA tool **Merge raster layers**. This tool can be found by navigating to **Processing Toolbox** | **SAGA** | **Grid-Tools** | **Merge raster layers**. This SAGA tool lets you determine how overlapping cells in the set of input rasters will be handled. You can choose to use the first value in the order of the grid list or the mean value. It also allows you to choose the interpolation method. See the following figure:

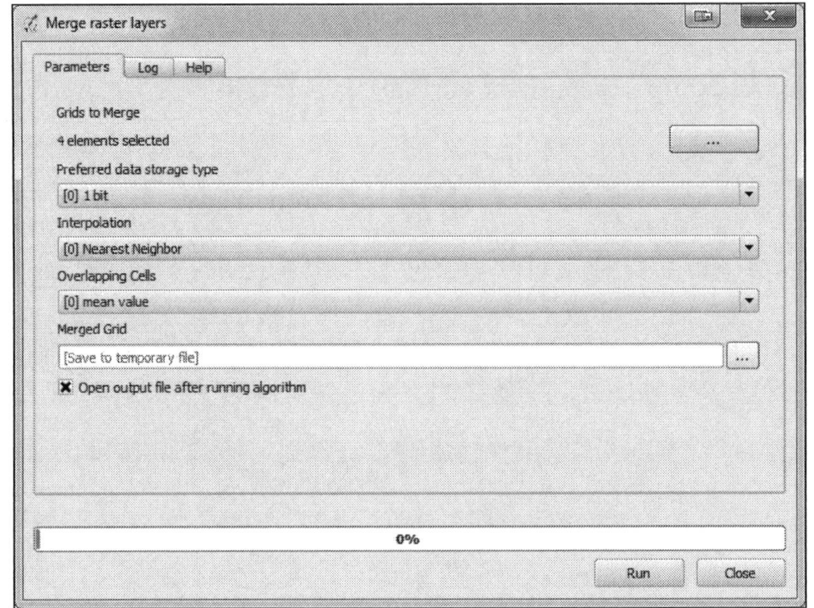

Generating raster overviews (pyramids)

A raster pyramid is a reduced-resolution version of a raster. The purpose of a pyramid is to reduce the time it takes to display a raster. Pyramids can be built at multiple levels to help strike a balance between the pyramid's file size and the display speed.

To build a raster overview in QGIS, click on **Build Overviews (Pyramids)** by navigating to **Raster | Miscellaneous**. This will open the **Build overviews (Pyramids)** tool window, as shown in the following screenshot:

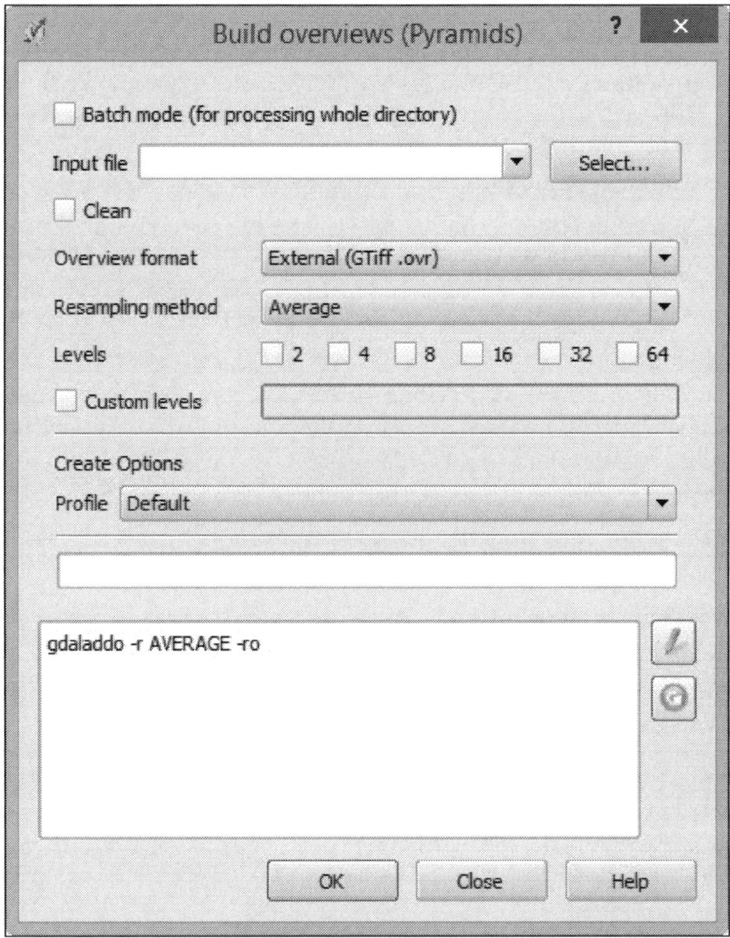

The Build overviews tool provides a few options as well as the ability to edit the GDAL command that will build the overviews. By selecting **Batch mode**, an entire directory of rasters will be processed, instead of the default of a single raster. In either case, the following options are available:

- **Input file**: The raster (or directory of rasters) that will have overviews built.
- **Clean**: If this is selected, any previously built overviews will be deleted.

- **Overview format**: The format of the built overviews. The options are as follows:
    - **External (GTiff.ovr)**: In this format, the overviews are stored in the external `.ovr` file. The file will have the same base name as the original input file.
    - **Internal (if possible)**: In this format, the overviews are stored within the raster file. Note that the **Clean** option will not remove previously built internal overviews.
    - **External (Erdas Imagine .aux)**: In this format, the overviews are stored in the external `.aux` file. The file will have the same base name as the original input file.
- **Resampling method**: The resampling method used to downsample the input raster.
- **Levels**: This provides the options for the levels for which the overviews should be built. The values represent the amount of reduction in resolution for each level. For instance, level 8 represents a resolution of one-eighth of the original raster. Multiple levels can be selected.
- **Custom levels**: A custom set of levels can be specified. Levels must be specified as positive integers that are separated by spaces.
- **Profile**: If External or Internal overview formats are selected, a compression profile can be selected. The profile sets parameters that are required to reach the selected compression level. Once a profile is selected, it appears underneath the text box.

The Build overviews tool is essentially a frontend for the `gdaladdo` GDAL command. So, at the bottom of the tool window, the GDAL command is displayed and modified when options are selected. To manually change the GDAL command, press the Edit button ( ) to make the GDAL command editable.

> The `gdaladdo` GDAL command builds or rebuilds pyramids for raster data. For more detailed information about this command and its parameters, visit the documentation page at `http://gdal.org/gdaladdo.html`.

Converting between raster and vector data models

QGIS provides tools to convert between raster and vector data models. In this section, we will convert between the two data models using a national land cover dataset of 2006 for the Dallas area in Texas.

Converting from raster to vector

To convert a raster to a vector format, QGIS provides the Polygonize tool. The Polygonize tool converts an input raster file into any supported type of vector file and writes the raster cell values to a field in the vector file. When the raster is polygonized, adjacent cells of the same value are aggregated to a single larger polygon.

To access the Polygonize tool, click on **Polygonize (Raster to Vector)** by navigating to **Raster** | **Conversion**. The Polygonize tool is shown in the following screenshot and uses the sample `DFW Land Cover.tif` file as input:

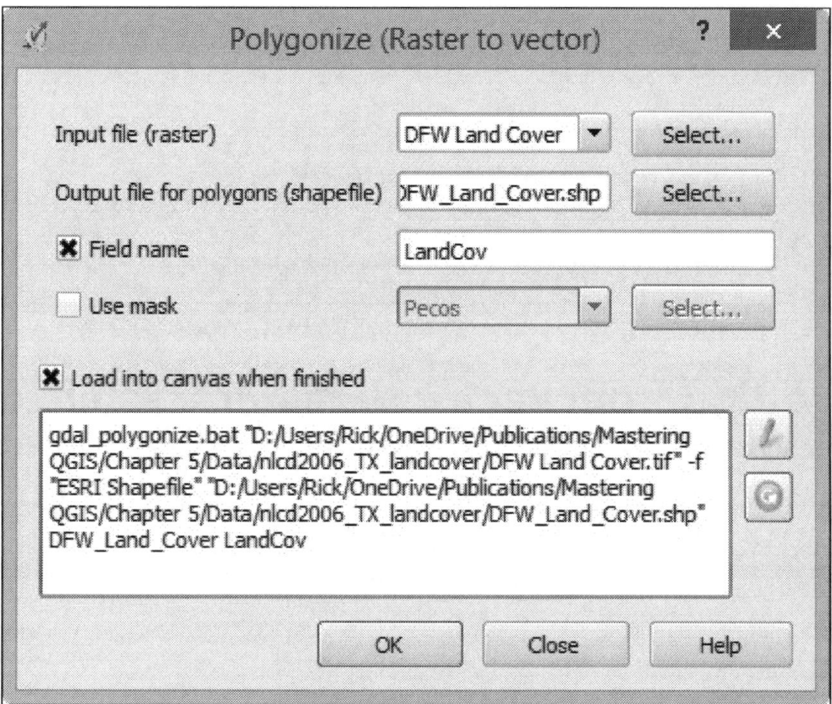

To convert a raster to a vector polygon, the following options are available:

- **Input file (raster)**: Input file to be polygonized.
- **Output file for polygons (shapefile)**: Name and extension of the output file that will hold the resulting polygons. Note that dozens of common vector formats are supported, so be sure to specify the extension for the format that you wish to use.
- **Field name**: The field name that will hold the cell values.
- **Use mask**: If selected, the specified file will be used to mask the input.
- **Load into canvas when finished**: Loads the output file into the QGIS canvas.

The Polygonize tool is essentially a frontend for GDAL. So, at the bottom of the tool window, the `gdal_polygonize` GDAL command is displayed and modified when the options are selected. To manually change the GDAL command, press the Edit button ( ) to make the GDAL command editable.

The `gdal_polygonize` GDAL command produces polygon features from raster data. For more detailed information about this command and its parameters, visit the documentation page at `http://gdal.org/gdal_polygonize.html`.

There is a similar GRASS tool in the Processing Toolbox named `r.to.vect` that converts a raster to a polygon, line, or a point-vector format. Complete documentation for this tool can be found on the GRASS GIS help pages at `http://grass.osgeo.org/grass65/manuals/r.to.vect.html`.

Converting from vector to raster (rasterize)

To convert a vector to a raster format, QGIS provides the Rasterize tool. This tool converts a shapefile to a raster and applies the values in a specified attribute field to the cell values. To access the Rasterize tool, click on **Rasterize (Vector to Raster)** by navigating to **Raster | Conversion**. The Rasterize tool, shown in the following figure, uses the `DFW_Land_Cover.shp` sample file as input.

To convert a vector to a raster, the following options are available:

- **Input file (shapefile)**: The input vector file to be converted. The tool supports multiple vector formats.
- **Attribute field**: The attribute field holds the value to assign to the raster cells.
- **Output file for rasterized vectors (raster)**: The output raster file. The tool supports multiple raster formats.
- **Keep existing raster size and resolution**: This is only selectable if the output file already exists. This sets the output raster size and resolution to match the existing output file.
- **Raster size in pixels**: This allows manual designation of raster width and height in pixels.

- **Raster resolution in map units per pixel**: This allows manual designation of raster width and height in the units of the map.
- **Load into canvas when finished**: Loads the output file in to the QGIS canvas.

The Rasterize tool is essentially a frontend for GDAL. So, at the bottom of the tool window, the `gdal_rasterize` GDAL command is displayed and modified when the options are selected. To manually change the GDAL command, press the Edit button ( ) to make the GDAL command editable.

The `gdal_rasterize` GDAL command burns vector geometries into the raster band(s) of a raster. For more detailed information about this command and its parameters, visit the documentation page at `http://gdal.org/gdal_rasterize.html`.

There are two similar GRASS tools in the Processing Toolbox named `v.to.rast.attribute` and `v.to.rast.value` that convert a vector to the raster format. The `v.to.rast.attribute` tool assigns attribute values to the output raster cells. The `v.to.rast.value` tool assigns a single value or calculated value to the output raster cells. Complete documentation for these tools can be found on the GRASS GIS help pages at `http://grass.osgeo.org/grass71/manuals/v.to.rast.html`.

Creating raster surfaces via interpolation

QGIS supports surface interpolation from vector points to a raster using the Interpolation plugin. The Interpolation tool supports **Inverse Distance Weighted (IDW)** and **Triangular Interpolation (TIN)**. To enable the Interpolation plugin, click on **Manage** and **Install Plugins** under **Plugins**.

As an example of how to use the Interpolation tool, let's use the `Pecos DEM Points.shp` sample file to interpolate a surface using IDW:

1. Add `Pecos DEM Points.shp` to the map canvas.
2. Open the Interpolation plugin tool by navigating to **Raster | Interpolation | Interpolation**. The tool is shown in the following figure and uses the `Pecos DEM Points.shp` sample file as the input vector layer:

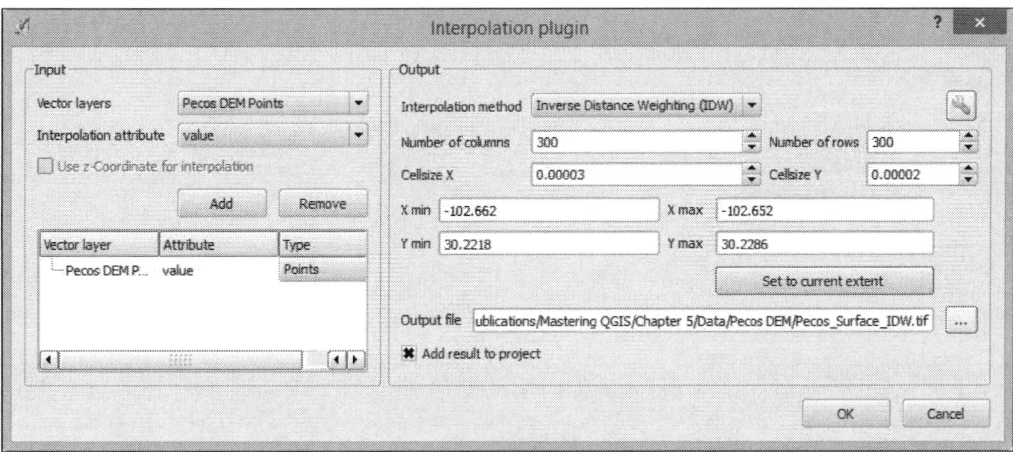

The interface of the Interpolation tool is identical whether IDW or TIN is chosen as the interpolation method. The only exceptions are the interpolation method parameters, which can be set by clicking on the configure button ( ). For this example, we will only cover the IDW parameter (distance coefficient); however, you must know that for TIN, you can set the Interpolation method (linear or cubic) and have the option to export the triangulation to shapefile.

3. In the **Input** area, the **Vector layers** combo box is populated with all the valid vector layers added to the QGIS project. Make sure that **Pecos DEM Points** is selected.
4. Select **value** as the interpolation attribute. This will be the value that is used as input for the interpolation method. If the input vector supports 3D geometry, we could optionally select **Use z-Coordinate for interpolation** instead of choosing an attribute.
5. Click on **Add** to add the vector layer and the selected attribute to the layer list. At this point, we could add additional input vector layers to use as inputs. The inputs will be combined into a single input.
6. Moving to the **Output** section, select **Inverse Distance Weighted (IDW)** as the interpolation method.
7. Click on the configure button ( ) to access the **Distance coefficient** (P value) parameter. Enter `3.0` to decrease the influence of distant points for the interpolation. Click on **OK** to set the value.
8. Set the **Number of columns** value to `200`. Note that as you type in the value, the **Cellsize X** value changes to `0.00005`. These two values are linked together and are automatically calculated based on the extent values listed (**X min**, **X max**, **Y min**, **Y max**).

9. Set the **Cellsize Y** value to `0.0005` to match the **Cellsize X** value. Again, note that as you type in the value, the **Number of rows** value changes to `127`.

   The extent values can be manually changed by typing in the desired values, or they can be automatically filled with the current extent of the map canvas by clicking on **Set to current extent**. The default extent is set to the extent of the input vectors.

10. Set the output file to **Pecos_IDW.tif**.
11. Select **Add result to project** to automatically add the interpolated raster to the map canvas. Click on **OK** to execute the IDW interpolation.

The following figure shows the resulting raster from the IDW interpolation with the `Pecos DEM Points.shp` input points on top:

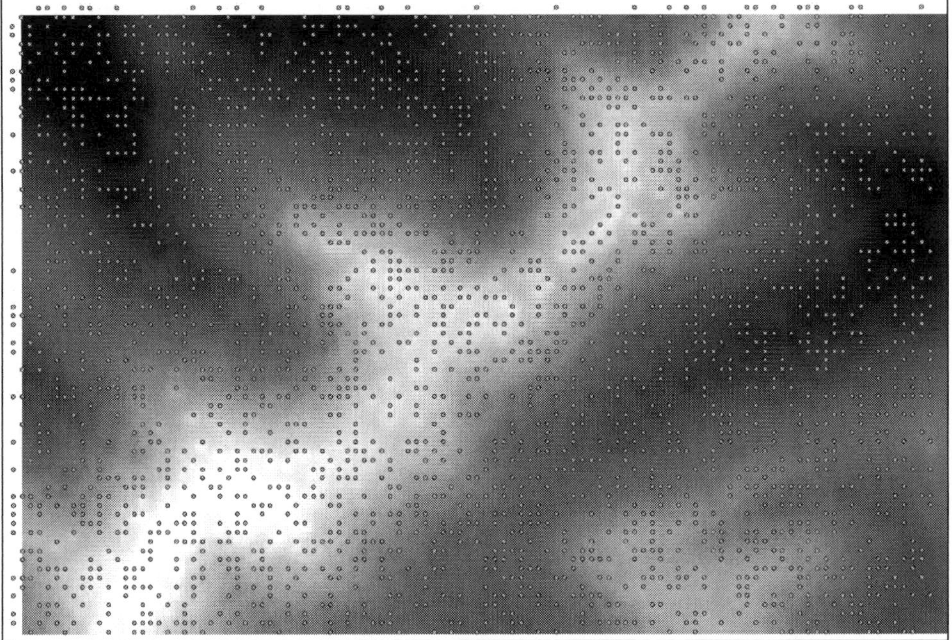

There are additional interpolation tools available via the Processing Toolbox. In the GRASS commands, there are `v.surf.bspline`, `v.surf.idw`, and `v.surf.rst`, which interpolate using the bicubic or bilinear spline, inverse distance weighted, and regularized spline, respectively. In the SAGA commands, there are many interpolation methods under the Grid - Gridding, Grid - Spline, and Kriging sections in the advanced interface of the Processing Toolbox.

Summary

This chapter provided steps and examples showing how to prepare raster data for further processing. This chapter covered common raster operations such as reclassification, resampling, rescaling, mosaicking, interpolation, and so on. Many of the tools shown in this chapter rely on GDAL to perform the calculations, while others are included as part of plugins or QGIS. Where applicable, alternative tools were noted in information boxes, as different tools may provide different functionality or parameters.

In the next chapter, we will switch from modifying and preparing existing data (as discussed in *Chapter 4, Preparing Vector Data for Processing,* and this chapter) to creating data. The next chapter will cover creating points from raw coordinate data, geocoding, georeferencing imagery, and topology operations.

6

Advanced Data Creation and Editing

This chapter will provide you with more advanced ways to create vector and raster data. There is a great deal of spatial data held in tabular format. Readers will learn how to map coordinate and address-based data. Other common sources of geospatial data are historic aerial photographs and maps in hard copy. Readers will learn how to georeference scanned imagery and transform it into a target coordinate reference system. The final portion of the chapter will cover testing topological relationships in vector data and correcting any errors via topological editing.

The topics that you will cover in this chapter are as follows:

- Creating points from coordinate data
- Geocoding address-based data
- Georeferencing imagery
- Checking the topology of vector data
- Repairing topological geometry errors via topological editing

Creating points from coordinate data

There is a lot of data with spatial components stored in spreadsheets and tables. One of the most common forms of tabular spatial data are *x* and *y* coordinates that are stored in a delimited text file. The data may have been collected with a GPS receiver, it may have been generated by a surveyor, or it may have been transcribed off topographic maps. Regardless, QGIS can map these coordinates as points by using the Add Delimited Text Layer tool ( ). This tool can be found by navigating to **Layer | Add Layer | Add Delimited Text Layer** or on the **Manage Layers** toolbar.

Delimited text data is simply a table with column breaks that are identified by a specific character such as a comma. With this tool, QGIS can accept either *x* and *y* coordinates or **Well-Known Text (WKT)** representations of geometry. WKT can contain point, line, or polygon geometry. The following is a sample data, `cougar_sightings.csv`, viewed in a text editor. This is a comma-delimited file with *x* and *y* coordinate values.

```
"SAMPID,C,20","SEX,C,10","UTM_X,N,19,11","UTM_Y,N,19,11"
PA087,F,115556.044021,3486272.88304
PA097,F,116870.543644,3489102.55056
PA098,M,116148.894117,3483420.50411
PN001,M,482000.018751,3700998.34463
PN002,M,296192.720405,4053069.38808
PN003,M,347990.948523,3990302.26593
PN004,F,431049.74714,3998099.74491
PN005,F,498461.953615,4013066.46126
PN006,F,319083.556347,3988585.77826
```

In this example, the first row contains the column names and definitions for the data type in each column. The column names and definitions are enclosed in quotes and are separated by commas. The first column reads `"SAMPID, C, 20"`. In this case, the field name is `SAMPID`. It is a text field signified by the letter `C`, which stands for character, with a width of `20` characters. The final two columns contain the coordinates. These are numeric fields signified by the `N` character. They have a precision of `19` and a scale of `11`.

QGIS has three requirements for the delimited text file to be mapped:

- The first row must be a delimited header row of field names
- The header row must contain field-type definitions
- If the geometry values are stored as x and y coordinate values, they must be stored as numeric fields

The **Create a Layer from a Delimited Text File** tool is simple but robust enough to handle many file-format contingencies. The following is the workflow for mapping data held in such a file:

1. Navigate to **Layer** | **Add Layer** | **Add Delimited Text Layer**.
2. Select the file name by clicking on **Browse...** and locate the delimited text file on your system. QGIS will attempt to parse the file with the most recently used delimiter.
3. Select **Layer name**. By default, this will be the prefix of the delimited text file.

4. Use the **File format** radio boxes to specify the format of the delimited text file. You will see how QGIS is parsing the file by the example at the bottom of the **Create a Layer from a Delimited Text File** window. The following are the options for **File format**:
   - Choose **CSV** if it is a standard comma-delimited file.
   - **Custom delimiters** can be checked to identify the specific character used. The choices are **Comma**, **Tab**, **Space**, **Colon**, **Semicolon**, or **Other delimiters**.
   - Choose the **Regular expression delimiter** option if you wish to enter the regular expression for the delimiter. For example, `\t` is the regular expression for the tab character.
5. The **Record options** section allows you to specify the number of header lines to discard. In most cases, this option will be set to **First record has field names**.
6. The **Field options** option allows you to control some field parameters:
   - Check **Trim fields** if you need to trim leading or trailing spaces from your data
   - Check **Discard empty fields** to prevent empty fields from being put into the output
   - If commas are also the separators for decimal place values, check **Decimal separator is a comma**
7. Once the file has been parsed, choose an appropriate value from the **Geometry definition** option:
   - If your file contains *x* and *y* coordinates, choose **Point coordinates** and identify the fields containing the *x* and *y* coordinates.
   - Choose **Well known text (WKT)**, if your file contains WKT geometries. For this option, you will also need to choose the field containing the WKT geometry definitions.
   - If the file does not contain any spatial information, choose **No geometry** and the table will be loaded simply as a table.
8. Additionally, you can choose to enable the following options:
   - **Use spatial index**: Creates a spatial index
   - **Use subset index**: Creates a subset index
   - **Watch file**: This setting watches for changes to the file by other applications while QGIS is running

9. After you click on **OK**, the **Coordinate Reference System Selector** dialog box will open. Use this dialog box to identify the coordinate reference system of the data. It is very important to correctly identify the CRS of the input data.

> There is a setting that can affect the behavior of the Coordinate Reference System Selector for both new layers and layers that are loaded into QGIS without a defined CRS. By navigating to **Settings | Options | CRS**, you can choose how these situations are handled. The choices are **Prompt for CRS, Use Project CRS**, or **Use default CRS displayed below**. The default setting is **Prompt for CRS**. However, if you have this set to **Use project CRS** or **Use default CRS displayed below**, then you will not be prompted to define the CRS as described earlier.

The following screenshot shows an example of a completed **Create a Layer from a Delimited Text File** tool.

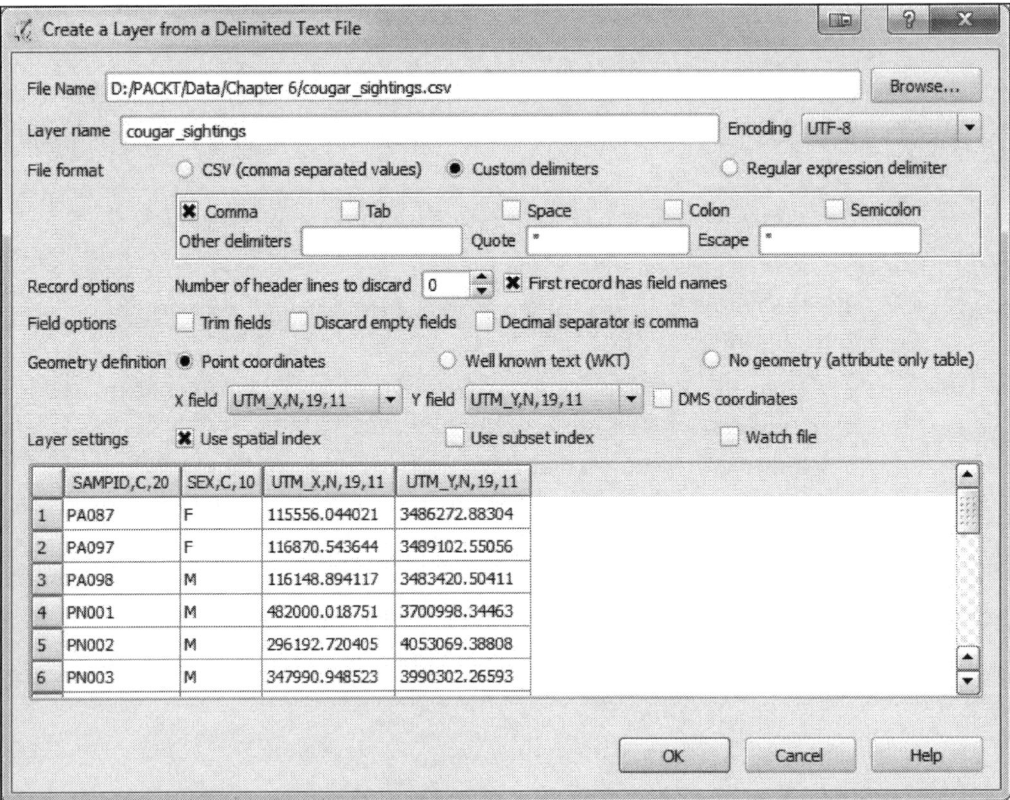

Once the tool has been run, a new point layer will be added to QGIS with all the attributes present in the original file (unless you chose to discard empty fields). However, this is not a standalone GIS layer yet. It is simply a rendering of the tabular data within the QGIS project. As such, it will behave like any other layer. It can be used as an input for other tools, records can be selected, and it can be styled. However, it cannot be edited. To convert the layer to a standalone shapefile or another vector format, click on **Save as** under **Layer** or right-click on the layer in the **Layers** panel and click on **Save as**. Here, you can choose any OGR supported file format along with an output CRS of your choice. The `cougar_sightings.csv` sample data has coordinates in UTM zone 13 NAD83 or EPSG:26913. The following screenshot shows the mapped data in the `cougar_sightings.csv` sample data:

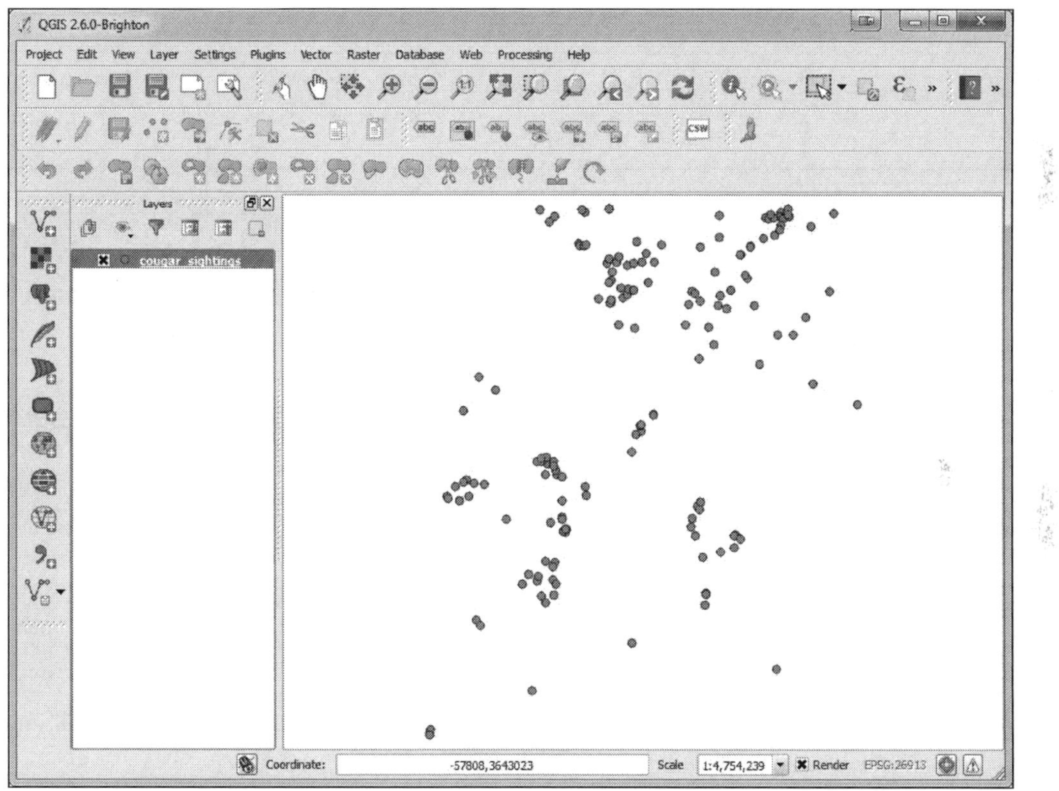

Sample data in `cougar_sightings.csv` mapped by *x* and *y* coordinate values

Mapping well-known text representations of geometry

As mentioned earlier, the Add Delimited Text Layer tool can also be used to map Well-Known Text (WKT) representations of geometry. WKT can be used to represent simple geometries such as Point, LineString, and Polygon along with MultiPoint, MultiLineString, and MultiPolygon. It can also represent more complex geometry types such as geometry collections, 3D geometries, curves, triangular irregular networks, and polyhedral surfaces. WKT geometries use geometry primitives such as Point, LineString, and Polygon followed by the coordinates of vertices that are separated by commas. For example, `LINESTRING (30 10, 20 20, 40 30)` would represent the line feature shown in the following screenshot:

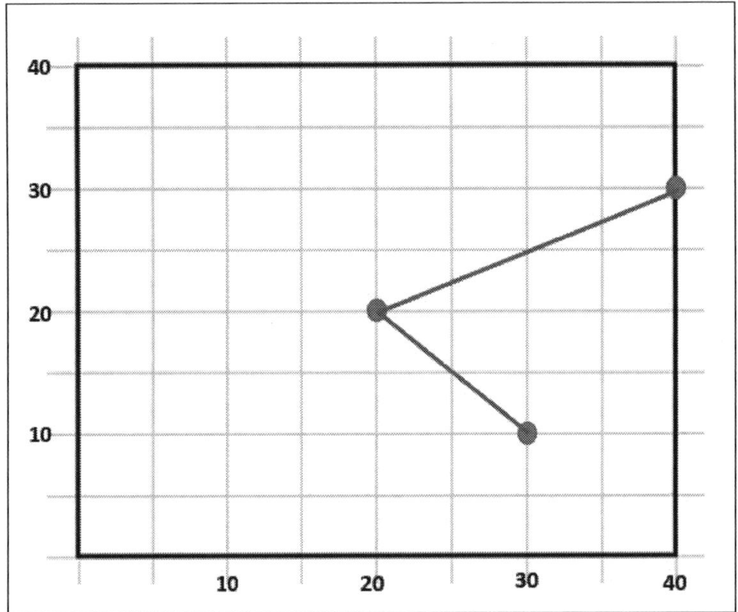

To demonstrate how WKT can be mapped via the Add Delimited Text Layer tool, we will map the `Parcels_WKT.csv` sample data file; this has WKT geometries for eight parcels (polygons):

1. Click on **Add Delimited Text Layer** by navigating to **Layer** | **Add Layer**.
2. Select the file name by clicking on **Browse...** and locate the delimited text file on your system. In this example, the `Parcels_WKT.csv` file is being used.
3. Choose an appropriate value for the **Layer name** field. By default, this will be the prefix of the delimited text file.

4. Use the **File format** radio buttons to specify the format of the delimited text file. This is a CSV file.
5. For **Record options**, set the **Number of header lines to discard** option as **1**.
6. Set the **Geometry definition** option to **Well known text (WKT)**.
7. Set the **Geometry field** option to **field_1**.
8. Click on **OK** and the Coordinate Reference System Selector will open. Use this dialog box to identify the coordinate reference system of the data. For this example, the data is in EPSG: 2903.

The following screenshot shows an example of a completed **Create a Layer from a Delimited Text File** tool set up to parse a WKT file:

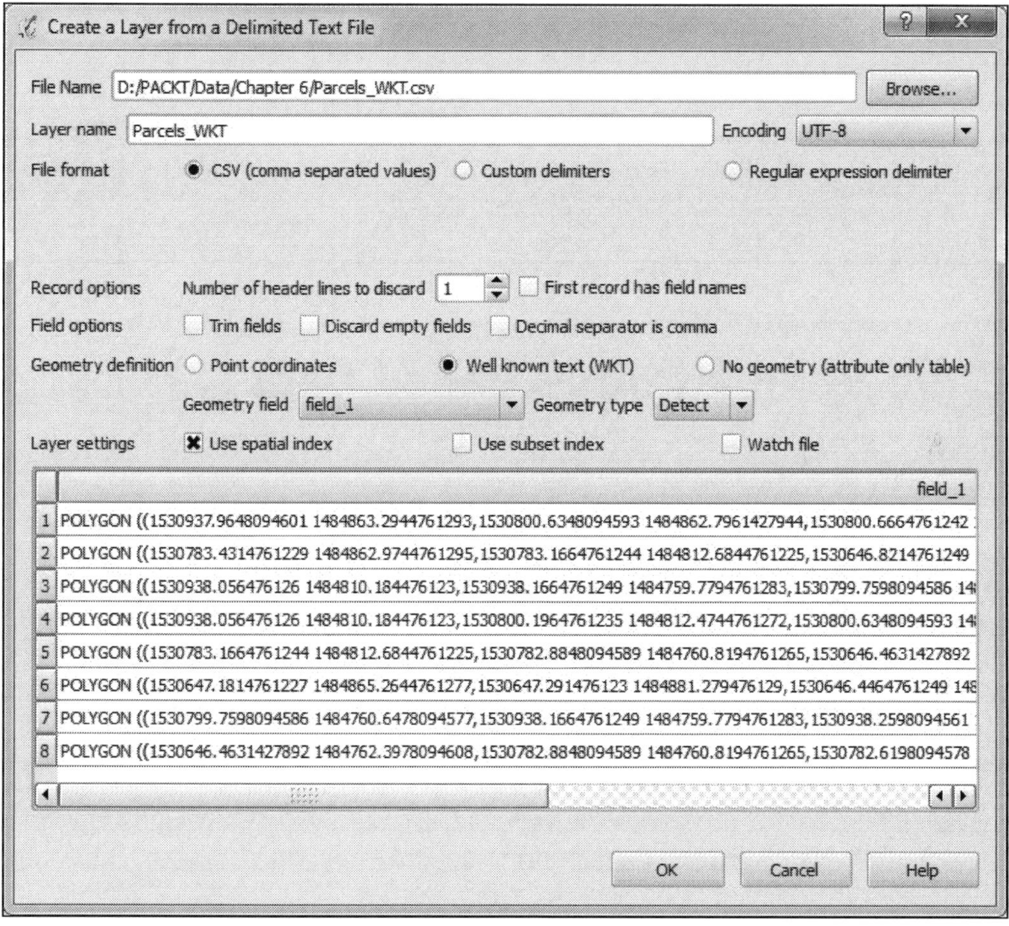

The data layer will be added to the **Layers** list and will behave like any other vector layer. The following figure shows the resulting parcel boundaries:

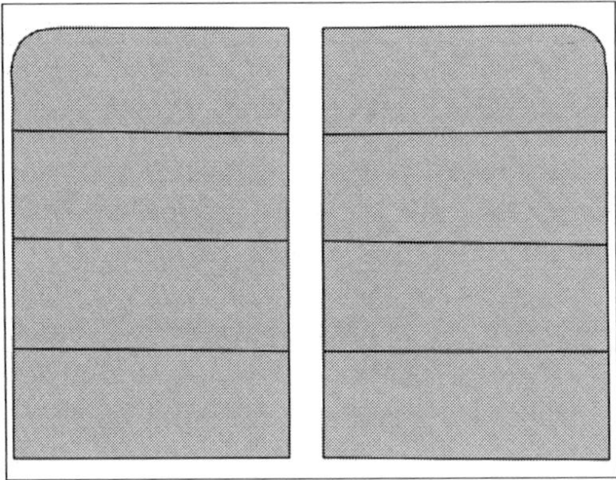

Well-known text representations of parcels mapped via the Add Delimited Text Layer tool

An easy way to explore WKT geometries is to use the getWKT plugin. This allows you to click on a selected feature (in the QGIS map canvas) and see the WKT for that feature. The WKT can be copied to the clipboard.

Geocoding address-based data

Another useful and common tabular spatial data source is a street address. Geocoding addresses has many applications such as mapping the customer base for a store, members of an organization, public health records, or incidence of crime. Once they are mapped, the points can be used in many ways to generate information. For example, they can be used as inputs to generate density surfaces, or they can be linked to parcels of land, and characterized by socio-economic data. They may also be an important component of a cadastral information system.

An address geocoding operation typically involves the tabular address data and a street network dataset. The street network needs to have attribute fields for address ranges on the left- and right-hand side of each road segment. You can geocode within QGIS using a plugin named MMQGIS (`http://michaelminn.com/linux/mmqgis/`). MMQGIS is a collection of vector data-processing tools developed by Michael Minn. To install the plugin, perform the following steps:

1. Navigate to **Plugins** | **Manage and Install Plugins**.
2. Click on the **All** tab and type MMQGIS into the search bar.
3. Install the plugin that manifests as the MMQGIS menu.

MMQGIS has many useful tools. For geocoding, you will use the tools found in **Geocode** under **MMQGIS**. There are two tools there: **Geocode CSV with Google/ OpenStreetMap** and **Geocode from Street Layer**. The first allows you to geocode a table of addresses using either the Google Maps API or the OpenStreetMap Nominatim web service. This tool requires an Internet connection but no local street network data. The web services provide the street network. The second tool uses a local street network dataset with address-range attributes to geocode the address data.

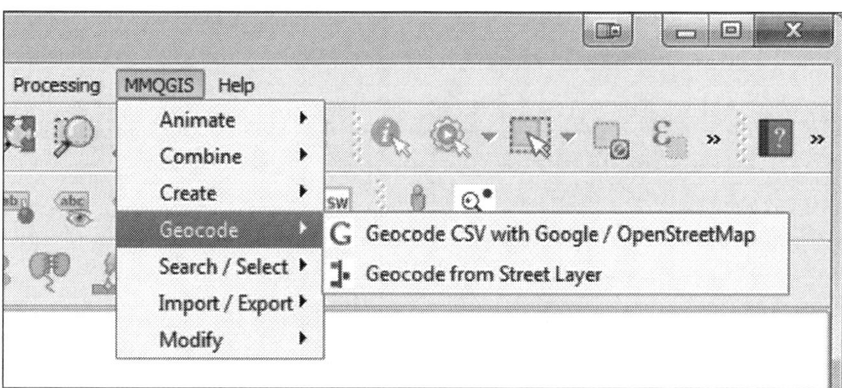

How address geocoding works

The basic mechanics of address geocoding are straightforward. The street network GIS data layer has attribute columns containing address ranges on both the even and odd side of every street segment. In the following example, you see a piece of the attribute table for the `Streets.shp` sample data. The columns `LEFTLOW`, `LEFTHIGH`, `RIGHTLOW`, and `RIGHTHIGH` contain the address ranges for each street segment.

Attribute table - Streets :: Features total: 41825, filtered: 41825, selected: 0

	LEFTLOW	LEFTHIGH	RIGHTLOW	RIGHTHIGH	STREETNAME	STREETDESI
13520	14301.00000000...	14305.00000000...	14300.00000000...	14302.00000000...	COPPER	AV
13581	14301.00000000...	14323.00000000...	14300.00000000...	14324.00000000...	STALGREN	CT
13805	14301.00000000...	14309.00000000...	14300.00000000...	14308.00000000...	MEL SMITH	DR
34181	14301.00000000...	14339.00000000...	14300.00000000...	14340.00000000...	BAUER	RD
34192	14301.00000000...	14321.00000000...	14300.00000000...	14320.00000000...	ENCANTADO	RD
34229	14301.00000000...	14321.00000000...	14300.00000000...	14320.00000000...	PIEDRAS	RD
34241	14301.00000000...	14335.00000000...	14300.00000000...	14334.00000000...	SKYLINE	RD
34255	14301.00000000...	14331.00000000...	14300.00000000...	14330.00000000...	OAKWOOD	PL
34293	14301.00000000...	14317.00000000...	14300.00000000...	14318.00000000...	ARCADIA	RD
34275	14297.00000000...	14331.00000000...	14296.00000000...	14314.00000000...	WINDSOR	PL
13153	14227.00000000...	14233.00000000...	14226.00000000...	14232.00000000...	GRAND	AV

In the following example, we are looking at **Easy Street**. On the odd side of the street, the addresses range from `101` to `199`. On the even side, they range from `102` to `200`. If you want to map `150 Easy Street`, QGIS would assume that the address is located halfway down the even side of that block. Similarly, `175 Easy Street` would be on the odd side of the street, roughly three-quarters of the way down the block. Address geocoding assumes that the addresses are evenly spaced along a linear network. QGIS should place the address point very close to its actual position, but due to variability in lot sizes not every address point will be perfectly positioned.

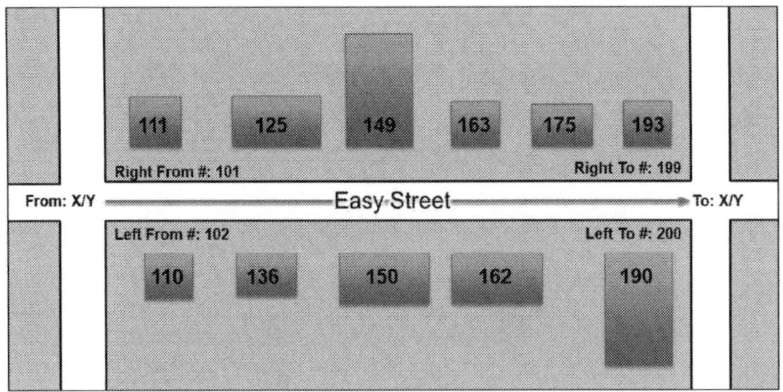

Now that you've learned the basics you'll see how each MMQGIS geocoding tool works. Here, both tools will be demonstrated against the `Addresses.csv` sample data. The first example will use web services. The second example will use the `Streets.shp` sample data. In both cases, the output will be a point shapefile containing all the attribute fields found in the source `Addresses.csv` files.

The first example – geocoding using web services

Here are the steps for geocoding the `Addresses.csv` sample data using web services.

1. Load the `Addresses.csv` and `Streets.shp` sample data into QGIS Desktop.
2. Open the `Addresses.csv` sample data and examine the table. These are addresses of municipal facilities. Notice that the street address (for example, `150 Easy Street`) is contained in a single field. There are also fields for the city, state, and country. Since both Google and OpenStreetMap are global services, it is wise to include such fields so that the services can narrow down the geography.
3. Install and enable the MMQGIS plugin.
4. Navigate to **MMQGIS | Geocode | Geocode CSV with Google/ OpenStreetMap**. The **Web Service Geocode** dialog window will open.

5. Select an appropriate value for the **Input CSV File (UTF-8)** field by clicking on **Browse...** and locating the delimited text file on your system.
6. Select the address fields by clicking on the drop-down menu and fill suitable values in the **Address Field**, **City Field**, **State Field**, and **Country Field** fields. MMQGIS may identify some or all of these fields by default if they are named with logical names such as `Address` or `State`.
7. Choose the web service.
8. Name the output shapefile by clicking on **Browse...**.
9. Select a value for the **Not Found Output List** field by clicking on **Browse...**. Any records that are not matched will be written to this file. This allows you to easily see and troubleshoot any unmapped records.
10. Click on **OK**. The status of the geocoding operation can be seen in the lower-left corner of QGIS. The word **Geocoding** will be displayed, followed by the number of records that have been processed.
11. The output will be a point shapefile and a CSV file listing the addresses that were not matched.

The following screenshot shows the completed **Web Service Geocode** tool:

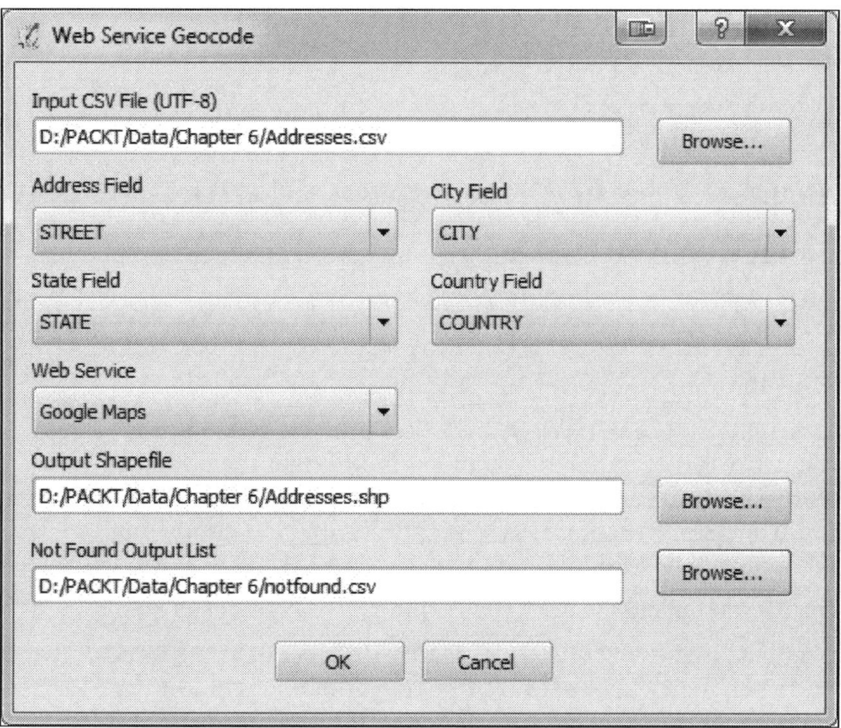

Two additional attribute columns will be added to the output address point shapefile: `addrtype` and `addrlocat`. These fields provide information on how the web geocoding service obtained the location. These may be useful for accuracy assessment.

`addrtype` is the Google `<type>` element or the OpenStreetMap class attribute. This will indicate what kind of address type was used by the web service (highway, locality, museum, neighborhood, park, place, premise, route, train station, university, and so on).

`addrlocat` is the Google `<location_type>` element or OpenStreetMap type attribute. This indicates the relationship of the coordinates to the addressed feature (approximate, geometric center, node, relation, rooftop, way interpolation, and so on).

If the web service returns more than one location for an address, the first of the locations will be used as the output feature.

Use of this plugin requires an active Internet connection. Google places both rate and volume restrictions on the number of addresses that can be geocoded within various time limits. You should visit the Google Geocoding API website (`http://code.google.com/apis/maps/documentation/geocoding/`) for more details, current information, and Google's terms of service.

Geocoding via these web services can be slow. If you don't get the desired results with one service, try the other.

The second example – geocoding using local street network data

Here are the steps for geocoding the `Addresses.csv` sample data using local street network data:

1. Load the `Addresses.csv` and `Streets.shp` sample data.
2. Open the `Addresses.csv` sample data and examine the table. This contains the addresses of municipal facilities. Notice that there is an address column (for example, `150 Easy Street`) along with separate columns for number (`150`) and street (`Easy`). This tool requires that the number and street address components be held in separate fields.
3. Install and enable the MMQGIS plugin.
4. Navigate to the **MMQGIS | Geocode | Geocode from Street Layer** menu and open the **Geocode from Street Layer** dialog window.

5. Select the `Addresses.csv` sample data as the **Input CSV File (UTF-8)** field by clicking on **Browse...** and locating the delimited text file on your system.
6. Select the street name field from the **Street Name Field** drop-down menu.
7. Select the number field from the **Number Field** drop-down menu.
8. Select the zip field from the **ZIP Field** drop-down menu.
9. Select the street GIS layer loaded in QGIS from the **Street Layer** drop-down menu.
10. Select the street name field of the street layer from the **Street Name Attribute** drop-down menu.

This tool allows geocoding from street address ranges or via **From X Attribute** and **To X Attribute** coordinates. The latter assumes that you have attribute columns with the `To` and `From` coordinates for each street segment. To geocode via `To` and `From` coordinates select the `From X Attribute`, `To X Attribute`, `From Y Attribute`, and `To Y Attribute` fields from the drop-down menu.

11. In this example, only address ranges will be used. Populate the **From X Attribute**, **To X Attribute**, **From Y Attribute**, and **To Y Attribute** dropdown menus with the **(street line start)**, **(street line end)**, **(street line start)**, and **(street line end)** option.
12. Since address ranges will be used for geocoding, select the **Left From Number**, **Left To Number**, **Right From Number**, and **Right To Number** attributes from the drop-down menu.
13. If the street data has left and right zip code attributes, select **Left Zip** and **Right Zip** from the drop-down menu. Since the `Streets.shp` sample data does not have zip code attributes, these options will the left blank **(none)**.
14. The **Bldg. Setback (map units)** option can be used to offset geocoded address points from the street centerline. This should represent how far buildings are from the middle of the street in map units. In this case, the map units are in feet. Enter a map unit value of **20**.
15. Name the output shapefile by clicking on **Browse...** button.

Geocoding operations rarely have 100 percent success. Street names in the street shapefile must match the street names in the CSV file exactly. Any discrepancy between the name of a street in the address table and the street attribute table will lower the geocoding success rate.

16. The tool will save a list of the unmatched records. Complete the **Not Found Output List** field by clicking on **Browse...** button name the comma delimited file. Any records that are not matched will be written to this file. This allows you to easily see and troubleshoot any unmapped records.
17. Click on **OK**.
18. The output will be a point shapefile and a CSV file listing the addresses that were not matched. In this example, the output shapefile will have 199 mapped address points. There will be four unmatched records described in the **Not Found CSV** list.

The following screenshot shows the completed **Geocode from Street Layer** tool:

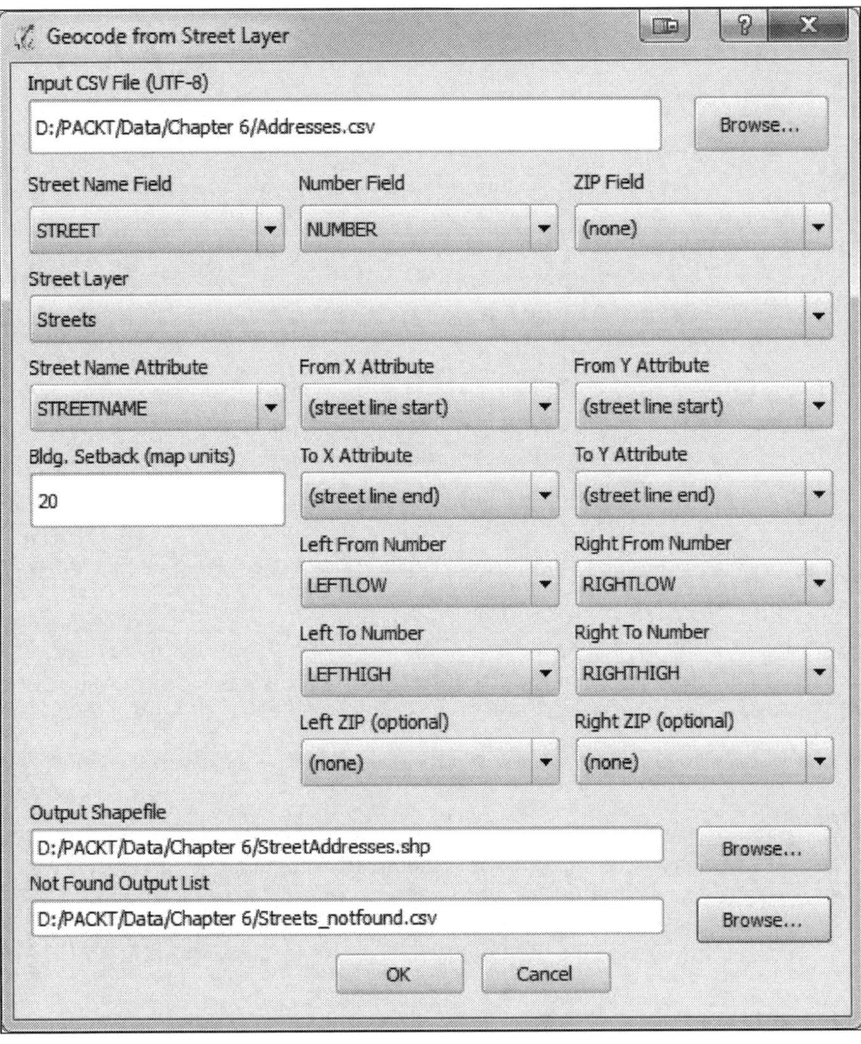

Geocoding is often an iterative process. After the initial geocoding operation, review the Not Found CSV file. If it's empty, then all the records were matched. If it has records in it, compare them with the attributes of the streets layer. This will help you determine why the records were not mapped. It may be due to inconsistencies in the spellings of street names. It may also be due to a street centerline layer that is not as current as the addresses. Once the errors have been identified, they can be addressed by editing the data or obtaining a different street centerline dataset. The geocoding operation can be rerun on the unmatched addresses. This process can be repeated until all the records are matched.

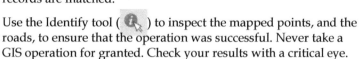

Use the Identify tool ( ) to inspect the mapped points, and the roads, to ensure that the operation was successful. Never take a GIS operation for granted. Check your results with a critical eye.

The following figure shows the results of geocoding addresses via street address ranges. The addresses are shown with the street network used in the geocoding operation.

Georeferencing imagery

Maps and aerial photographs in hard copy have a lot of valuable data on them. When this data needs to be brought into a GIS, they are digitally scanned to produce raster imagery. The output of a digital scanner has a coordinate system, but it is a local coordinate system created by the scanning process. The scanned imagery needs to be georeferenced to a real-world coordinate system before it can be used in a GIS.

Georeferencing is the process of transforming the **coordinate reference system (CRS)** of a raster dataset into a new coordinate reference system. Often, the process transforms the CRS of a spatial dataset from a local coordinate system to a real-world coordinate system. Regardless of the coordinate systems involved, we'll call the coordinate system of the raster to be georeferenced as the *source CRS* and the coordinate system of the output as the *destination CRS*. The transformation may involve shifting, rotating, skewing, or scaling the input raster from source coordinates to destination coordinates. Once a data set has been georeferenced, it can be brought into a GIS and aligned with other layers.

Ground control points

Georeferencing is done by identifying **ground control points** (**GCP**). These are locations on the input raster where the destination coordinate system is known. Ground control points can be identified in one of the following two ways:

- Using another dataset covering the same spatial extent that is in the destination coordinate system. This can be either a vector or a raster dataset. In this case, GCPs will be locations that can be identified on both the datasets.
- Using datums or other locations with either printed coordinates or coordinates that can be looked up. In this case, the locations are identified and the target coordinates are entered.

Once a set of ground control points has been created, a transformation equation is developed and used to transform the raster from the source CRS to the destination CRS.

Ideally, GCPs are well distributed across the input raster. You should strive to create GCPs near the four corners of the image, plus several located in the middle of the image. This isn't always possible, but it will result in a better transformation.

Using the Georeferencer GDAL plugin

The Georeferencer GDAL plugin is a core QGIS plugin, meaning it will be installed by default. It is an implementation of the GDAL_Translate command-line utility. To enable it, navigate to **Plugins | Manage and Install Plugins** and then click on the **Installed** tab and check the box to the left of **Georeferencer GDAL** plugin. Once enabled, you can launch the plugin by clicking on **Georeferencer** under **Raster**. The **Georeferencer** window has two main windows: the image window and the ground control point (GCP) table window. These windows are shown in the following screenshot:

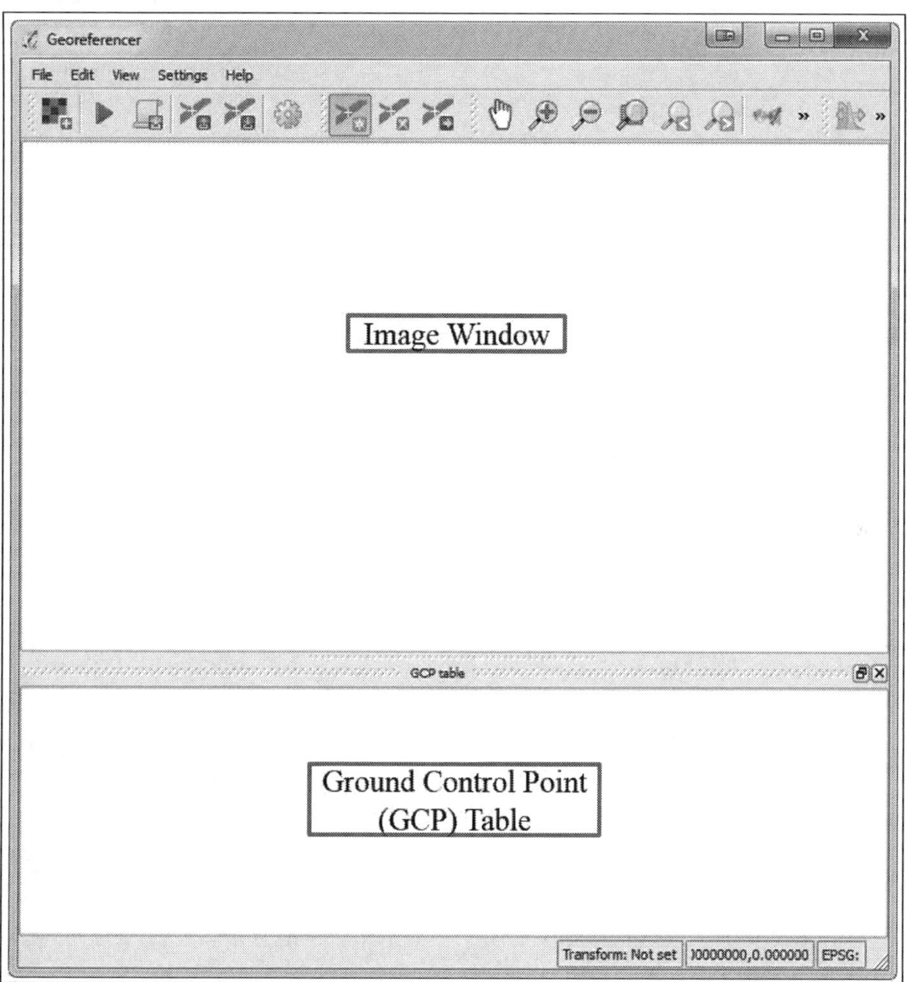

The general procedure for georeferencing an image is as follows:

1. Load the image to be georeferenced into the Georeferencer image window by clicking on **Open Raster** under **File** or by using the Open raster button ().
2. If you are georeferencing the raster against another dataset, load the second dataset into the main QGIS Desktop map canvas.
3. Begin to enter ground control points with the Add point tool (This tool, , is also available via **Edit | Add point**) Regardless of which of the two ground control point scenarios you are working with, you need to click on the GCP point within the **Georeferencer** image window. Use the zoom and pan tools so that you can precisely click on the intended GCP location.
4. Once you click on the input raster with the Add point tool, the **Enter map coordinates** dialog box will open:

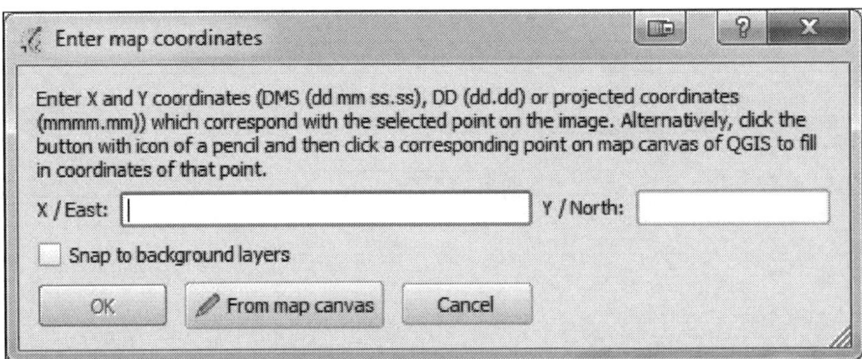

You are now halfway done entering the GCP. Follow the appropriate directions below. These will be different workflow depending on whether you are georeferencing against a second loaded dataset or against benchmarks, datums, or other printed coordinates on the input raster.

If you are georeferencing against a second loaded dataset, you need to follow these steps:

1. Click on the **From map canvas** button.
2. Locate the same GCP spatial location on the data loaded in the main QGIS Desktop map canvas. Click on that GCP location.
3. Use the zoom and pan tools so that you can precisely click on the intended GCP location.
4. If you need to zoom in to the dataset within the QGIS Desktop map canvas, you will have to first zoom in and then click on the **From map canvas** button again to regain the **Add point** cursor and enter the GCP.

5. The **Enter map coordinates** dialog box will reappear with the **X / East** and **Y / North** coordinates entered for the point where you clicked on the QGIS Desktop map canvas:

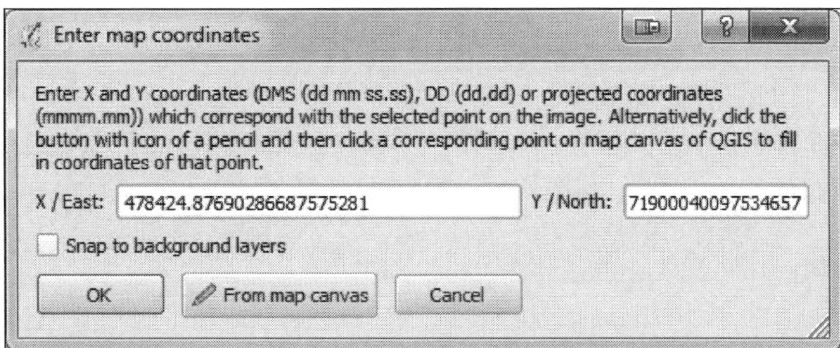

6. Click on **OK**.
7. As you enter GCP information for the source (**srcX/ srcY**) and destination (**dstX/ dstY**) coordinates, they will be displayed in the **GCP Table** window in the **Georeferencer** window:

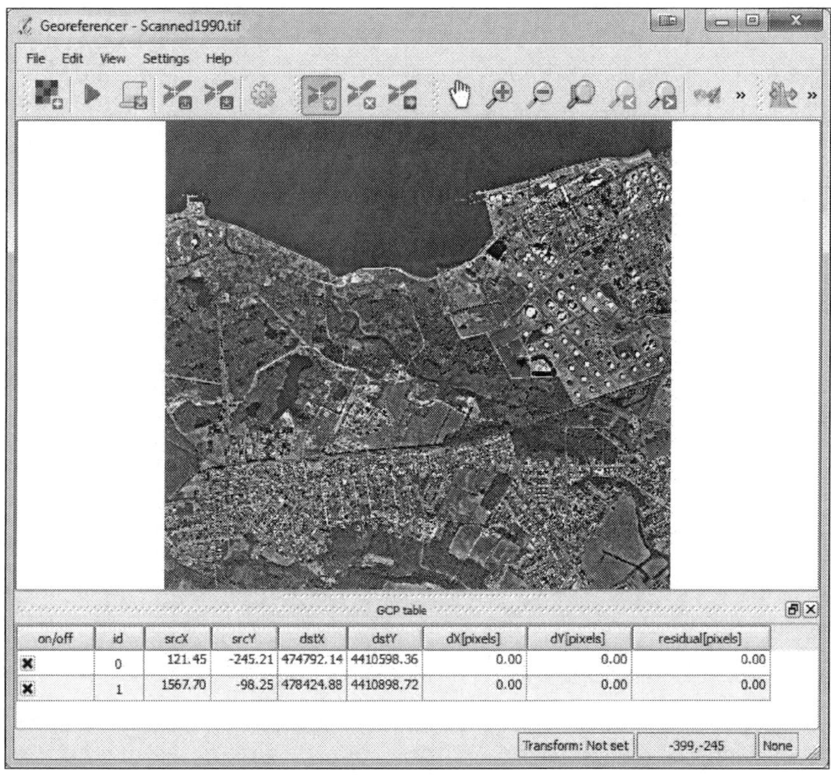

8. Repeat steps (1-4 and 1-7 above) to enter the remaining GCPs.

If you are georeferencing against benchmarks, datums, or other printed coordinates on the input raster, you need to perform the following steps:

1. Enter the **X / East** and **Y / North** coordinates in the appropriate boxes.
2. Click on **OK**.
3. Repeat steps (1-4 and 1-2 above) to enter the remaining GCPs.

Now that you've learned the basic procedure for georeferencing in QGIS, we will go through two examples in greater detail. Here, you will learn all the options for using the Georeferencer GDAL plugin.

The first example – georeferencing using a second dataset

In this example, the `scanned1990.tif` aerial photograph will be georeferenced by choosing ground control points from a more recent aerial photograph of the `bridgeport_nj.sid` area. The `scanned1990.tif` image is the result of scanning a hard copy of an aerial photograph. The `bridgeport_nj.sid` image file covers the same portion of the planet and is in the EPSG:26918 - NAD83 / UTM zone 18N CRS. Once the georeferencing operation is completed, a new copy of the `scanned1990.tif` image will be created in the EPSG:26918 - NAD83 / UTM zone 18N CRS.

Getting started

1. Launch QGIS Desktop and load the `bridgeport_nj.sid` file into the QGIS Desktop map canvas. (Note that you may need to navigate to **Properties** | **Style** for this layer and set the **Load min/max values** option to **Min / max** so that the image renders properly.)
2. Click on **Georeferencer** under **Raster** to launch the plugin. The Georeferencer window will open.
3. Load the `scanned1990.tif` aerial photograph into the Georeferencer image window by clicking on **Open Raster** under **File** or by using the Open raster button. The Coordinate Reference System Selector window will open. This is because the `scanned1990.tif` image does not have a defined CRS. Set the CRS to EPSG:26918 - NAD83 / UTM zone 18N and click on **OK**.
4. Arrange your desktop so that QGIS Desktop and the **Georeferencer** window are visible simultaneously.
5. Familiarize yourself with both datasets and look for potential GCPs. Look for precise locations such as piers, corners of roof tops, and street intersections.

Entering the ground control points

1. Zoom in to the area, using the zoom-in button ( ), where you will enter the first GCP in both the QGIS Desktop and Georeferencer windows. Zooming in will allow you to be more precise.
2. Enter the first GCP into the Georeferencer image window using the Add Point tool( ).
3. After clicking on the image in the Georeferencer image window, the **Enter map coordinates** window will open. Click on the **From map canvas** button. The entire Georeferencer window will momentarily disappear.
4. Click on the same location in QGIS Desktop.

If you have not first zoomed in to the GCP area in QGIS Desktop, you can still do so. After zooming in you will need to click on the **From map canvas** button again to regain the Add Point cursor.

5. The **Enter map coordinates** window will reappear with the destination coordinates, populating the **X / East** and **Y / North** boxes. Click on **OK** to complete the Ground Control Point.
6. The GCP table in the **Georeferencer** window will now be populated with the source and destination coordinates for the first ground control point. The control point will also be indicated in both the Georeferencer image window and QGIS Desktop by a red dot.

If a GCP has not been precisely placed, the Move GCP Point tool ( ) can be used to adjust the position of the control point in either the Georeferencer image window or the QGIS Desktop map canvas.

GCPs can be deleted in two ways, as follows:

- Using the Delete point tool ( ) and clicking on the point in the Georeferencer image window
- By right-clicking on the point in the GCP table and choosing **Remove**

The following figure QGIS Desktop and the Georeferencer window with a single GCP entered.

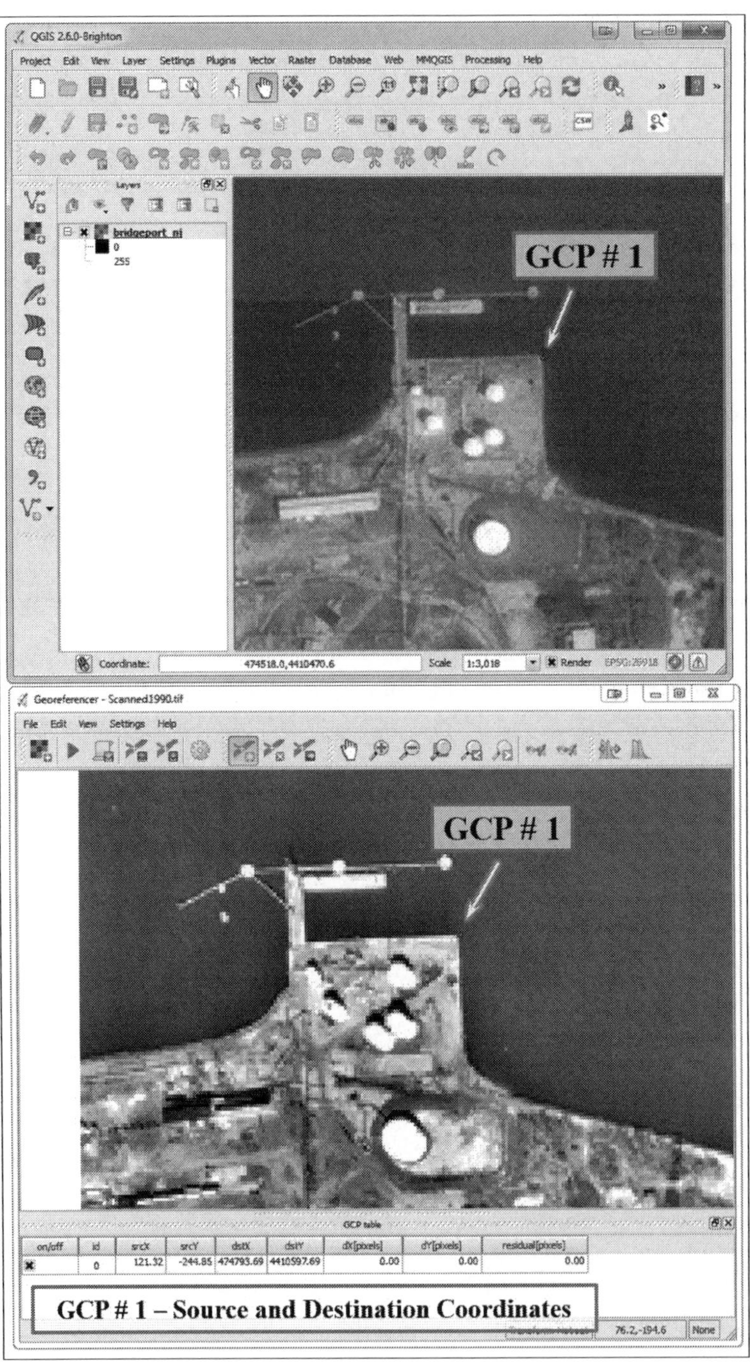

7. Repeat steps 6 to 11 for the remaining ground control points until you have entered eight GCPs.
8. Use the pan and zoom controls to navigate around each image, as needed:

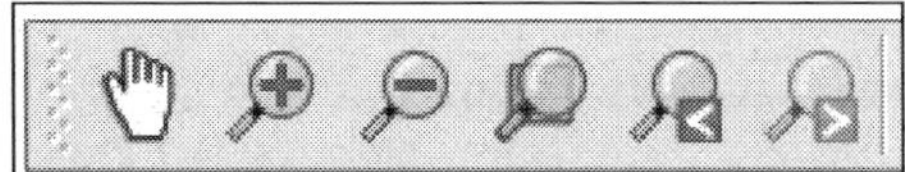

9. Once all the points have been entered, the Save GCP Points As button ( ) can be used to save the points to a text file with a `.points` extension. These can serve as part of the documentation of the georeferencing operation and can be reloaded with the Load GCP Points tool ( ) to redo the operation at a later date.

Transformation settings

The following steps describe how to set the Transformation settings.

1. Once all the eight GCPs have been created, click on the Transformation settings button ( ).
2. Here, you can choose appropriate values for the **Transformation type**, **Resampling method** fields, and other output settings. There are seven choices for **Transformation type**. This setting will determine how the ground control points are used to transform the image from source to destination coordinate space. Each will produce different results and these are described as follows; for this example, choose **Polynomial 2**:
    - **Linear**: This algorithm simply creates a world file for the raster and does not actually transform the raster. Therefore, this option is not sufficient for dealing with scanned images. It can be used on images that are already in a projected coordinate reference system but are lacking a world file. It requires a minimum of two GCPs.
    - **Helmert**: This performs a simple scaling and rotational transformation. This option is only suitable if the transformation simply involves a change from one projected CRS to another. It requires a minimum of two GCPs.

- **Polynomial 1, Polynomial 2, Polynomial 3**: These are perhaps the most widely used transformation types. They are also commonly referred to as first (affine), second, and third order transformations. The higher the transformation order the more complex the distortion that can be corrected and the more computer power it requires. **Polynomial 1** requires a minimum of three GCPs. It is suitable for situations where the input raster needs to be stretched, scaled, and rotated. **Polynomial 2** or **Polynomial 3** should be used if the input raster needs to be bent or curved. **Polynomial 2** requires six GCPs and **Polynomial 3** requires 10 GCPs.
- **Thin Plate Spline**: This transforms the raster in a way that allows for local deformations in the data. This may give similar results as a higher-order polynomial transformation and is also suitable for scanned imagery. It requires only one GCP.
- **Projective**: This is useful for oblique imagery and some scanned maps. A minimum of four GCPs should be used. This is often a good choice when Georeferencing satellite imagery such as Landsat and DigitalGlobe.

There is no one best **Transformation type**. You may need to try several and then determine which generated the most accurate transformation for your particular dataset.

The following screenshot shows setting the **Transformation type** setting within the **Transformation settings** window.

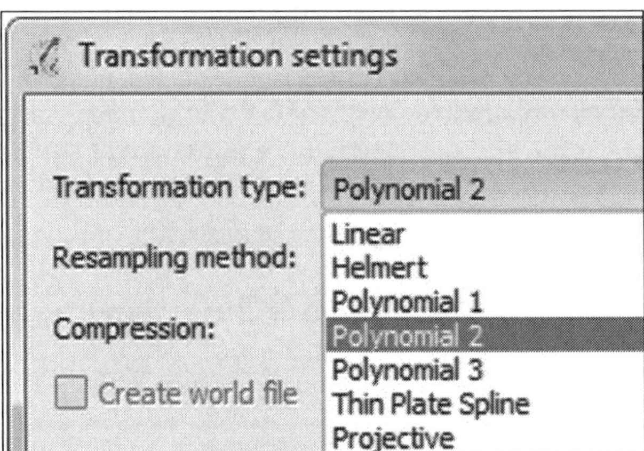

1. There are five choices for **Resampling method**. During the transformation, a new output raster will be generated. This setting will determine how the pixel values will be calculated in the output raster. Each is described here; for this example, choose **Linear**:

    - **Nearest neighbour**: In this method, the value of an output pixel values will be determined by the value of the nearest cell in the input. This is the fastest method and it will not change pixel values during the transformation. It is recommended for categorical or integer data. If it is used with continuous data, it produces blocky output.
    - **Linear**: This method uses the four nearest input cell values to determine the value of the output cell. The new cell value is a weighted average of the four input cell values. It produces smooth output because high and low input cell values may be eliminated in the output. It is recommended for continuous datasets. It should not be used on categorical data because the input categories may not be maintained in the output.
    - **Cubic**: This is similar to **Linear**, but it uses the 16 nearest input cells to determine the output cell value. It is better at preserving edges, and the output is sharper than the **Linear** resampling. It is often used with aerial photography or satellite imagery and is also recommended for continuous data. This should not be used for categorical data for the same reasons that were given for the **Linear** resampling.
    - **Cubic Spline**: This algorithm is based on a spline function and produces smooth output.
    - **Lanczos**: This algorithm produces sharp output. It must be used with caution because it can result in output values that are both lower and higher than those in the input.

The following figure shows setting the **Resampling method** setting within the **Transformation settings** window.

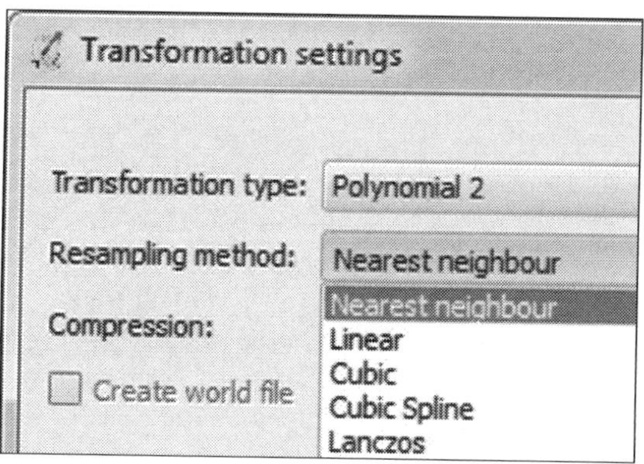

As is the case with **Transformation type**, there is no best **Resampling method**. Choosing the most appropriate algorithm depends on the nature of the data and how that data will be used after it has been georeferenced. **Nearest neighbour**, **Linear**, and **Cubic** are the most frequently used options.

2. Since raster data tends to be large, it may be desirable to choose a compression algorithm. There are four choices for **Compression**. Some choices offer better reductions in file size while others offer better data access rates. For this example, use **None**. The choices are as follows:
    - **None**: This offers no compression
    - **LZW**: This offers the best compromise between data access times and file size reduction
    - **Packbits**: This offers the best data access times but the worst file size reduction
    - **Deflate**: This offers the best file size reduction
3. Name the output raster by clicking on the **Browse** button.
4. Choose the target SRS by clicking on the **Browse** button. A window for choosing the target coordinate reference system will open. For this example, choose **EPSG: 26918**.
5. If an output map and output report are desired in the PDF format, click on the browse button next to the **Generate pdf map** and **Generate pdf report** options and specify the output name for each. The report includes a summary of the transformation setting, GCPs used, and the root mean square error for the transformation.
6. Click on the **Set Target Resolution** box to activate the **Horizontal** and **Vertical** options for output pixel resolution in map units. For this example, leave this option unchecked.
7. The **Use 0 for transparency when needed** option can be activated if pixels with the value of `0` should be transparent in the output. For this example, leave this option unchecked.
8. Click on **Load in QGIS when done** to have the output added to the QGIS Desktop map canvas.

The Georeferencer tool can be configured by clicking on **Configure Georeferencer** under **Settings** in the Georeferencing window. Here, there are options for adding tips (labels) for the GCPS, choosing residual units, and specifying sheet sizes for the PDF report.

9. Click on **OK** to set the transformation settings:

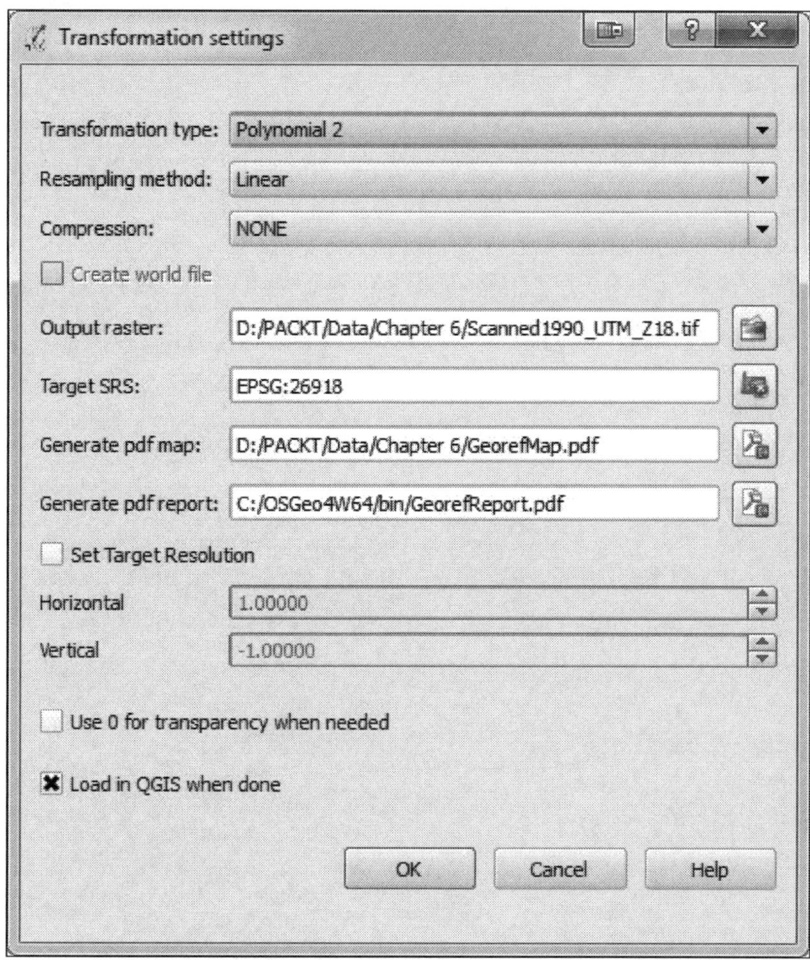

10. Once the **Transformation Settings** values have been set, the `residual [pixels]` column in the GCP table will be populated. This column contains the **root mean square error** (**RMSE**) for each GCP. The mean RMSE for the transformation will be displayed at the bottom of the **Georeferencer** window.

> RMSE is a metric that indicates the quality of the transformation. It will change depending on the **Transformation type** value chosen. The general rule of thumb is that the RMSE should not be larger than half the pixel size of the raster in map units. However, it is only an indication. Another indication is how well the georeferenced imagery aligns with other datasets.

11. Additionally, the Link Georeferencer to QGIS tool (icon) and Link QGIS to Georeferencer tool (icon) will be activated. These will join the Georeferencer window to the QGIS Desktop map canvas, and they will be synched together when you use the pan and zoom tools.

The following screenshot shows the image in the Georeferencer window with 8 GCP's entered. Their location is identified by numbered boxes within the image window. The To and From coordinates are displayed in the GCP table window along with the RMSE values.

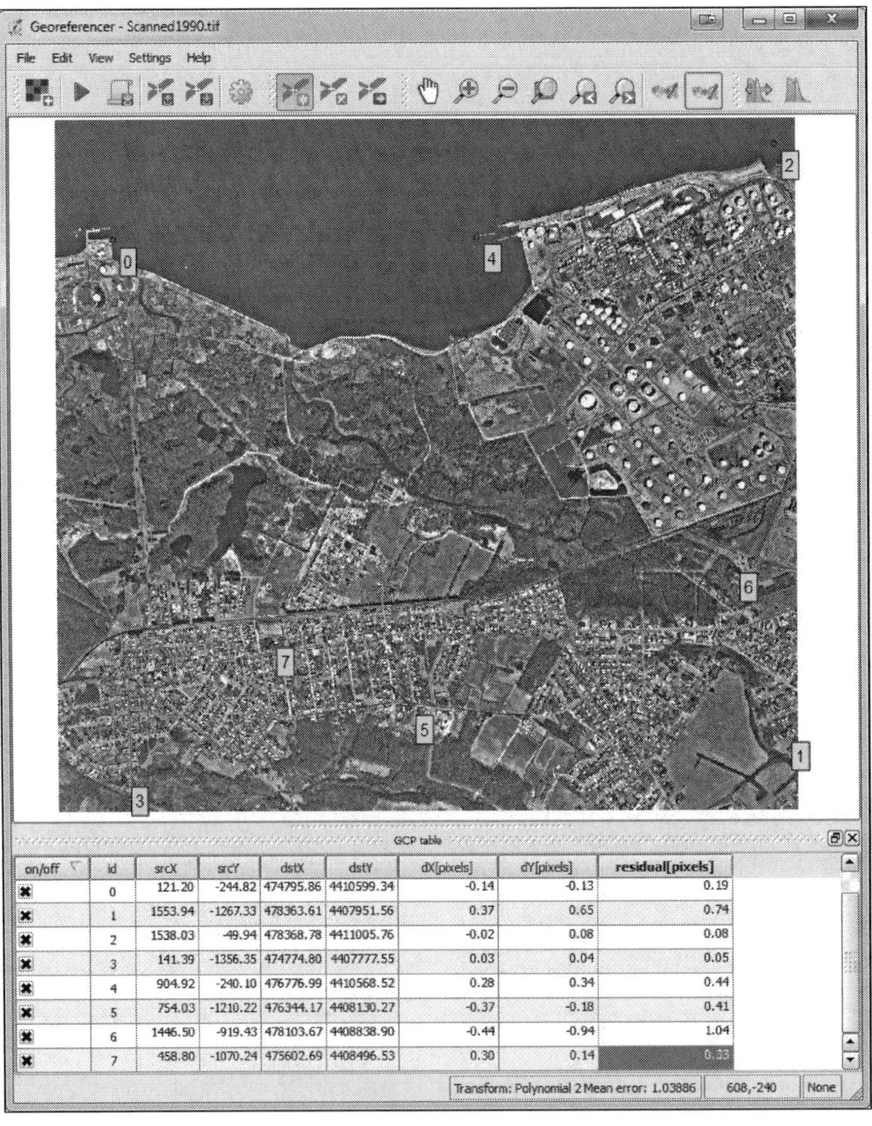

Georeferencer - Scanned1990.tif
File Edit View Settings Help
0
1
2
3
4
5
6
7
GCP table
on/off | id | srcX | srcY | dstX | dstY | dX[pixels] | dY[pixels] | residual[pixels]
0 | 121.20 | -244.82 | 474795.86 | 4410599.34 | -0.14 | -0.13 | 0.19
1 | 1553.94 | -1267.33 | 478363.61 | 4407951.56 | 0.37 | 0.65 | 0.74
2 | 1538.03 | -49.94 | 478368.78 | 4411005.76 | -0.02 | 0.08 | 0.08
3 | 141.39 | -1356.35 | 474774.80 | 4407777.55 | 0.03 | 0.04 | 0.05
4 | 904.92 | -240.10 | 476776.99 | 4410568.52 | 0.28 | 0.34 | 0.44
5 | 754.03 | -1210.22 | 476344.17 | 4408130.27 | -0.37 | -0.18 | 0.41
6 | 1446.50 | -919.43 | 478103.67 | 4408838.90 | -0.44 | -0.94 | 1.04
7 | 458.80 | -1070.24 | 475602.69 | 4408496.53 | 0.30 | 0.14 | 0.33
Transform: Polynomial 2 Mean error: 1.03886
608,-240
None

Completing the operation

1. Click on the Start Georeferencing button (▶) button to complete the operation. The georeferenced raster will be written out and added to the QGIS Desktop map canvas if the option was checked in the **Transformation Settings** window.

> The Generate GDAL Script tool ( ) will write out the GDAL command-line syntax for the current georeferencing operation. This code can be copied to the clipboard and used to write out to a file:

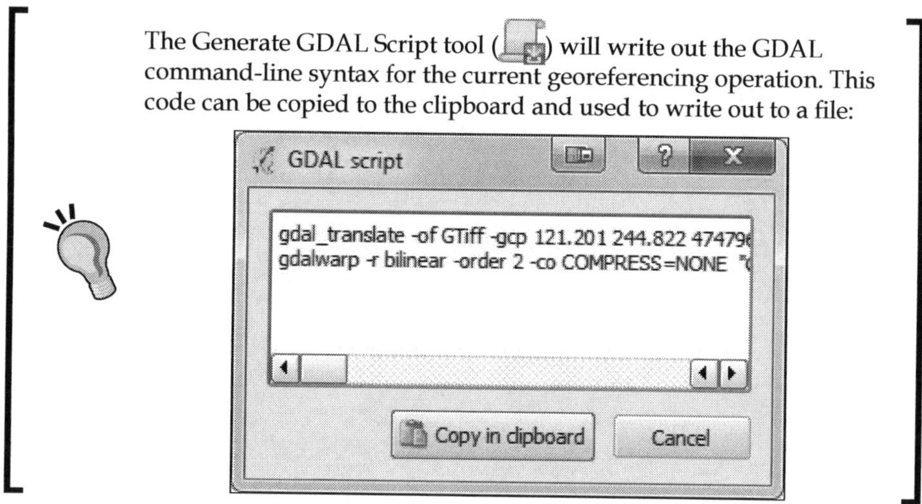

The second example – georeferencing using a point file

This example will use the `zone_map.bmp` image. It displays zoning for a small group of parcels in Albuquerque, New Mexico. This image has five geodetic control points that are indicated by small points with labels (for example, `I25 28`). These control points are maintained by the U.S. National Geodetic Survey (NGS). Here, you will learn how to load a precompiled set of ground control points to georeference the image:

1. Load the image into the Georeferencer window.
2. Choose EPSG:2903 - NAD83(HARN) / New Mexico Central (ftUS) for the CRS.
3. Click on the Load GCP Points tool ( ) and choose the `zone_map.points` file. The destination coordinates for the locations in this file were obtained from the NGS website (`http://www.ngs.noaa.gov/cgi-bin/datasheet.prl`). From the website, the Station Name link under DATASHEETS was used, and a station name search conducted for each. The destination coordinates are in EPSG:2903 - NAD83(HARN) / New Mexico Central (ftUS).

The following figure shows the image in the Georeferencer window with 5 GCP's entered based off of datums whose destination coordinates were looked up online. Their location is identified by numbered boxes within the image window. The To and From coordinates are displayed in the GCP table window along with the RMSE values.

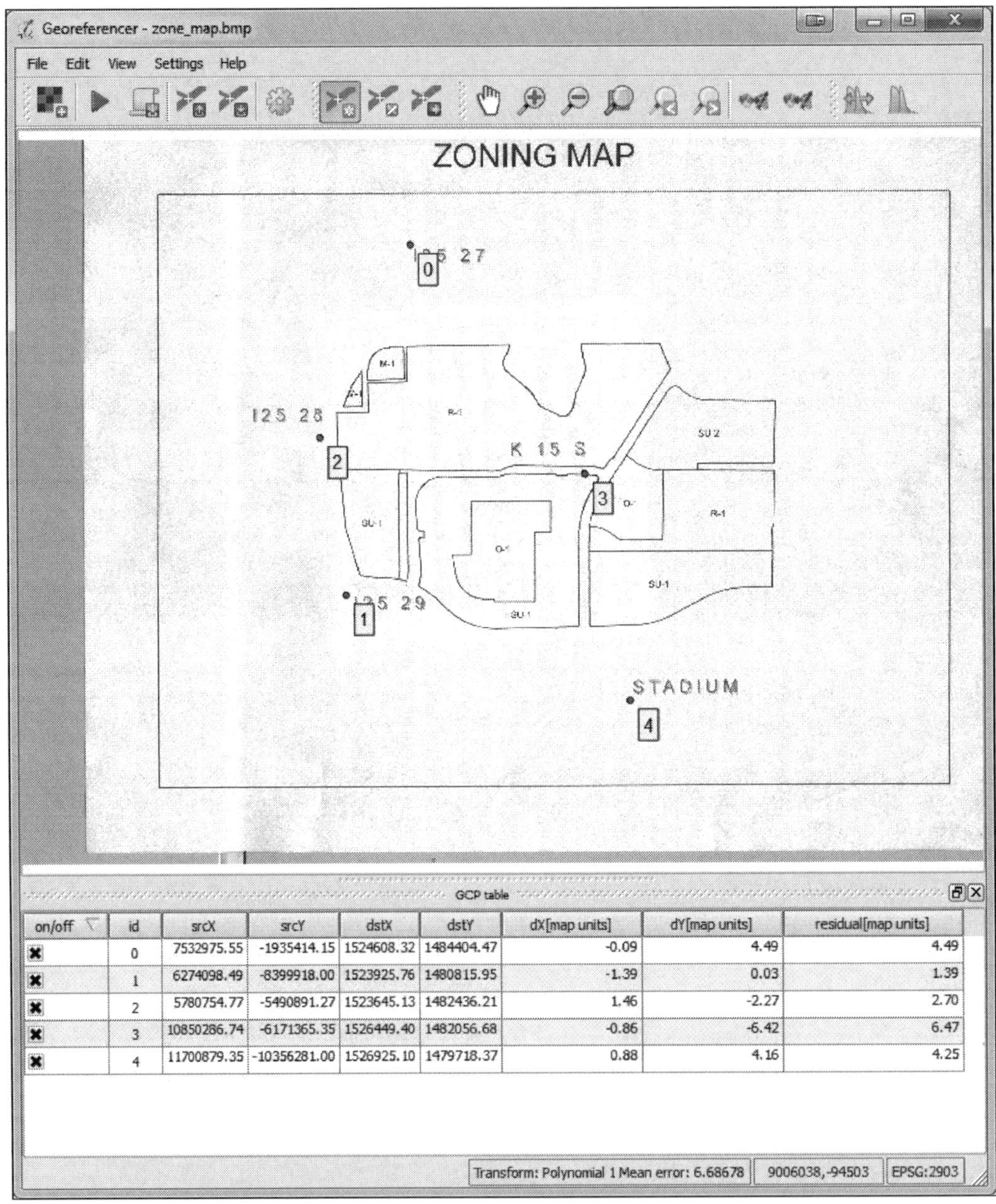

4. The `zone_map.points` file consists of five columns in a comma-delimited text file. The columns **MapX / MapY** are the destination coordinates. Columns **pixelX / pixelY** are the source coordinates, and **enable** column has a value of `1` if the GCP is to be used in the transformation and a value of `0` if it is not to be used. The following are the contents of this points file:

```
mapX,mapY,pixelX,pixelY,enable
1524608.32,1484404.47,7532975.55,-1935414.15,1
1523925.76,1480815.95,6274098.49,-8399918.00,1
1523645.13,1482436.21,5780754.77,-5490891.27,1
1526449.40,1482056.68,10850286.74,-6171365.35,1
1526925.10,1479718.37,11700879.35,-10356281.00,1
```

5. Click on **Transformation Settings** under **Settings** and set the following parameters:
    - Choose **Polynomial 1** as the **Transformation type**
    - Choose **Nearest neighbour** as the **Resampling method**
    - Choose a **Compression** of **None**
    - Name the output raster
    - Choose **EPSG: 2903** as the **Target SRS**
    - Complete the **Generate pdf map** and **Generate report pdf** fields
    - Check **Load in QGIS when done**
    - Click on **OK**

The following figure shows the completed **Transformation settings**.

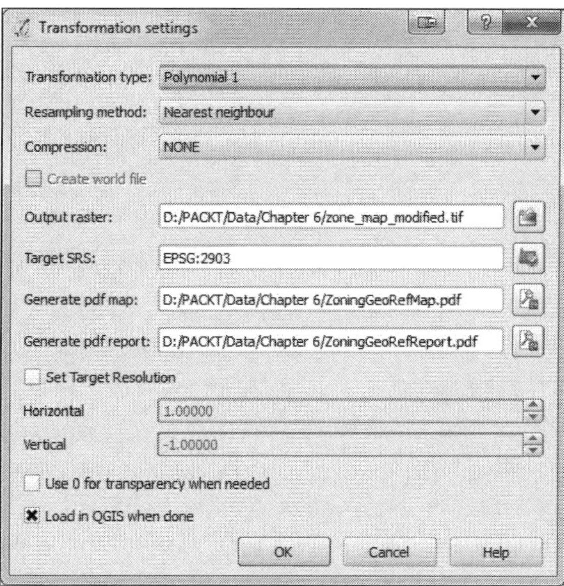

6. Click on the Start Georeferencing button (▶) to complete the operation. The georeferenced raster will be written out and added to the QGIS Desktop map canvas.

Checking the topology of vector data

In GIS, there are two main data models: vector and raster. They are called models because they are not real but are representations of the real world. It is important that we ensure our data is modeling the world as accurately as possible. Vector datasets often have hundreds or thousands of features making it nearly impossible to verify each feature. However, using topology rules, we can let QGIS evaluate the geometry of our datasets and ensure that they are well constructed.

Topology is the relationship between contiguous or connected features in a GIS. Here, you will be introduced to the Topology Checker plugin. This plugin allows you to test topological relationships in your data and ensure that they are modeling the real world accurately. An example of a topological relationship rule is *polygons must not overlap*. Imagine a country boundaries dataset. It is not possible for a point to be in two countries at once. Therefore, polygons in such a dataset should not overlap. The Topology Checker plugin can be used to test whether there are any overlapping polygons.

Installing the Topology Checker

Here are the steps for installing the Topology Checker plugin:

1. Navigate to **Plugins** | **Manage and Install Plugins** and click on the **All** tab.
2. In the search bar, type `topology`.
3. Select the **Topology Checker** plugin and click on **Install plugin**.
4. Once enabled, the Topology Checker plugin can be found by navigating to **Vector** | **Topology Checker**.
5. When the **Topology Checker** window opens, it appears as a panel in QGIS Desktop.

Topological rules

Different sets of topological rules are available depending on the feature geometry: point, line, or polygon. Some rules test for relationships between features in a single layer and some test the relationships between features of two separate layers. All participating layers need to be loaded into QGIS. The following topological rule tests are available.

Rules for point features

The rules for point features are as follows:

- **must be covered by**: This relationship test evaluates how a point layer interacts with a second vector layer. Points that do not intersect the second layer are flagged as errors.
- **must be covered by endpoints of**: This relationship test evaluates how a point layer interacts with a line layer. Points that do not intersect the endpoints of the second layer are flagged as errors.
- **must be inside**: This evaluates how a point layer interacts with a second polygon layer. Points not covered by the polygons are flagged as errors.
- **must not have duplicates**: This evaluates if point features are stacked on top of one another. Additional points are with the same *x* and *y* position (stacked) as the first point queried are flagged as errors.
- **must not have invalid geometries**: This checks whether the geometries are valid and if they are not, then it flags those features as errors.
- **must not have multi-part geometries**: This flags all multi-part points as errors.

Rules for line features

The rules for line features are as follows:

- **end points must be covered by**: This relationship test evaluates how a line layer interacts with a second point layer. The features that do not intersect the point layer are flagged as errors.
- **must not have dangles**: This test will flag features that are dangling arcs.
- **must not have duplicates**: This flags additional duplicate line segments (stacked) as errors.
- **must not have invalid geometries**: This checks whether the geometries are valid and if they are not, then it flags those features as errors.
- **must not have multi-part geometries**: This flags features that have a geometry type of multi-line as errors.
- **must not have pseudos**: This tests lines for the presence of pseudo nodes. This is when there is a pair of nodes where there should only be one. These can interfere with network analysis. The features with pseudo nodes will be flagged as errors.

Rules for polygon features

The rules for polygon features are as follows:

- **must contain**: This checks whether the target polygon layer contains at least one node or vertex from the second layer. If it doesn't, it is flagged as an error.
- **must not have duplicates**: This flags additional duplicated stacked polygons as errors.
- **must not have gaps**: This flags adjacent polygons with gaps as errors. Watersheds or parcel boundaries would be suitable for this test.
- **must not have invalid geometries**: This checks whether the geometries are valid. Some of the rules that define a valid geometry are as follows:
    - Polygon rings must close
    - Rings that define holes should be inside rings that define exterior boundaries
    - Rings should not self-intersect (they may neither touch nor cross one another)
    - Rings should not touch other rings, except at a point
- **must not have multi-part geometries**: This flags all multi-part polygons as errors.
- **must not overlap**: This flags adjacent polygon features in the same layer that overlap one another as errors. Watersheds or parcel boundaries would be suitable for this test.
- **must not overlap with**: This relationship test evaluates how polygon features from the target layer interact with polygon features from a second polygon layer. Those that do will be flagged as errors.

Using the Topology Checker

The `parcels.shp` sample data will be used to demonstrate how to set up and test topological relationships. Here, the parcels polygon shapefile is loaded and the **Topology Checker** panel has been enabled by clicking on **Topology Checker** under **Vector**. The following figure shows the `parcels.shp` sample data loaded into QGIS desktop and the **Topology checker** plugin enabled.

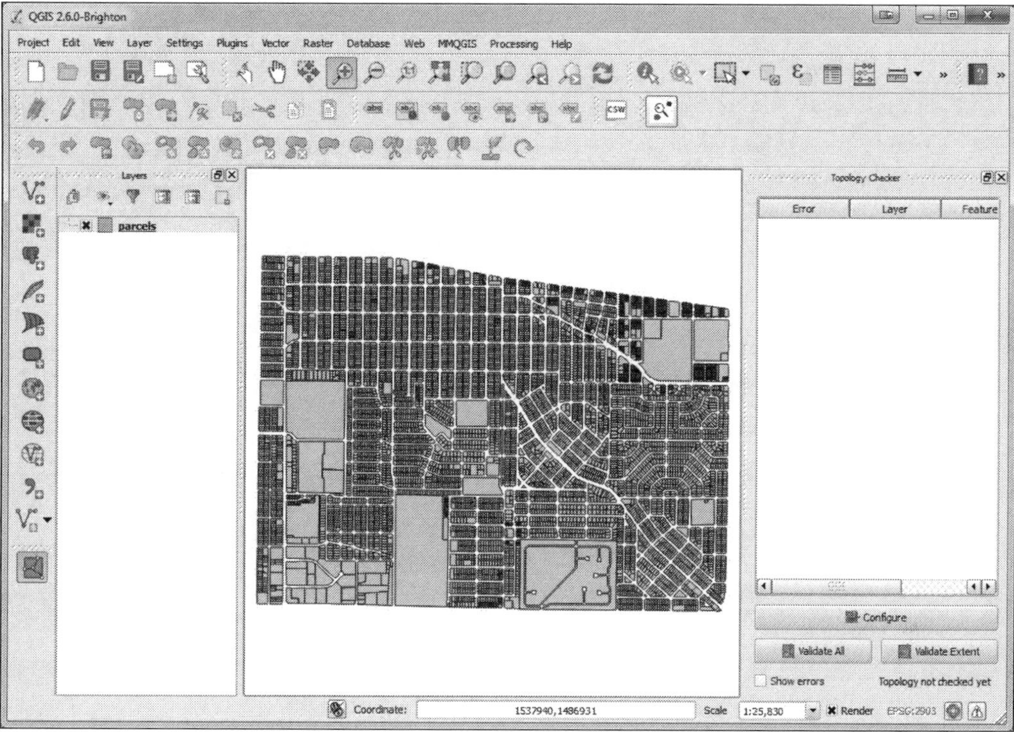

Here are the steps for configuring the **Topology Checker** plugin and evaluating the topology of the `parcels.shp` sample data.

1. Click on the **Configure** button in the **Topology Checker** panel to open the **Topology Rule Settings** dialog.
2. To set a rule, choose the target layer, **parcels**.
3. Next, choose the **must not have gaps** rule from the central drop-down menu:

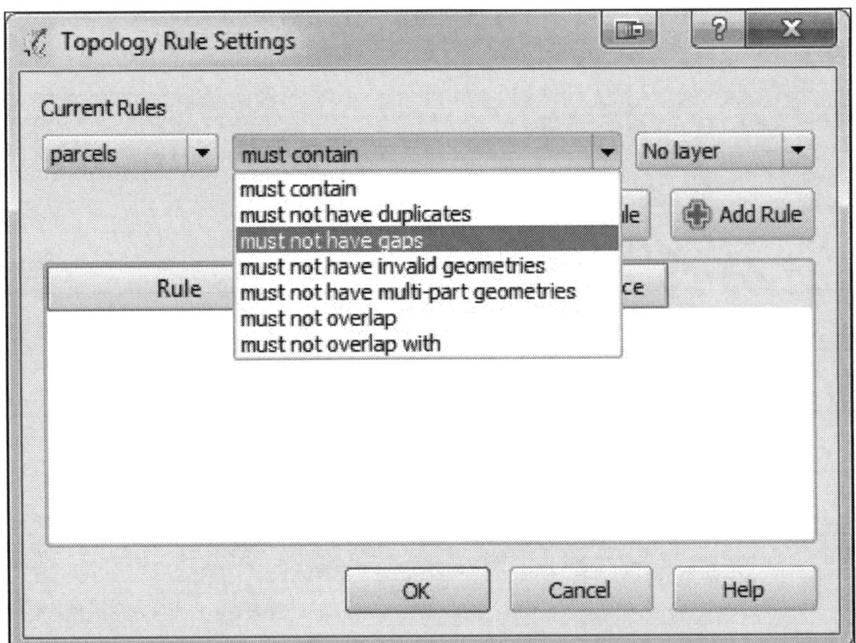

The list of available rules changes depending upon which target layer is chosen.

4. Since this rule involves only the target layer, the final drop for a second layer disappears.
5. Now, we will add a second rule. Set the target layer to **parcels** and the rule as **must not overlap**.
6. Click on the **Add Rule** button (Add Rule).
7. For the third rule, again set the target layer to **parcels** and set the rule as **must not have duplicates**.

8. Click on the **Add Rule** button.
9. For this example, we will test three rules against the parcels layer:
    - **must not have gaps**
    - **must not overlap**
    - **must not have duplicates**
10. The rules that have been established are summarized in the **Topology Rule Settings** dialog box:

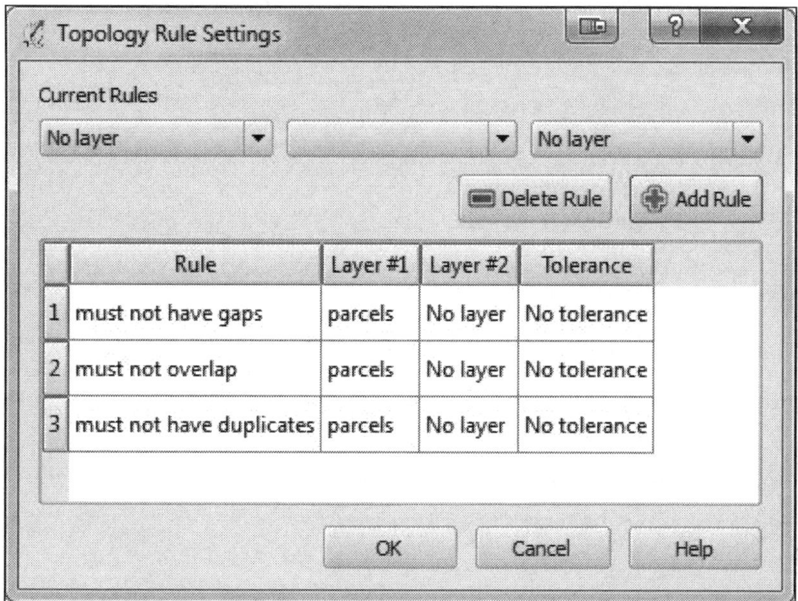

11. A rule can be deleted by selecting it and choosing **Delete Rule** (Delete Rule).
12. Click on **OK** when the topological rules have been defined.

> As of version 0.1 of the **Topology Checker** plugin, the **Tolerance** setting is not operational. If it were, it would allow a tolerance to be set in map units. For example, one could test whether a bus stop's layer (point) is within 50 feet of the centerline of a road (line) by setting a tolerance of 50 feet and using the **must be covered by** rule.

13. Once the topology rules have been set, you can choose to validate the topology for the entire layer (**Validate All**) or just within the current map extent (**Validate Extent**).
14. For this example, choose **Validate All**.
15. The topology errors are displayed in the **Topology Checker** panel. In this case, 17 errors are found including 6 gaps, 9 overlaps, and 2 duplicate geometries, as shown in the following screenshot:

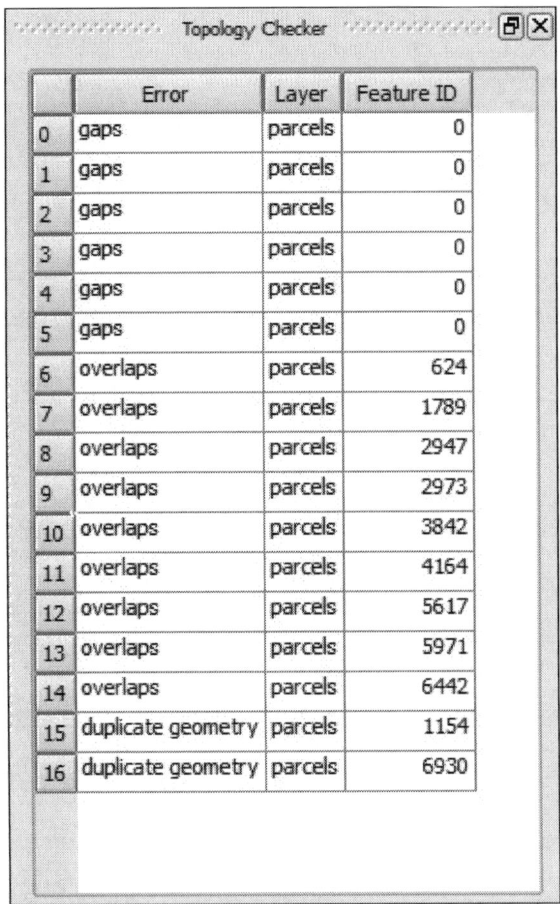

Topology Checker

	Error	Layer	Feature ID
0	gaps	parcels	0
1	gaps	parcels	0
2	gaps	parcels	0
3	gaps	parcels	0
4	gaps	parcels	0
5	gaps	parcels	0
6	overlaps	parcels	624
7	overlaps	parcels	1789
8	overlaps	parcels	2947
9	overlaps	parcels	2973
10	overlaps	parcels	3842
11	overlaps	parcels	4164
12	overlaps	parcels	5617
13	overlaps	parcels	5971
14	overlaps	parcels	6442
15	duplicate geometry	parcels	1154
16	duplicate geometry	parcels	6930

16. The **Show errors** box can be checked to see where in the dataset the errors occur. Errors will be highlighted in red, as shown in the following figure:

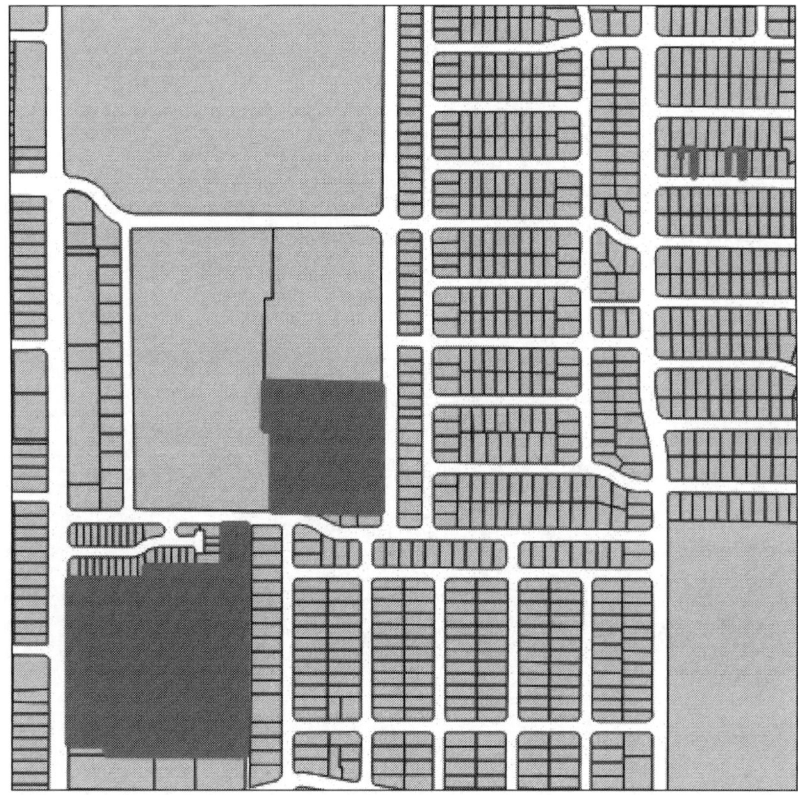

Repairing topological errors via topological editing

Once the geometry errors have been identified, the work of repairing the layer begins. In *Chapter 1, A Refreshing Look at QGIS*, we covered basic vector data editing that included layer-based snapping. In this final section, we will cover how to repair topological geometry errors via topological editing. We will continue to use the `parcels.shp` data as an example.

Topological editing only works with polygon geometries.

The editing approach taken depends on the topological error you are addressing. In the last section, three types of errors were found: gaps, overlaps, and duplicate geometries. These are three of the most common errors associated with polygon data and we will look at how to repair these three types of errors.

Example 1 – resolving duplicate geometries

Duplicate geometries are the most straightforward errors to address. Here are the step by step directions for resolving this type of topological conflict.

1. Toggle the editing option on for the **parcels** layer.
2. Double-click on the first instance of a duplicate geometry in the **Topology Checker** error table to zoom to it.
3. Use the Select Features by Rectangle tool ( ) to select the duplicate parcel.
4. Open the attribute table.
5. Change the display filter in the lower-right corner to **Show Selected Features**:

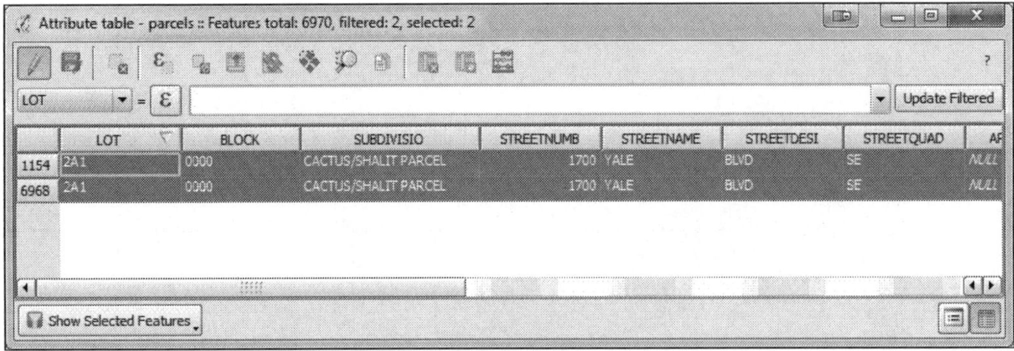

6. Notice that all the attributes are identical. It is wise to verify this to ensure you do not delete any unique data.
7. Select the feature with the higher row number and click on the Delete selected button ( ).
8. Toggle off editing for this layer and save the changes.

Example 2 – repairing overlaps

To repair overlaps, there are some editing parameters with which you should familiarize yourself and set.

Setting the editing parameters

1. Click on **Snapping Options** under **Settings** to check the snapping tolerances.
2. Click the checkbox to the left of the **parcels** layer to select it. Choose **to vertex and segment** in the **Mode** field and a value of **10 map units** in the **Tolerance** field.

3. Besides layer-based snapping options, you can also enable topological editing from the **Snapping Options** dialog box. Click on the **Enable topological editing** checkbox. Checking this option allows you to edit common boundaries in adjacent polygons. QGIS will detect shared polygon boundaries and vertices on these shared boundaries; they will only have to be moved once and both polygons will be edited together.
4. There are two other editing options available here:
    - **Avoid intersections**: This can be checked for a particular layer to avoid creating overlaps when digitizing new polygons. With this option checked, you can digitize a new polygon adjacent to an existing one so that the new polygon intersects the existing feature. QGIS will cut the new polygon to create the shared boundary.
    - **Enable snapping on intersection**: This allows you to snap to an intersection of another background layer.

    For this example, leave the above two options unchecked.
5. Click on **OK** to close the **Snapping options** window.

    The completed **Snapping options** are displayed in the following screenshot:

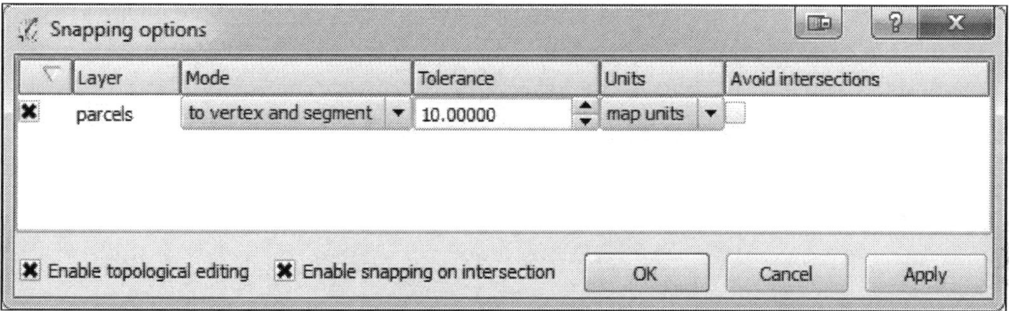

6. There are additional editing parameters that need to be set from **Options** under **Settings** on the **Digitizing** tab. Set the value for **Search radius for vertex edits** field to **10 pixels** as shown in the figure below. Setting this value to something larger than zero helps to ensure that QGIS finds the correct vertex during an editing operation.

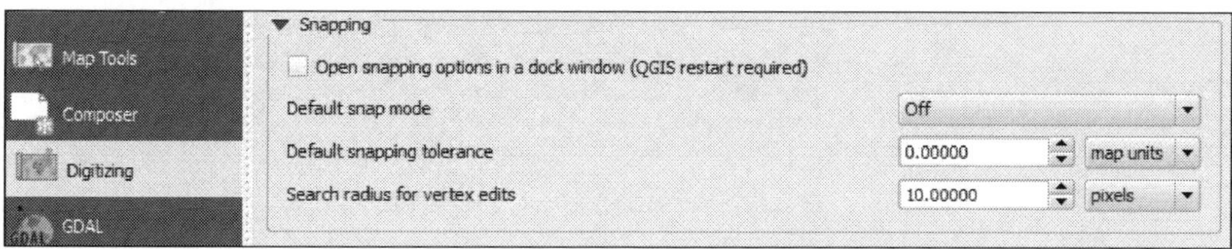

Adjusting the layer transparency can help when you work with overlaps. A 50 percent transparency setting will allow the overlaps to be visible.

7. Uncheck the **Show errors** option on the **Topology Checker** panel. This declutters the map canvas.
8. Here, we will work on the first overlap in the list that has a feature ID value of 624. To find this error, double-click on this record in the **Topology Checker** error table. QGIS will zoom to the location of the error shown in the following figure. Here we can see two parcels overlapping. The parcel on the right will be moved to the right to eliminate the overlap with the left parcel.

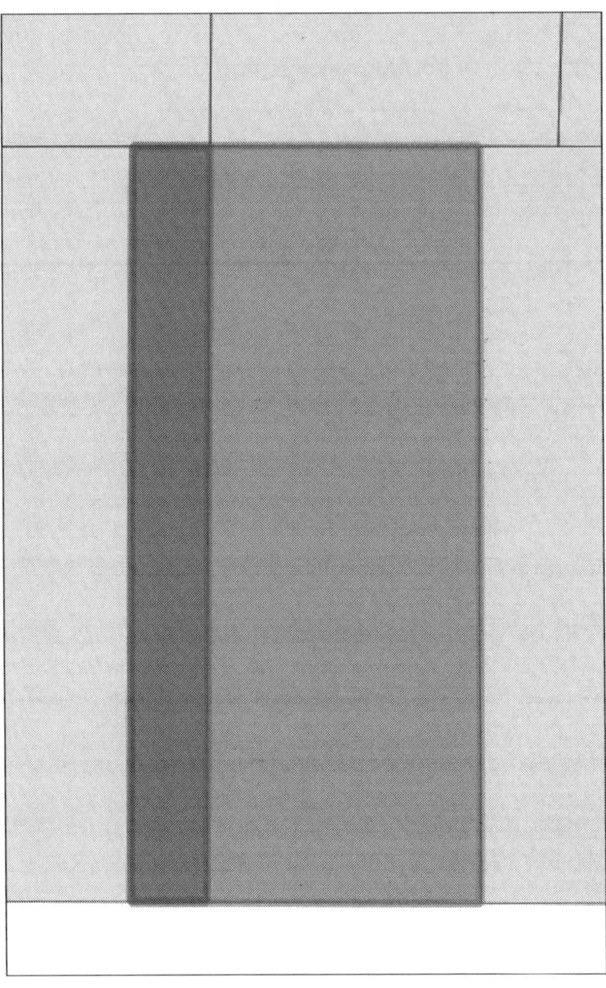

Overlapping parcel polygons

Repairing an overlap between polygons

Here are the step by step directions for repairing the overlaps found in the sample `parcels.shp` data.

1. Toggle on editing option on for the parcels layer and select the polygon to edit with the Select Feature by Rectangle tool ( ). Each vertex will be displayed as red graphic Xs.
2. The Node tool ( ) will be used to move the leftmost parcel and eliminate the overlap. It allows individual vertices to be moved.
    1. Click on one of the parcel corners and the vertices will appear as red boxes.
    2. Click on the lower-left vertex of the right-hand side parcel to select it. It will turn blue.
    3. Drag the selected vertex until it snaps to the boundary of the parcel it is overlapping. A blue line will appear showing the location of virtual polygon boundary as you edit it, as shown in the following figure:

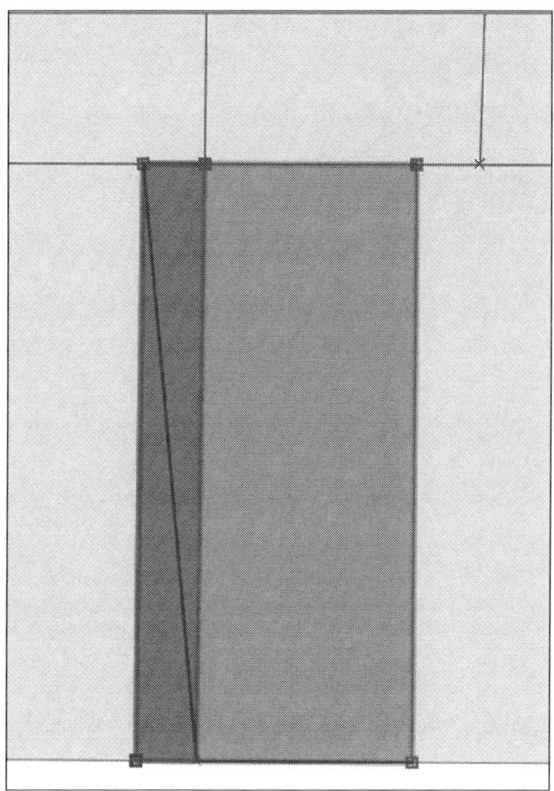

Vertex of the right-hand overlapping parcel being moved

3. Repeat the actions in the previous step for the vertex in the top-left corner.
4. Now, the vertices have been snapped to the boundary of the left-side parcel and the overlap has been repaired. Click on **Validate Extent** in the **Topology Checker** panel to ensure that the overlap has been solved. If so, no errors will be listed in the **Topology Checker** error table.
5. Any remaining overlaps can be fixed repeating steps 1-4.

The repaired parcel is shown in the following figure:

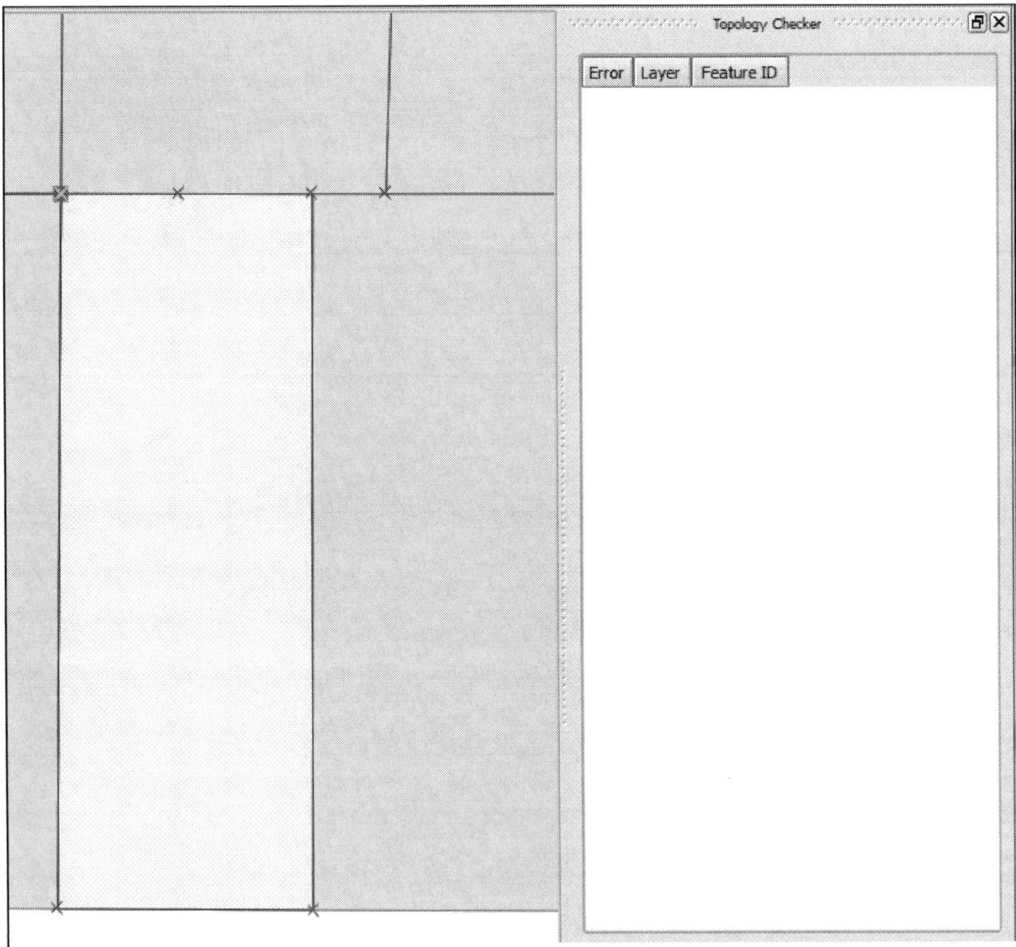

Overlap repaired

Example 3 – repairing a gap between polygons

This example we will continue to work with the `parcel.shp` polygon layer. Here, we will focus on the first gap error listed in the **Topology Checker** error list. It has a feature ID of 0.

1. Ensure that editing is still toggled on for the **parcels** layer.
2. Double-click on the error in the table so that QGIS will zoom to the area. You will see a small horizontal gap between two parcel polygons, as shown in the following figure:

A small gap between two parcels

3. The same editing parameters that were set in Example 2 will be used here.
4. Zoom in a bit closer to the problem area.
5. Select the parcel to the north with the Select Feature by Rectangle tool.
6. Using the node tool, select the lower-left vertex and drag it to snap with the other two parcels and close the gap.

Moving a vertex to repair or close the gap

7. Verify that the issue has been resolved by clicking on **Validate Extent** in the **Topology Checker** panel.
8. The remaining gaps can be repaired using these steps 1-7.
9. Toggle off editing for the parcels layer and save the edits.

> If you have too many topological errors to repair manually, you can import your data into a GRASS database. GRASS has a topological vector data model. The GRASS command v.clean will repair a lot of errors. The cleaned GRASS vector can then be exported into the file format of your choosing.

Summary

This chapter covered more advanced ways to create GIS data from different sources. We provided explanations and step-by-step examples of mapping raw coordinate data, geocoding address-based data, georeferencing imagery, validating vector data with topological rules, and topological editing. With the topics covered to this point, you will be able to work with a variety of vector, raster, and tabular input data.

In the next chapter, we will switch from preparing and editing data to performing spatial analyses. We will cover the QGIS processing toolbox. We will begin with a comprehensive overview and a description of layout of the toolbox. We will then explore the various algorithms and tools that are available in the toolbox with real-world examples.

7
The Processing Toolbox

In this chapter, we will explore the structure of the QGIS processing toolbox, identify which algorithm providers are available, and how to use these specialized algorithms. To accomplish these goals, we will ensure that the toolbox is properly configured, use a variety of specialized vector and spatial algorithms from the GRASS and SAGA libraries, and perform hydrologic analyses using the **Terrain Analysis Using Digital Elevation Models** (**TauDEM**) library. We will cover the following topics in this chapter:

- Introduction to the toolbox
- Configuring the toolbox
- Structure of the toolbox
- Performing spatial analyses using GRASS and SAGA
- Performing a hydrologic analyses with TauDEM

About the processing toolbox

The processing toolbox serves as a one-stop-shopping GUI for accessing algorithms from both native QGIS tools and many third-party providers. Historically, the algorithms from other geospatial packages were only accessible within the native software environment or through a command-line environment. Algorithms from the following providers are accessible using the toolbox:

- QGIS geoalgorithms
- GDAL/OGR
- GRASS
- SAGA
- TauDEM
- LAStools
- R
- Orfeo Toolbox
- Models
- Scripts

We will not make use of all the algorithm providers or explore all the available algorithms in this chapter; however, the last two entries in the list offer additional options for creating reusable graphical models and running Python scripts, which are covered in *Chapter 8, Automating Workflows with the Graphical Modeler*, and *Chapter 9, Creating QGIS Plugins with PyQGIS and Problem Solving*, respectively.

Configuring the processing toolbox

In this section, we will ensure that the processing toolbox is correctly configured to access and execute the algorithms within the GRASS, SAGA, TauDEM, and LAStools libraries. Many of the required libraries are automatically installed, but configuring these tools will vary depending on your operating system and how you choose to install QGIS.

Finding support for your installation

To use some of the GRASS algorithms in this chapter, you will need to make sure that you properly install GRASS 7. If you used the OSGeo installer, you can use the advanced installer option to add GRASS 7 to your installation, otherwise you will need to manually install GRASS 7 and set the path directory in the processing toolbox.

In-depth instructions for configuring SAGA are provided in *Chapter 5, Preparing Raster Data for Processing*.

Instructions for configuring most third-party algorithms on different operating systems can be found on the QGIS website at `http://docs.qgis.org/2.6/en/docs/user_manual/processing/3rdParty.html`.

Support for installing LAStools on Windows, Mac OS X, and Linux can also be found at `http://rapidlasso.com/category/tutorials/`.

To begin configuring the toolbox, we need to click on **Options and configuration** under **Processing**, which is illustrated in the following screenshot. Note that if you are using a Linux distribution, this configuration can be found by navigating to **Processing** | **Options** | **Providers**.

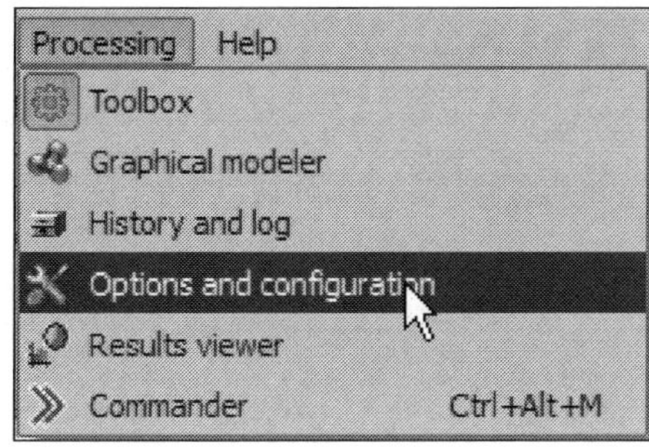

To get started, you need to make sure that each of the providers that you intend to use are activated, and depending on your operating system and installation approach, you may need to specify the necessary folders to run TauDEM, LAStools, and R. The next screenshot illustrates that each of the algorithms are activated and the necessary folders are specified:

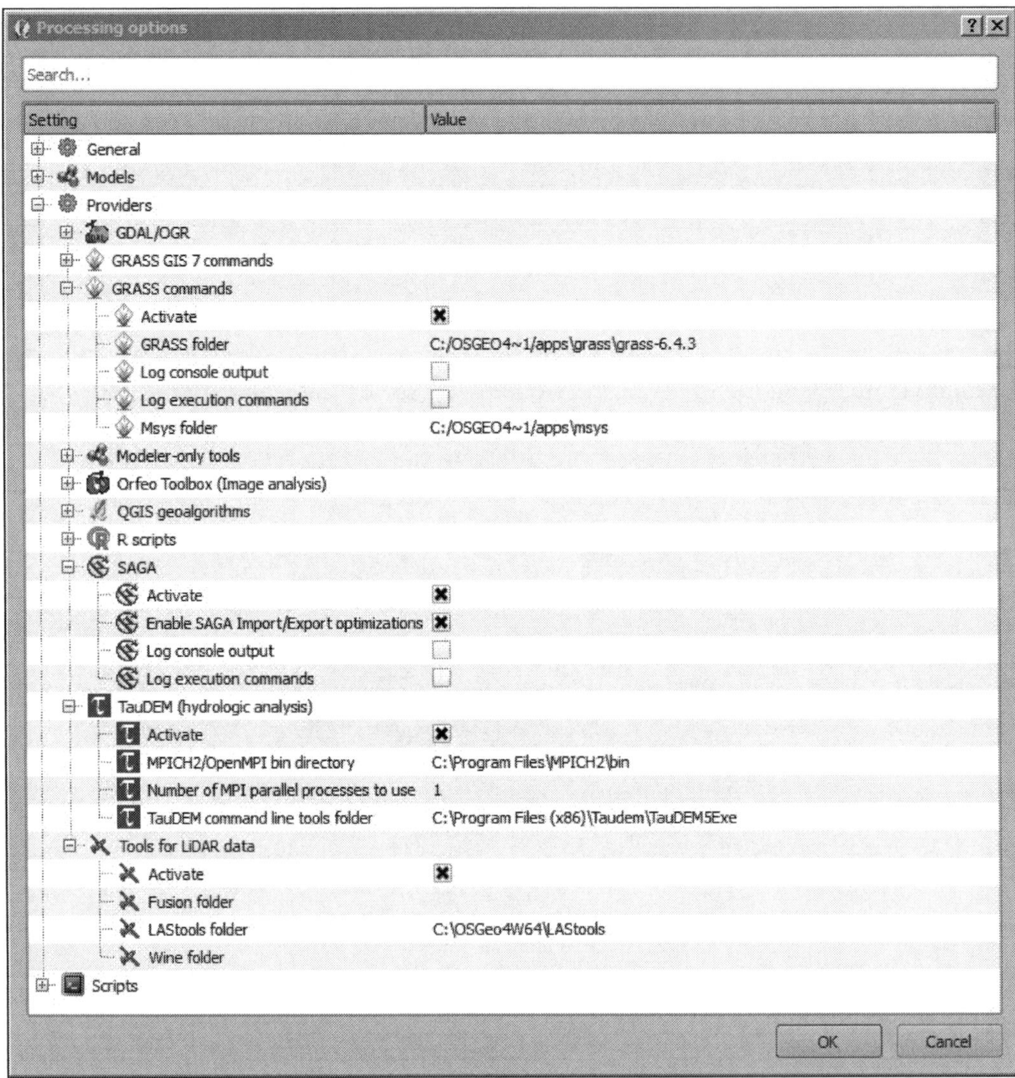

Once you click on **OK**, QGIS will update the list of algorithms accessible through the processing toolbox. The next section will provide you with an overview of the structure and organization of the toolbox interface.

Understanding the processing toolbox

In this section, we will explore the organization and establish a common language for describing the various components of the toolbox. Until this point, we haven't actually seen the interface itself. We merely configured and possibly installed the required dependencies to make the toolbox function. To view the toolbox, you need to click on **Toolbox** under **Processing**, as illustrated in this screenshot:

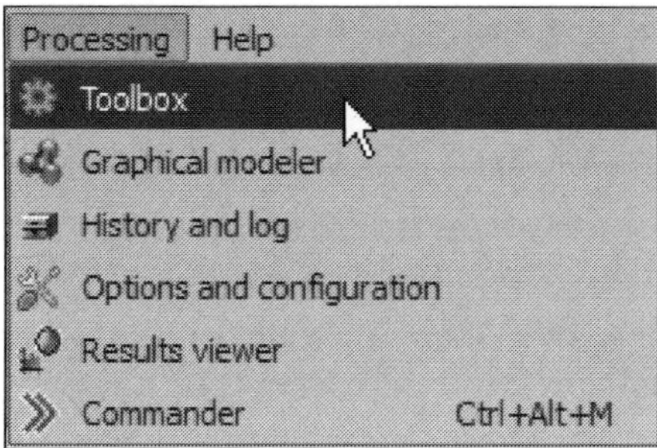

The processing toolbox will appear on the right-hand side of the QGIS interface; however, by default most algorithm providers are not visible. You need to click on the **Simplified interface** option that is visible in the next screenshot in the lower right-hand corner, which will then display the option to select the **Advanced interface** option:

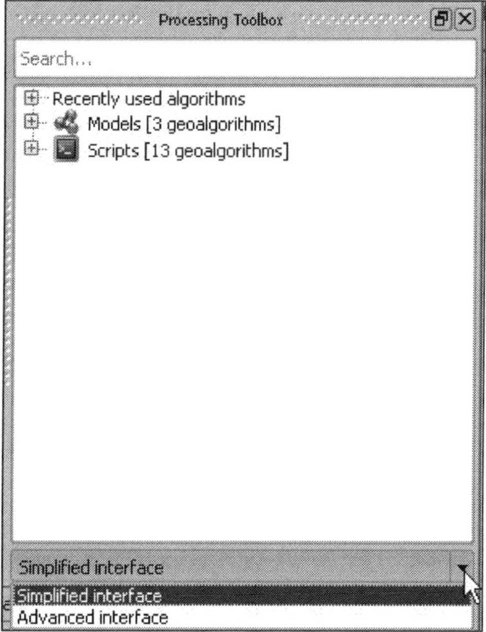

After selecting the **Advanced interface** option, you will finally have access to the full list of algorithms that the toolbox provides, as illustrated in this screenshot:

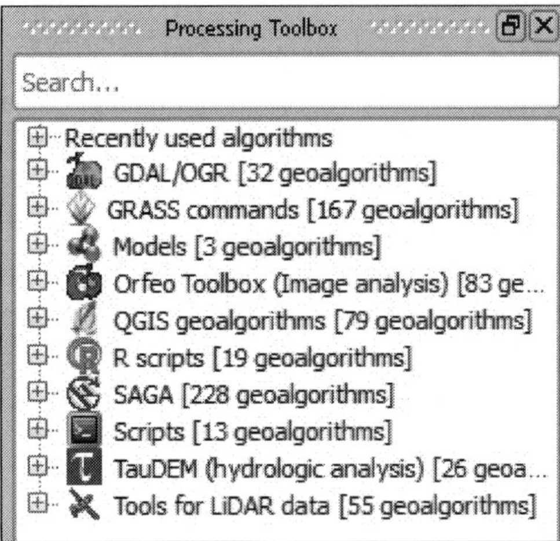

Initially, you will only see a list of the various providers and a summary of the total algorithms available from each provider. When you click on the **+** icon next to any of the entries, the list expands to reveal subdirectories that group related tools. In addition to manually navigating these directories, there is a search box at the top of the toolbox. So, if you are already familiar with these third-party packages or are looking for a specific tool, this may be a more efficient way to access the algorithms of interest.

You can search algorithms by topic

Even if you aren't familiar with the algorithm providers, you can still use the search box to explore what tools are available from multiple providers. For example, if you are interested in finding different ways to visualize or explore topographic relationships, you could search for it by typing "*topographic*" in the text box and discover that there are ten tools from three different providers that relate to topography!

To open any algorithm of interest, you just need to double-click on the name and the algorithm dialog interface will open. It looks similar to other tools that we have already used in QGIS. For example, click on the **+** icon next to the **GDAL/OGR** entry and double-click on **Aspect**. You will see the dialog interface as shown in the following screenshot:

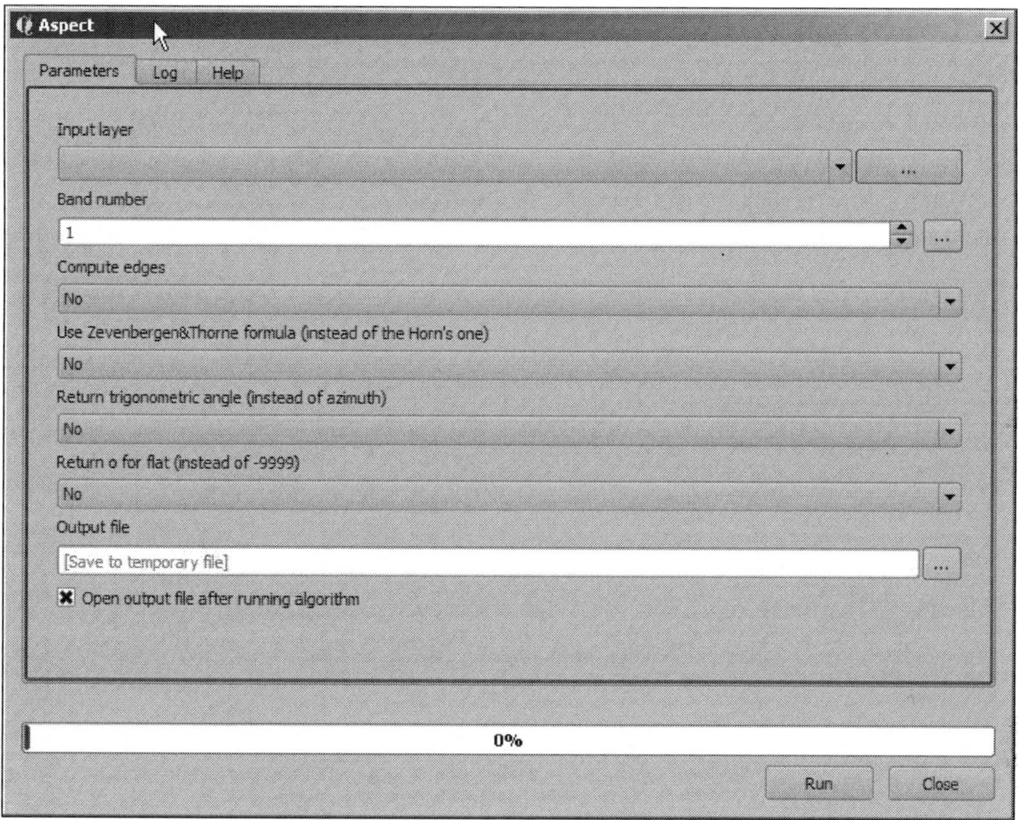

Any algorithm that you select will present you with a similar algorithm dialog box, so it is worth exploring the functionality of the interface. Similar to other tools that we have already used, clicking on any inverted black triangle will reveal drop-down options that will allow us to select an option that is passed to the algorithm. The dialog boxes within the processing toolbox also provide two additional tabs that may provide additional information. The **Log** tab will record the history of any operations performed using the tool, which is often useful for debugging errors, and the **Help** tab provides a brief summary of the functionality and explanation of the various options presented in the interface. However, if we click on the **Help** tab for the **Aspect** tool, we are presented with the message "Sorry, no help is available for this algorithm". This is not an uncommon experience; so, if the functionality or optional parameters are unclear, we need to visit the website of the algorithm provider.

You can explore the functionality of each of the algorithms that we are going to use in this section by going to the official website of each provider:

- **GRASS**: `http://grass.osgeo.org/`
- **SAGA**: `http://www.saga-gis.org/en/index.html`
- **TauDEM**: `http://hydrology.usu.edu/taudem/taudem5/`
- **LAStools**: `http://rapidlasso.com/LAStools/`

The processing toolbox also provides one additional option for accessing the underlying algorithms and that is through **processing commander**. To access this tool, click on **Commander** under **Processing** and you will be presented with an interface as shown in the following screenshot:

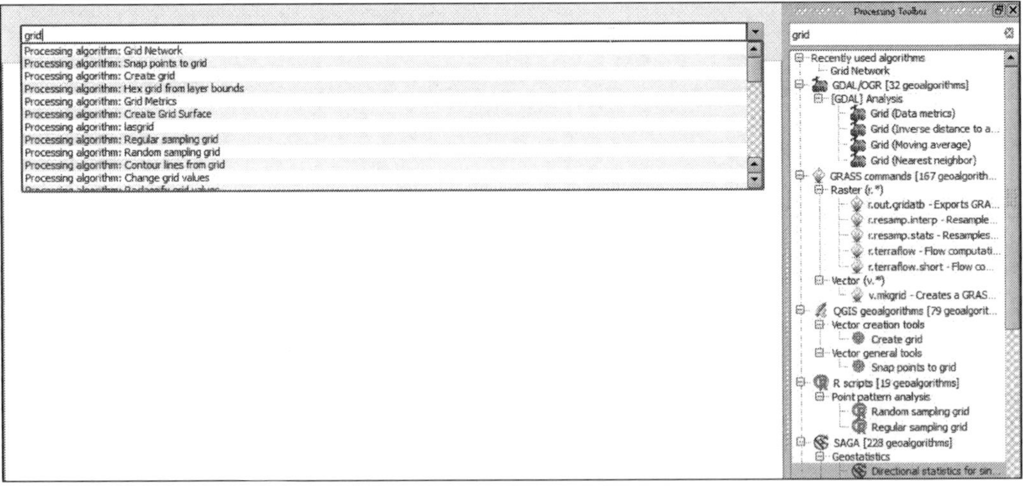

Notice that by typing "grid" in either the commander box or the search box, we are presented with a list of available algorithms. The primary difference between the two is that when a tool is selected in the commander drop-down list, it automatically opens. Therefore, once we develop a familiarity with the names of specific tools, the processing commander may increase workflow productivity.

Now that the QGIS processing toolbox is properly configured and we have a basic understanding of its overall functionality and organization, we can begin using it to utilize tools that weren't historically available within the QGIS environment. The intent with these exercises isn't to provide a comprehensive overview of all the providers or algorithms but to illustrate the power and flexibility that the toolbox brings to QGIS.

Using the processing toolbox

We will begin by using some of the GRASS algorithms and focusing primarily on tools that aren't available through default plugins or drop-down menus. For example, even though GRASS has the ability to calculate aspect, this functionality is already available in QGIS and it can be found by navigating to **Raster | Terrain Analysis**.

The original data used in this chapter can be obtained from these sources:

- `http://oe.oregonexplorer.info/craterlake//data.html`
- `http://www.mrlc.gov/`

Performing raster analyses with GRASS

The GRASS (short form for Geographical Resources Analysis Support System) environment represents one of the first available open source GIS options. It has a long history of providing powerful geospatial tools that were often overlooked because the GRASS interface and data organization requirements weren't as intuitive as other—often proprietary—options. The integration of GRASS algorithms within the processing toolbox provides access to these powerful tools within an intuitive GUI-based interface.

To explore the types of GRASS algorithms available through the toolbox, we will work through a series of hypothetical situations and perform the following analyses:

- Calculating a least-cost path across a landscape
- Evaluating a viewshed

Please make sure that you have downloaded, unzipped, and added the necessary data to QGIS and set the project CRS value to `EPSG: 26710`. We need to organize this data so that the elevation layer is at the bottom of the data layer panel as illustrated in the next screenshot:

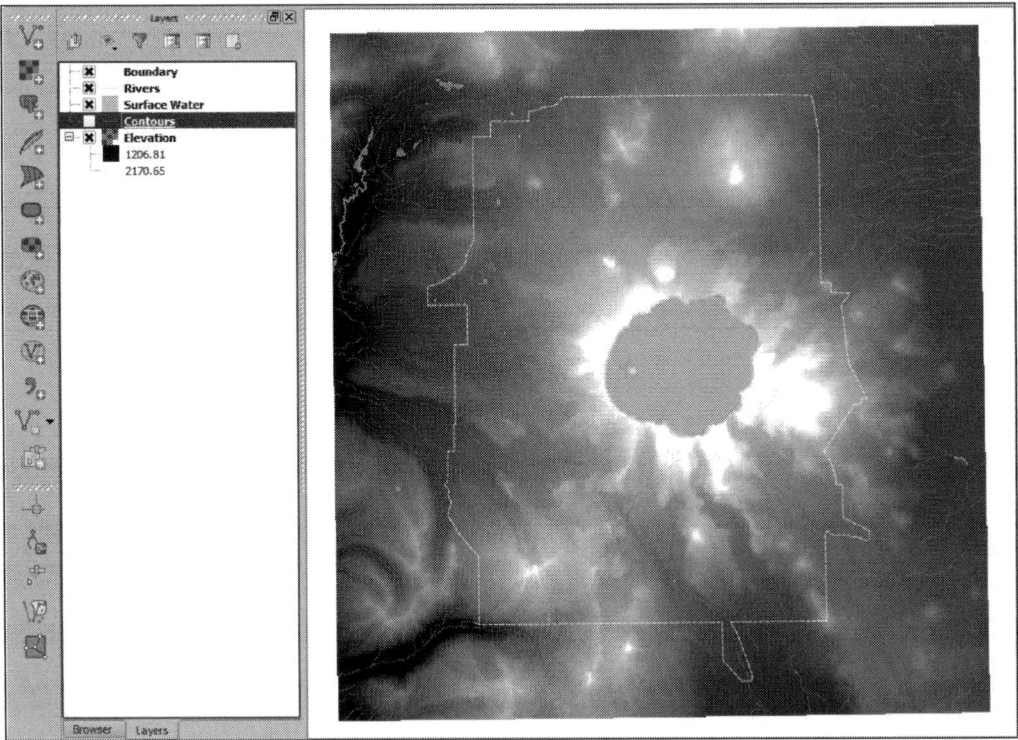

The ZIP folder contains the following files:

- Elevation file (`dems_10m.dem`)
- Boundary file (`crlabndyp.shp`)
- Surface water file (`hydp.shp`)
- Land use file (`lulc_clnp.tif`)
- Search and rescue office file (`Start.shp`)
- Injured hiker file (`End.shp`)
- Fire towers file (`towers.shp`

Calculating shaded relief

The basic requirement for many of the tools within the GRASS library is a **digital elevation model (DEM)** or **digital terrain model (DTM)**. However, since a DEM is a layer that contains continuous data representing elevation, when we load a DEM into QGIS, or any GIS for that matter, it has a flat appearance. Therefore, it is sometimes difficult to visually evaluate how topography might influence the results of our analyses.

So, our first foray into the GRASS library will make use of the **r.shaded.relief** tool to create a shaded relief map or hillshade, which can provide some topographic context for spatial analyses. Remember that you can access this algorithm by using the **processing commander**, **search bar**, or by navigating through the GRASS GIS commands list. Once the dialog box is open, we need to select the elevation layer of interest (in this case, the elevation layer). Leave all the default parameters the way they are (as illustrated in the next screenshot) and click on **Run**.

Changing the default save option

By default QGIS saves any new layer as a temporary file in memory. To save all your output files to a directory, you need to click on the small button containing three dots and specify the location where file needs to be saved.

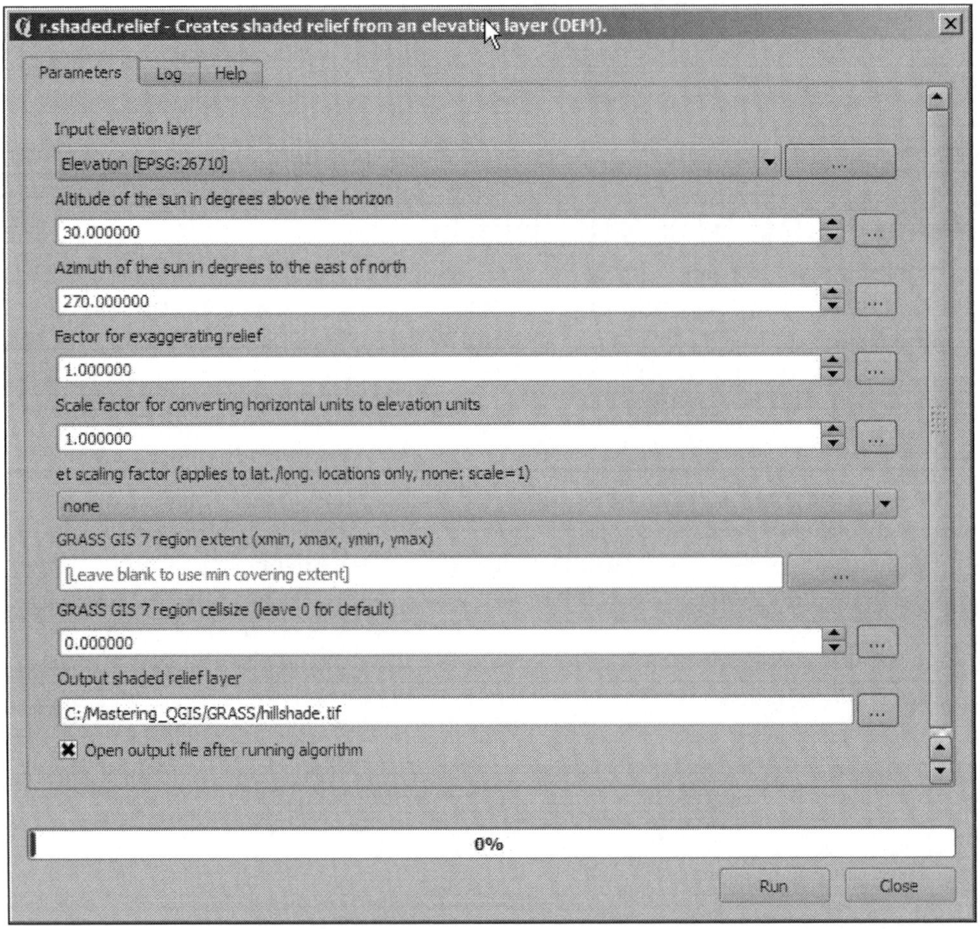

We could have easily used the built-in **Terrain Analyses** tools and executed the **Hillshade** tool by navigating to **Raster | Terrain Analyses**, but the decision to use GRASS was deliberate to illustrate that, more often than not, algorithms in the processing toolbox offer more optional parameters for better control over the resulting output. In this case, the output can be moved to the bottom of the data layer panel and the blending mode of the *elevation* layer can be set to `Darken`. The results of this blending operation are shown in the following screenshot:

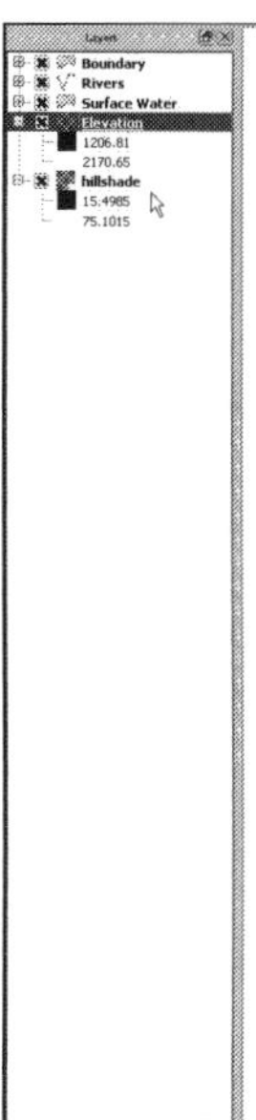

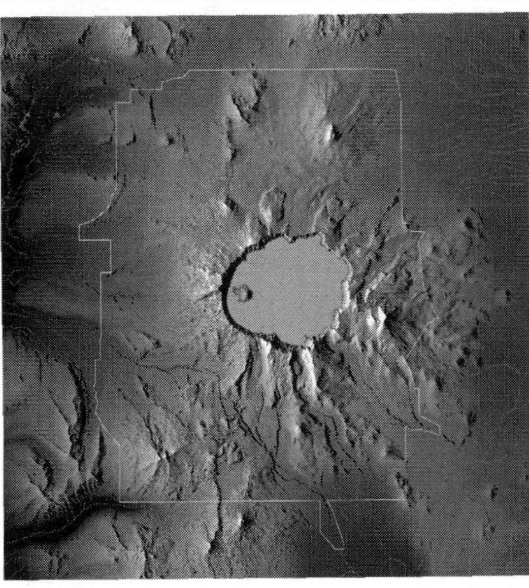

Although this tool would typically be considered more of a geoprocessing action than an analytical tool, this type of algorithm has been used to evaluate topographic shading at various times throughout a given year to estimate the persistence of snow and characterize potential habitat. If the intent is to merely show a visual and not perform any spatial analyses, remember (from *Chapter 3, Styling Raster and Vector Data*) that we can symbolize the elevation layer using colors rather than greyscale to better visualize changes in elevation.

Adjusting default algorithm settings for cartographic reasons

The default altitude and azimuth settings specify the position of the sun relative to the landscape, which isn't an unrealistic value for Crater Lake. However, it is possible to move the sun to an unrealistic position to achieve better contrast between topographic features.

For an extensive exploration of shaded relief techniques, visit `http://www.shadedrelief.com/`.

To calculate accurate azimuth and elevation values for varying latitudes, visit `http://www.esrl.noaa.gov/gmd/grad/solcalc/azel.html`.

Calculating the least-cost path

Least-cost path (LCP) analyses have been used to model historical trade routes and wildlife migration corridors, plan recreation and transportation networks, and maximize safe backcountry travel in avalanche-prone areas to name just a few applications. To perform a LCP analysis in QGIS, we are going to use a variety of tools from the processing toolbox and combine the resulting output from the tools.

Although there are numerous useful geoprocessing algorithms in the `GRASS` library, we are going to focus on more advanced spatial analyses that better demonstrate the analytical power residing in the processing toolbox. We are going to calculate a least-cost path for a hypothetical situation where a search and rescue team has been deployed to Crater Lake National Park to extract an injured hiker. The team may be able to use roads for part of their approach but would like to identify the least cost or the least rigorous approach to the hiker. Essentially, we are going to make some simplistic assumptions about how much effort will be required to move across the landscape by incorporating slope and land use into a raster layer representing the cost of movement. This cost layer will then be used to identify the least-cost path from the search and rescue office to the injured hiker.

In order to accomplish this analysis, we need to complete the following steps:

1. Calculate slope using **r.slope**.
2. Reclassify new slope raster using rules in `slope_recode.txt`.
3. Reclassify the land use raster using rules in `lulc_reclass.txt`.
4. Combine reclassified slope and land use layers.
5. Calculate cumulative cost raster using **r.cost**.
6. Calculate cost path using `least-cost paths`.

Calculating the slope using r.slope

The necessary settings for calculating slope are illustrated in the following screenshot:

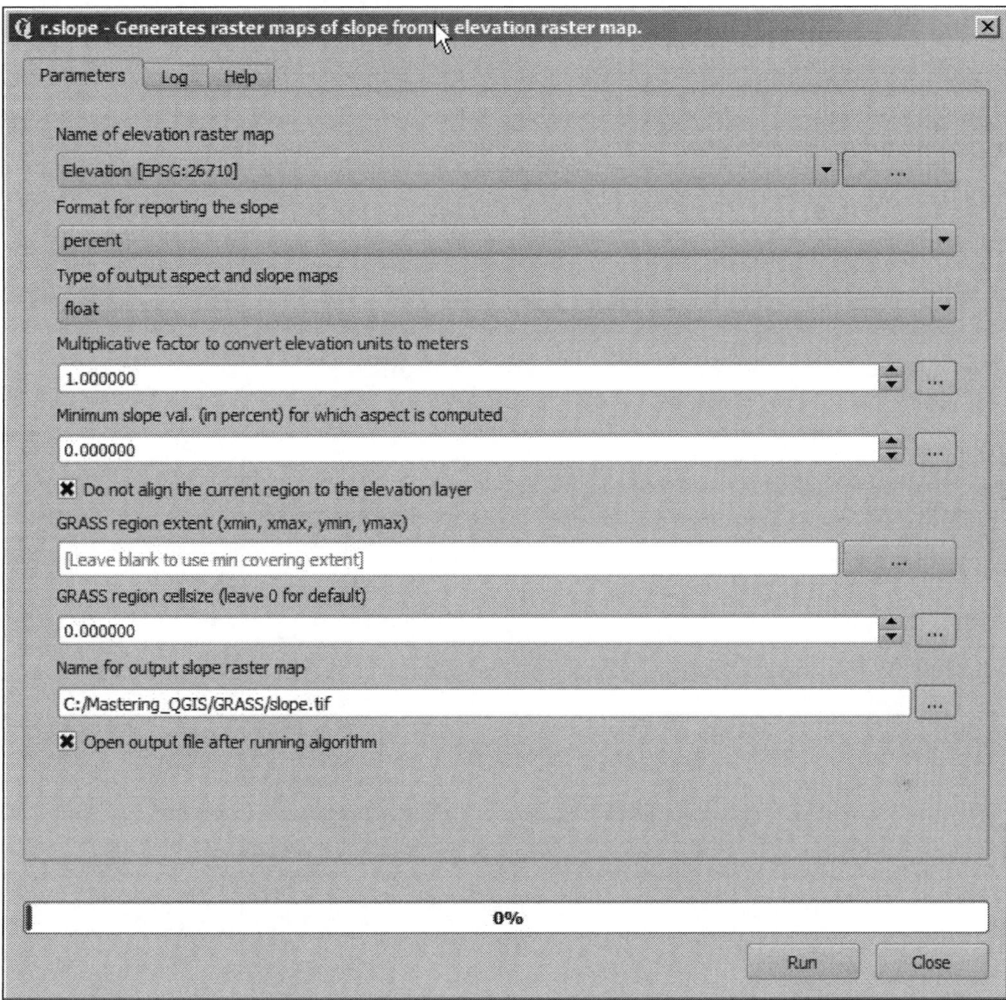

This dialog box indicates that slope is being calculated in percent, which will need to be reflected in the rule set used to reclassify this layer. Essentially, we are making the assumption that increasing slope values equate to increased physical exertion and thus inflicts a higher cost on members of the search and rescue team.

Reclassifying a new slope raster and the land use raster

To accomplish this, we are going to input the slope raster into **r.recode** and use the `slope_recode.txt` file to inform the tool how to reclassify the slope values. It is worth opening up the `slope_recode.txt` file to understand the GRASS formatting requirements and evaluate the assumptions within this reclassification scheme, which are also summarized in the following table:

Land use/Land class type	Land use/Land class code	Travel cost assumption	Recode value
Water	11	Highest cost	1000
Developed open land	21	Lowest cost	1
Developed low intensity	22	Lowest cost	1
Developed medium intensity	23	Lowest cost	5
Developed high intensity	24	Moderate cost	20
Barren land	31	Lowest cost	1
Deciduous forest	41	Moderate cost	20
Evergreen forest	42	Moderate cost	50
Mixed forest	43	Moderate cost	20
Shrub/scrub	52	Low cost	10
Grassland	71	Lowest cost	5
Pasture/hay	81	Lowest cost	5
Cultivated crops	82	Moderate cost	20
Woody wetlands	90	Highest cost	1000
Wetlands	95	Highest cost	1000

The following screenshot illustrates how to populate the **r.recode** algorithm:

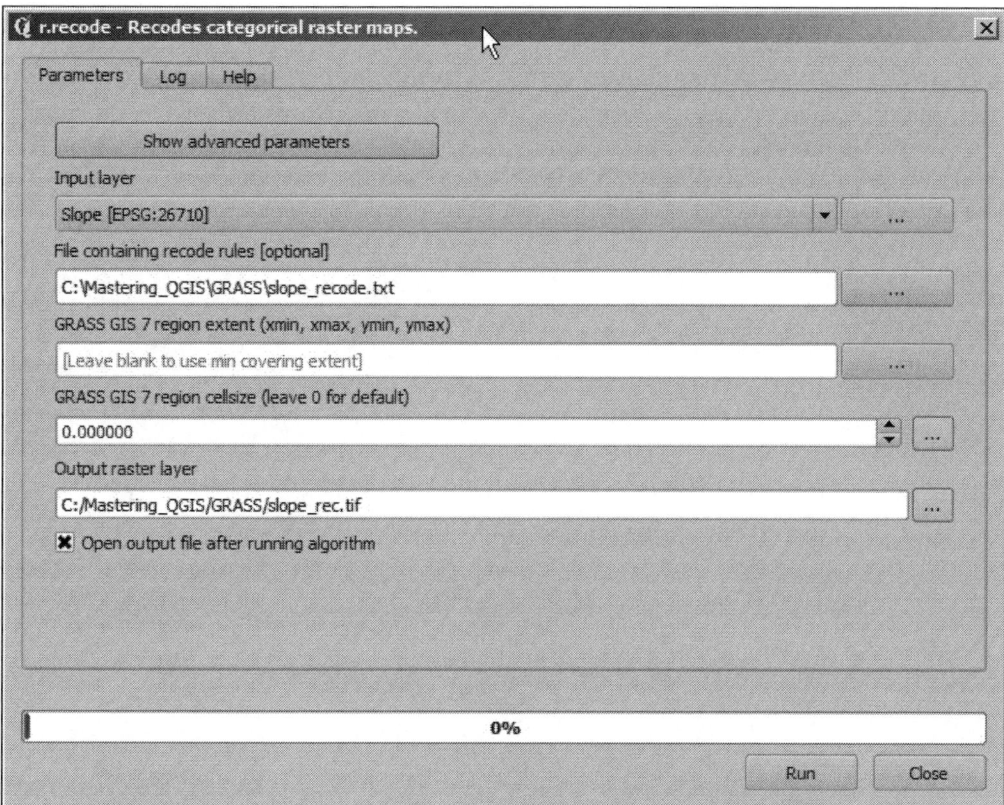

We need to use this same tool to recode the values of the provided land use layer using the `lulc_recode.txt` rule set. Again, it is worth exploring this file to evaluate the assumptions made about the costs for moving through each land use classification. For example, we have assumed that water has the highest cost and developed open space has the lowest cost. To properly explore this layer, you will need to import the `lulc_palette.qml` QGIS style file, which will categorize land use by name (for example, water, mixed forest, and so on).

Combining reclassified slope and land use layers

Once we have created both the slope and land use cost grids, we can combine them using the native QGIS **Raster calculator** tool to use with the **r.cost** algorithm. Since neither layer contains any zero values, which would need to be preserved through multiplication, we can combine them using addition as shown in the next screenshot. We could also use the **r.mapcalculator** tool to combine these layers, but this demonstrates how easy it is to move between native QGIS tools and those housed in the processing toolbox.

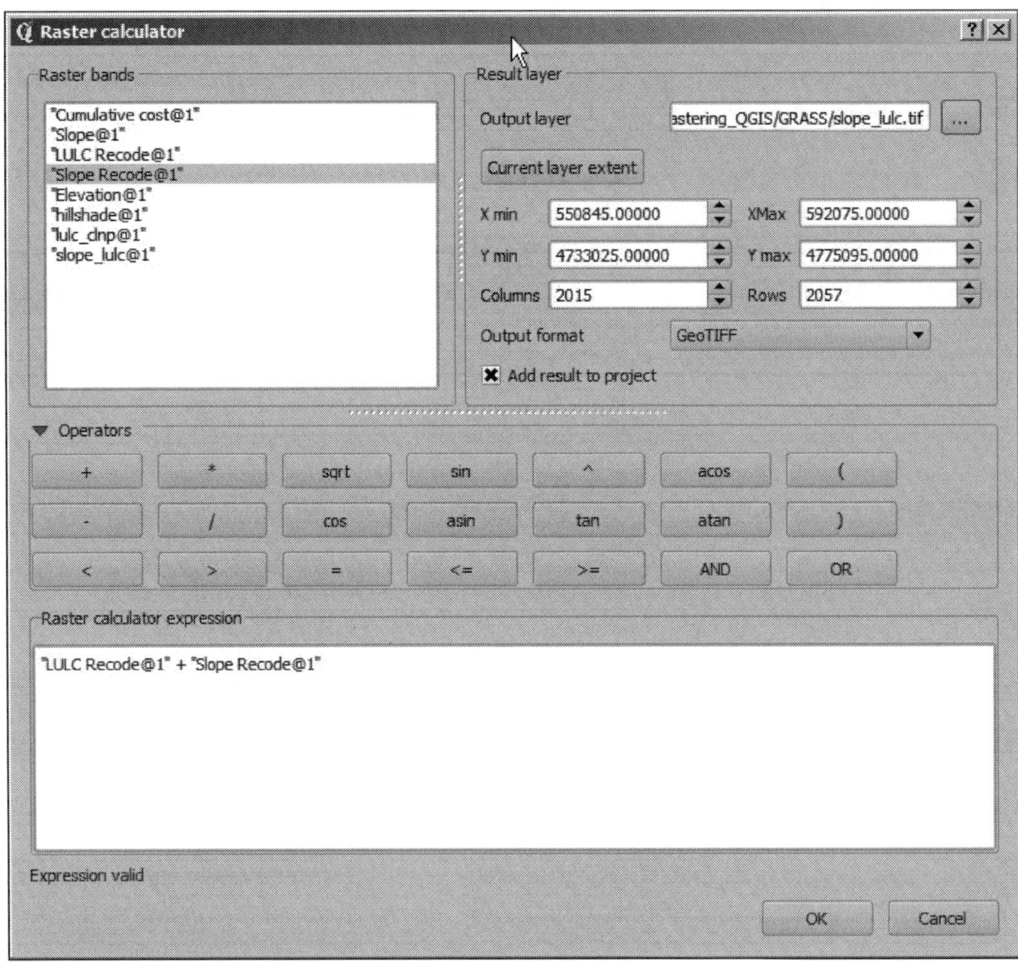

In this example, we used **r.cost** to create a new layer representing the cost of traveling across the landscape. If we know that the path will be traveled exclusively on foot, it may make more sense to use the **r.walk** algorithm available through the GRASS library. For more information about this, visit `http://grass.osgeo.org/grass63/manuals/r.cost.html`.

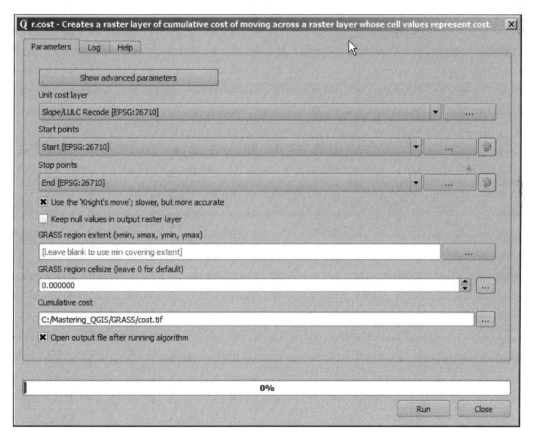

Calculating the cumulative cost raster using r.cost

To summarize our progress so far, we have reclassified the slope and land use layers and combined them so that we can now create a cost grid that can be used to evaluate the cost associated with moving between individual cells. This analysis requires two additional inputs, a starting and ending point that are provided as separate shapefiles, `Start.shp` and `End.shp`. These points serve as a guide for how the algorithm should characterize the cost of moving through an area of interest. The following screenshot illustrates how to populate the **r.cost** tool:

r.cost - Creates a raster layer of cumulative cost of moving across a raster layer whose cell values represent cost.
Parameters | Log | Help
Show advanced parameters
Unit cost layer
Slope/LULC Recode [EPSG:26710]
Start points
Start [EPSG:26710]
Stop points
End [EPSG:26710]
Use the 'Knight's move'; slower, but more accurate
Keep null values in output raster layer
GRASS region extent (xmin, xmax, ymin, ymax)
[Leave blank to use min covering extent]
GRASS region cellsize (leave 0 for default)
0.000000
Cumulative cost
C:/Mastering_QGIS/GRASS/cost.tif
Open output file after running algorithm
0%
Run | Close

Calculating the cost path using least-cost paths

This land use layer can now be used to calculate the least-cost path between each individual cell. To accomplish this, we are going to make use of a tool from the SAGA library, which is explored in more depth later in this chapter. This approach again demonstrates the flexibility of the processing toolbox and how easy it is to combine tools from various libraries to perform spatial analyses. We need to search the toolbox for least-cost paths and identify the relevant point (in this example, there will be only two point layers, so SAGA finds them by default), specify the cost grid, and then define an output for the resulting least-cost path as illustrated in the following screenshot:

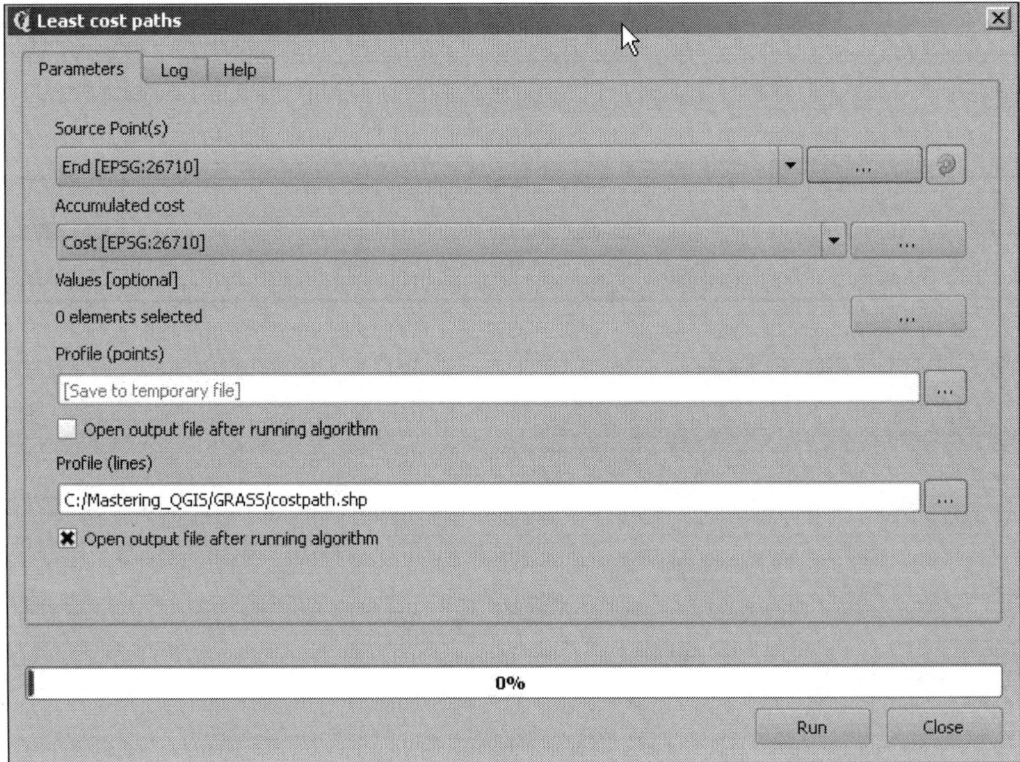

Now, we just need to organize the relevant layers, as shown in the next screenshot, to inform the Crater Lake search and rescue team about the least-cost approach to the injured hiker:

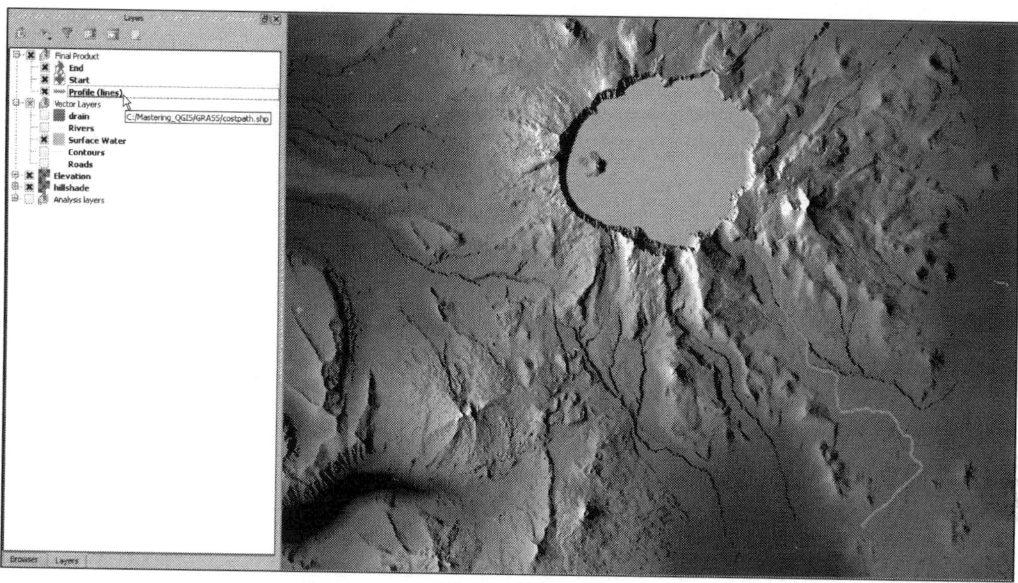

In this exercise, we made use of both GRASS and SAGA algorithms to calculate a least-cost path. These algorithms allowed us to calculate a hillshade and slope, reclassify raster layers, combine raster layers, create a cost grid, and calculate a least-cost path from this cost grid. Although this exercise was clearly hypothetical and limited in the number of parameters used to evaluate cumulative cost, it hopefully demonstrates how easy it is to perform this type of analysis. Least-cost path analyses have been used to model historical trade routes (Howey, 2007), wildlife migration corridors (Morato et al. 2014), plan recreation and transportation networks (Gurrutxaga and Saura, 2014), and maximize safe backcountry travel in avalanche prone areas (Balstrøm, 2002) to name just a few applications.

For more information please see the following references:

- *Howey, M. (2007). Using multi-criteria cost surface analysis to explore past regional landscapes: a case study of ritual activity and social interaction in Michigan, AD 1200–1600. Journal of Archaeological Science, 34(11): 1830-1846*
- *Morato, R. G., Ferraz, K. B., de Paula, R. C., & Campos, C. d. (2014). Identification of Priority Conservation Areas and Potential Corridors for Jaguars in the Caatinga Biome, Brazil. Plos ONE, 9(4), 1-11. doi:10.1371/journal.pone.0092950*
- *Gurrutxaga, M. and Saura, S. (2014) Prioritizing highway defragmentation locations for restoring landscape connectivity. Environmental Conservation, 41(2), 157-164. doi:10.1017/S0376892913000325*
- *Balstrøm, T. (2002). On identifying the most time-saving walking route in a trackless mountainous terrain, 102(1), 51-58. 10.1080/00167223.2002.10649465*

Evaluating a viewshed

Another advanced spatial analysis technique involves evaluating viewsheds to address the intervisibility between features or the potential visual impact of vertical structures such as wind turbines and radio or cell towers. This type of analysis is often incorporated into an environmental impact evaluation but the technique has other applications, such as evaluating which proposed viewing platform offers the greatest viewable area or determining how best to position observers during an aerial threat assessment. Although this tool has a specific niche application, working through this section will allow us to make use of additional algorithms that have broader applications.

We will begin by creating a new QGIS project and adding the following files:

- Elevation file (`dems_10m.dem`)
- Boundary file (`crlabndyp.shp`)
- Surface water file (`hydp.shp`)
- Fire towers file (`towers.shp`)

In this application, we are going to assume that the National Park Service has asked us to evaluate the visual impact of building three proposed fire towers. We need to perform a viewshed analysis and provide an estimate of the total area impacted within the park.

In order to accomplish this analysis, we need to complete the following steps:

1. Clip elevation to the boundary of the park using GDAL.
2. Calculate viewsheds for towers using **r.viewshed**.
3. Combine viewsheds using **r.mapcalculator**.
4. Calculate raster statistics using **r.stats**.

Clipping elevation to the boundary of a park using GDAL

To reinforce the concept that we can make use of a variety of algorithms within the processing toolbox to accomplish our analyses, we will use the clip raster by mask layer tool that is available through the GDAL/ORG algorithms. We will clip the elevation layer to the park boundary so that we save processing time by only evaluating the viewshed within the park. We can find this tool by typing `clip` in the search bar. The following screenshot illustrates how to set the parameters for this tool:

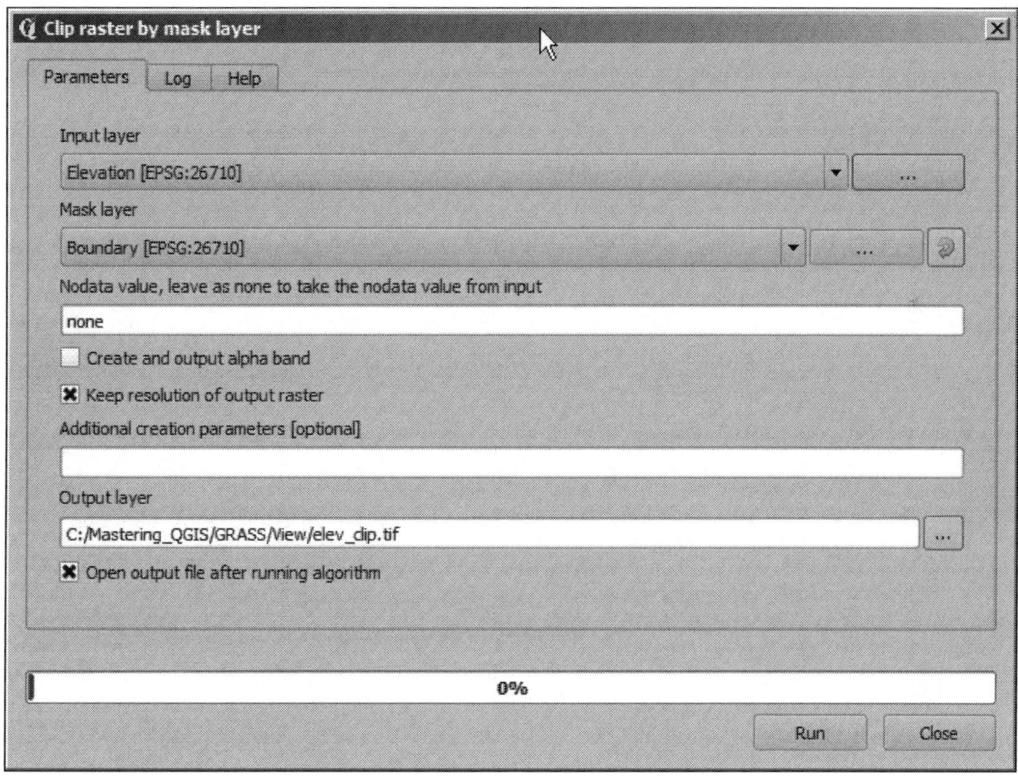

Calculating viewsheds for towers using r.viewshed

Once we have a clipped elevation layer, we can set the transparency of the value 0 to 100 percent in the transparency tab of the **Layer Properties** interface and begin the process of calculating the viewshed using the **r.viewshed** tool. If you open this tool using the processing commander or double-click on the entry within the toolbox, you will be presented with a dialog box that contains the option to enter a coordinate identifying the viewing position. However, we have three towers of interest, and although we could manually execute this tool three different times, most of the algorithms in the toolbox have the option to execute as batch process. By right-clicking on the tool, we can select this option as illustrated in the following screenshot:

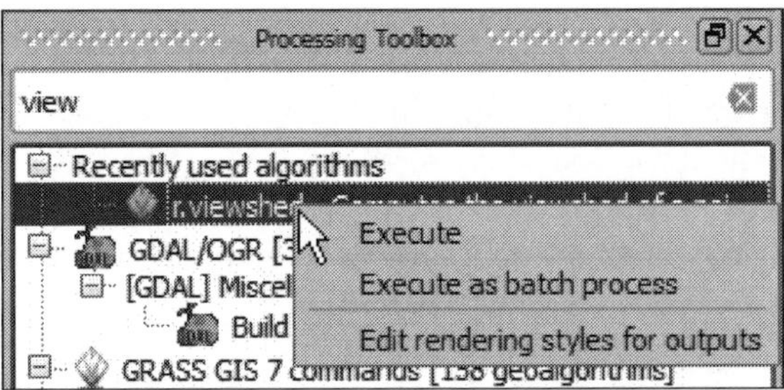

The resulting batch-processing interface allows us to enter the coordinates for all three towers and export a separate viewshed for each tower. The toolbox options can be set to the following values:

- **Elevation**: This is the elevation for the park
- **Coordinate identify viewing position**: This contains the coordinates for each tower
- **Viewing position height above ground**: This is the viewing position height, for example, `20`
- **Maximum distance from the viewing point**: This is the maximum distance from the viewing point, for example, `32000`
- **Consider Earth Curvature**: This contains a `Yes` value if Earth's curvature should be considered
- **GRASS GIS Region 7 extent**: This option is set to `default`
- **GRASS GIS 7 region cellsize**: This option is set to `0.0`
- **Output raster layer**: Set output names as `tower1, tower2, tower3`
- **Load in QGIS**: This option is set to `Yes` if viewshed loads in QGIS

If we had more than three towers, we could click on the **Add row** button at the bottom of the batch-processing interface.

We can begin entering the necessary parameters using the coordinates provided in the following table and the guidelines:

Tower number	Coordinates
1	574599.082827, 4749967.314004
2	580207.025953, 4752197.343687
3	571656.050455, 4750321.28697

It is worth exploring the rationale behind some of the input parameters. The first two are hopefully obvious: we need an elevation layer and observer points to evaluate viewshed for any assumptions. However, setting the position height above ground to 20 meters is an average value for typical fire towers. The maximum distance of 32,000 meters is the greatest distance between any of the towers and the edge of the park elevation layer, and including Earth's curvature—even for small areas—at worst increases processing time but provides a more accurate representation of visibility.

If you have a lot of observers, completely fill out the information for the first observer and after you set the **Output raster layer parameter**, you will be prompted to autofill the input boxes. If you select yes, the interface will automatically populate the parameters and you will only need to adjust the parameters that are different. For example, the coordinates will need to be updated, and perhaps not all observers have the same height.

The output from this algorithm will need to be renamed since they will all be added with the same name; fortunately, if you hover the mouse over each entry, QGIS will report the full path name, as illustrated in the following screenshot:

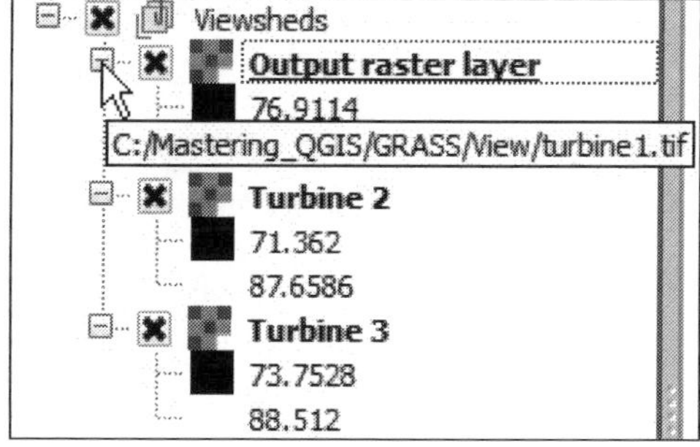

Combining viewsheds using r.mapcalculator

In order to evaluate the cumulative visual impact of all the three towers, we need to add them together. However, the algorithm outputs a grid that contains either a degree angle representing the vertical angle with respect to the observer or null values. If we attempt to add three layers that contain null values, the resulting output will not accurately reflect the total visible area within the park. To address this issue, we need to make use of the `isnull` function within **r.mapcalculator**. We will use this function within a conditional statement to identify where there are null values and replace them with a zero so that we can accurately combine all the three layers. We need to open **r.mapcalculator** and use this conditional statement:

```
if(isnull(A),0,1)+ if(isnull(B),0,10) + if(isnull(C),0,100)
```

The query that we are asking the calculator to execute is if layer A is null, then replace it with a value of zero, otherwise give the resulting grid a value of `1` and then add it to the results from the other three layers, which are also evaluated for null values. By replacing the original values with either 0, 1, 10, or 100, we are able to evaluate the total cumulative viewshed and also differentiate between the impacts of individual towers. The following screenshot illustrates how to ask these questions within the raster calculator:

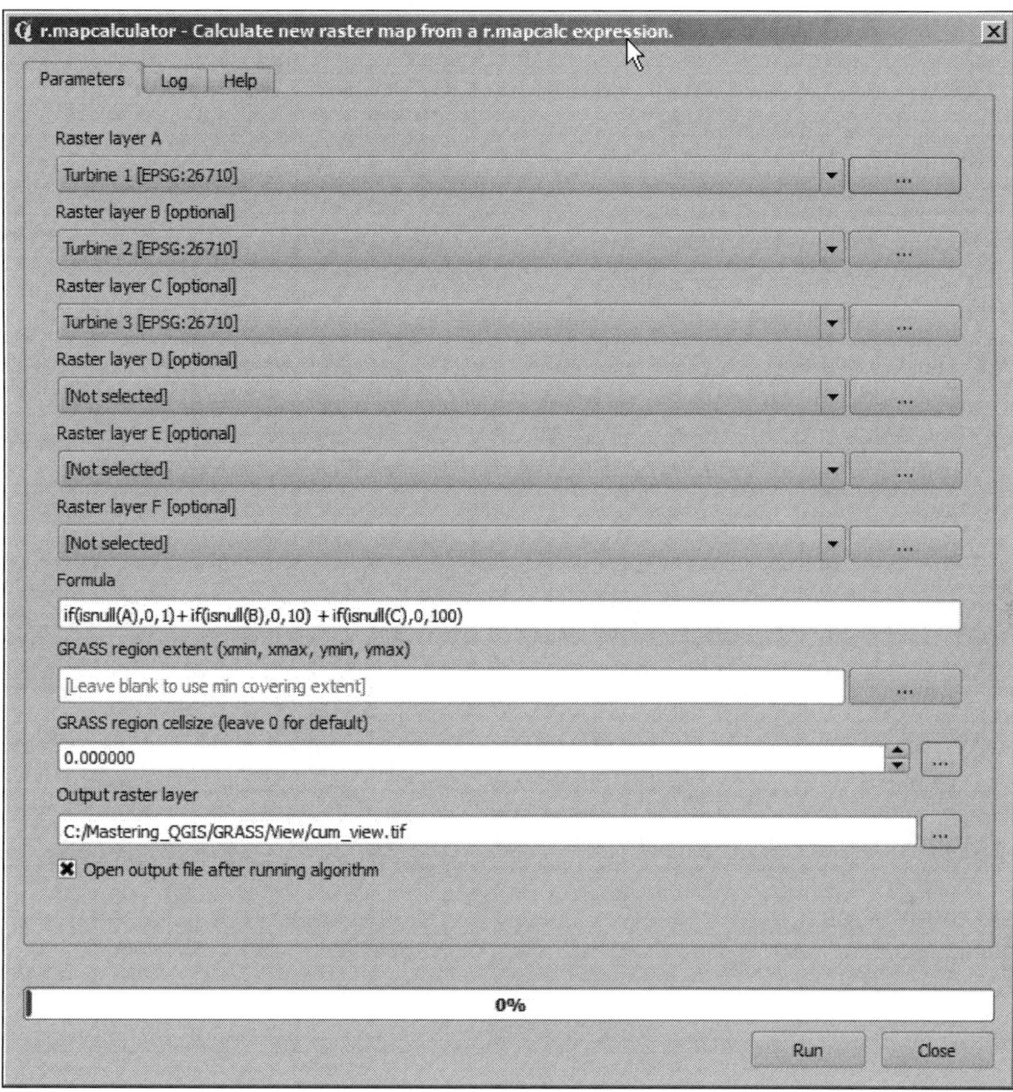
r.mapcalculator - Calculate new raster map from a r.mapcalc expression.
Parameters
Log
Help
Raster layer A
Turbine 1 [EPSG:26710]
Raster layer B [optional]
Turbine 2 [EPSG:26710]
Raster layer C [optional]
Turbine 3 [EPSG:26710]
Raster layer D [optional]
[Not selected]
Raster layer E [optional]
[Not selected]
Raster layer F [optional]
[Not selected]
Formula
if(isnull(A),0,1)+if(isnull(B),0,10) +if(isnull(C),0,100)
GRASS region extent (xmin, xmax, ymin, ymax)
[Leave blank to use min covering extent]
GRASS region cellsize (leave 0 for default)
0.000000
Output raster layer
C:/Mastering_QGIS/GRASS/View/cum_view.tif
Open output file after running algorithm
0%
Run
Close

The resulting output will contain values that can be used to interpret which towers contribute to the cumulative viewshed. These values are summarized in the following screenshot. To better visualize the cumulative viewshed within the park, you can load the `view_style.qml` layer and adjust the colors to your preference as follows:

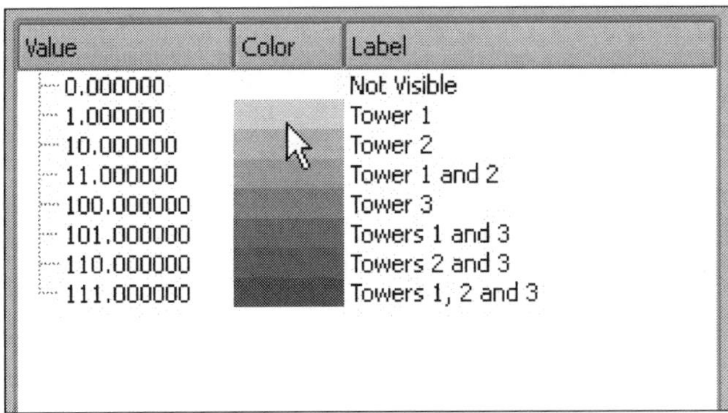

Value	Color	Label
0.000000		Not Visible
1.000000		Tower 1
10.000000		Tower 2
11.000000		Tower 1 and 2
100.000000		Tower 3
101.000000		Towers 1 and 3
110.000000		Towers 2 and 3
111.000000		Towers 1, 2 and 3

Calculating raster statistics using r.stats

To evaluate the total cumulative impact, we can use **r.stats** to summarize the number of pixels with these eight corresponding values. In the **r.stats** dialog, we need to select the cumulative viewshed as the input raster, make sure that the **Print area totals** and **Print Category labels** options are checked, and set an output filename. By default, the **One cell (range) per line** option is checked and we need to uncheck this option. The results of this algorithm will summarize the area in square meters by category. In this case, the categories are equal to the eight values in the previous screenshot. We can then sum the area for each combination to calculate the total visual impact of these three towers in Crater Lake National Park as follows:

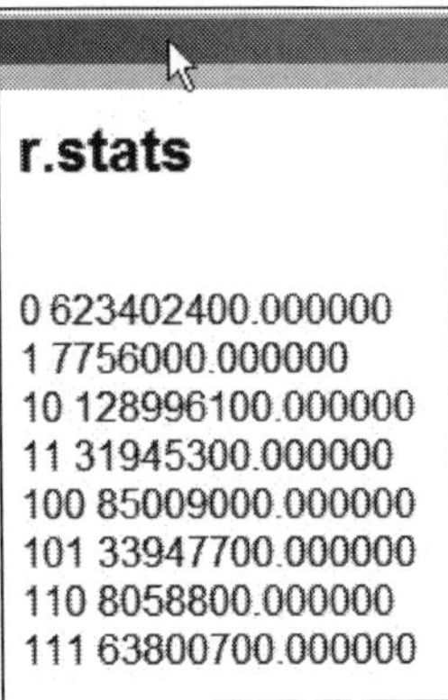

We can also provide a more informative visual depiction of the impact, as demonstrated in the next screenshot, using this approach, rather than the traditional binary visible/not-visible viewshed maps:

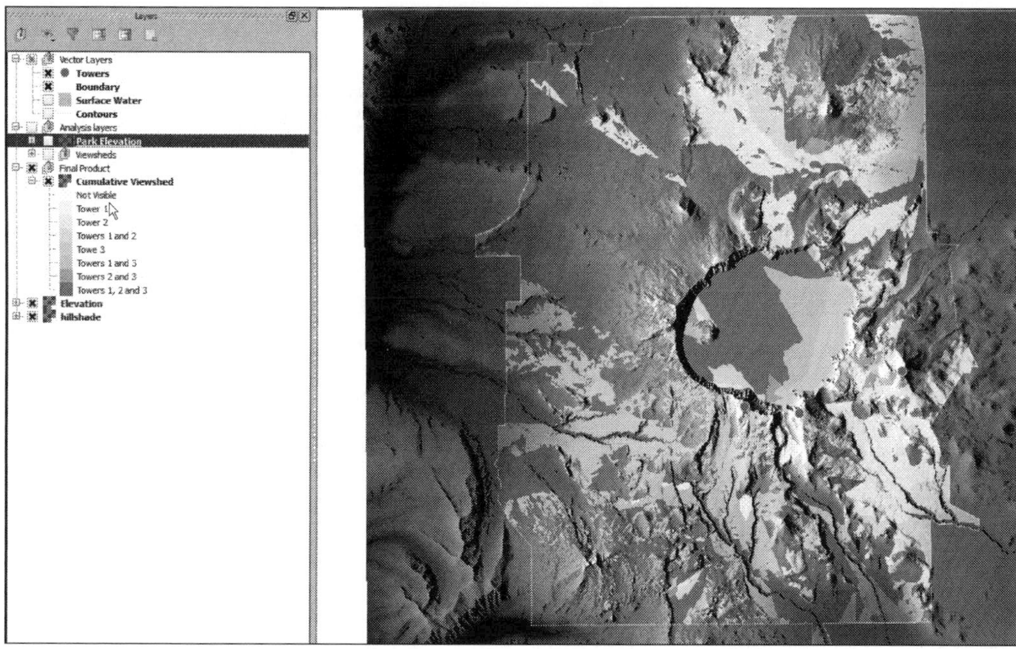

In this exercise, we used a variety of GRASS algorithms to explore the analytical power of the processing toolbox. We performed both common geoprocessing and advanced spatial analyses to arrive at hypothetical scenarios that would be time consuming to address without the support of a GIS; these analyses included the following:

- Creating a shaded relief map using **r.shaded.relief**
- Calculating slope using **r.slope**
- Reclassifying raster data using **r.recode**
- Creating a cost grid using **r.cost**

- Calculating a least-cost path using least-cost paths
- Calculating viewshed using **r.viewshed**
- Utilizing raster calculation functions within **r.mapcalculator**
- Summarizing raster attributes using **r.stats**

In the next section, we will continue exploring the types of analyses that are possible using the SAGA algorithms that are available through the toolbox.

SAGA

The SAGA (short form for System for Automated Geoscientific Automation) environment contains powerful tools, some of which have very specific applications; for example, geostatistical analyses and fire or erosion modeling. However, we will explore some of the SAGA tools that have broader applications and often dovetail nicely with tools from other providers. Similar to GRASS, integrating the SAGA algorithms within the processing toolbox provides access to powerful tools within a single interface.

To explore some of the SAGA algorithms available through the toolbox, we will work through a hypothetical situation and perform the analysis to evaluate the potential roosting habitat for the Northern Spotted Owl.

We are going to continue using data from the provided ZIP file, and we will need the following files:

- Elevation file (`dems_10m.dem` available in the `GRASS` data folder)
- Hillshade file (`hillshade.tif` created in the GRASS section)
- Boundary file (`crlabndyp.shp`)
- Surface water file (`hydp.shp`)
- Land use file (`lulc_clnp.tif` available in the `GRASS` data folder)

Evaluating a habitat

GIS has been used to evaluate potential habitat for a variety of flora and fauna in diverse geographic locations. Most of the habitats are more sophisticated than the approach we will take in this exercise, but the intention is to demonstrate the available tools as succinctly as possible. However, for simplicity's sake, we are going to assume that the resource management office of Crater Lake National Park has requested an analysis of potential habitat for the endangered Northern Spotted Owl. We are informed that the owls prefer to roost at higher elevations (approximately 1,800 meters and higher) in dense forest cover, and in close proximity to surface water (approximately 1,000 meters).

In order to accomplish this analysis, we need to complete the following steps:

1. Calculate elevation ranges using the SAGA **Raster calculator** tool.
2. Clip land use to the park boundary using **Clip grid** with **polygon**.
3. Query land use for only surface water using SAGA **Raster calculator**.
4. Find proximity to surface water using GDAL **Proximity**.
5. Query the proximity for 1,000 meters of water using GDAL **Raster calculator**.
6. Reclassify land use using the **Reclassify grid values** tool.
7. Combine raster layers using SAGA **Raster calculator**.

Calculating elevation ranges using the SAGA Raster calculator

There are multiple ways to create a layer that represents elevation ranges or, in this case, elevation zones that relate to potential habitat. One method would be to use **r.recode** as we did in the GRASS exercise; another would be to use the **Reclassify grid values** tool provided by SAGA, which we will use later in this exercise; but, another very quick way is to only identify the areas above a certain elevation—in this case, greater than 1,800 meters—using a raster calculator. This type of query will produce a layer with a binary level of measurement, meaning the query is either true or false. To execute the raster calculator, select the layer representing elevation only in the park, enter the formula `gt(a, 1800)`, name the output file, and click on **OK**.

The syntax we entered in the formula box tells the SAGA algorithm to look at the first grid—in this case a—and if it has a value greater than (`gt`) 1,800 meters, the new grid value should be one, otherwise it should be zero. The following screenshot illustrates how this appears in the SAGA **Raster calculator** window. We could have also used the native QGIS **Raster calculator** tool. So, the intent here is to demonstrate that there are numerous tools at our disposal in QGIS that often perform similar functions. However, the syntax is slightly different between the QGIS, GRASS, and SAGA raster calculators; so, it is important to check the **Help** tab before executing each of the tools.

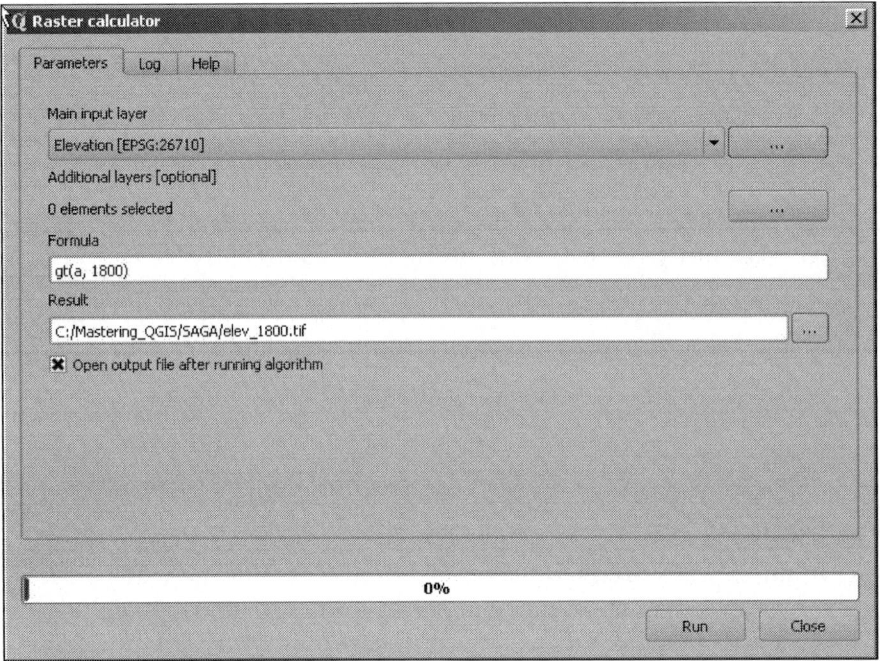

Clipping land use to the park boundary using Clip grid with polygon

After executing this tool, we will be presented with a new raster layer that identifies the elevations above 1,800 meters with a value of `1` and all other values with a value of `0`. The next step is to clip the land use layer using the SAGA **Clip grid with polygon** tool. If you remember, we clipped a raster layer in a previous exercise using the native **GDAL Clipper** tool, so again this is merely demonstrating the number of options we have to perform spatial operations.

We need to select land use (`lulc_clnp`) as our **input's** raster layer, the park boundary as our **polygon's** layer, name the output file as `lulc_clip.tif`, and click on **OK**. Remember from an earlier exercise that you can load the `lulc_palette.qml` file if you would like to properly symbolize the land use layer, but this step isn't necessary.

Querying land use for only surface water using the SAGA Raster calculator

Now, we can query this layer for the areas that represent surface water. We can again use the SAGA **Raster calculator** tool and enter `(a, 11)` in the **Formula** box, as illustrated in the next screenshot. In this example, we are stating that if the land use layer (that is `a`) is equal to 11, the resulting output value will be 1, otherwise it will be 0.

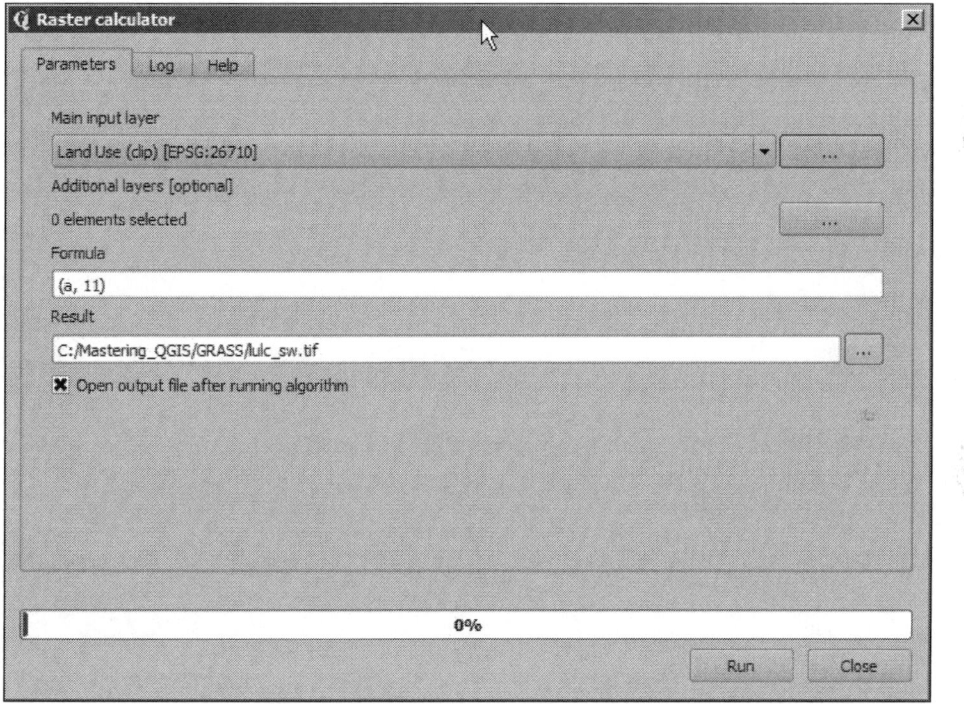

Now, we have a raster layer that we can use to identify potential habitat within 1,000 meters of surface water.

Finding proximity to surface water using GDAL Proximity

To accomplish this, we need need to create a layer representing proximity to surface water and query that layer for areas within 1,000 meters of any surface water. Our first step is to execute the GDAL **Proximity (raster distance)** tool in the processing toolbox. We need to select the binary (true or false) layer representing surface water (`lulc_sw.tif`), set the **Values** field to `1`, leave the **Dist units** field as **GEO**, change the **Output raster type** to **Int32**, leave all the other defaults as they are, and name the output layer as illustrated in the next screenshot:

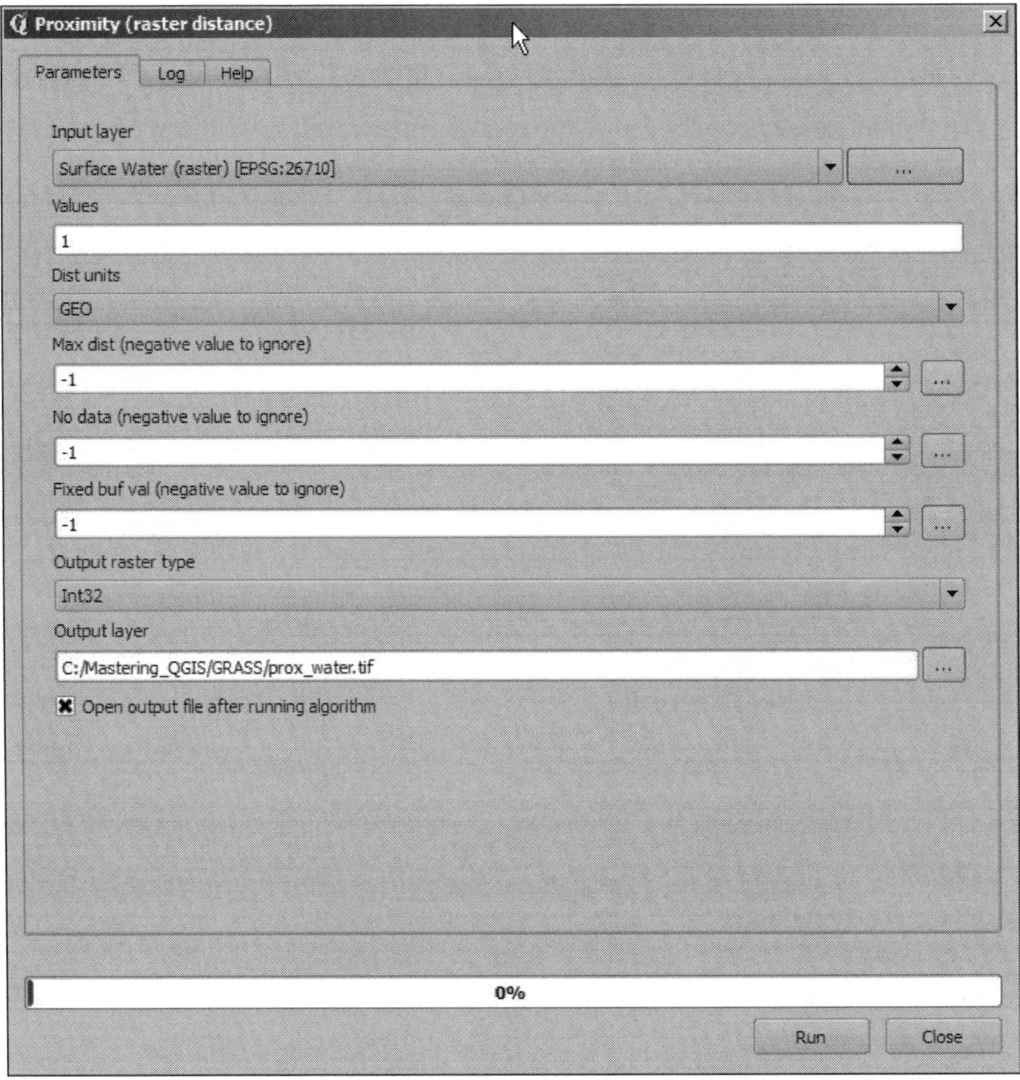

The rationale for setting **Values** to `1` and **Dist units** to **GEO** is that we are asking the algorithm to assume that the distance is measured in increments of 1 based on the geographic distance—in this case meters—and not on the number of pixels. We can now query the resulting grid for the area that is within 1,000 meters of surface water, but it is important to recognize that we want to identify the areas that are less than 1,000 meters of surface water but greater than 0. If we just query for values less than 1,000 meters, we will produce an output that will suggest that the roosting habitat exists within bodies of water.

Querying the proximity for 1,000 meters of water using the GDAL Raster calculator

The easiest way to perform this query is by using the native QGIS **Raster calculator** tool by clicking on **Raster Calculator** under **Raster**. The following screenshot illustrates how to enter the `"Proximity to Water@1" > 0 AND "Proximity to Water@1" <= 1000` syntax to identify a range between 0 and 1,000 meters:

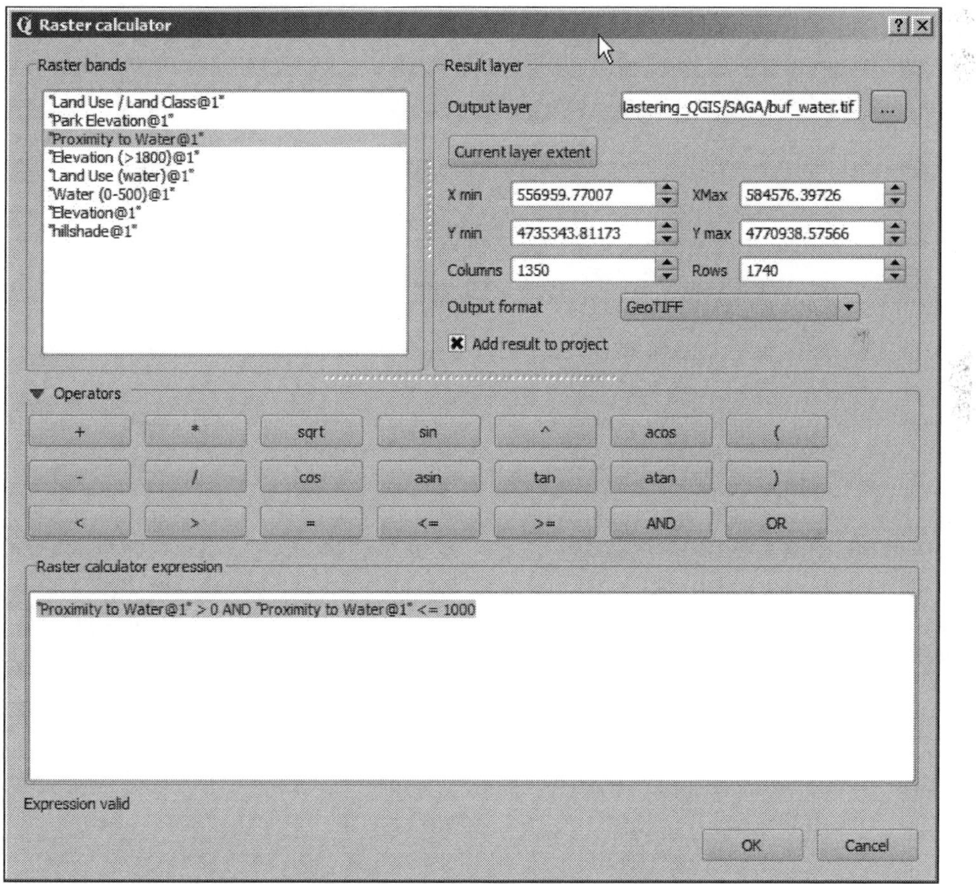

The resulting output will contain the values of 0 and 1, where 1 represents the cells that are within 1,000 meters of surface water and 0 represents those that are beyond 1,000 meters. The next screenshot illustrates what this layer looks like after you set the value of zero to transparent and the buffer itself to red:

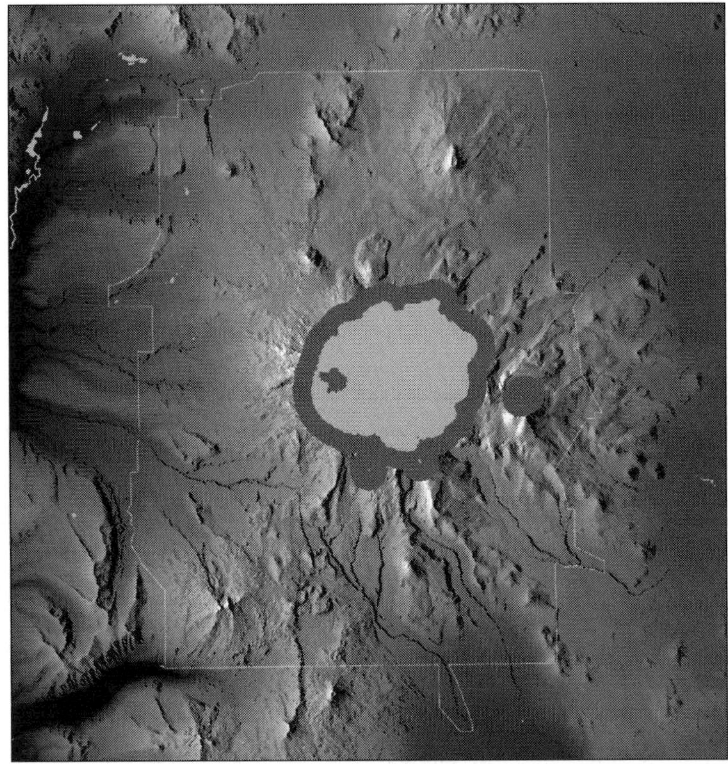

The last habitat variable that we need to evaluate is the preference towards roosting in dense forest cover. We are going to reclassify or recode the land use layer assuming that the owls will make use of three primary classes that are deciduous, evergreen, and mixed forest types in decreasing preference. This means that we are going to use a simple ordinal ranking scheme to assign a new value of 3 to grid cells that represent evergreen forest, a value of 2 for shrub cover, a value of 0 for water, and a value of 1 for the remaining land types. We could assume zero for all other cover types, but owls are unpredictable.

Reclassifying land use using the Reclassify grid values tool

To accomplish this, we could use **r.recode** as we did in a previous exercise, but instead, we are going to use the SAGA **Reclassify grid values** tool. The advantage of this tool is that we can enter our reclassification rules directly in the tool interface, rather than reading them into the algorithm from a separate file. The following screenshot provides the necessary values to reclassify the land use layer where `11` represents surface water, `42` represents evergreen forest, `52` represents shrub cover, and all other values are equal to `1`:

Fixed Table

minimum	maximum	new
0	11	1
11	12	0
12	42	1
42	43	3
43	52	1
52	53	2
53	255	1

Add row
Remove row
OK
Cancel

If your version of QGIS doesn't allow you to add or remove rows, remember that you can also use the GRASS **r.recode** tool after creating a recode rule file. This might be a good exercise to work through to make sure you understand the formatting requirements for GRASS recode rule files. For a more in-depth explanation, visit `http://grass.osgeo.org/grass65/manuals/r.recode.html`.

To use the SAGA **Reclassify grid values** tool, we need to provide an input grid, which in this case is the clipped land use layer (`lulc_clip.tif`), and set **Method** to `[2] simple table`. The values that need to be reclassified (shown in the previous screenshot) can be entered by clicking on the **Fixed table 3x3** button. Make sure you provide a name for the new reclassified grid, for example, `lulc_rec.tif`.

Combining raster layers using the SAGA Raster calculator

Now, we have all the necessary layers to finalize our simplistic model of Northern Spotted Owl habitat. Since we have zero values that need to be preserved, that is, places where owls will never roost, we will multiply the three layers together using the SAGA **Raster calculator** tool. The next screenshot illustrates how to populate the raster calculator by selecting the reclassified elevation layer (`elev_1800.tif`) as the main input layer and the reclassified water proximity (`buf_water.tif`) and land use (`lulc_rec.tif`) layers as the two additional reclassified layers:

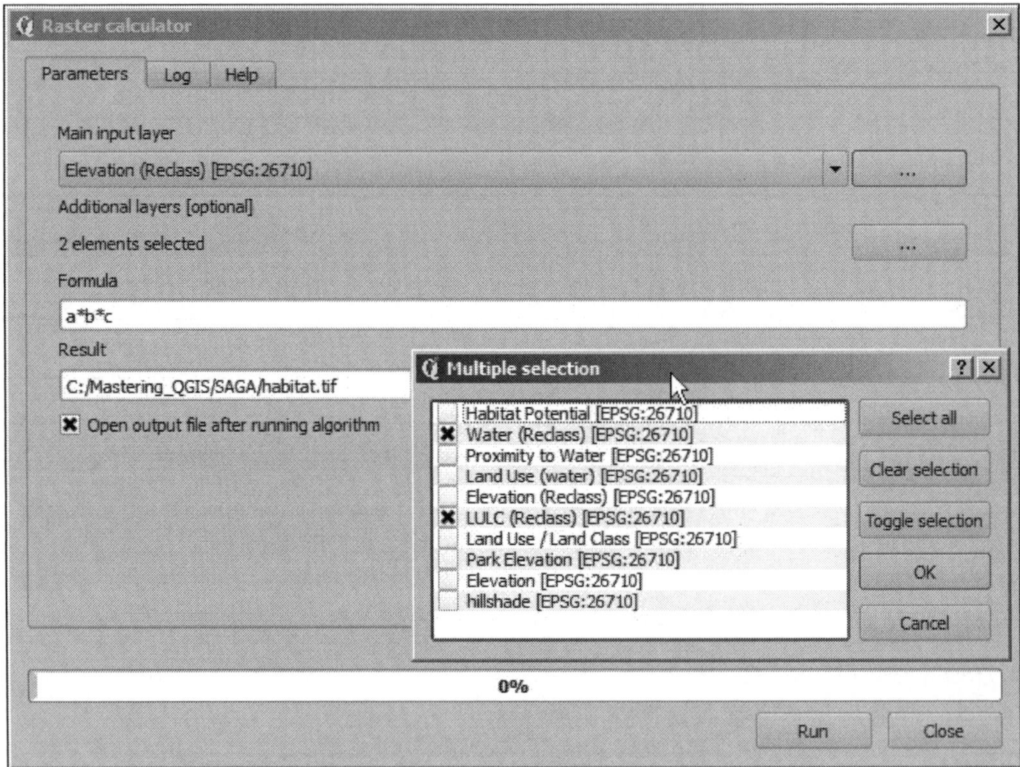

We could have used the native GDAL **Raster calculator** tool or the GRASS **r.mapcalculator** tool, but once again, this demonstrates how easy it is to switch between the various toolbox options. Similar to the GRASS syntax, the SAGA algorithm identifies the inputs in the order they are selected as a, b, and c. To ensure that we understand the values reported in the resulting output from this calculation, we need to remember the reclassified water and elevation layers are binary, so it will have the values of 0 and 1, while the reclassified land use layer contains the values from 0 to 3. Therefore, the new layer can only contain values of from 0 to 3 where 0 indicates no habitat, 1 indicates poor habitat potential, 2 indicates moderate habitat potential, and 3 indicates good habitat potential, as illustrated in the next screenshot:

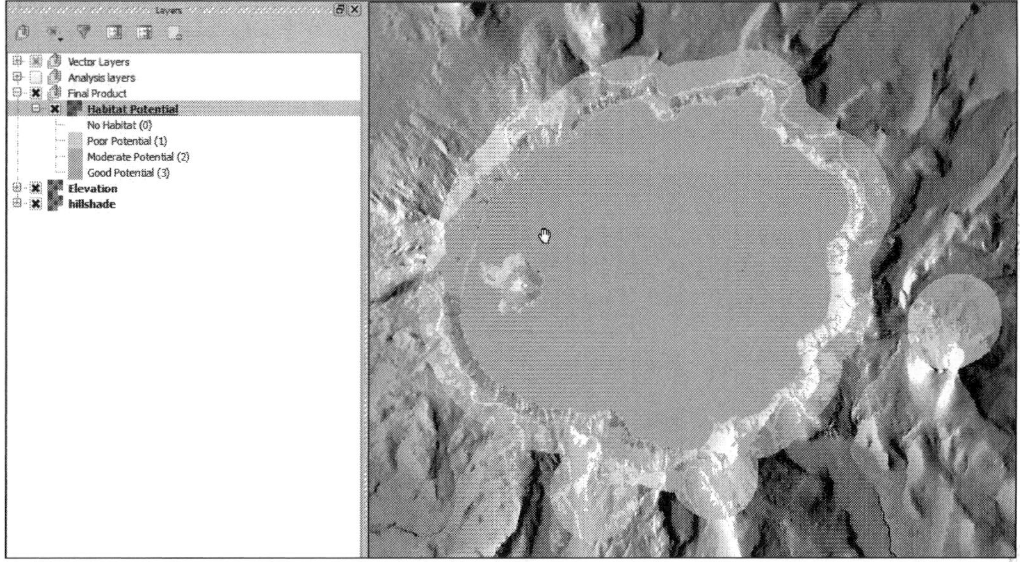

Hopefully, it is clear that this is a very simple model with many assumptions that any ornithologist who actually studies the Northern Spotted Owl would not actually use to evaluate habitat. However, the various tools and general approach that has been taken to evaluate this hypothetical scenario could be applied by paying more rigorous attention to the underlying assumptions about the variables that influence potential habitat. The goals of working through this type of analysis were threefold: to showcase a variety of useful SAGA algorithms, to demonstrate that there are similar tools with subtle differences that are available through the toolbox, and to illustrate how easy it is to switch between native QGIS tools and those found in the toolbox.

Exploring hydrologic analyses with TauDEM

The TauDEM (short form for Terrain Analysis Using Digital Elevation Models) environment contains a suite of tools with a specific emphasis on hydrologic and surface flow analysis. GRASS and SAGA also contain some algorithms that calculate similar parameters, but TauDEM has a comprehensive suite of tools in a single location.

We are going to continue using data from the provided ZIP file, and we will need the following files:

- Elevation file (`dems_10m.dem`, available in the `GRASS` data folder)
- Gauge shapefile (`gauge.shp`)
- Rivers file (`hydl.shp`)

To explore the functionality of TauDEM, we will characterize the watershed of Sun Creek upstream to the town of Fort Klamath, California. To accomplish this, we will perform the following tasks:

1. Remove pits from the DEM.
2. Calculate flow directions across the landscape.
3. Calculate the upstream area above Fort Klamath.

4. Calculate a stream network raster grid.
5. Create a watershed-specific vector stream network.

Reminder about installing TauDEM

Using TauDEM requires you to carefully follow the instructions for your particular operating system, as described at `http://docs.qgis.org/2.6/uk/docs/user_manual/processing/3rdParty.html`. This particular library is easier to install and run on Windows and Linux than Mac OS X.

TauDEM requires the initial input to be a `.tif` file rather than the `.dem` file that we used throughout this chapter. So, our first task is to export our original Crater Lake elevation layer to a `.tif` file. We can accomplish this by right-clicking on the DEM and clicking on **Save As**. By default, QGIS offers GTiff as the export option. We just need to specify a new output file and we can begin using the TauDEM tools.

Reminder about accessing additional libraries

Remember that in order to access any of the algorithms available through additional providers, we need to make sure that the processing toolbox is set to the **Advanced Interface**.

Removing pits from the DEM

Before using any hydrologic algorithms, regardless of the algorithm provider, we need to make sure that the DEM is hydrologically corrected. This means that we need to ensure that it behaves like the natural landscape where surface flow moves across the landscape and does not get trapped in pits, or depressions, in the DEM. To accomplish this, we are going to use the **Pit Remove** tool on our new DEM file as illustrated in the next screenshot.

Note that the DEM won't necessarily look any different, but the cells will behave in a more appropriate fashion for modeling surface flow.

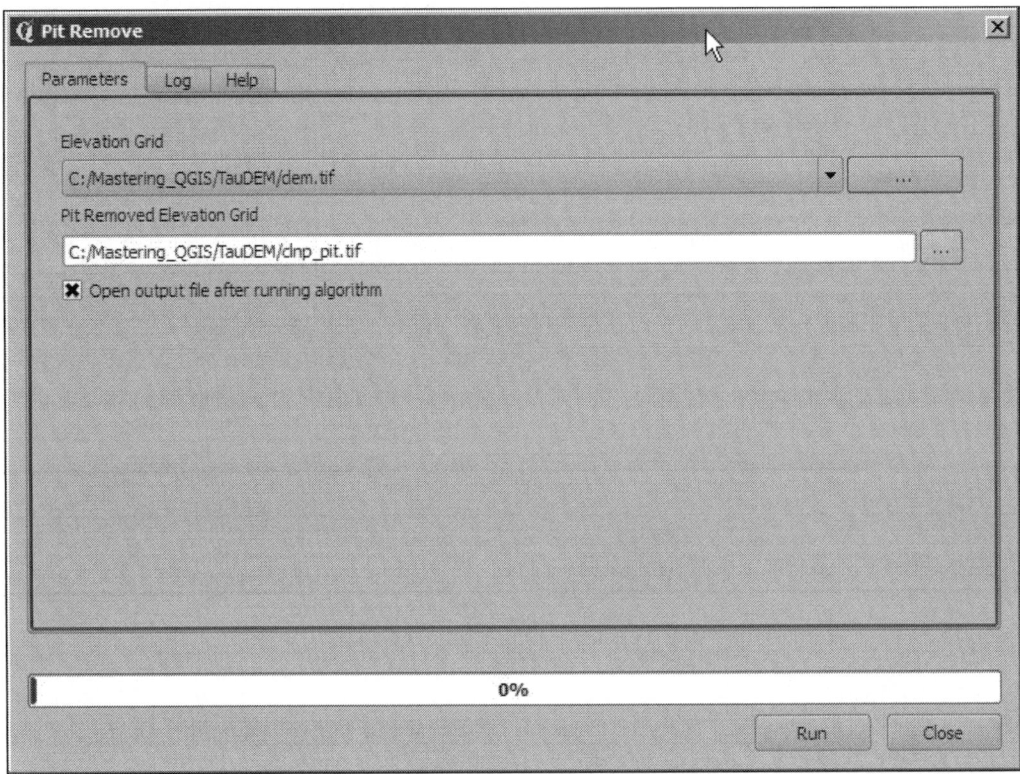

Calculating flow directions across the landscape

This is the elevation grid that we will use to perform the remaining calculations. Our next step is to use the **D8 Flow Directions** tool that creates two grids: a D8 flow direction grid, which calculates what direction the data would flow in each grid cell, and a D8 slope grid, which calculates a slope value for each grid cell. For illustration purposes, we are only going to use the D8 tools, but there are additional options for using the D-Infinity algorithms. The next screenshot illustrates how to populate this tool with the new pitremoved elevation layer:

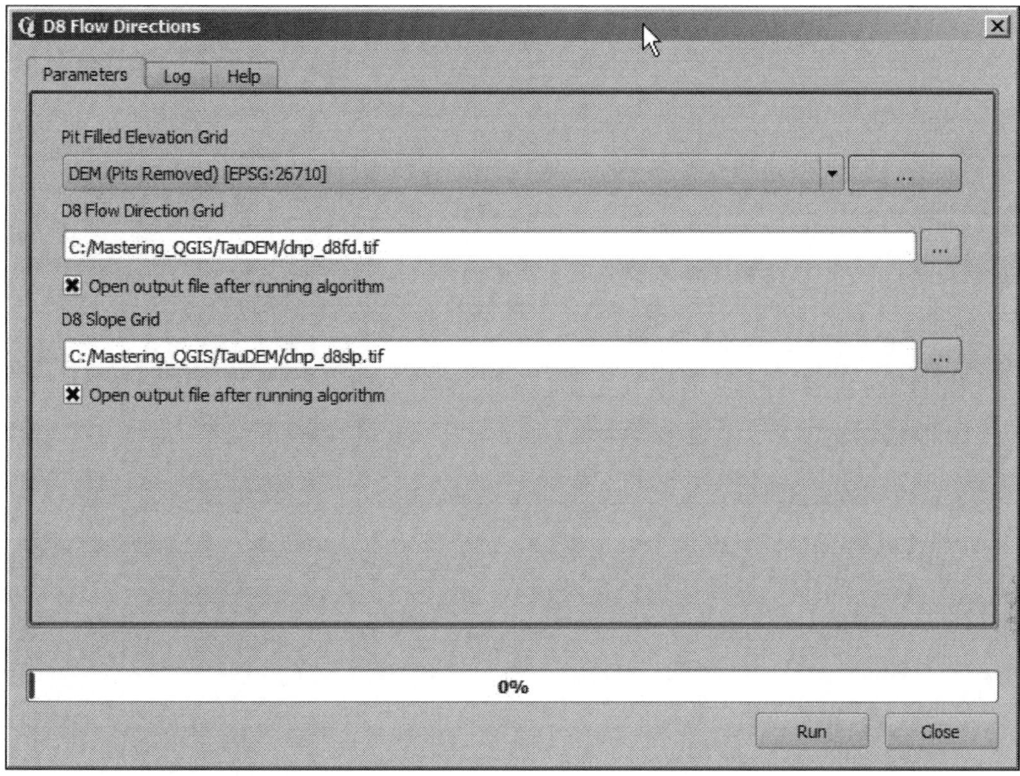

Calculating the upstream area above Fort Klamath

These two grids cover the entire area of the DEM, but we are only interested in evaluating what the watershed looks like along Sun Creek upstream of Fort Klamath. Many rivers are monitored by USGS gauging stations, which can be used as points of interest to delineate the upstream contributing area. However, more often than not, smaller streams typically aren't monitored, even though they are important for local communities. So, we can create arbitrary outlet points that are defined along the stream network. To focus our analyses on Sun Creek, we will make use of the Gauge shapefile and use as our outlet what is often called a pour point. We will use the **D8 Contributing Area** tool to identify the cells that drain through this pour point. In other words, we are going to calculate the watershed above this particular point on Sun Creek. The following screenshot indicates that we need the D8 flow direction and the Gauge shapefile as input. For simplicity, we are going to use all the algorithm defaults, but it is important to clarify that these parameters may need to be changed depending on local conditions.

Before using any shapefile to calculate upstream contributing area, it is worthwhile to ensure that every point is located on a grid cell representing the stream network, otherwise the algorithm won't be able to accurately characterize surface flow. To make sure each point is located on the network, we can use the **Move Outlets To Streams** tool, which will move each point to the nearest cell representing the network.

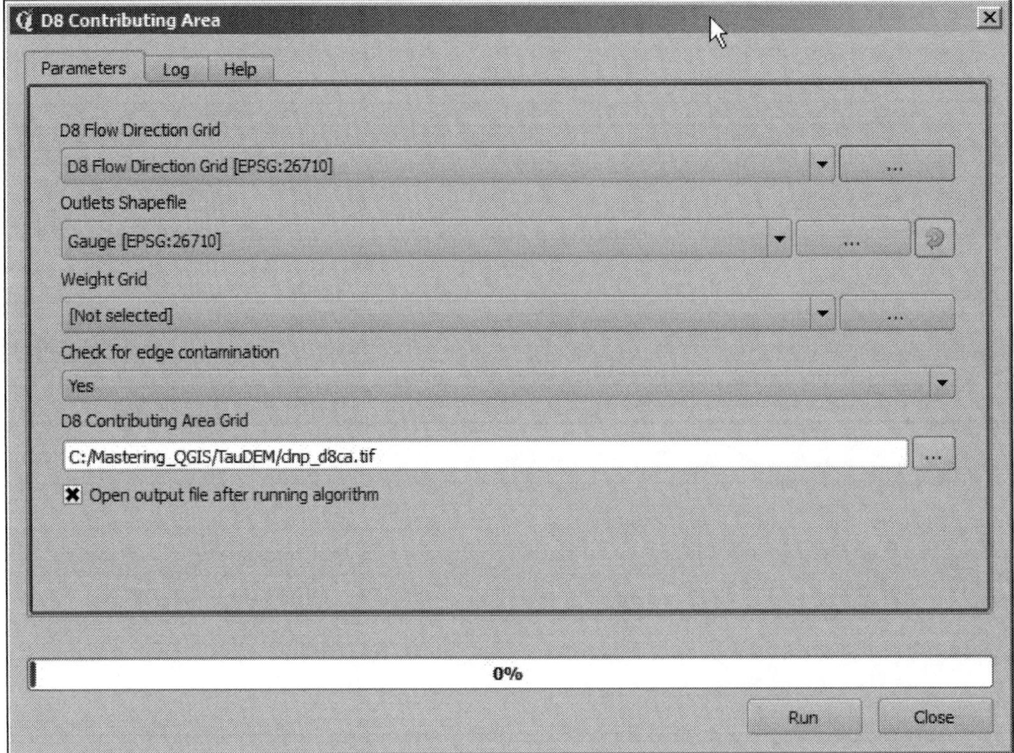

Calculating a stream network raster grid

The resulting output looks similar to a watershed boundary and could easily be converted to a polygon using the **r.to.vect** tool. However, in addition to identifying the contributing watershed area, we can also model the potential stream network that drains this watershed. If we make the provided River (`hydl.shp`) visible, we can see that it has relatively low resolution and, for a watershed of this size, there are likely to be other smaller tributaries that we can extract from the topography. To accomplish this, we are going to use the **Stream Definition By Threshold** tool and input the D8 contributing area for Sun Creek, as illustrated in the next screenshot:

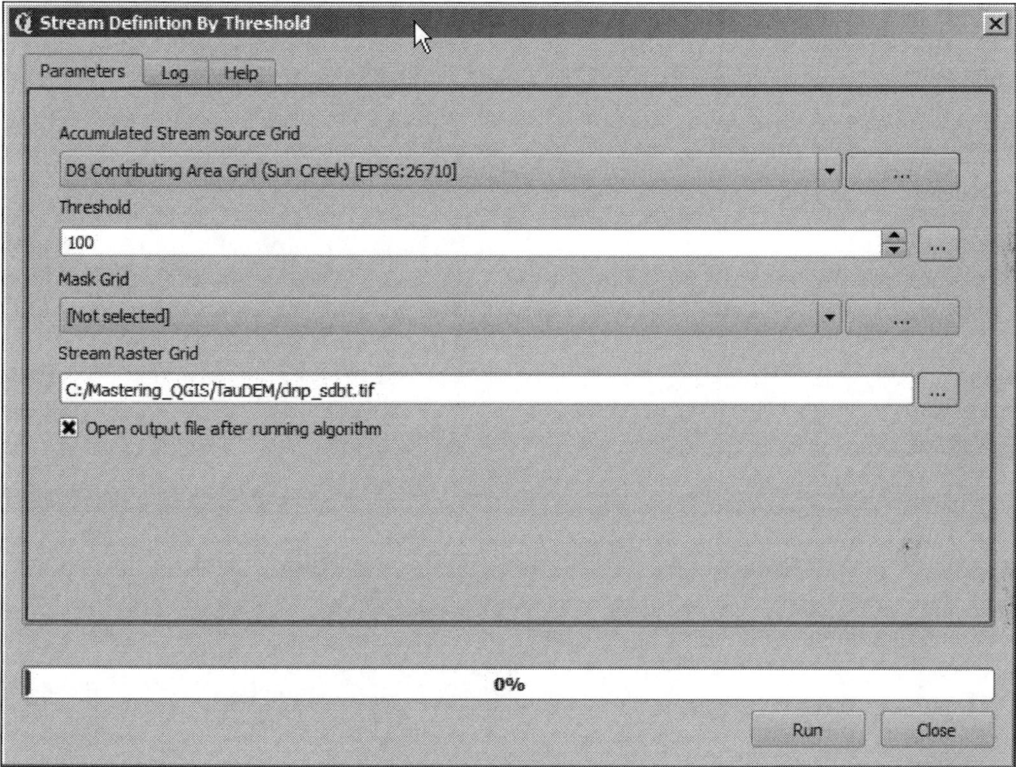

Creating a watershed-specific vector stream network

Essentially this algorithm identifies grid cells that have values greater than the default threshold of 100. Cells with values greater than the threshold represent areas of high flow accumulation; in other words, areas of the landscape that accumulate surface flow and represent potential river networks. Our last step is to extract a vector layer from this raster stream network. To accomplish this, we are going to use the **Stream Reach And Watershed** tool and populate the interface, as shown in the next screenshot:

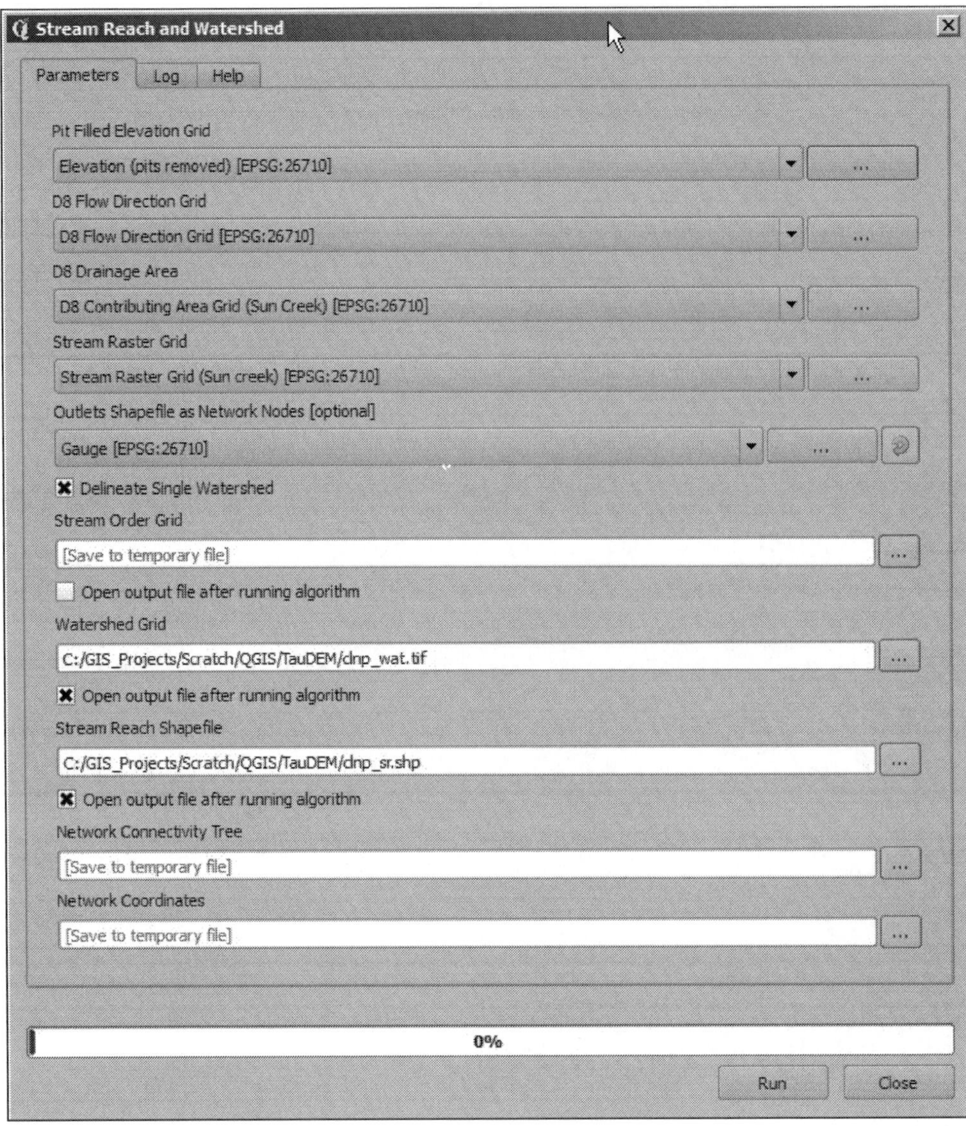

In this example, we chose to create a single watershed. However, if we wanted to identify sub-watersheds for each individual reach, we could select **No** for the **Delineate Single Watershed** option. The resulting watershed and stream reach shapefile are shown in the next screenshot with the original river's layer, illustrating the improved visualization of potential surface flow upstream of the town:

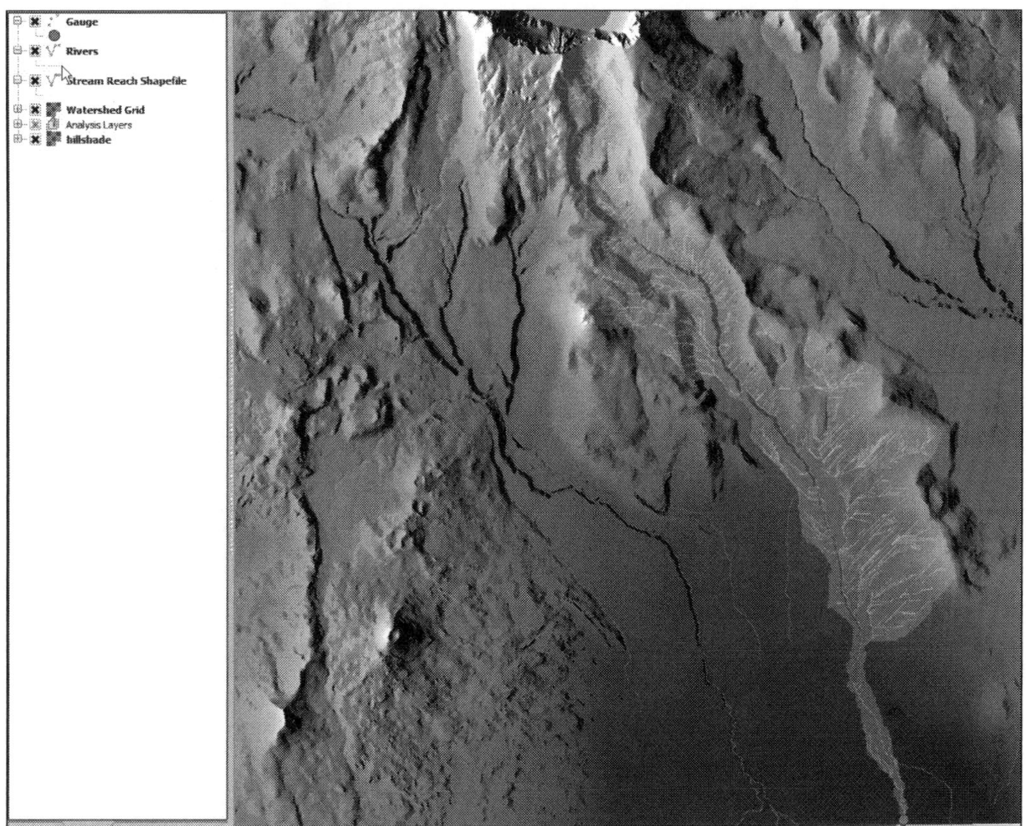

Hopefully, this brief exercise demonstrates the potential applications of TauDEM for exploring hydrologic conditions using high-resolution elevation data. Although the final output consists of only models of how water might flow across the surface, the clear alignment with the provided river's shapefile and the resulting stream network shapefile suggests that the default assumptions are useful for delineating watersheds from user-specified pour points and for estimating potential stream networks within this watershed.

R

R is a standalone open source language and environment that is useful for performing statistical analyses and graphically visualizing data. Users typically make use of this language within a command-line interface or a GUI-based software such as RStudio. Within either environment, users can work with geospatial data by installing additional packages such as SP, RGDAL, SpatioTemporal, and so on. However, we can also access a number of these powerful statistical tools through the processing toolbox.

Similar to all the previous algorithm providers, we need to make sure that R is properly configured. Although QGIS gets installed with the required R scripts, in order to run them, we also need to download and install R from `http://www.r-project.org/`.

The integration of R within QGIS offers access to some highly specialized spatial analysis tools that are focused on home range analysis and point pattern analysis. To explore some of the R algorithms available through the toolbox, we will use our existing data to perform some common statistical tasks that are useful for evaluating spatial data. We will use the following data layers in this section:

- Elevation file (`dems_10m.dem`, available in the GRASS data folder)
- Hillshade file (`hillshade.tif`, created in the GRASS section)
- Rivers (`hydl.shp`)
- Volcanic Vents file (`vents.shp`, in the R data folder)
- Slope file (`slope.tif`, created in GRASS section)

Exploring summary statistics and histograms

A common starting point for exploring spatial data is to evaluate the range of values within a given data layer. Although QGIS offers similar information natively for vector data when you navigate to **Vector** | **Analysis Tools** | **Basic Statistics** and for raster layers through the **Histogram** window under **Properties**, R offers a few more options and the ability to better visualize the data. For example, we might be interested in the range of values for stream length within a given watershed.

To evaluate this using R, we can use the **Summary statistics** tool, select the river's layer as our input, and define an output file to produce a text summary of the underlying data, as illustrated in the following screenshot:

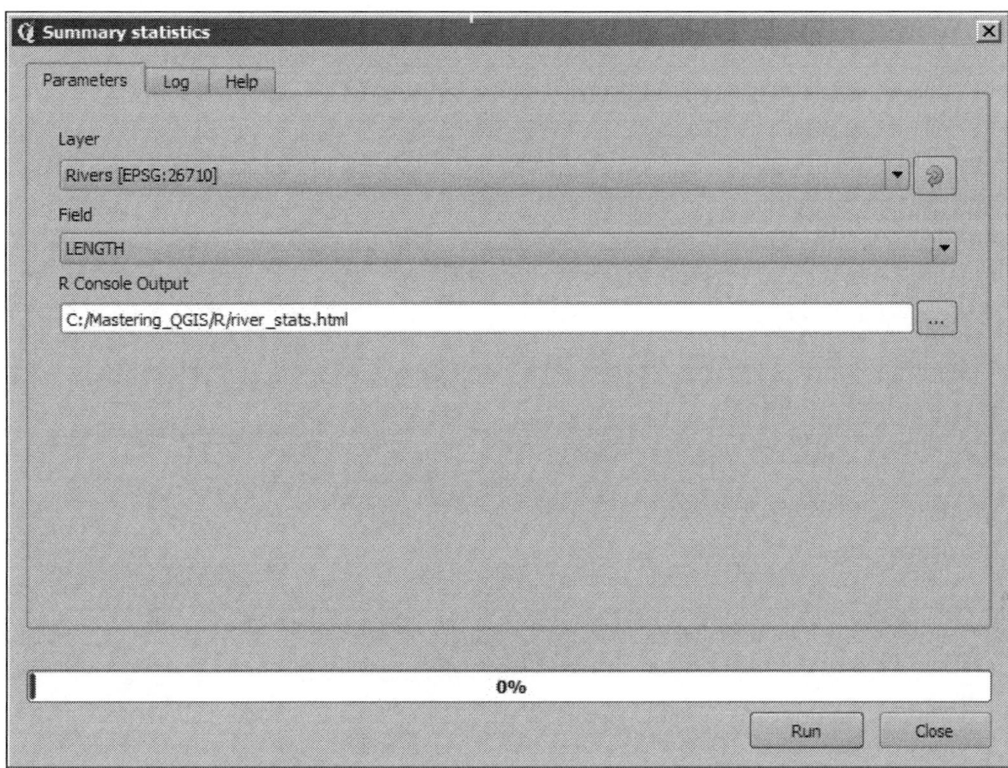

The following screenshot illustrates the summary produced as a result of running the **Summary statistics** tool:

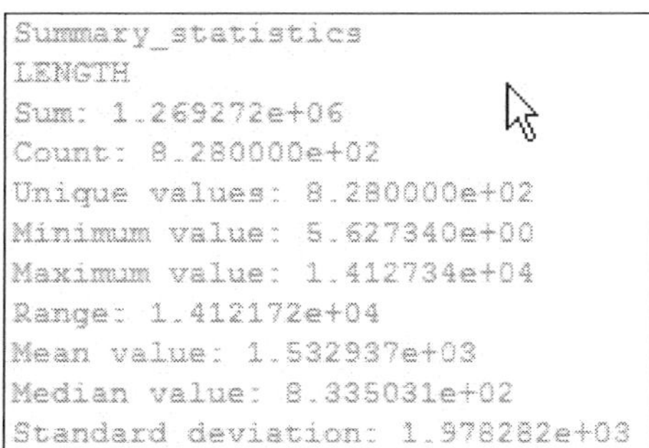
Summary_statistics
LENGTH
Sum: 1.269272e+06
Count: 8.280000e+02
Unique values: 8.280000e+02
Minimum value: 5.627340e+00
Maximum value: 1.412734e+04
Range: 1.412172e+04
Mean value: 1.532937e+03
Median value: 8.335031e+02
Standard deviation: 1.978282e+03

However, often a more informative way of evaluating this type of data is through a histogram to see how frequently a feature or characteristic of a feature occurs. In this case, we can use the **Histogram** tool under **Vector Processing** to produce a visual that summarizes the most and least frequently occurring stream length. This is one parameter that is often used to characterize the surface hydrology of a given watershed. The following screenshot illustrates the input parameters:

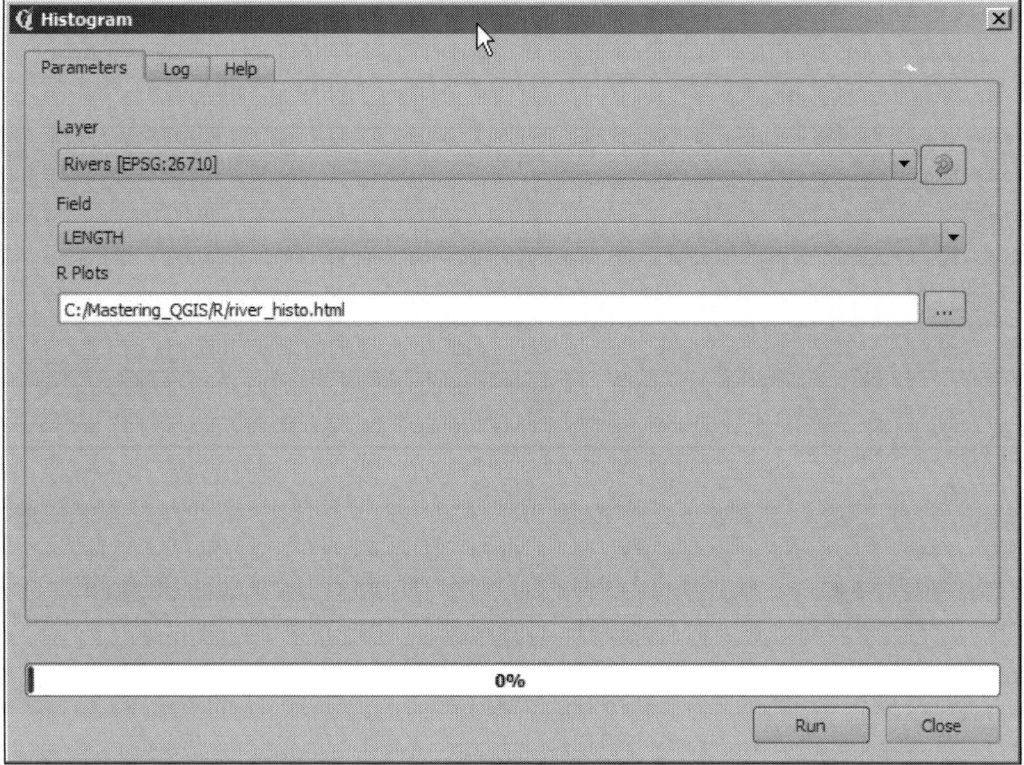

The following screenshot illustrates the resulting histogram:

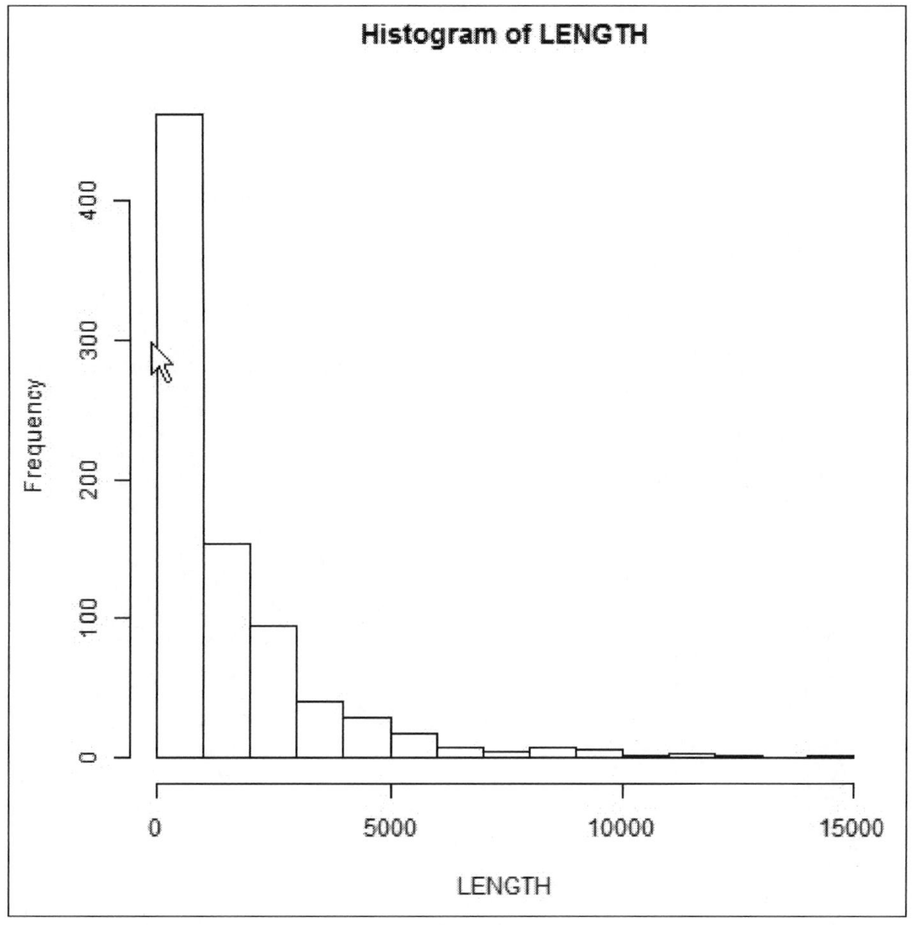

For this particular case, we see a higher frequency of shorter stream segments, which makes sense in this particular topography because they typically represent numerous small tributaries within a radial drainage network. Longer and more continuous river segments would more likely be found in areas with less topographic variation. This is illustrated in the next screenshot, which highlights stream segments that are less than 1,000 meters long:

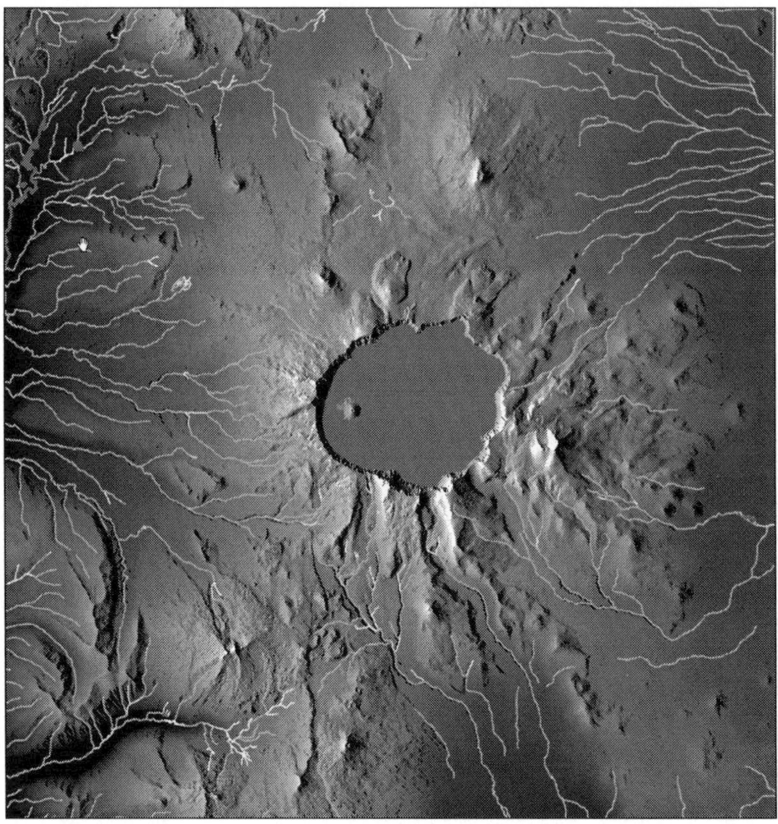

We can perform a similar analysis with raster layers by using the **Raster Histogram** tool under **Raster Processing**. For example, we might be interested in exploring the variation in elevation or slope within a given region for evaluating development potential or landslide susceptibility. The next screenshot illustrates the resulting output after running this tool on the elevation layers:

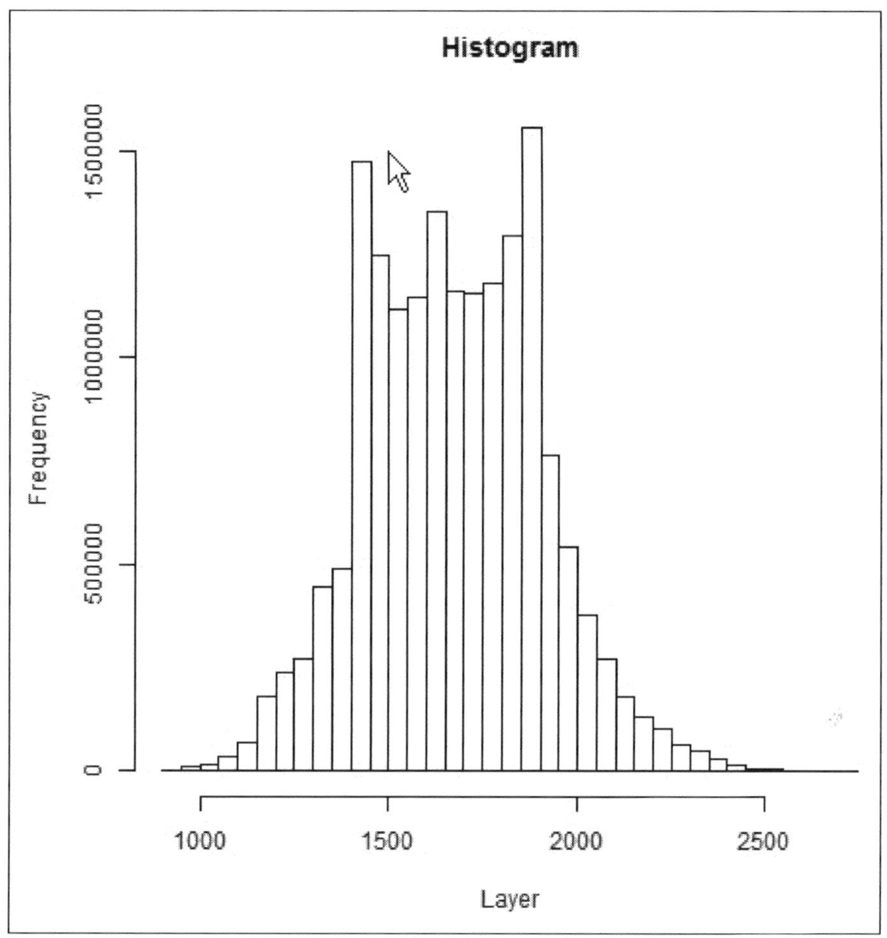

The next screenshot illustrates the resulting output after running this tool on the slope layers:

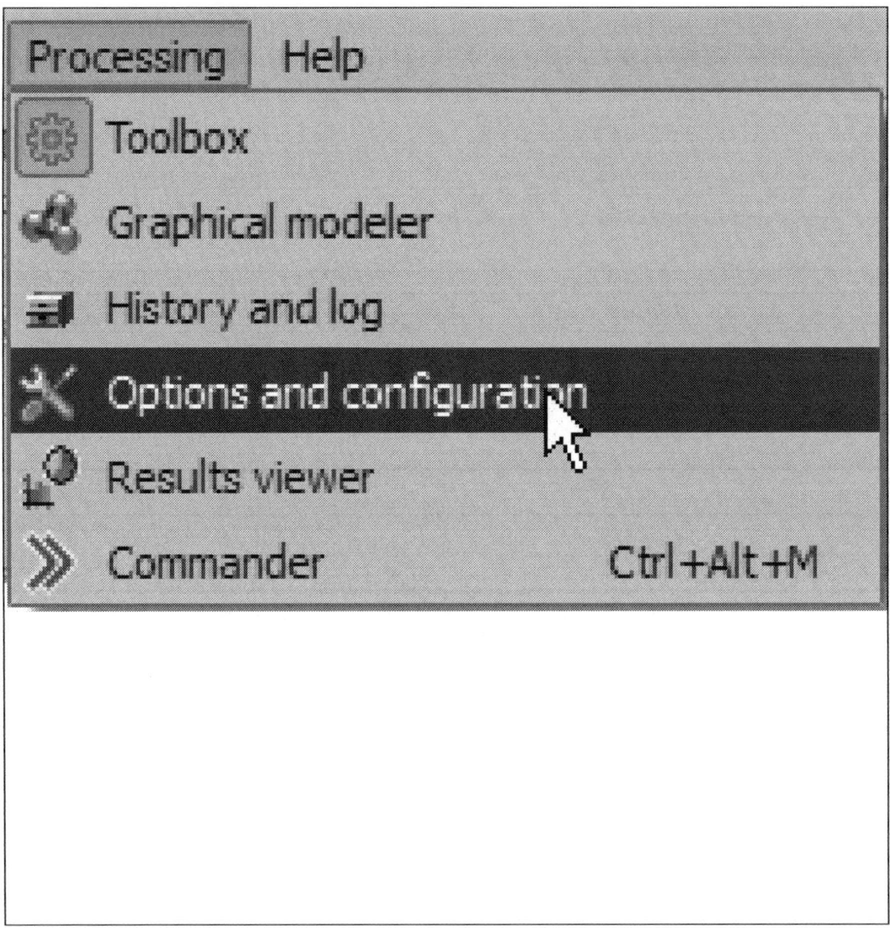

From these two simple histograms, we can quickly surmise that although there is a lot of variation in the elevation throughout the Crater Lake National Park region, the slope is rather unimodal and indicates a great occurrence of gentler slopes. As previously mentioned, QGIS has a built-in viewer for exploring similar information, but it is often less visually concise.

Summary

This chapter provided an overview of the structure within the processing toolbox and an introduction to the variety of advanced spatial analyses tools than can be accessed through the toolbox. You specifically learned how to create a shaded relief map, calculate the least-cost path, evaluate a viewshed, reclassify raster layers, query and combine raster layers, and calculate raster statistics using GRASS algorithms. You then learned how to crop raster layers using a polygon mask and reclassify, query, and combine raster layers using SAGA algorithms. You learned how to delineate a watershed and extract a vector stream network from a DEM using TauDEM algorithms. And in our last exercise, we explored the integration of spatial statistics using R packages to identify characteristics of landscape features. Perhaps most importantly, we saw how interoperable the native QGIS tools are with the tools executed from within the processing toolbox.

Although we explored these tools through hypothetical scenarios to illustrate how these analyses might be applied to real-world questions, it is important to clarify that this chapter is by no means exhaustive in its coverage of the complete suite of tools or their various applications. There are additional powerful algorithms provided by the R and LAStools environments.

In the next chapter, you will learn how to automate geospatial workflows using the graphical modeler within the processing toolbox. We will explore the various types of input options and available algorithms and develop an example model that we can add to the toolbox as a reusable tool. You will also learn how to export models to Python in preparation for the last chapter, which will explore Python scripting within QGIS.

8

Automating Workflows with the Graphical Modeler

This chapter will provide you with an overview of the **graphical modeler** (GM). First, we will introduce the modeler and explore the various inputs and algorithms available for models. Then, we will demonstrate via step-by-step examples how to develop a model that can be added to the Processing Toolbox. We will also cover more advanced topics, including nesting models and executing models iteratively. The specific topics that we will cover in this chapter are as follows:

- An introduction to the graphical modeler
- Opening the graphical modeler
- Configuring the modeler and naming a model
- Adding inputs
- Adding algorithms
- Running a model
- Editing a model
- Documenting a model
- Saving, loading, and exporting models
- Executing model algorithms iteratively
- Nesting models
- Using batch processing with models
- Converting a model into a Python script

An introduction to the graphical modeler

A typical spatial analysis involves a series of GIS operations, with the output of one operation as the input for the next one, until the final result is generated. Using the graphical modeler, you can combine these individual steps into a single process. The interface to the GM allows you to visually draw inputs, GIS algorithms, and outputs. The entire analysis is then ready to run as a custom tool within the Processing Toolbox. The custom tool will look like other tools in the Processing Toolbox. After assigning the inputs, and naming the outputs, the entire analysis will run in a single step.

A major benefit of this approach is that the completed analytical workflow can be modified and rerun. This allows stakeholders to understand how changing thresholds or input values affect the results of an analysis. Let's assume that you were assigned the task of developing a site-selection model for a new coffee shop. To match one of the site-selection criteria, you buffered railroads by one kilometer. However, a stakeholder later asks you how the result would change if the one-kilometer distance was changed to half a kilometer. If you had completed the original analysis with a traditional step-by-step approach, without using a model, you would have to start from scratch to answer this question. However, if you developed this problem as a model, you can simply change the distance parameter in the tool and rerun the entire site-selection model. Similarly, the site-selection model can also be run in a different city or neighborhood simply by pointing to different (but equivalent) input layers. The model can also be shared with others.

Opening the graphical modeler

The graphical modeler can be opened from QGIS Desktop using either of the following two ways:

- By clicking on **Graphical Modeler** under **Processing**
- By enabling the **Processing Toolbox** panel, navigating to **Models | Tools**, and then clicking on **Create new model**

The processing modeler opens as a new window. On the left-hand side of the window, there are two tabs: **Inputs** and **Algorithms**. These are used to add both types of elements to the modeler canvas that takes up the remainder of the window. Above the modeler canvas, there are the **[Enter model name here]** and **[Enter group name here]** input boxes to enter the model name and the group name. The buttons for managing models can be found above the **Input** and **Algorithm** tabs, as shown in the following screenshot:

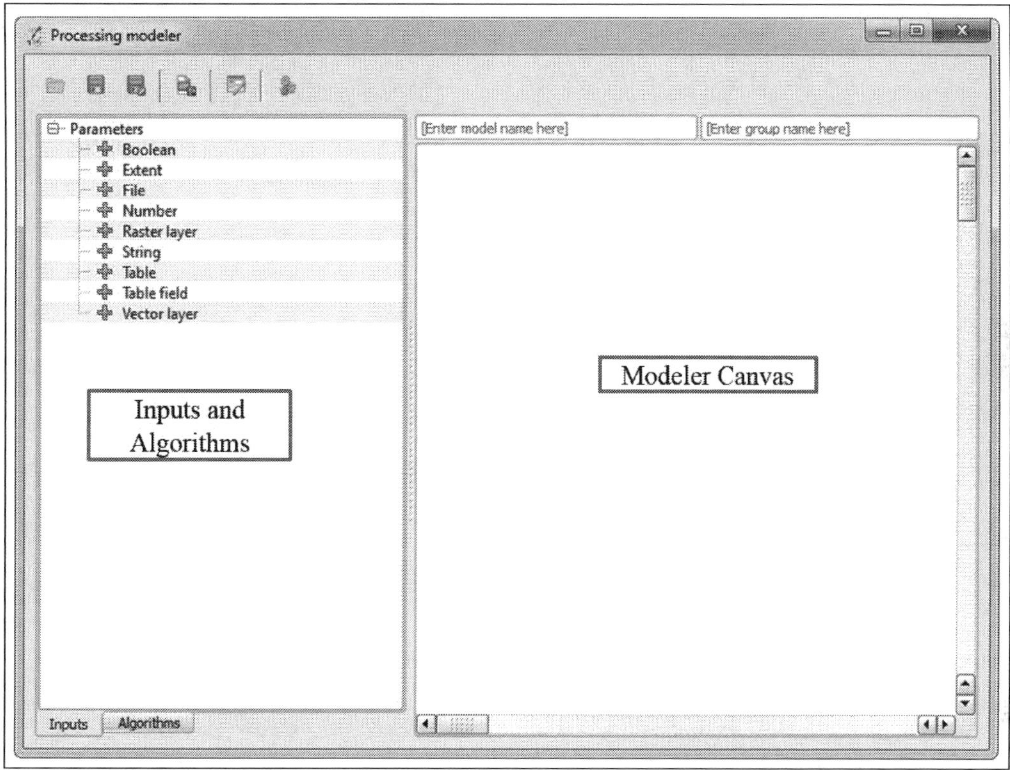

The window itself is called processing modeler, and not graphical modeler.

Configuring the modeler and naming a model

Before starting a model, it is a good practice to configure the modeler. Models are saved as JSON files with a `.model` extension. When you save a model, QGIS will prompt you to save the model file to the **Models folder**. You can set the location of the **Models folder** by navigating to **Processing** | **Options** in QGIS Desktop. Under the **Models** section of the **Processing options** window, you can specify the location of the **Models folder**. Click on the default folder path and the browse (ellipses) button will appear, allowing you to select a different location:

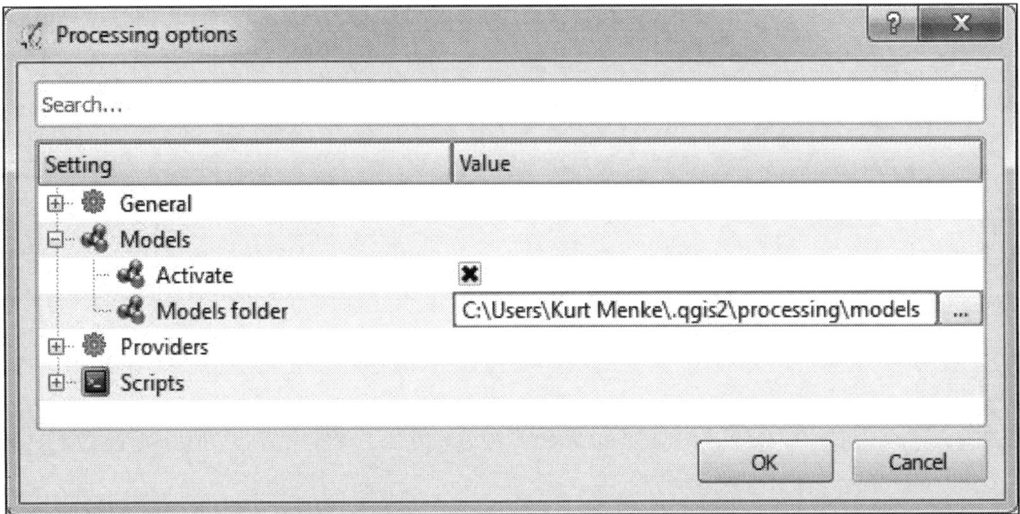

To demonstrate the basics of using the graphical modeler, we will use a simple example that identifies riparian tree stands in Alaska. It will have three inputs and two algorithms. First, we will give our model a name and a group name. For this example, as shown in the following screenshot, we have opened the graphical modeler and named the model as **Riparian trees** and the model group as **Landcover**. This is the group and the name by which the model will be displayed within the Processing Toolbox.

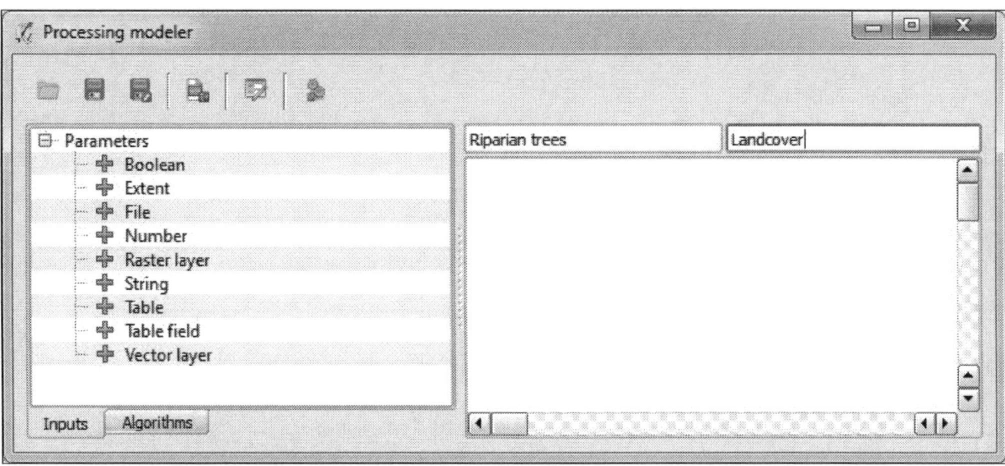

Graphical modeler with the model named as **Riparian trees** and the group named as **Landcover**

Then, we will click on the save button (). The **Save Model** dialog will open, defaulting to the **Models folder**. Here, you need to choose a name for the `*.model` file. We are naming it as `RiparianTreeClipper.model`.

> The model name and group name must be set before the model can be saved.

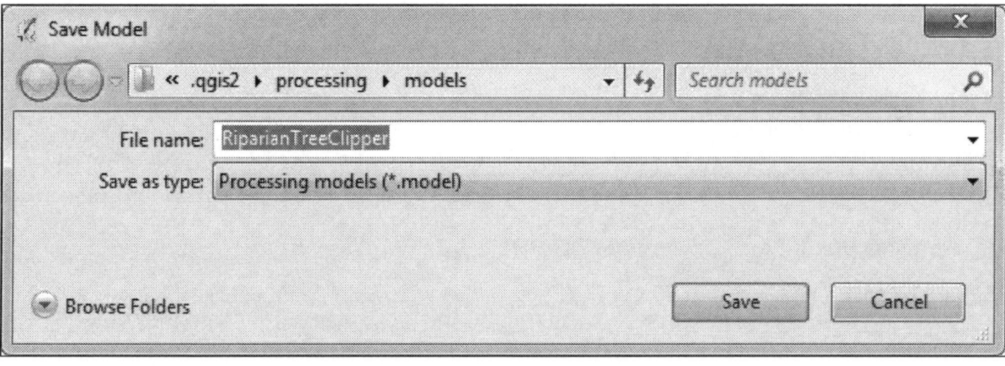

If models are saved to the **Models folder**, they will appear as model tools in the Processing Toolbox panel. Once a model has been named and saved to the **Models folder**, it will appear under its group in the **Processing Toolbox**. Again, the model will appear with the name that was entered into the graphical modeler versus the name of the `*.model` file. Models can be saved outside the **Models folder**, but they won't appear in the **Processing Toolbox** panel.

You will need to close the model before it appears in the **Processing Toolbox** panel.

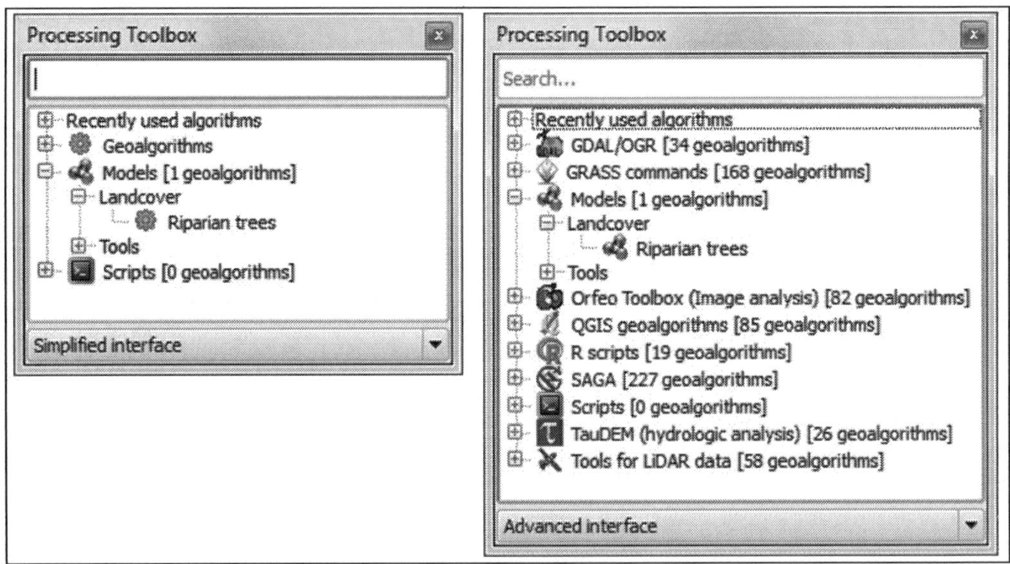

The Processing Toolbox showing the **Models** category with the **Landcover** group and the **Riparian trees** model.

The simplified interface is shown on the left and the advanced interface is on the right.

Adding inputs

To begin a model, you will need to define the inputs. The graphical modeler will accept the following:

- Boolean
- Extent
- File
- Number
- Raster layer
- String
- Table
- Table field
- Vector layer

To add an input, either double-click on the appropriate category from the **Inputs** tab or drag the input onto the modeler canvas. The **Parameter definition** dialog will open. Give the parameter a name and fill in any other details, which change depending on the input that is chosen. When an input parameter is defined and added to the model, it is essentially a conceptual parameter. It will not actually be connected to a GIS data layer until you are ready to run the model.

For this example, we will add a vector layer. We will specify the geometry of the vector data and classify it as a required parameter:

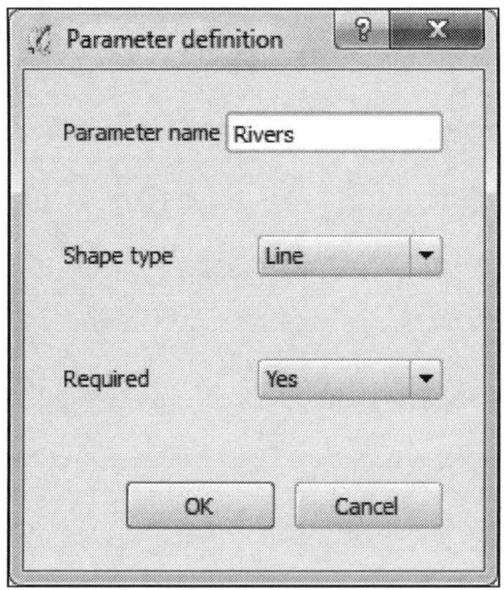

Once you click on **OK**, the input object is added to the modeler canvas. All the objects in the modeler canvas can be selected with a mouse click and dragged to reposition. Clicking on the pencil icon of an input will open the **Parameter definition** dialog so that changes can be made to it. Clicking on the close button (**X**) will delete the input from the model.

For our example, we will add a second vector layer. Trees is added as a required polygon layer. Finally, we will add a number input. This will allow us to expose the buffer distance value as an input that can be changed when the model is executed. It will be named `Buffer distance` and it will be given a default value of `100`, since 100 meters is the distance that we initially want to use.

In the graphical modeler, distances are expressed in coordinate reference system units.

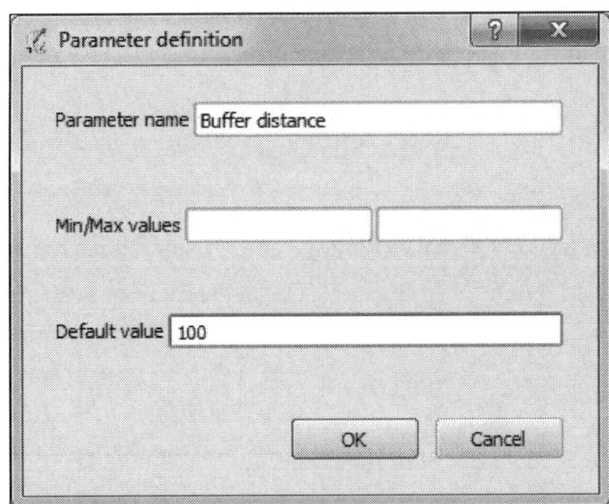

The following screenshot shows the model with the two vector layer inputs and a number input:

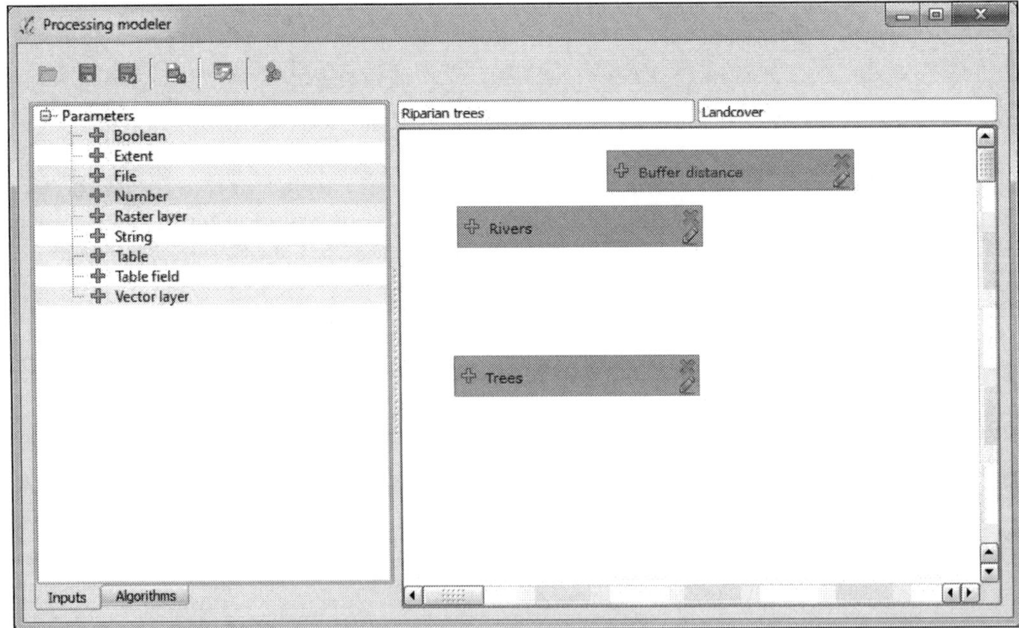

A model with three inputs

Adding algorithms

Algorithms are added to the graphical modeler in the same way as inputs. Find the algorithm from the **Algorithms** tab, and either double-click on it or drag it onto the modeler canvas. You can search for tools as you would in the Processing Toolbox. Type the name into the search box at the top of the **Algorithm** tab.

The Processing Toolbox has two interface settings: Advanced and Simplified. The interface setting that is currently being used in the Processing Toolbox determines how the algorithms in the graphical modeler will be organized. This setting cannot be changed from within the graphical modeler. Instead, to change the setting, the GM has to be shut down, the interface setting has to be changed in the Processing Toolbox, and then the graphical modeler has to be reopened. Other than this, finding algorithms is the same as it is within the Processing Toolbox.

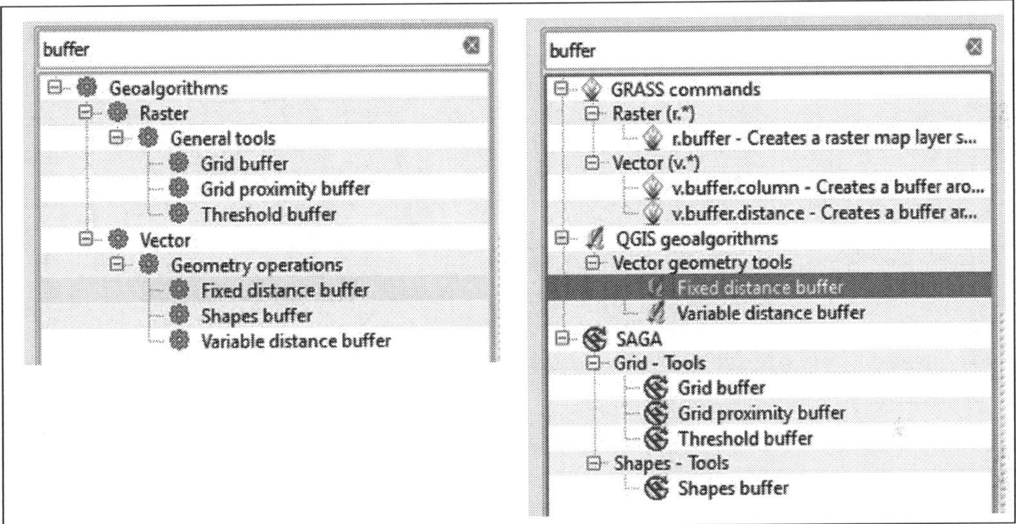

The **Algorithms** tab with `buffer` being used as the search term. The simplified interface is shown on the left and the advanced interface is on the right.

In the **Algorithms** tab, there is a special category named **Modeler-only tools**. The three tools—**Calculator**, **Raster layer bounds**, and **Vector layer bounds**—do not appear in the Processing Toolbox. They are tools that only make sense when they are used in the context of the graphical modeler.

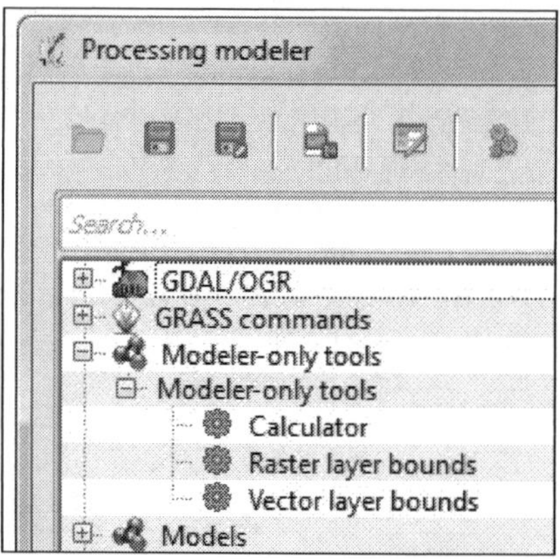

The **Calculator** tool is perhaps the most commonly used of the three tools. It allows you to perform arithmetic calculations on numeric outputs from other algorithms. For example, if you use one of the statistical output tools such as **Raster layer statistics** in your model or if you have numeric inputs, the associated numeric values will be available to the **Calculator** algorithm. The calculator lists the available numeric values within the model. They are labeled from a to x with the description to the right. Below this is a text box for entering a formula. For example, the formula given in the following screenshot divides the **Canopy density** value by the **Owl Habitat Acres** value and multiplies the result with the standard deviation from the **Raster layer statistics** algorithm. The output from the **Calculator** algorithm can be fed into other algorithms.

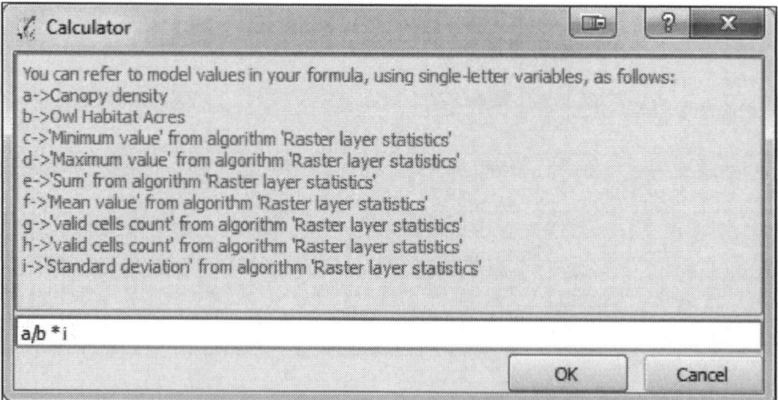

The algorithm dialog will look very similar to how it would if you were running it from the Processing Toolbox. There are inputs, tool parameters, and outputs. However, there are some important differences because the graphical modeler is a self-contained universe of data inputs. The differences are as follows:

- Input layers are limited to those that have been added to the model.
- Output can be left blank if it is an intermediate result that will be used as an input for another algorithm. If the output is a layer that needs to be saved, enter the name of this layer in the text box. When naming an output layer, you won't actually need to provide an output filename. This will be done when the tool is run. Instead, you just need to enter the name of the layer (for example, `stream buffer`).
- Numerical values or string-value parameters can be entered as numbers or strings. They can also be chosen from other inputs of the `Number` or `String` type.
- The fields of an attribute table (or other standalone table) can be specified by typing the field name or by using the **Table field** input. These fields will be chosen when the model is run.
- **Parent algorithms** is an additional parameter found only in tools that are run from graphical modeler. It allows you to define the execution order of algorithms. Setting an algorithm as a parent forces the graphical modeler to execute this parent algorithm before the current algorithm can be run. When you set the output of one algorithm as the input for the next one, you automatically sets the first algorithm as the parent. However, in complex models, there may be several branches, and it may be necessary for an operation in a separate branch of the model to be completed before another operation can run.

For this example, we will be buffering streams by 100 meters and then clipping trees by that buffer layer. The first algorithm that we will add is **Fixed distance buffer**. Double-click on the tool from the **Algorithm** tab and the tool dialog will open. The tool will be filled like the following screenshot. Notice that instead of setting an explicit buffer distance, the `Buffer distance` input is being used. Also, note that no output is named since this output will be considered as an intermediate dataset.

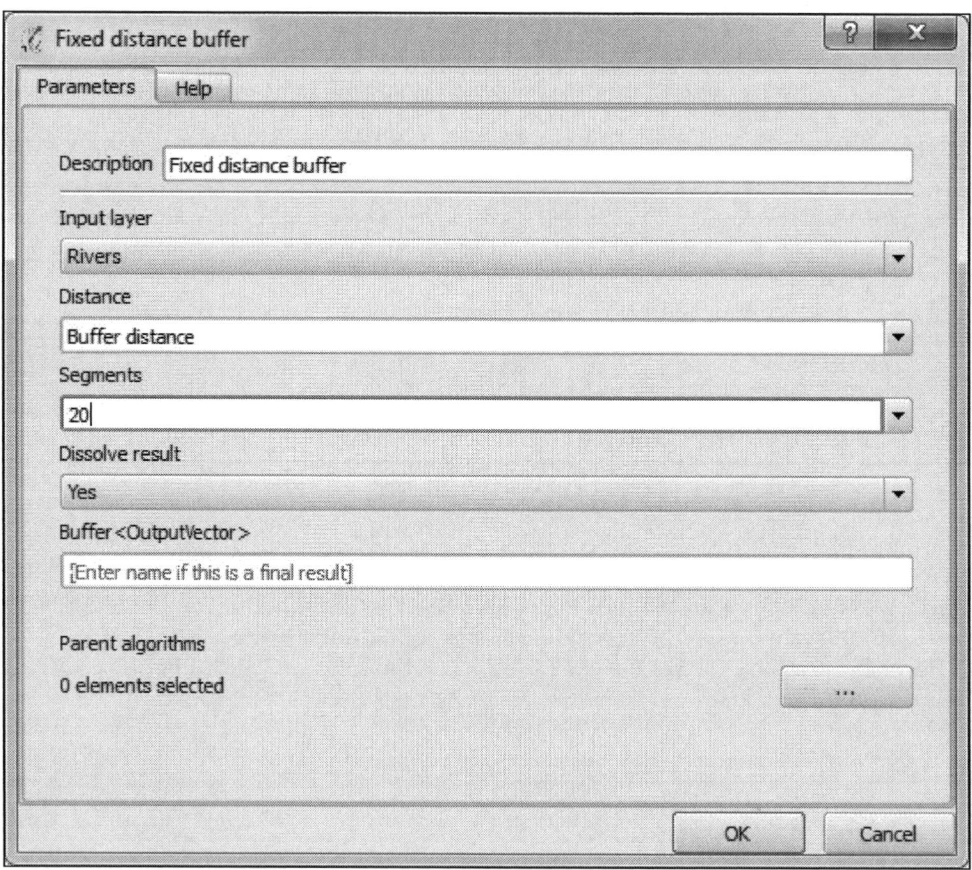

Next, we'll add the `Clip` tool to the model using the following parameters:

- Set the **Input layer** field to **Trees**
- Set the **Clip layer** field to **'Buffer' from algorithm 'Fixed distance buffer'**
- Type `Riparian Trees` under **Clipped<OutputVector>**
- Finally, click on **OK**

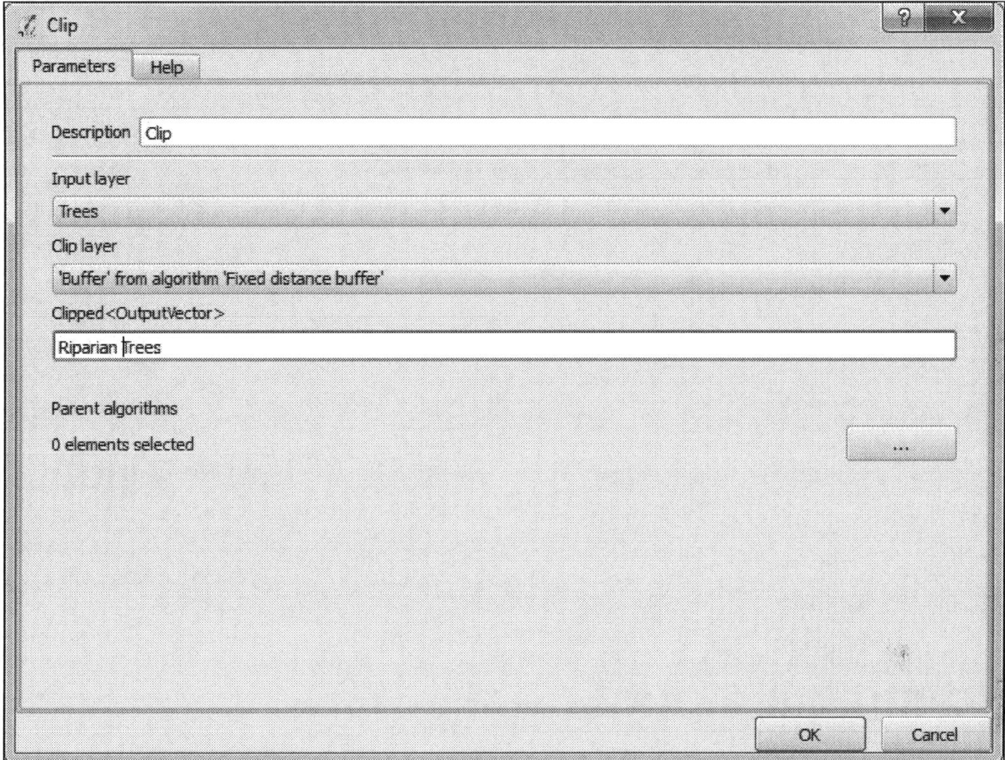

The final model looks like the following screenshot. The connecting lines show how elements are connected in the workflow. The input, output, and algorithm elements have different-colored boxes so that they can be distinguished. The algorithm boxes will also include an icon representing the source library. For example, the **Fixed distance buffer** and **Clip** tools are QGIS algorithms and have the Q icon within the element box.

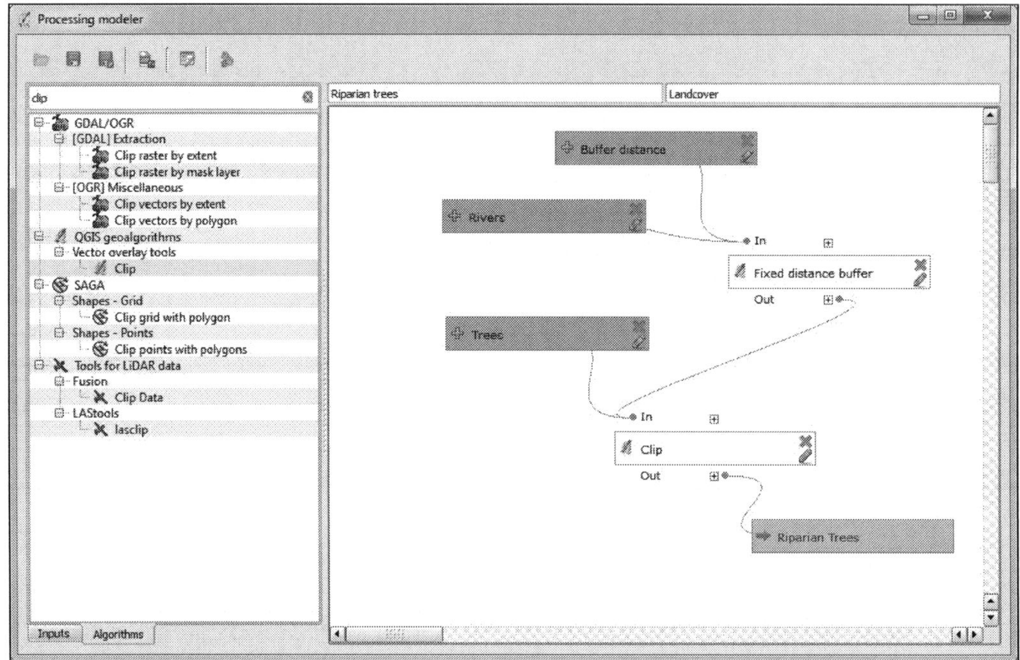

Running a model

The model can be run either from the **Processing modeler** window or from the **Processing Toolbox** panel. To run a model from the **Processing modeler** window, click on the Run model button ( ). To run a model from the **Processing Toolbox** panel, first save and close the model. Then, find the model by navigating to **Processing Toolbox | Models**, right-click on it, and choose **Execute** from the context menu. In our example, the model will be found in the **Landcover** group.

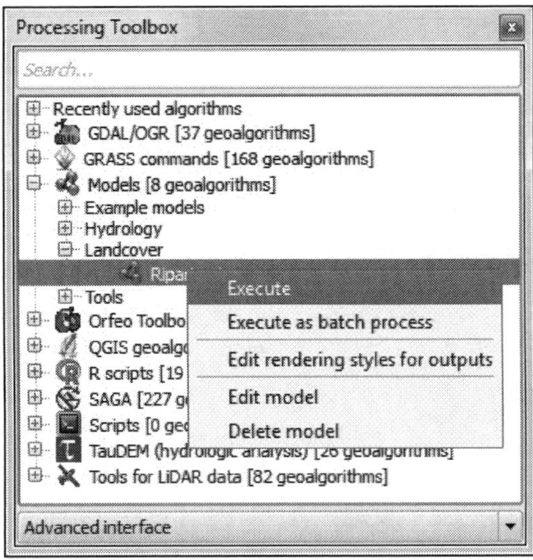

The model dialog will open with the listed inputs. For the data layer input, you can choose data loaded into QGIS by using the drop-down arrow or you can use the browse button (...) to locate the data on disk. For this example, we are using the `AKrivers.shp` and the `trees.shp` sample data. The **Buffer distance** field is set to `100` since this was the default value set for the number input. For the output, you can choose to have the layer as a temporary one or choose a location and filename for it. Here, the data is being saved as a shapefile. Click on **Run** to execute the model.

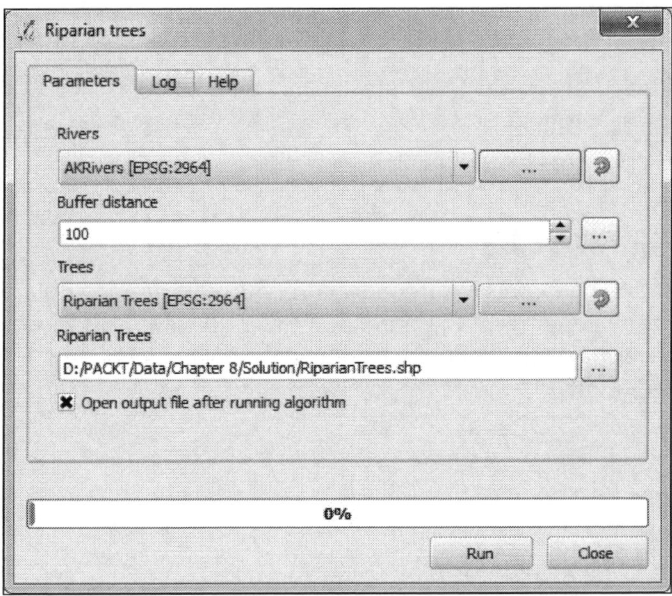

As the model runs, the dialog will switch to the **Log** tab, which provides output as it runs.

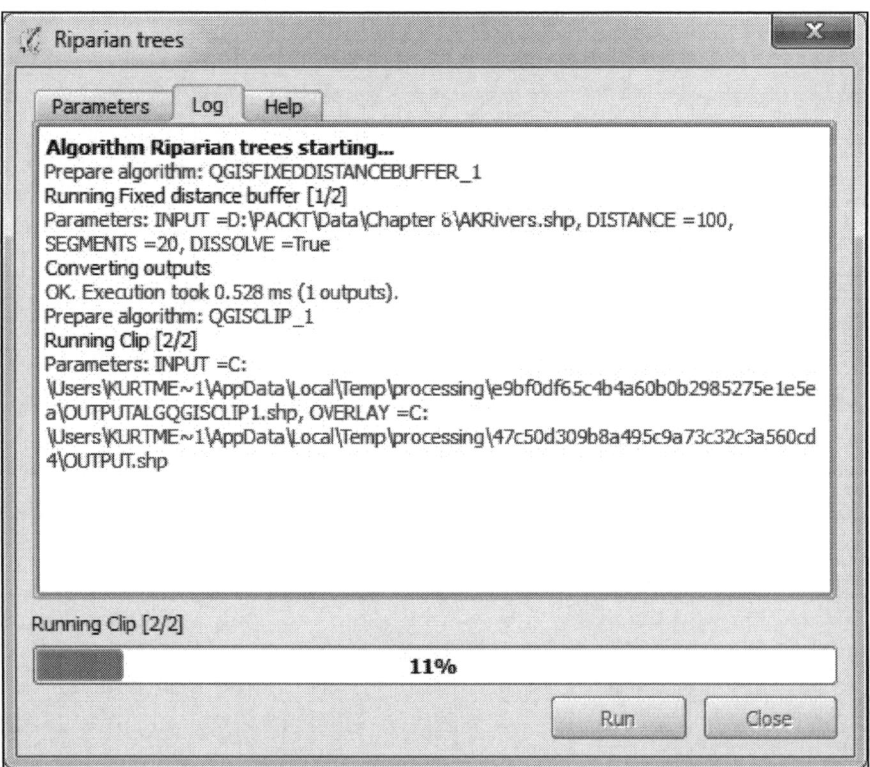

All the model files and data inputs discussed in this chapter are included with the *Mastering QGIS* sample data.

Editing a model

Existing QGIS models can be modified as needed. Right-clicking on a model in the **Processing Toolbox** panel opens a context menu. Choosing **Edit model** will open the model in the **Processing modeler** window. The model can also be deleted here by clicking on **Delete model**.

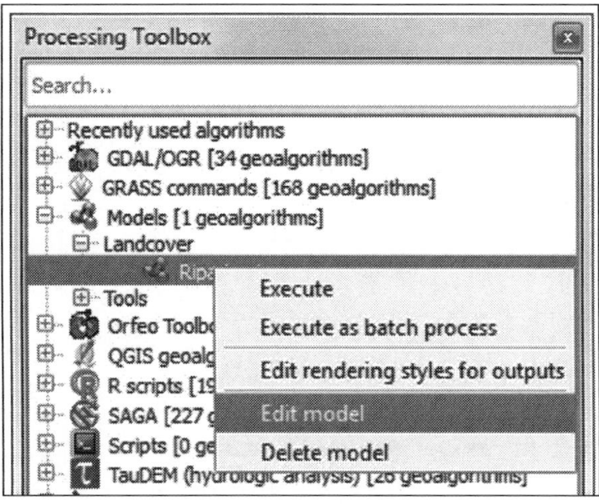

If a model is opened in the **Processing modeler** window, individual model input and algorithms can be modified. As we mentioned in the *Adding inputs* section of this chapter, clicking on the pencil icon of a model's input will open the **Parameter definition** dialog so that changes can be made. Clicking on the close button (**X**) will delete the input from the model.

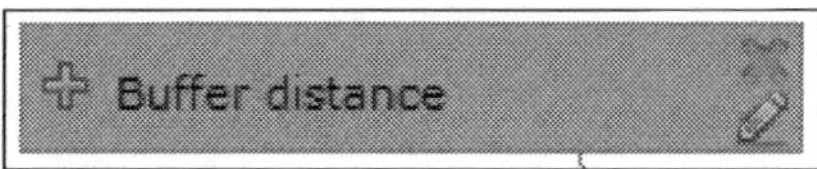

From the modeler canvas, information about algorithm parameters can be exposed by clicking on the + signs above and below an algorithm. This is a convenient way to see algorithm parameters without opening each algorithm. Right-clicking on an algorithm opens a context menu, as you can see in the following screenshot. Clicking on **Remove** deletes the algorithm from the model as long as there are no other algorithms depending on its output.

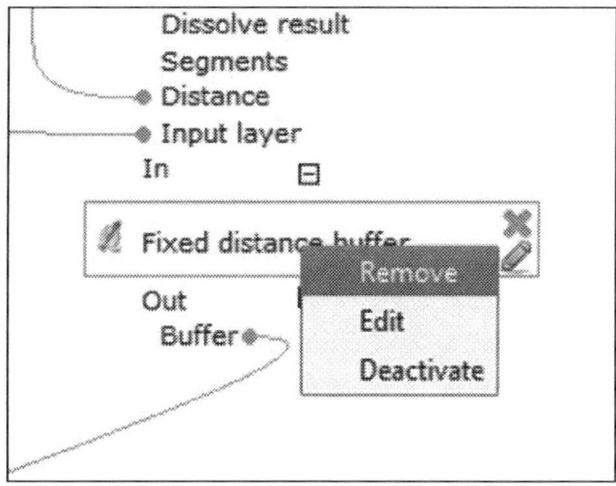

If you attempt to delete an algorithm in the middle of a workflow, you will see the following message. The dependent downstream elements will have to be deleted prior to deleting the algorithm.

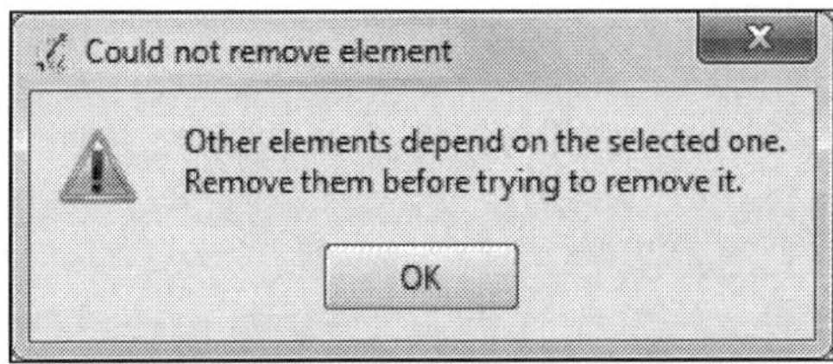

Clicking on **Edit** from the algorithm context menu opens the algorithm dialog so that changes can be made to the model. After editing an algorithm, the connections to other model elements in the canvas will be updated. The algorithm parameters exposed by clicking on the + signs above and below the algorithm will also be updated.

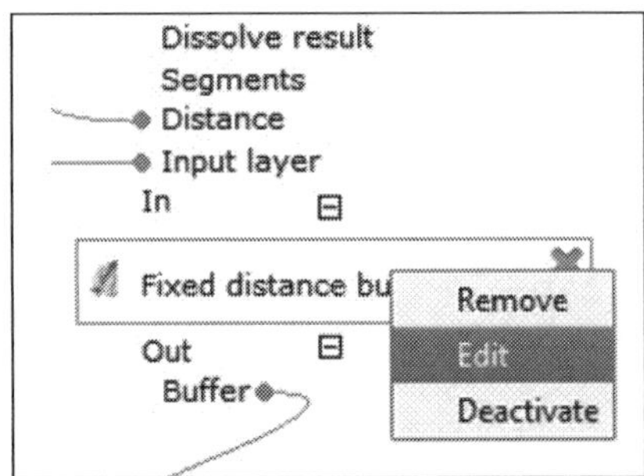

Clicking on **Deactivate** from the algorithm context menu will deactivate the algorithm and all algorithms downstream that depend on that algorithm. An algorithm can be reactivated at any point by right-clicking on it and choosing **Activate**. When you do this, any other downstream algorithms that were deactivated earlier will have to be individually reactivated.

Documenting a model

Model help can be written for any model by clicking on the Edit model help button ( ) within the **Processing modeler** window. This will open the **Help editor** window that has three panels. At the top is an HTML page with placeholders for the **Algorithm description**, **Input parameters**, and **Outputs** sections. At the bottom-left corner, there is an element selection box and there is a box for entering text at the bottom-right corner. To edit an element, select it in the **Select element to edit** box. Once it is selected, use the **Element description** box to type a description or necessary documentation. Click on **OK** when finished.

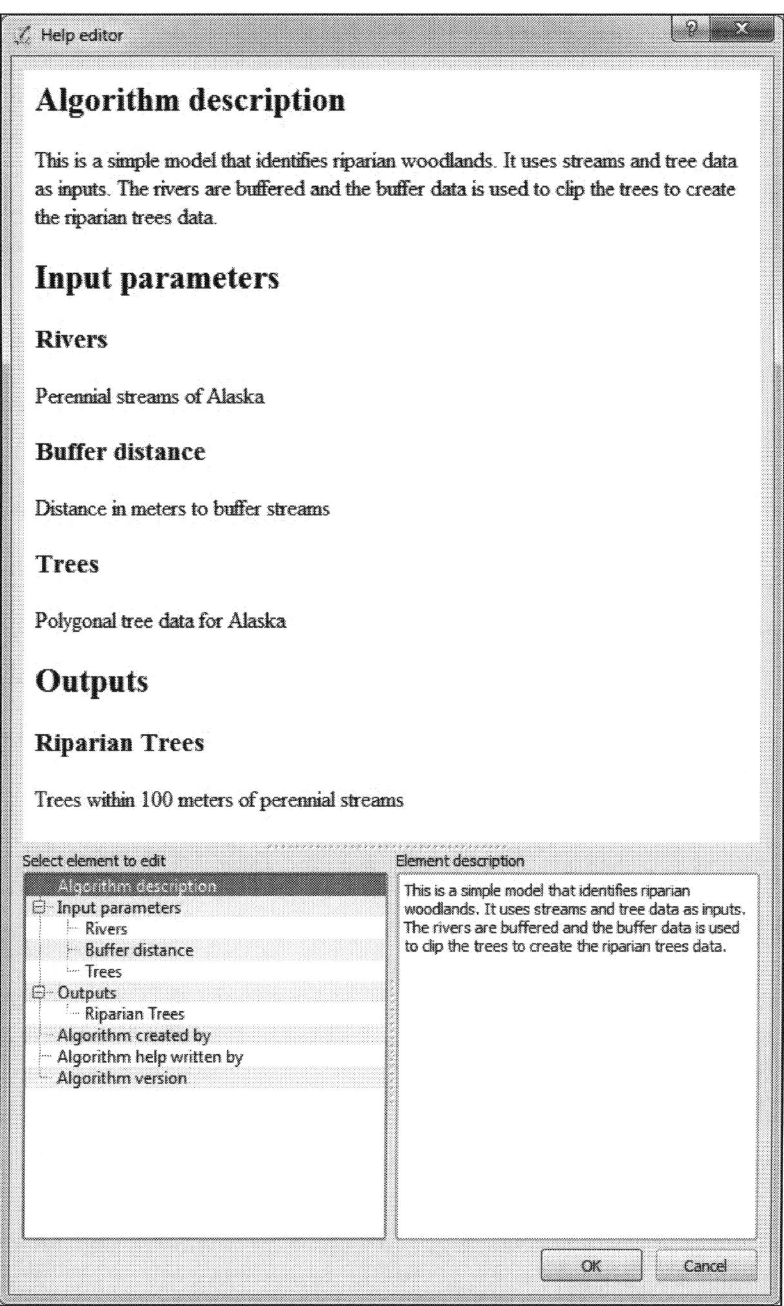
Help editor
Algorithm description
This is a simple model that identifies riparian woodlands. It uses streams and tree data as inputs. The rivers are buffered and the buffer data is used to clip the trees to create the riparian trees data.
Input parameters
Rivers
Perennial streams of Alaska
Buffer distance
Distance in meters to buffer streams
Trees
Polygonal tree data for Alaska
Outputs
Riparian Trees
Trees within 100 meters of perennial streams
Select element to edit
Algorithm description
Input parameters
Rivers
Buffer distance
Trees
Outputs
Riparian Trees
Algorithm created by
Algorithm help written by
Algorithm version
Element description
This is a simple model that identifies riparian woodlands. It uses streams and tree data as inputs. The rivers are buffered and the buffer data is used to clip the trees to create the riparian trees data.
OK
Cancel

This help information will then be available on the **Help** tab when the tool is in the execution mode:

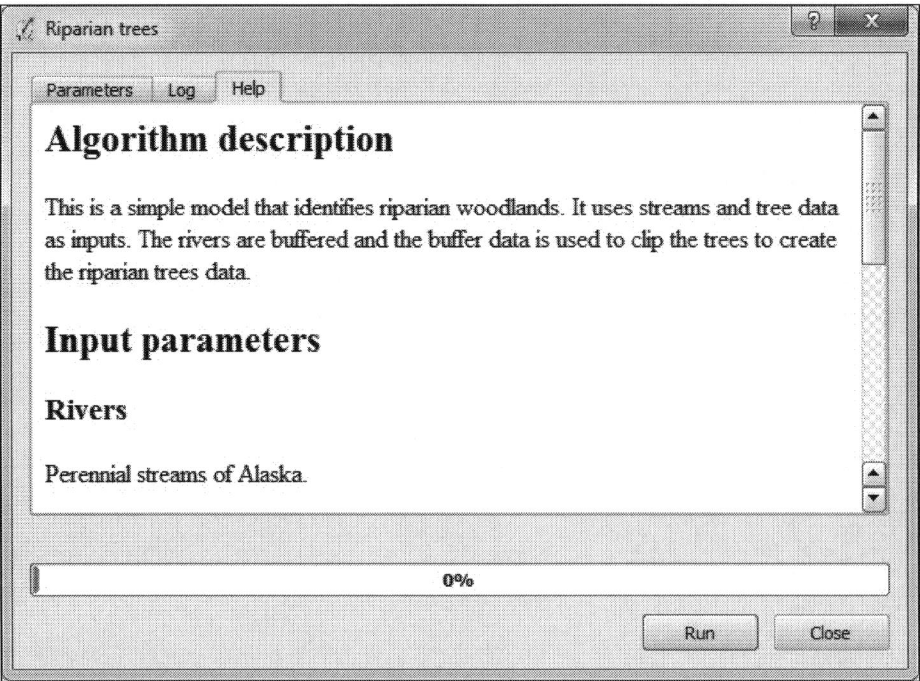

Saving, loading, and exporting models

Models can be saved anytime by clicking on the Save button ( ) in the **Processing modeler** window. It is best to save early and often when working on a model. As we mentioned in the *Configuring the modeler and naming a model* section of this chapter, the first time a model is saved, you will be prompted to name the model file. Subsequent saves update the existing `*.model` file. There is also a Save as button ( ) that can be used to save a new version of a model.

Models that are not saved to the **Modeler folder** can be opened using either of the following two ways:

- By enabling the **Processing Toolbox** panel, navigating to **Models | Tools**, and then double-clicking on **Add model from file**
- By using the **Processing modeler** window, and clicking on the Open model button ( )

  In either case, navigate to the `*.model` file.

Models can also be exported as image files. This is useful if the workflow needs to be presented or included in a report. To export a model, click on the Export as image button ( ) in the **Processing modeler** window. The model will be saved as a PNG file.

QGIS now has an online collection of models and scripts that can be loaded. From the **Processing Toolbox** panel, navigate to **Models** | **Tools** and double-click on **Get models from on-line scripts collection**. The **Get scripts and models** window will open. Choose the models to load and click on **OK**. The new models will be loaded in the **Models** section of the **Processing Toolbox** panel under the **Example models** group. This collection of online models will be continually expanded by QGIS users.

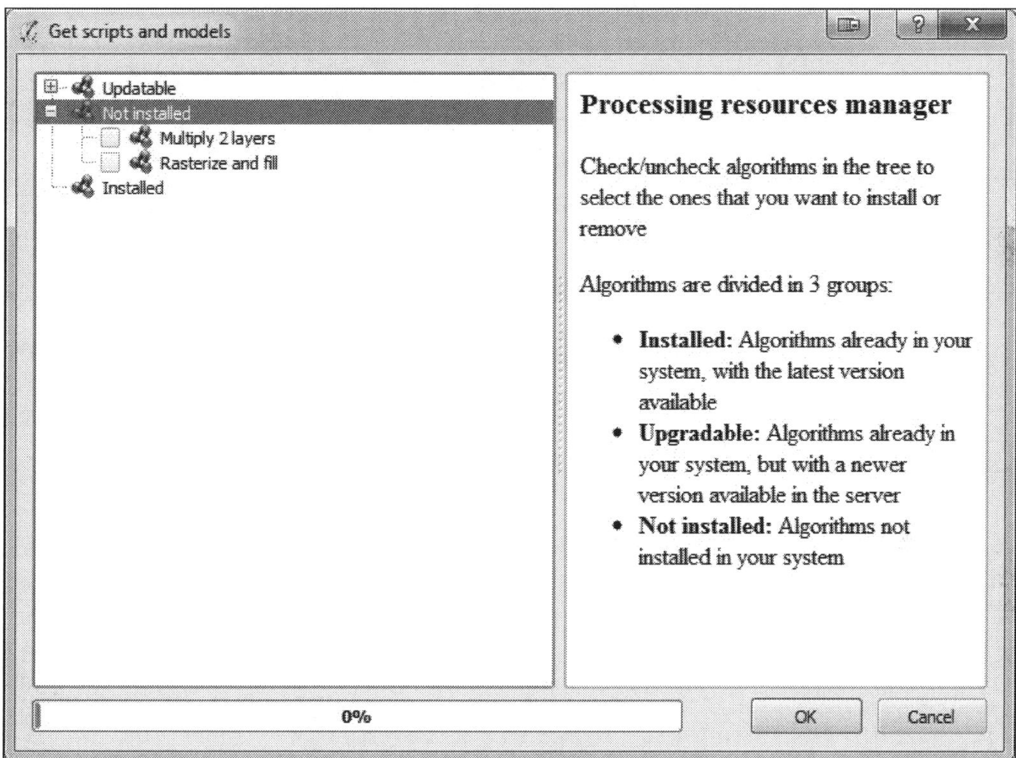

Executing model algorithms iteratively

Models, like all QGIS algorithms, can be executed iteratively. Here, we will demonstrate this feature with one of the QGIS example models: `DEMs_Clipped_to_Watersheds.model`. We will use two inputs, a DEM covering Taos, New Mexico and a watersheds polygon layer for the area. The `elevation.tif` and `watersheds.shp` sample data will be used.

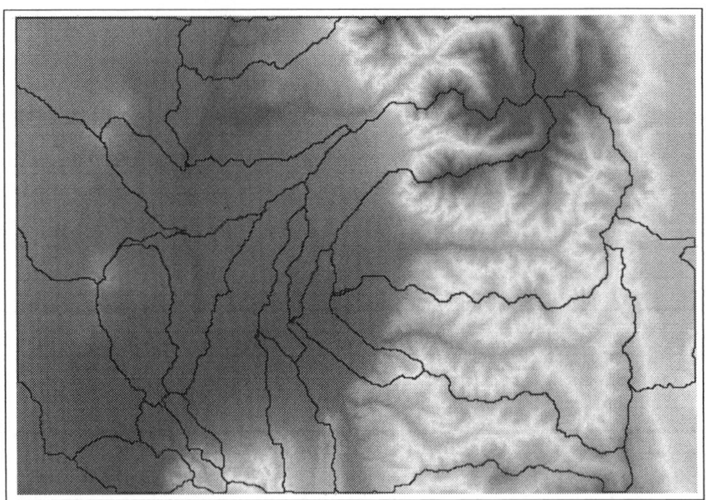

Input data: watersheds and a DEM

The model has just one algorithm. It uses the **Clip grid with polygon** tool to clip the DEM to watersheds. There are 21 watersheds covering this area.

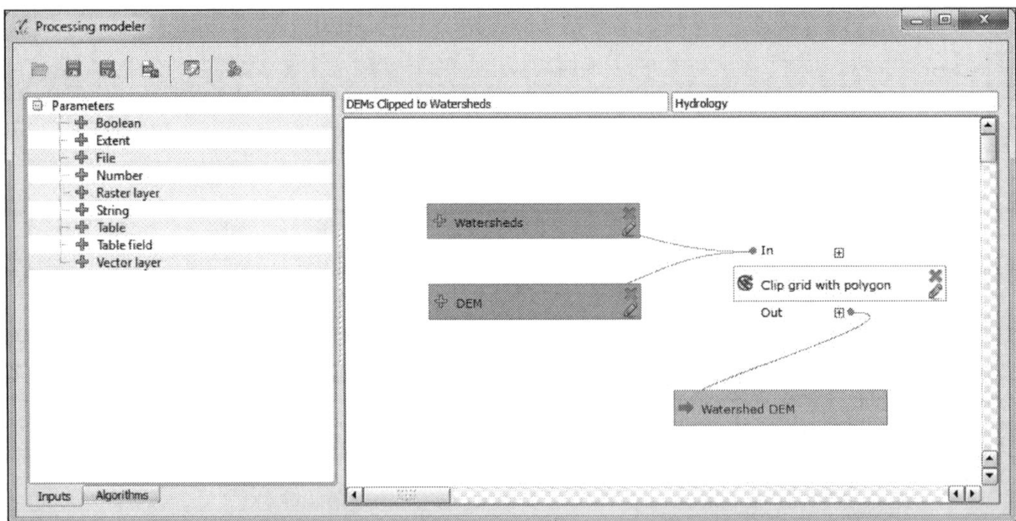

If the model is run normally, it will clip the DEM to the extent of all 21 watersheds and produce one output elevation raster. However, if the Iterate over this layer button ( ) is clicked (see the following screenshot), the model will cycle through each feature in the watershed layer and output a DEM that covers each individual watershed. This will result in 21 individual elevation rasters. This sort of automation is very easy to generate and can save you a lot of time.

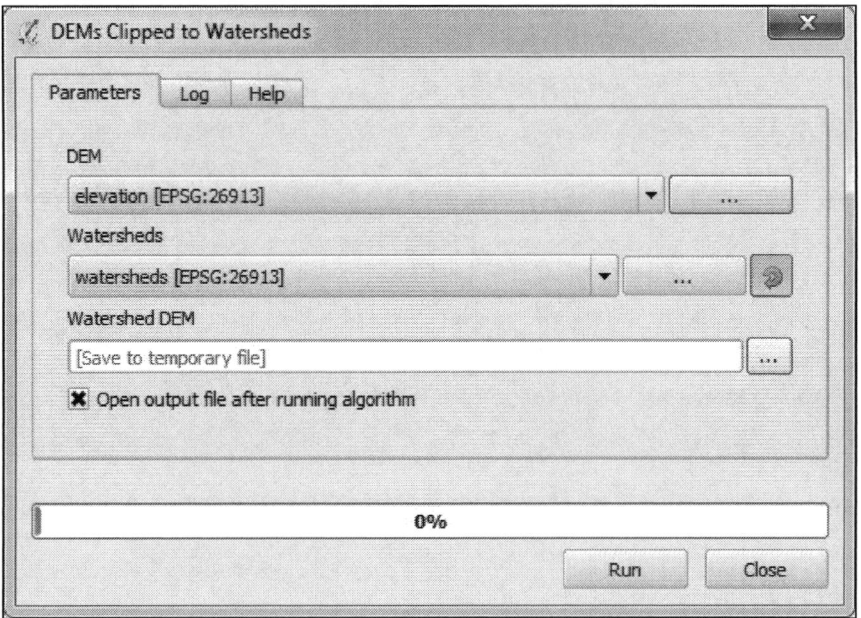

The following figure shows the resulting 21 DEMs that are clipped to individual watersheds:

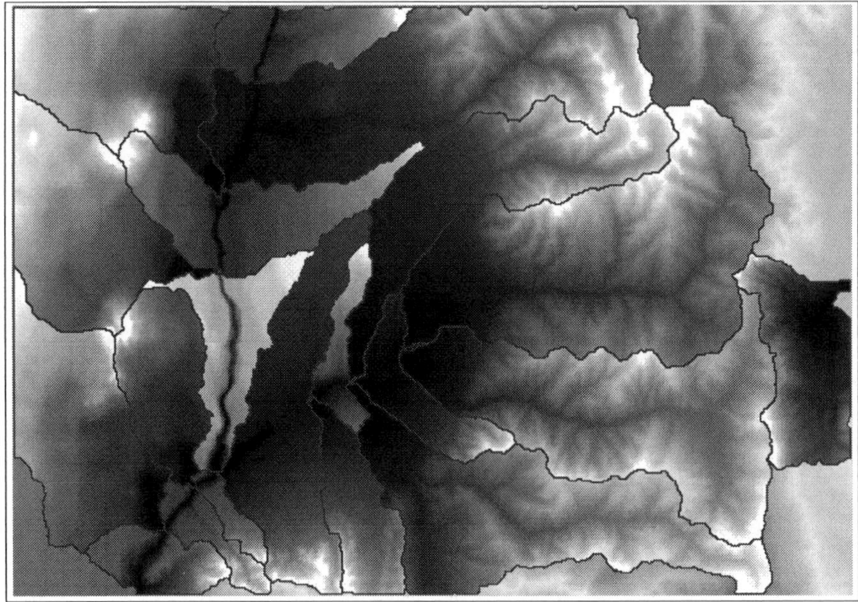

The resulting 21 clipped DEMs

Nesting models

As we previously covered, when a model is saved to the **Models folder**, it will appear in the **Models** category of the **Processing Toolbox** panel. What we didn't mention earlier was that it will also appear in the **Algorithms** tab of the **Processing modeler** window. This means that a previously written model can be used as an algorithm in another model.

Models won't appear as algorithms if some of their component algorithms are not available. This can happen if an algorithm provider is deactivated in **Providers**, and you can find this by navigating to **Processing | Options**. For example, if you have used a SAGA tool in a model but have subsequently deactivated SAGA tools, that model will not be available. As long as all the algorithms in a model are visible in the **Processing Toolbox** panel, a model will be available as an algorithm.

To demonstrate this feature, we will build on the model that we used in the previous section. The model clipped elevation data by watershed boundaries. With a DEM, you can generate a metric called **Topographic Wetness Index** (**TWI**). The QGIS sample model (`TWI_from_DEM.model`) shown in the following screenshot takes one input, a DEM. From this input, it generates slope and catchment areas. These then feed into the Topographic Wetness Index algorithm.

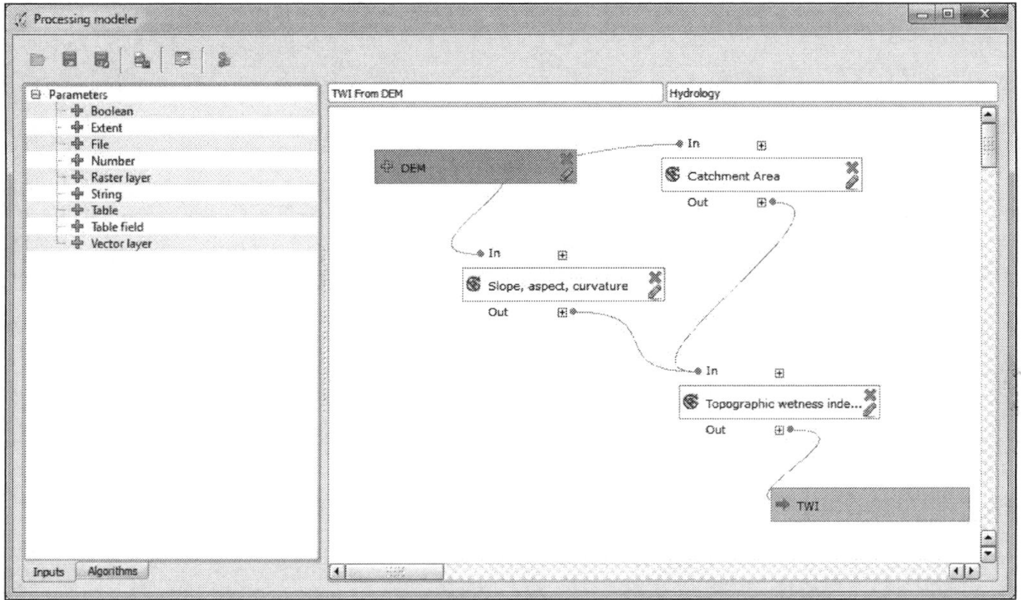

First, we will create a new copy of the **DEMs Clipped to Watersheds** model using the save as button. We will name this new model file as `TWI_for_watersheds.model`. The **TWI From DEM** model is located in the **Algorithms** tab and is added as an algorithm to our new model. (Remember that models need to be saved to the **Models folder** to appear as algorithms.) You will notice that the model icon in the modeler canvas for the **TWI From DEM** algorithm identifies the algorithm as a model:

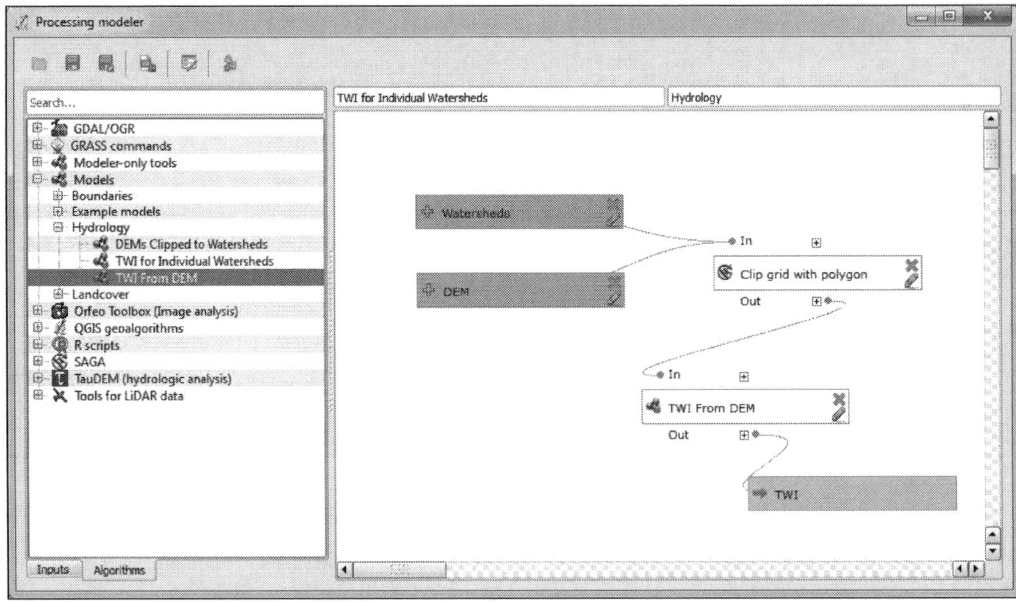

The DEM will be clipped to the watersheds layer, and the clipped DEM will be the input to the **TWI From DEM** algorithm. This will create one output, a TWI raster covering the watersheds. However, if the **Iterate over this layer** setting is used, the DEM will be clipped to each of the 21 watersheds and the TWI will be calculated for each. This will use both a nested model and the iterate feature in the same model.

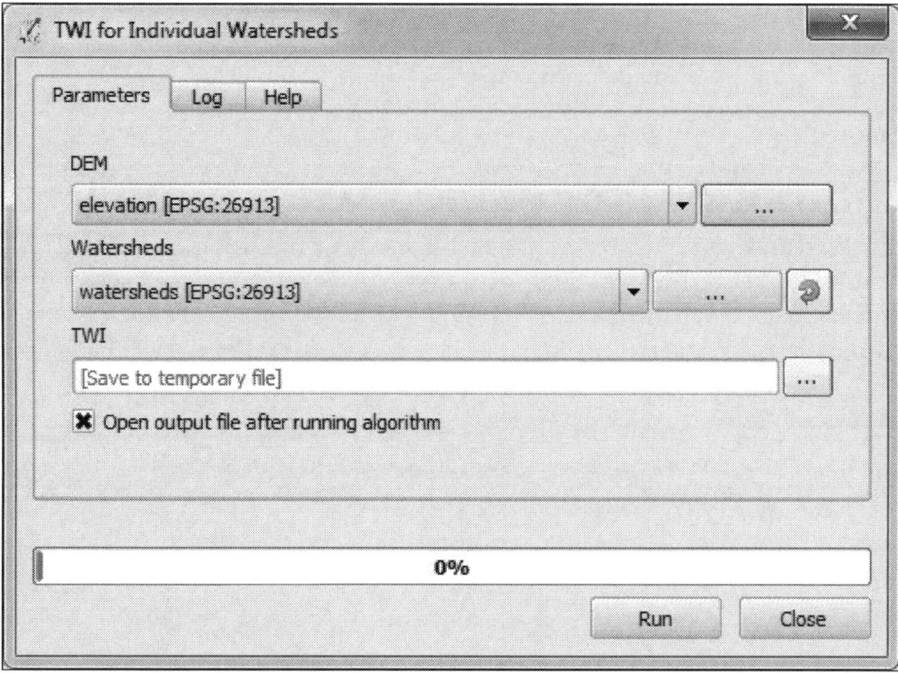

The following figure shows the output of the TWI for Individual Watersheds nested model using the iterator feature:

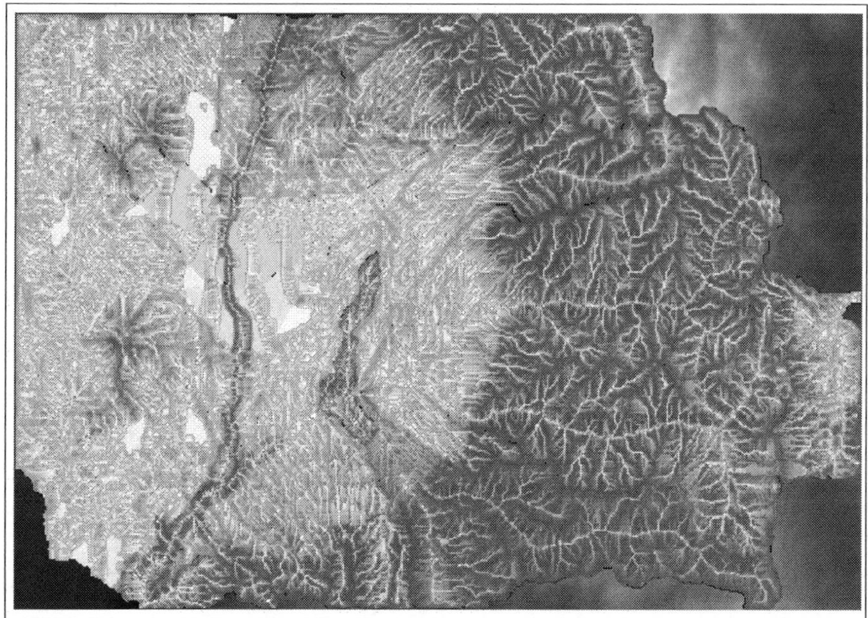

As of version QGIS 2.6, you can have as many levels of nested models as you wish. There is no limit!

Using batch processing with models

Models can also be used in batch mode just like other processing algorithms. To do this, simply locate the model in the **Processing Toolbox** panel, right-click on it, and choose **Execute as batch process**, as shown in the following screenshot:

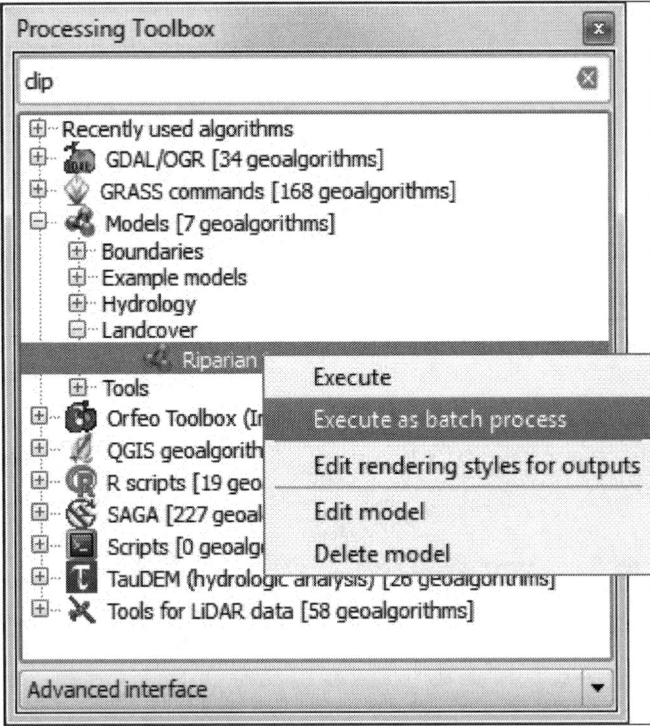

The tool will operate like any other geoalgorithm in QGIS. You can click on **Add rows**, **Delete rows**, and **Run** when ready. With this method, the model can be utilized on datasets from different geographies. This technique is also useful in cases where you have to repeat several geoprocessing steps on a collection of files.

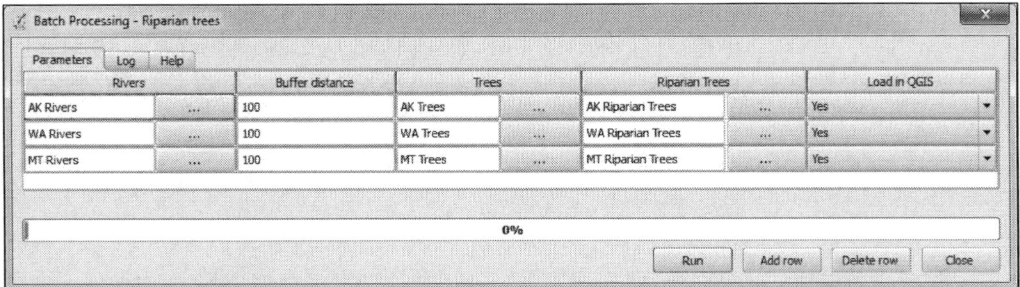

Converting a model into a Python script

In QGIS version 2.4, it was possible to convert a model tool to a Python script. It was done by right-clicking on the model in the **Processing Toolbox** panel and choosing **Save as Python script**. During the development of QGIS 2.6, the underlying code for the graphical modeler was completely rewritten. As a result, there are many changes and improvements in the new modeler. For example, `*.model` files are now stored as JSON instead of XML, there is no depth limit to nesting models within models, and algorithms and inputs can be dragged and dropped onto the modeler canvas. The modeler is also more stable and less buggy. Unfortunately, the ability to export a model as a Python script has not yet been implemented in the updated modeler. There simply was not enough time to get this piece completed before the release of QGIS 2.6. This functionality is expected to be implemented in a future QGIS release. However, since models are algorithms, they can be executed from the Python Console. This topic is covered in *Chapter 10, PyQGIS Scripting*.

Summary

In this chapter, we covered automating workflows with the QGIS graphical modeler. We showed you how to set up, edit, document, and run a model. You learned how to add inputs and algorithms to models. We also covered how to execute models iteratively, nest models within models, and run them in batch mode. With what has been covered to this point, you should understand how to work with a variety of vector, raster, and tabular data. You should also be well versed with the geoprocessing and analytic capabilities of QGIS.

In the next chapter, we will switch from conducting analyses with the graphical modeler and the Processing Toolbox to expanding the functionality of QGIS with Python. In *Chapter 9, Creating QGIS Plugins with PyQGIS and Problem Solving*, you will learn how to create a QGIS plugin from scratch. The chapter will begin with a primer on PyQGIS. You'll learn where you can get API information and other PyQGIS help. We will then explore plugin file structure and the available functions. The chapter will conclude with a simple step-by-step example of writing a QGIS plugin. This will also include information on debugging your code.

9

Creating QGIS Plugins with PyQGIS and Problem Solving

This chapter focuses on the basic information necessary to start developing a QGIS plugin. Topics that will be approached will include the following:

- Where to get help to solve your PyQGIS problems
- How to setup a development environment that can resolve PyQGIS and PyQt API names during code editing
- How to interactively test your snippet using the QGIS Python console and some useful classes that can be used everywhere
- Creating a basic plugin using Plugin Builder
- Analyze your first basic plugin to know its structure
- Setting up a runtime debugging environment that can be useful in developing complex plugins

Webography - where to get API information and PyQGIS help

One of the characteristics of most free software projects is that their documentation is freely available and can be used for learning. QGIS is one of the best-documented projects, thanks to training material, a coding cookbook, and the automatic documentation of its **Application Programming Interfaces** (**APIs**).

In this chapter, we will focus on main resources that are available on the web to learn how to script QGIS and how to solve your scripting problems.

PyQGIS cookbook

The main resource is a community content-driven cookbook that gives a general introduction to scripting QGIS. You can find this documentation at `http://www.qgis.org/en/docs/index.html`.

You have to choose the QGIS target version of your plugin and then choose the PyQGIS Developer Cookbook link. If you are interested in the latest QGIS APIs, you have to choose the testing version or directly go to `http://docs.qgis.org/testing/en/docs/pyqgis_developer_cookbook/`.

If you need a copy on your system, you can also download a PDF version of the cookbook from `http://docs.qgis.org/<qgis version or testing>/pdf/`.

For example, if you need the documentation for the version 2.2, you have to direct your browser to `http://docs.qgis.org/2.2/pdf/`.

However, if you need documentation of a version under development, you can visit `http://docs.qgis.org/testing/pdf/`.

Once you open the PDF documentation page, you can choose your preferred translation.

QGIS even versions (for example, 2.2, 2.4, 2.6, and so on) are always stable versions. Odd versions are always developing versions (for example, 2.3 or 2.5). Odd versions are generally known as testing versions.

API documentation

APIs are the doors that use the components of a software program. As a program evolves, the APIs can change affecting, in our case, all the plugins that directly use them.

The biggest QGIS API changes append jumping from version 1.8 to 2.0, but moving from one version to another, there are new APIs added and others are deprecated because of the normal development life cycle of a complex software. Generally, deprecation and new APIs are added to satisfy new features (for example, multithreading visualization added in version 2.4 or the newer legend engine added in version 2.6) or due to code refactoring (refer to `http://en.wikipedia.org/wiki/Code_refactoring`).

So, depending on API changes and on what QGIS version you want to integrate your code into, you should use one API set or another, or better, write code that can be executed in multiple QGIS versions.

API documentation is automatically generated from the QGIS code and can be found at `http://qgis.org/api/`, where you can look for the class that you need.

For example, if you need to know public methods of the `QgsVectorLayer` class in QGIS 2.4, you can refer to `http://qgis.org/api/2.4/classQgsVectorLayer.html` or for the latest development version, `http://qgis.org/api/classQgsVectorLayer.html`.

It should be mentioned that QGIS is mainly written in C++ and its API documentation follows C++ notation. Most of the methods of the QGIS classes are available as a Python bind. The way to discover if a method is exported to Python is to test it in the QGIS Python Console or read about its class documentation in the QGIS Python Console, as described in the next chapter.

The QGIS community, mailing lists, and IRC channel

One of the advantages of the open source project is that you can talk directly to other developers and frequently with the core developers of the project. QGIS has three official ways to support development and problem resolution.

Mailing lists

All official mailing lists are listed at `http://qgis.org/en/site/getinvolved/mailinglists.html`.

There are two extremely important lists from the user's point of view, one for developers (QGIS core and plugin developers) and the other for users. Depending on your profile, choose one list:

- **Developer list**: For this, refer to `http://lists.osgeo.org/mailman/listinfo/qgis-developer`
- **User list**: For this, refer to `http://lists.osgeo.org/mailman/listinfo/qgis-user`

These lists can be read and searched for using an online service at `http://osgeo-org.1560.x6.nabble.com/Quantum-GIS-f4099105.html`, where you can also find lists of other QGIS sub-projects or the mailing lists of several other local QGIS user groups.

If you don't find your nearest local QGIS user group, first ask in the user or developer mailing lists and, depending on the answer, try to create a new QGIS local group and announce it to the community.

IRC channel

Internet Relay Chat (**IRC**) is a fantastic way to get real-time support from users and developers. Remember that this help is always voluntary and the answers depend on your politeness and the available time of the connected users.

You can connect to the #qgis channel at the `http://www.freenode.net` server with your preferred IRC client via `http://webchat.freenode.net/?channels=#qgis`.

The philosophy of IRC problem solving is condensed in the first chat message sent to you by the #qgis channel: it will be "Don't ask to ask, just ask and hang around a while to see if someone answers. Please refer to `http://osgeo.pastebin.com/` instead of pasting more than five lines."

The StackExchange community

Technical social networks like StackExchange have a GIS sub-project that can be accessed from `http://gis.stackexchange.com`. Here you can look for problems reported by other users about QGIS and the answers that are given by other users or directly by QGIS core developers.

Messages relating to QGIS can be found looking for the `qgis` tag; for example, `http://gis.stackexchange.com/?tags=qgis`.

Sharing your knowledge and reporting issues

In StackExchange, the IRC channel, and the mailing lists, you can actively support other users who have problems that you have have already solved.

An important way to support a QGIS project, other than funding it, is by reporting bugs that are packaged with a detailed use case and data that allows others to replicate the problem. This will speed up bug fixing.

There are two kinds of issues: those that are related to QGIS or its core plugins (such as Processing) and those that are related to third-party plugins that you can install with Plugin Manager.

To report a QGIS issue or a core plugin issue, you need an OSGeo account, created at `https://www.osgeo.org/cgi-bin/ldap_create_user.py`, using which you can log in to the QGIS Redmine bug tracker to report issues at `http://hub.qgis.org/projects/quantum-gis/issues`.

Beware! Check to make sure your issue hasn't already been reported by looking in the issues list.

A good guide to reporting a QGIS issue is available at `http://qgis.org/en/site/getinvolved/development/index.html#bugs-features-and-issues`.

Reporting a third-party plugin issue depends on the plugin developer and where he/she decides to host the bug tracker. You can find this information in the plugin manager as shown in the following screenshot:

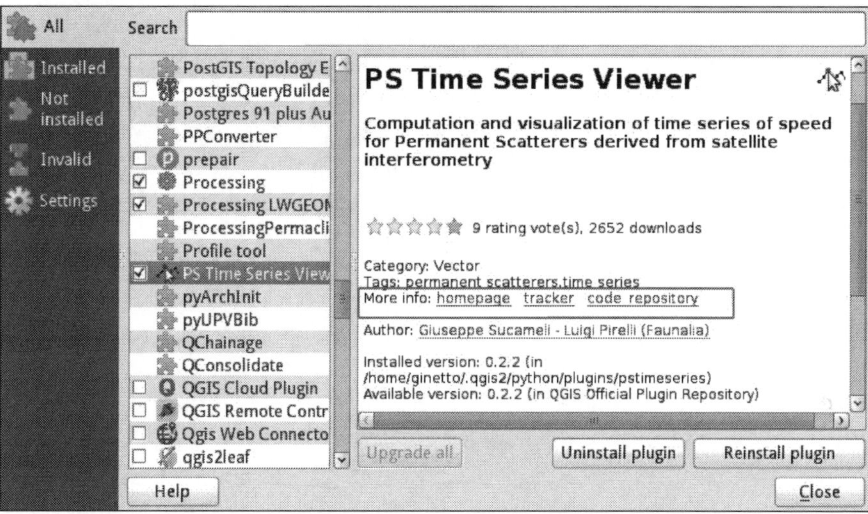

If you are looking for the link tracker, it will be found in the area marked by the red box in the second link, **tracker**. Other useful links can be found in the area marked in red. The first link points to the **homepage** plugin, where the plugin is described. The third link points to the the **code repository** of the plugin. In the QGIS plugin central repository, every plugin is accepted only if it has a lease tracker and a code repository.

The Python Console

The Python Console is a wonderful instrument to explore and learn PyQGIS. It's available in every QGIS installation and can be opened by selecting the **Python Console** voice in the **Plugins** menu.

The Python Console is a dockable interface, and like all dockable interfaces, you can change its position inside QGIS or separate it. You can try moving the console by dragging and dropping it.

The console is shown in this screenshot:

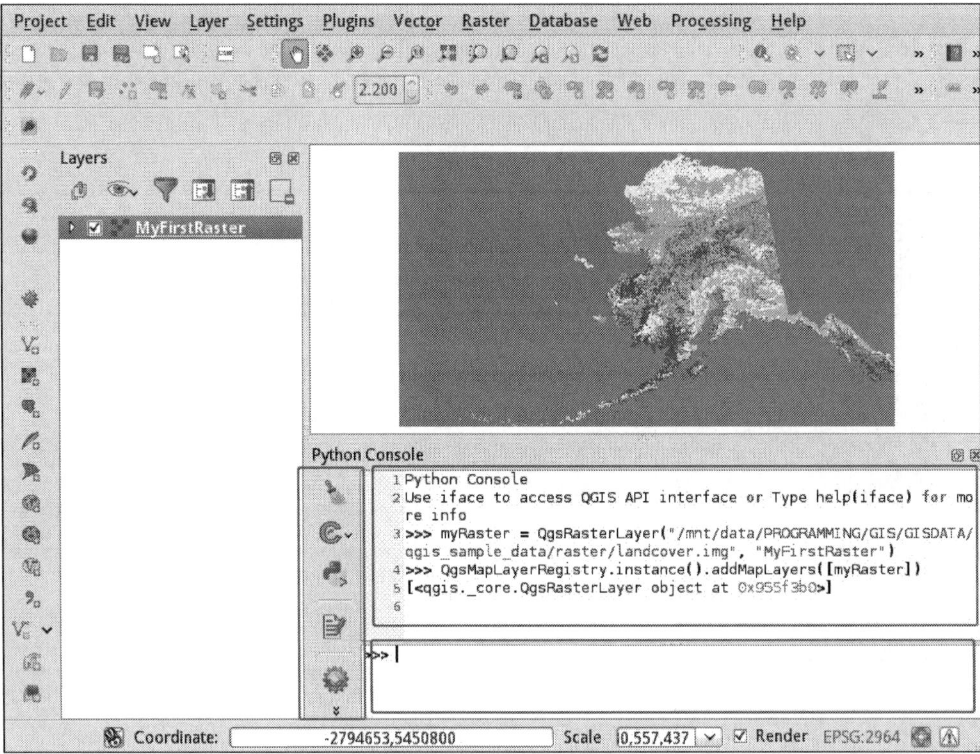

As you can see, the console is composed of a button toolbar marked by the red box. The bigger Python Console is marked by the upper-right red box and is where all the command results are shown, and finally a bottom command line, marked by the bottom-right red box, is where you can edit commands.

Here, we describe how to test code interactively and explore the PyQGIS classes. However, we will not explain all the possibilities of the Python Console. These are well documented and you can find them at `http://docs.qgis.org/testing/en/docs/pyqgis_developer_cookbook/intro.html#python-console`.

Getting sample data

To continue experimenting with PyQGIS we need a test dataset. The QGIS project has training material and sample data that we'll use in our snippet.

The QGIS sample data can be downloaded from `http://qgis.org/downloads/data/`.

My first PyQGIS code snippet

To break the ice, we will create our first PyQGIS code to show the unique ID of a selected layer loaded in QGIS.

1. To start with, we will first load the layer, `airports.shp`, which is available in the `shapefiles` directory of `qgis_sample_data`.
2. After it has been loaded successfully, select it in the list of layers; doing this will make it the active layer for QGIS. We can also do this by writing the following line in the the Python Console command line:

   ```
   layer = iface.activeLayer()
   ```

3. After editing the code and hitting *Return*, the edited command code is shown in the console.
4. The reference of the current active layer is archived in the variable named `layer`. Now, we can show the layer ID by typing the following code command in the command line after pressing *Return*:

   ```
   print layer.id()
   ```

The output will display something similar to **airports20141001174143539**.

My second PyQGIS code snippet – looping the layer features

In this paragraph, we'll introduce how to loop in Python and how to apply loops to explore the content of the layer loaded in the previous paragraph.
Write the following snippet in the Python Console, taking special care with the code indentation:

```
for feature in layer.getFeatures():
    print "Feature %d has attributes and geometry:" % feature.id()
    print feature.attributes()
    print feature.geometry().asPoint()
```

This will print a pattern like the following:

```
Feature with id 21 has attributes and geometry:
[22, u'US00342', 858.0, u'Airport/Airfield', u'PATL', u'TATALINA
    LRRS', u'Other']
(-328415,4.71636e+06)
```

The `layer.getFeatures()` method returns an object that can be iterated inside a `for` Python instruction, getting a `QgsFeature` instance for every loop. The `feature.attributes()` method returns a list (inside the brackets, `[]`) of the integer and unicode strings (the u'' values). The `feature.geometry()` method returns `QgsGeometry` that is converted in `QgsPoint` to be printed as a tuple (inside the `()` parenthesis) of coordinates.

It is strongly recommended that you explore the preceding classes. You can also practice by referring to the documentation at `http://qgis.org/api/`. Start by exploring the `QgisInterface` and `QGis` classes.

Indentation is an important part of the Python language; in fact nesting the code in Python is done using indentation as specified in the standard followed globally. You can find this at `http://legacy.python.org/dev/peps/pep-0008/`.

Exploring iface and QGis

The `iface` class used in the preceding snippets is important in every PyQGIS code; it is used to access most graphical QGIS components, from displayed layers to the toolbar buttons.

> The `iface` class is a Python wrapper for the C++ class, `QgisInterface`, which is documented at `http://qgis.org/api/classQgisInterface.html`. Most QGIS classes have a `Qgs` prefix. Some special classes can have the `Qgis` or `QGis` prefixes.
>
> The prefix `Qgs` is the Qt namespace registered by Gary Sherman, the QGIS creator, so `Q` stands for Qt and `gs` stands for Gary Sherman.

The most common use of the `iface` class is to get a reference of the canvas where maps are displayed:

```
canvas = iface.mapCanvas()
```

The class can also be used as a shortcut to load raster or vector layers; for example loading the raster, `path/to/my/raster.tif`, and naming it `myraster` in the legend panel. This can be done by typing the following command:

```
iface.addRasterLayer("path/to/my/raster.tif", "myraster")
```

> Pay attention to writing paths with Windows. A path string, such as `C:\path\to\raster.tif`, has the special escape character, \, so rewrite it by double escaping `C:\\path\to\raster.tif` or using the Unix notation, `C:/path/to/myraster.tif`, or notify Python with a raw string adding an "r" as in `r, C:\path\to\raster.tif`. Generally, it's good practice to create path strings using a Python library like `os.path`.

`QGis` is another class that contains some useful constants, such as a QGIS version or some default values. We can find out the QGIS version name running on our system by typing in the following command:

```
print QGis.QGIS_RELEASE_NAME, QGis.QGIS_VERSION_INT
```

For example, if the output is `Chugiak 20400`, then this value represents the version name and the version integer representation (which is version 2.4). This is useful to programmatically create a plugin that can run on different QGIS versions. The following snippet helps to distinguish the code among them:

```
if Qgis.QGIS_VERSION_INT < 20400:
    <here the code compatible with older version>
else:
    <here the code compatible with version higher or equal to 2.4>
```

Exploring a QGIS API in the Python Console

The QGIS APIs can be browsed in the documentation web page, but if you want to access the documentation directly in the Python Console, you can use some useful Python commands. The `help` command shows a synthesis of the API information available in the web documentation. Try to edit Python Console with the command:

```
help(iface)
```

The console will show all the methods of the `QgisInterface` class and a synthetic example of how to use this in Python syntax instead of C++ syntax. For example, if you want to show the result type of the call `iface.activeLayer` type:

```
help(iface.activeLayer)
```

The following lines will be displayed:

```
Help on built-in function activeLayer:
activeLayer(...)
QgisInterface.activeLayer() -> QgsMapLayer
```

This shows that the `activeLayer` call returns data that is a `QgsMapLayer` data type.

The Python `dir()` function gives you more detailed information, showing a list of all the methods belonging to a class.

Try typing `dir(iface)` and compare it with the result of the previous `help(iface)` command.

Creating a plugin structure with Plugin Builder

A QGIS plugin can be created manually with a simple editor, but the simplest and most complete way to start to create a plugin is to use another Python plugin called Plugin Builder.

Plugin Builder generates the file infrastructure of the plugin, thus avoiding writing repetitive code. Plugin Builder creates only basic and generic plugins, which can be modified to add specific user functionalities.

It is a graphical interface used to introduce the main parameters to create a plugin. It will generate a generic plugin with the following interface:

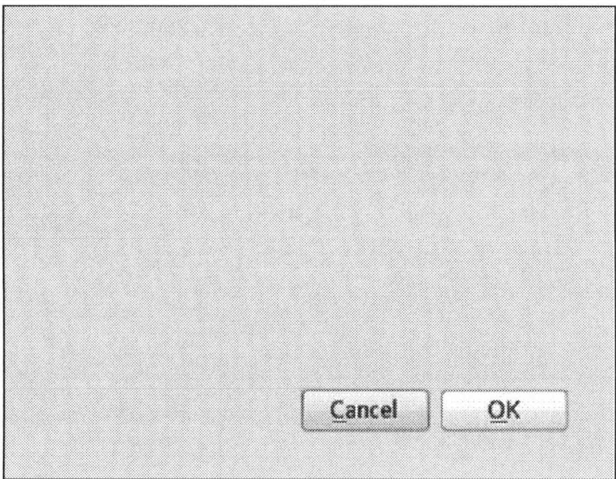

This is an almost empty dialog with two buttons. Every piece of this interface can be modified and customized to reach the plugin goal.

Installing Plugin Builder

The first step is to install Plugin Builder using the Plugin Manager by navigating to **Plugins | Manage and Install Plugins...**.

It's strongly suggested you install the experimental version of the plugin, as it is more complete and is the simplest to use. Its version should be greater than version 2.0.3.

To find the experimental version of the Plugin Builder in Plugin Manager, it's necessary to configure the manager to show the experimental plugin by ticking the checkbox when you navigate to **Settings | Show also experimental plugins**.

Locating plugins

The Plugin Builder, as every third-party Python plugin is by default, is installed in your home directory at the following path:

```
<your home path>/.qgis2/python/plugins/
```

Over here, you'll find your Plugin Builder code at the `pluginbuilder` directory. You will notice that each installed plugin has a proper code directory. We'll create a new plugin that, to be loaded by default by QGIS, has to be created in the Python plugin directory. It's possible to change the default plugin directory path, but this is outside the scope of this topic.

Creating my first Python plugin – TestPlugin

Starting the Plugin Builder will open a GUI to insert the basic parameters to set up the generation of your first QGIS plugin. The interface is shown in the following screenshot:

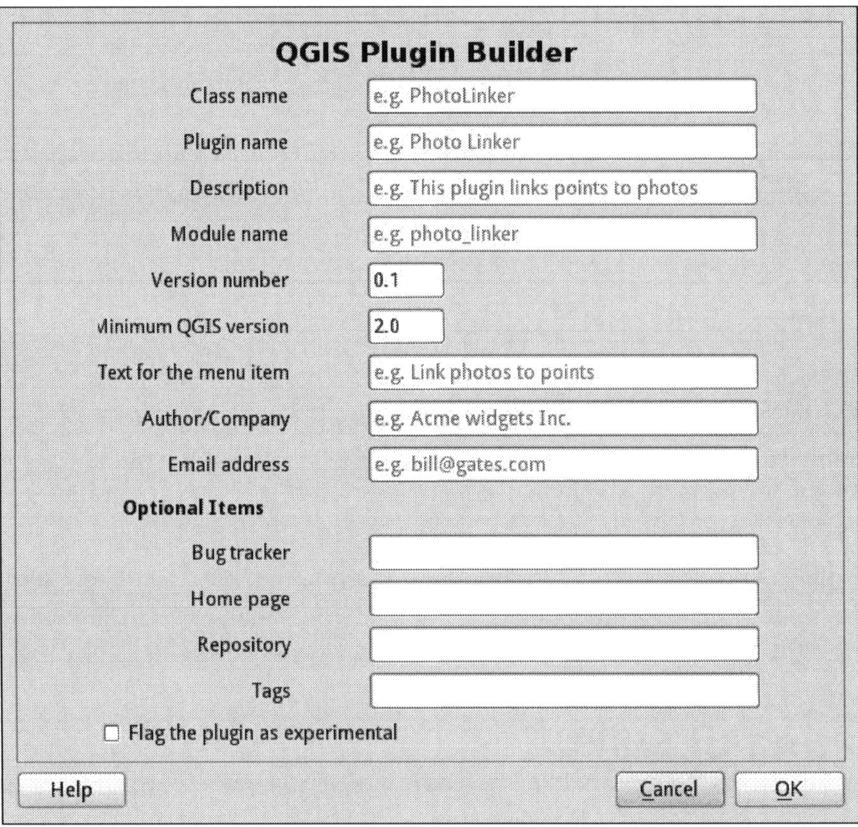

Each parameter is self-explanatory through tooltips and can be seen by moving the cursor on each parameter line.

Setting mandatory plugin parameters

There is a set of mandatory parameters that are always checked by the QGIS plugin repository when a plugin is uploaded. These parameters are also manually checked by QGIS members to approve the plugin officially in the central repository. The parameters are as follows:

- **Class name**: This is the name of the class that will contain the plugin business logic. It will be named in the CamelCase format (refer to http://en.wikipedia.org/wiki/CamelCase) to be aligned with the Python standard. This name will be used by Plugin Builder to generate a directory that will contain the generated code. Edit the value, TestPlugin.
- **Plugin name**: This refers to the colloquial name of the plugin and is what will be shown in the Plugin Manager and in the QGIS Plugins menu. Enter the value, My First Test Plugin.
- **Description**: This is a string containing the description or the plugin scope. Enter the value, This is the description of the plugin.
- **Module name**: In Python, a group of classes can be addressed and imported as a module. The module name should be in lowercase and, if necessary, with underscores to improve readability. We shall insert the value, test_plugin.
- **Version number**: This is the version number of the plugin. It can be any number. Generally, the versioning has this format,<MAJOR>.<MINOR>.<PATCH>,where:
    - A MAJOR version will specify that there are incompatible API changes from the previous majors
    - A MINOR version will specify that there are new functionalities in a backwards compatible manner
    - A PATCH version will specify that there are backwards compatible bug fixes

  At the moment, we can leave the default value set at 0.1.

- **Minimum QGIS version**: This refers to the minimum QGIS version in which the plugin will run. Each QGIS version has its own API set; the plugin can be compatible with a specified newer version but not with older ones if it's not programmed to be compatible. The minimum QGIS version is used by the QGIS plugin manager to show only plugins that are compatible with the running QGIS. This means that in QGIS 2.0 it's not possible to see the plugin for 1.8 or plugins that are designed to work only with 2.4 or newer versions. We can leave the default value 2.0.

- **Text for the menu item**: This refers to the text of the submenu opened under the voice, **Plugin Name**, described previously. We can insert the `Test Plugin starter` value.
- **Author/Company** and **Email address**: The parameters are obvious and are used to contact the developer if a user finds problems in the plugin. For example, you can set your name, surname, or company name, and your e-mail address.

Setting optional plugin parameters

There are also optional parameters that are really useful if your plugin would be available for other users. The parameters are as follows:

- **Repository**: A repository can be added later; it is the location where the plugin code is located. Its common to use a **Version Control System** (**VCS**) repository to maintain your code. Some popular VCSs are **Git** or **Subversion** and some related to Git. There are famous online services available at `http://www.github.com or https://bitbucket.org/`, where you can upload your project and maintain modifications. For example, the repository of the code of the Plugin Builder is `https://github.com/g-sherman/Qgis-Plugin-Builder`. For our plugin, we can leave this blank for now.
- **Bug tracker**: It's good practice to maintain a service to track the bugs of the plugin. Plugin users can file issues by preparing test cases that help to reproduce the bug. Tracking traces of the bugs and their solutions help us to know the evolution of the plugin. Usually the use of a VCS web service as shown previously, provides a bug-tracking service. For example, the bug tracker for the plugin called Plugin Builder is provided by the QGIS infrastructure and can be found at the `http://hub.qgis.org/projects/plugin-builder/issues`. For our plugin, we can leave this blank at the beginning.
- **Home page**: If the plugin has a web page where it is described, its good practice to add a plugin home page where you can leave usage instructions and the usages of the plugin. We can leave this blank at the start.
- **Tags**: This field is really important to allow QGIS users to find the plugin. It's used by the plugin manager to look for plugin keywords. For example, if the plugin is managing GPS data, its tags could be: `gps`, `gpx`, `satellite`, and so on. Try to find the tags that best describe the plugin and edit them separated with commas.

- The last checkbox of the Plugin Builder interface is checked if the plugin is in the experimental stage. By default, the Plugin Manager shows only plugins that are not experimental. To list the experimental plugins, it's necessary to tick the relative checkbox option in the Plugin Manager configuration. During the first developmental stage of the plugin, it's good practice to set it as experimental.

Generating the plugin code

After setting all the necessary plugin parameters, it's time to generate the code by clicking on the **OK** button, which will open a path selection dialog, which will select the location of the new plugin. Selecting the same directory that contains the plugin, Plugin Builder allows QGIS to find the new plugin. The default path should be is:

```
<your home path>/.qgis2/python/plugins/
```

However, you can create your plugin anywhere. Just remember to link or deploy it in the plugin directory to allow QGIS to load it.

After selecting a path, the code will be generated, creating a new directory in the selected path. In our case, the new directory will have the name, `TestPlugin`.

At the end of the code generation, there will appear a dialog with a message explaining the steps to complete plugin creation.

The generated plugin is not available yet; it's necessary to restart QGIS and activate it in the Plugin Manager interface. The plugin is now fully functional, but after the first activation, its button in the QGIS toolbar will be without an icon.

Compiling the icon resource

To make the icon visible, it's necessary to compile the icon resource so as to have it available in Python. Resource compilation is a process to render an icon's platform independent of the Qt framework, which is the graphical infrastructure on which QGIS is built.

To compile the icon resource, it's necessary to have installed the GNU `make` and the `pyrcc4` command.

In Windows, using the OSGeo4W QGIS installation, this command will be automatically installed and can be addressed only inside the OSGeo4W shell. On other platforms, they have to be installed using another command

The `make` command is usually available in every Linux operating system distribution.

The `pyrcc4` command is the Qt resource compiler for Qt4 and it's available in the pyqt4-dev-tools qt4-designer packages.

After the `make` and `pyrcc4` commands are installed, `make` has to be called inside the directory of the plugin. The `make` command will use the instructions included in the file called `Makefile` that instructs us about all the aspects of plugin compilation. The result of the `make` command is shown in this next screenshot:

```
OSGeo4W Shell
2014-09-24  04:29 PM               934 README.txt
2014-09-24  04:29 PM               101 resources.qrc
2014-09-24  05:05 PM             5,443 resources_rc.py
2014-09-24  05:09 PM             1,932 resources_rc.pyc
2014-09-02  01:26 PM    <DIR>          scripts
2014-09-24  04:29 PM    <DIR>          test
2014-09-25  01:56 PM             8,309 test3.py
2014-09-29  11:51 AM             8,167 test3.pyc
2014-09-25  12:52 PM             7,896 test3_csv_nonfunziona.py
2014-09-25  01:13 PM             2,295 test3_dialog.py
2014-09-25  01:13 PM             2,767 test3_dialog.pyc
2014-09-25  10:20 PM             2,396 test3_dialog_base.ui
2014-09-25  10:13 AM             3,504 ui_used_in_developing.py
2014-09-24  05:40 PM             1,455 __init__.py
2014-09-24  05:42 PM             1,662 __init__.pyc
              19 File(s)         68,933 bytes
               6 Dir(s)  23,884,546,048 bytes free

C:\Users\gino\.qgis2\python\plugins\Test3>MAKE
pyrcc4 -o resources_rc.py  resources.qrc

C:\Users\gino\.qgis2\python\plugins\Test3>make
pyrcc4 -o resources_rc.py  resources.qrc

C:\Users\gino\.qgis2\python\plugins\Test3>_
```

In the preceding screenshot, we can see that the `make` command instructs `pyrcc4` to compile the `resources.qrc` file, generating the Python version, `resources_rc.py`.

After compiling the icon resource and restarting QGIS, the plugin button will have an icon which is the default icon set by the Plugin Builder.

To change the icon, just change `icon.png` with a new image leaving the filename unchanged, and then recompile the icon resource.

[It's possible to change the filename and add more icon resources, but this is out the scope of the current chapter, so please refer to the Qt documentation for this.]

The plugin file structure – where and what to customize

Our `TestPlugin` code has been created in this folder:

```
<your home path>/.qgis2/python/plugins/
```

Here, we can find a complex file structure, where only a subset of files are strictly necessary for plugins and are in the scope of this book. The basic files are the following ones:

- `__init__.py`
- `metadata.txt`
- `Makefile`
- `icon.png`
- `resources.qrc`
- `resources_rc.py`
- `test_plugin_dialog_base.ui`
- `test_plugin_dialog.py`
- `test_plugin.py`

Each file has its own role inside the plugin, but only a few of them have to be modified to develop a custom plugin.

Other than basic files, the Plugin Builder generates other files and directories useful to manage more complex plugin projects. The files and directories are as follows:

- `help/`
- `i18n/`
- `scripts/`
- `test/`
- `pylintrc`
- `plugin_upload.py`
- `README.html`
- `README.txt`

Exploring main plugin files

Here, we will describe the role of each of the main files that compose a plugin:

- The `__init__.py` file is the common Python module starting file and it's also the entry point for QGIS to load the plugin. Usually, it doesn't have to be modified to create a plugin.
- The `metadata.txt` file is a text file containing all the information about the plugin. This file is read by Plugin Manger to manage the plugin inside QGIS. For example, in this file there are the plugin classification tags or the minimum QGIS version in which the plugin can be run.
- `Makefile` is a set of instructions used by the `make` command to compile resources and to manage some shortcuts to compile documentation or to clean previously compiled files, and so on. Usually, it's not necessary to edit it.
- The `icon.png` file is the plugin icon. As explained previously, it would be modified with a definitive plugin icon.
- The `resources.qrc` file is the file that instructs Qt about how to manage the icon. Usually, it's not necessary to edit it other than adding more icons or changing the filename of the `icon.png` file. More information about the resource file can be found in the Qt documentation at `http://qt-project.org/doc/qt-4.8/resources.html`.
- The `resource_rc.py` file is the compiled version of the `resource.qrc` file, and it's generated after compilation with the `make` command.
- The `test_plugin_dialog_base.ui` file is a file in XML format, describing the layout of the user interface of the plugin. It's strictly necessary only if the plugin needs its own GUI. The GUI structure can be edited manually, but usually it's better to use the Qt framework to edit it. The framework is called Qt Designer or Qt Creator and it can be downloaded from `http://qt-project.org/downloads`. The GUI design with the Qt framework is beyond the scope of this book, but the framework has good tutorials explaining how to customize graphic interfaces.
- The `test_plugin_dialog.py` file contains the logic of the preceding plugin GUI layout. This is the place where you add the logic of the plugin related to the GUI. For example, buttons that are disabled when a specific value is inserted, and so on.
- The `test_plugin.py` file is the container of the business logic of the plugin. It is complex, but usually only some parts have to be modified to insert the plugin logic. Modifying how this code will be managed will be dealt with shortly.

Plugin Builder generated files

The Plugin Builder generates more than basic files because it creates a template to manage complex Python plugin projects. A project can involve unit testing, detailed documentation, translation, code analysis, and so on. Here is a summary of these files:

- The `help` directory contains all the files necessary to automatically generate documentation in different formats, from HTML to PDF.
- The `i18n` directory contains files where we can add translations in other languages.
- The `script` directory contains some tools to facilitate the plugin development and deployment.
- The `test` directory contains unit tests for the plugins. It also contains utility classes to support unit testing.
- The `pylintrc` file is a configuration file for Pylint, a framework of code analysis.
- The `plugin_upload.py` file is a command-line utility to upload the plugin in the QGIS plugin repository.
- The `README` files contain the messages displayed at the end of plugin generation.

A simple plugin example

The goal of this section is to customize TestPlugin to classify the loaded layers in the raster and vectors and respectively populate two comboboxes with the layer names.

Adding basic logic to TestPlugin

As said previously, to customize TestPlugin, we have to modify some code portions in the files, `test_plugin_dialog_base.ui` for the GUI layout, `test_plugin_dialog.py` for the GUI logic, and `test_plugin.py` for the plugin logic.

Modifying the layout with Qt Designer

The default plugin GUI layout has only two buttons, **Ok** and **Cancel**. Here, we will add two comboboxes that will be populated by the logic of the plugin in `test_plugin.py`.

To edit the `test_plugin_dialog_base.ui` GUI layout, open it with Qt Designer, which will show the interface of the following screenshot:

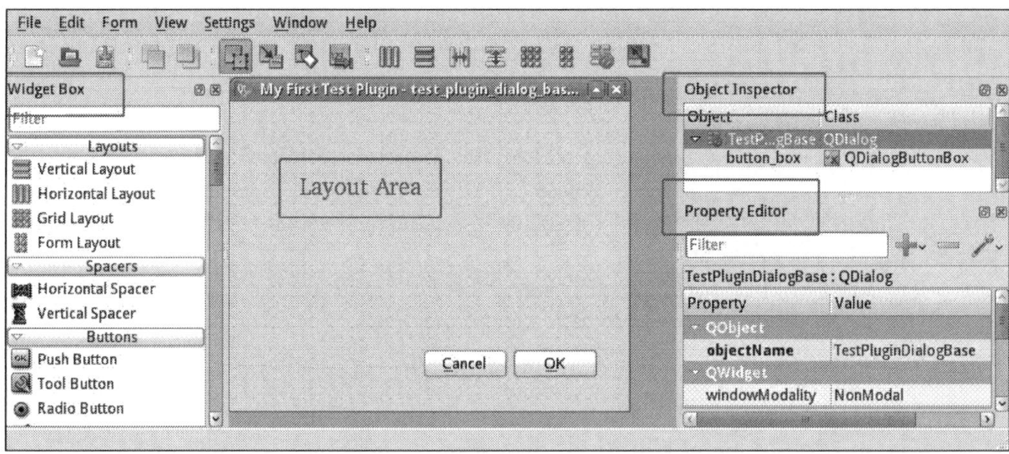

This is the graphical representation of the `test_plugin_dialog_base.ui` XML file. With Qt designer we can reorganize the layout, adding new graphical elements and also connect events and triggers related to the interface. In the preceding screenshot, the four red boxes mark the Designer sections:

- The **Layout Area** is the area where the plugin GUI is rendered.
- The **Widget Box** section contains the list of predefined GUI components. Here, we'll look for the combobox to add to the GUI layout.
- The **Object Inspector** section gives the hierarchy of graphical components composing the GUI layout.
- The **Property Editor** section gives a list of all the properties of the graphical components that can be customized.

Adding two pull-down menus

The next steps will be to create the layout as shown in the following screenshot:

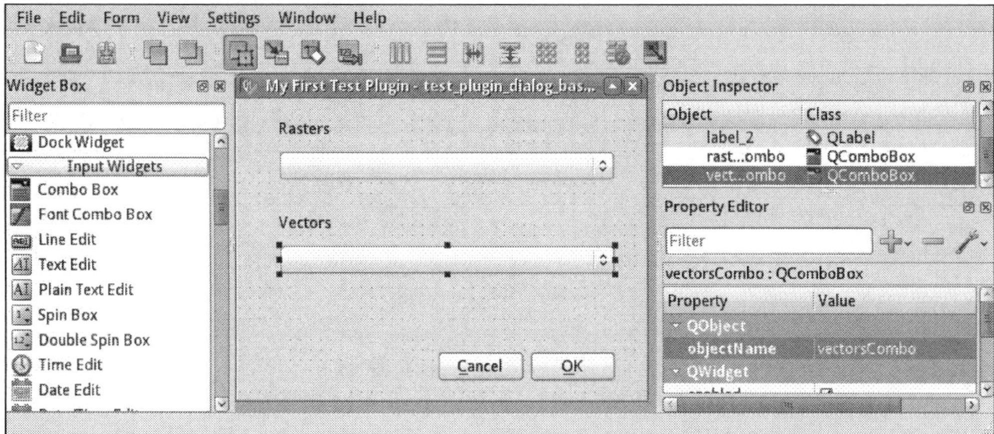

To create this layout, drag two comboboxes to the central GUI layout. The **Combo Box** option can be found by scrolling in the **Widget Box** section. In the same way, we'll add two labels on the top of each combobox.

To edit the labels, just double-click on them to enter into the label edit mode. This action is equivalent to changing the **Text** property in the **Property Editor** section.

After creating the layout, we can associate each combobox with an object name that will be used to distinguish the function of each combobox. To do this, we will change the **objectName** property in the **Property Editor** section. For example, we can set the name of the raster combobox as `rastersCombo`. In the same, way we rename the vector combobox as `vectorsCombo`.

The string used as **objectName** will be the name of the Python variable that refers to the graphical element. It will be used in the Python code when we want to get or set some property of the graphical element.

Modifying the GUI logic

Our plugin doesn't need modification in the dialog code, `test_plugin_dialog.py`, because all the GUI updates will be guided by the `test_plugin.py` code directly populating the `rasterCombo` and `vectorsCombo` elements. This is a design decision; in other cases, it could be better or cleaner to have the logic inside the dialog code to hide combo names using the dedicated function added to the dialog.

Modifying the plugin logic

Our core plugin logic has to be added. This can be done by modifying the `test_plugin.py` code. In many cases, such as in simple plugins or batch-processing instructions, only the `run(self)` function has to be modified inside the plugin code.

The `run()` function is the function that is called every time the plugin button is clicked on in the QGIS toolbox or the plugin is run from the plugin menu. In the `run()` function we have to:

- Collect all loaded layers
- Classify in raster and vector layers
- Populate the comboboxes in the plugin GUI
- Show the GUI with the new values loaded

To get all the listed layers, we'll have to ask the container of all the displayed layers, that is, the `QgsMapLayerRegistry` class. To do this, we will use the following code:

```
from qgis.core import QgsMapLayerRegistry
layersDict = QgsMapLayerRegistry.instance().mapLayers()
```

The first line imports the class, `QgsMapLayerRegistry`, from the Python module `qgis.core`.

You can import classes everywhere in the code, but it's good practice to import them at the beginning of the file.

Forgetting to import the class will cause an error during runtime. The error will be as follows:

```
Traceback (most recent call last):
File "<input>", line 1, in <module>
NameError: name 'QgsMapLayerRegistry' is not defined
```

In the second line, the result variable, `layersDict`, is a Python dictionary; it contains a set of key-value pairs where the key is the unique ID of the layer inside QGIS, and the value is an instance of the `QgsMapLayer` class that can be a vector or raster layer.

The variable, `layersDict`, has the suffix, `Dict`, only for a didactic reason, but it could simply be named `layers`.

Classifying layers

The next step is creating a list of vector and raster layer names. This can be achieved by looping `layersDict` in the following way:

```
from qgis.core import QgsMapLayer
vectors = []
rasters = []
for (id, map) in layersDict.items():
    if (map.type() == QgsMapLayer.VectorLayer):
        vectors.append( map.name() )
    elif (map.type() == QgsMapLayer.RasterLayer):
        rasters.append( map.name() )
    else:
        print "Not Raster nor Vector for layer with id:", id
```

The first line, which is the import line, is necessary to allow the use of the `QgsMapLayer` class.

The next two lines initialize two empty Python lists that will be filled with the layer names. Adding an element to an array is done with the Python command, `append`.

The layers are looped, separating each key-value couple directly into a couple of variables named `id` and `map`. The `id` variable is used to display a warning message in line 10.

The `map` variable is used with the methods, `type()` and `name()`, of the `QgsMapLayer` class. The `map.type()` call returns an enumerator value that can be `0`, `1`, or `2`, but it's better to compare it with the symbolic name of this constant to allow more readability.

Populating the combobox

After classifying the loaded layers, we set the values of the combobox of the plugin interface. This can be done with the following code:

```
self.dlg.rastersCombo.insertItems(0, rasters)
self.dlg.vectorsCombo.insertItems(0, vectors)
```

We named our comboboxes with object names, `rastersCombo` and `vectorsCombo`, in the two code lines earlier; comboboxes are populated with a standard QComboBox with the `insertItems(...)` call passing the two lists of layers. The `0` parameter is the index where we start to add new elements.

Understanding self

In the two preceding lines, there is the keyword, `self`, that may confuse everyone when approaching object-oriented programming for the first time. To explain it, try to follow where the `TestPluginDialog()` interface is created and saved.

At the beginning of the `test_plugin.py` code, the function, `__init__(self, iface)`, is where the Plugin GUI is created for the first time with the instruction:

```
self.dlg = TestPluginDialog()
```

This means that the result of the creation of the dialog, the `TestPlugiDialog()` constructor call, is saved in the `dlg` variable that belongs to the current instance of the plugin. In this case, `dlg` is called an object or instance variable, where the instance of the plugin is referred to with the `self` variable.

The variable, `self` ,is almost always available in every Python function; this allows us to access the `dlg` variable everywhere in the code.

Showing and running the dialog

We don't have to write any code here, because it will be generated by the Plugin Builder. The action to show how a dialog is saved in the `self.dlg` instance variable is shown here:

```
# show the dialog
self.dlg.show()
# Run the dialog event loop
result = self.dlg.exec_()
# See if OK was pressed
if result:
    # Do something useful here - delete the line containing pass and
    # substitute with your code.
    pass
```

This code is self-explanatory by the comments generated by the Plugin Builder

Some improvements

As you can see for yourself, the plugin doesn't work well if it is run more than one time. The content of comboboxes grow on every run of the plugin. It's left to the reader to find a solution how to avoid this behavior.

More detail of the code

The complete code of this example, as usual, can be obtained from the source code of the book.

Here, we'll give a bird's-eye view in the `test_plugin.py` source code that contains the `TestPlugin` class. This class has other methods than `run(self)`; these are as follows:

- `__init__(self, iface)`
- `tr(self, message)`
- `initGui(self)`
- `add_action(self, icon_path, text, callback, enabled_flag=True, add_to_menu=True, add_to_toolbar=True, status_tip=None, whats_this=None, parent=None)`
- `unload(self)`

The following provides a brief description of these methods:

- The `__init__(self, iface)` method is always present in every Python class and it is the constructor, which means that it is called every time you find a call, such as `TestPlugin(iface)`, as you can find in the `__init__.py` code.

  In our case, the constructor needs the `iface` variable passed as a parameter during construction.

  The constructor has the role of initializing the current translation, creating the plugin dialog GUI, and also creating the toolbar where the plugin button is to be added.

- The `tr(self, message)` method is just a shortcut to access the Qt translation engine of string messages.
- The `initGui(self)` method gets the icon resource and instructs how to interact with QGIS menu calling the `add_action(...)` method. This method is always called when the plugin is loaded in QGIS.

> It is important to remember the difference between loading a plugin and running a plugin.
>
> Loading is done using the Plugin Manager or automatically at the start of QGIS if the plugin was already loaded in the previous session.
>
> Running the plugin is when the user starts the plugin by clicking on the plugin icon or activating it in the plugin menu.

- The `add_action(...)` method has a lot of parameters that allow for fine configuration, but most of them are used with their default values, `True` or `None`. The main goal of this method is to create the menu in the plugin menu and to create the button to call the `run()` method. In Qt, these kind of buttons are objects of the `QAction` class.
- The `unload(self)` method is used to unroll all the QGIS GUI elements added with the previous `add_action(...)` method.

  This method is always called when the plugin is unloaded in QGIS using the Plugin Manager.

Setting up a debugging environment

Software development is a complex task and there's no software without bugs. Debugging is the process to remove software failures. Debugging is a task that can involve some other software to facilitate the debugging process.

A plugin can become complex, requiring debugging tools to discover problems. The complexity of the debugging process can start by inserting some prints inside the code or adding log messages to finish controlling the execution instructions by instructing how to find execution problems.

Inserting a breakpoint to stop the execution at a certain point of the code of a third-party QGIS plugin can be useful to discover how it works.

What is a debugger?

There is a set of possible tools to debug the Python code, but we'll focus only on PyDev, which reduces the number of installation steps and allows remote debugging without modification of the plugin code.

PyDev is an Eclipse plugin, where Eclipse is a free software programmable framework used to develop almost everything. PyDev can be added to a local installation of Eclipse, adding it from the marketplace, but to reduce the number of installation steps, it's suggested that you install Aptana Studio 3, an Eclipse customization with PyDev already installed.

Installing Aptana

Aptana Studio 3 can be downloaded from the project homepage at `http://aptana.com/`. Just unzip the folder and execute the executable file, `AptanaStudio3`, inside the unzipped folder.

The installation version of Aptana Studio 3 should be at least version 3.6.1, because some previous versions have bugs that don't facilitate code writing. If a version greater than 3.6 is not available, then it's necessary to upgrade to the beta version. To upgrade, follow the instructions mentioned at `http://preview.appcelerator.com/aptana/studio3/standalone/update/beta/`.

Setting up PYTHONPATH

To allow QGIS to be connected with the PyDev daemon, it's necessary that the PyDev daemon path be added to the `PYTHONPATH` environment variable.

To find the path to add, look for the `pydevd.py` file; it will be in the `AptanaStudio` installation path. If you find more than one version, get the path that has the highest version number.

For example, in my Linux installation there are the following paths:

```
/users/ginetto/Aptana_Studio_3.6/plugins/org.python.
pydev_3.0.0.1388187472/pysrc/pydevd.py
/users/ginetto/Aptana_Studio_3.6/plugins/org.python.
pydev_3.8.0.201409251235/pysrc/pydevd.pyc
```

In this case, we should use the following path:

```
/users/ginetto/Aptana_Studio_3.6/plugins/org.python.
pydev_3.8.0.201409251235/pysrc
```

This path can be added in the session, `PYTHONPATH`, or directly in the QGIS environment by modifying `PYTHONPATH` by navigating to **Options** | **System** in the **Environment** section, as shown in the following screenshot:

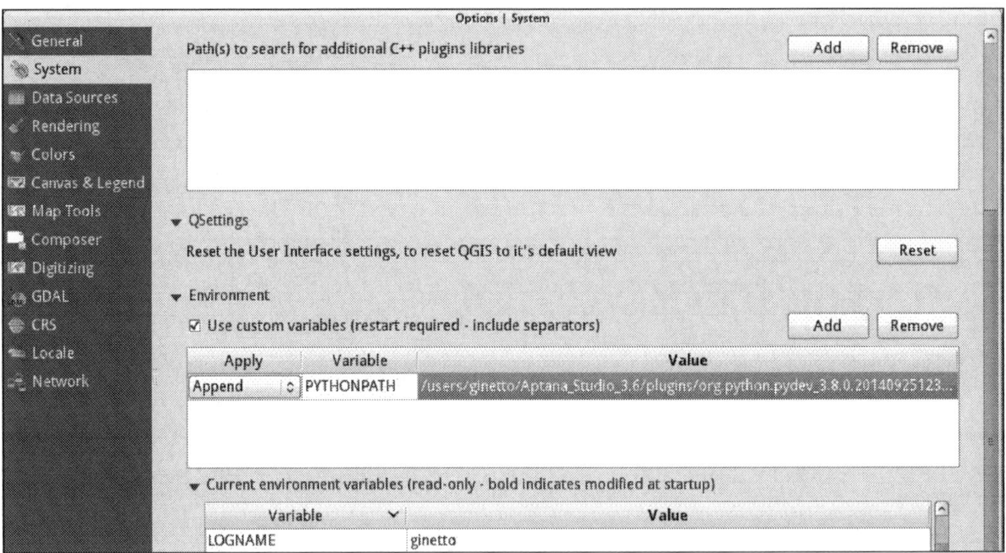

This way it will be possible to import the Python module, `pydevd`, in the QGIS Python Console and set the connection to the PyDev debug server, as described in the next paragraph.

To test if the path is set correctly, try to type the following code in the QGIS Python Console:

```
import pydevd
```

If it generates an error, it means that `PYTHONPATH` is not set correctly with the path of the `pydevd` module.

Starting the Pydevd server

The first step to connect to PyDev server is to start the server in the Aptana environment. This can be achieved by opening the Debug perspective of Aptana and then starting the server with the relative start/stop buttons. The buttons and Debug perspective are shown here:

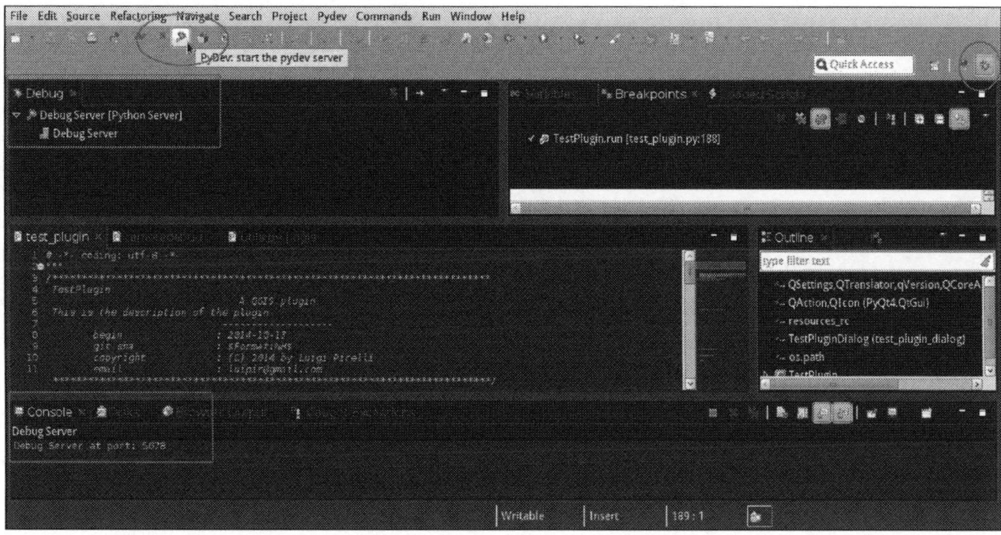

The Debug perspective can be opened by clicking on the right-hand side button circled in red. If the Debug perspective button is not available, it can be added to the Aptana menu. Navigate to **Window** | **Open Perspective** | **Other**.

The Start/Stop server button is pointed out by the red circle on the left.

While starting the server, some messages will appear in the **Debug** window highlighted by the red box in the upper-left section; this means that the server is running. In the **Debug** window, all connected clients will be listed.

In the red box on the bottom, the Aptana console window shows that the server answers to the port, `5678`; this is the information that we'll use to connect from QGIS.

Connecting QGIS to the Pydevd server

After running the PyDev server we'll connect to it from QGIS. In the QGIS Python Console, type the following code:

```
import pydevd
try:
    pydevd.settrace(port=5678, suspend=False)
except:
    pass
```

The preceding code first imports the `pydevd` module and then connects to the server with the `settrace` method. The connection is inside try/catch to allow catching an exception raised in case `settrace` cannot connect. The connection will take some seconds to connect. If the connection fails, the Python Console will show a message similar to the following one:

```
Could not connect to 127.0.0.1: 5678
Traceback (most recent call last):
File "/mnt/data/PROGRAMMING/IDE/Aptana_Studio_3/plugins/org.python.
pydev_3.8.0.201409251235/pysrc/pydevd_comm.py", line 484, in
StartClient
s.connect((host, port))
File "/usr/lib/python2.7/socket.py", line 224, in meth
return getattr(self._sock,name)(*args)
error: [Errno 111] Connection refused
```

If the connection is successful, the Aptana Debug Perspective will change showing the connected clients.

Debugging session example

Here, we will show how to debug the TestPlugin remotely. We'll also learn how to insert a code breakpoint, to stop executions, and to show variable values during executions.

The steps to follow are as follows:

1. Create a PyDev project that points to the source code of the TestPlugin.
2. Add a breakpoint to the `TestPlugin run()` function in the Aptana Debug Perspective.
3. Start the PyDev Debug server.
4. Connect to the PyDev server from QGIS.
5. Run the plugin.
6. Explore the variable values.
7. Continue the execution of the plugin.

Creating a PyDev project for TestPlugin

To be able to add code breakpoints it's necessary to load `test_plugin.py`. This can be simply opened as a file, but it's better to learn how to have a view of the entire plugin as a PyDev project. This allows us to use Aptana as a debug and develop environment.

This is done in two steps:

1. Creating a PyDev project in Aptana Studio 3.
2. Linking the source code to the project.

Creating a PyDev project called `TestPlugin` is done by navigating to **File** | **New Project**. This will open a wizard where we'll have to look for a **PyDev Project** entry. Select it and click on the **Next** button at the bottom. Here, the wizard will pass to the phase to insert the project name, `TestPlugin`, and then click on the **Finish** button at the bottom. A new project called `TestPlugin` will be shown in the **PyDev Package Explorer** Aptana section.

The next step is to add the folder of our `TestPlugin` code inside the project. To add it, select the **TestPlugin** PyDev project; right-click on it to add a new folder, as shown in this following screenshot:

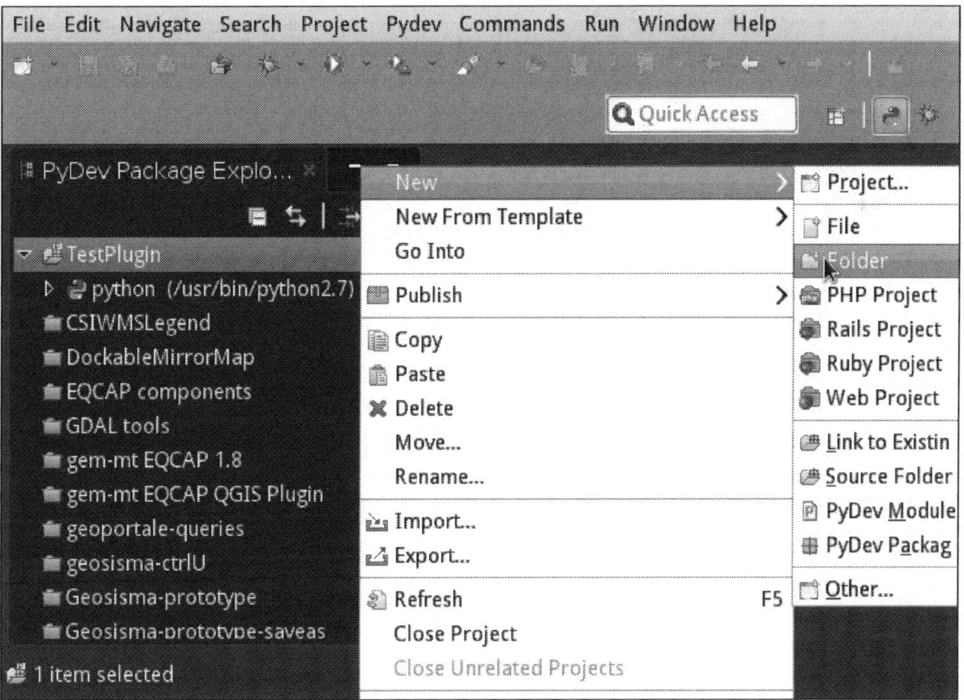

Here, we can see the contextual menu to add a new folder for the selected project. This action will open a GUI where we can create or link a new folder. In our case, it's useful to link to the existing plugin code, which can be done using the **Advanced** features of the GUI, as shown here:

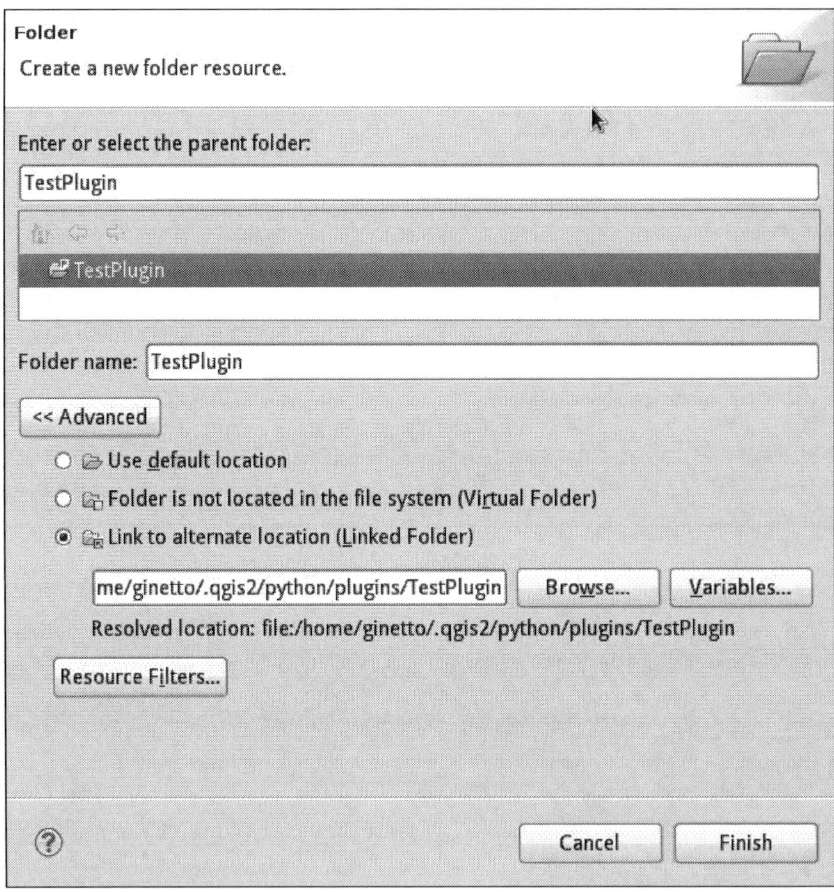

After linking the folder, it will appear under the `TestPlugin` PyDev project where we can look for the `test_plugin.py` code. Double-click on the file; it will be opened on the right-hand side of Aptana, as shown in the following screenshot:

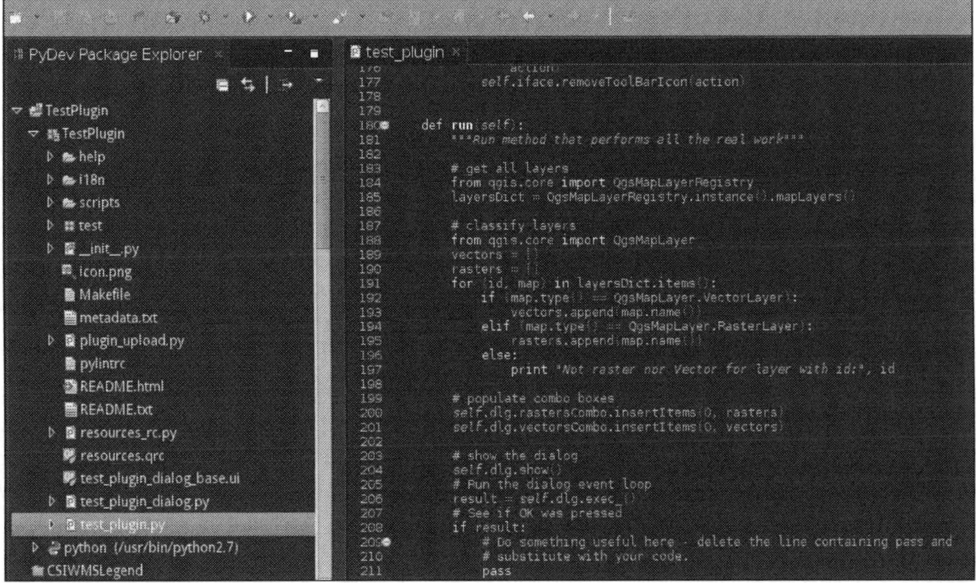

Adding breakpoints

Breakpoints are debugger instructions to stop execution at a specified line to allow users to investigate variable values and eventually change their values manually.

Our scope is to add a simple breakpoint and check that the plugin execution stops exactly at that point, passing the control to the remote debugger.

To add a breakpoint, open the Debug perspective and double-click on the left-hand side of the line number, for example, the line with the `for (id, map)` code in `layersDict.items()`. Aptana will add a breakpoint, as shown in this screenshot:

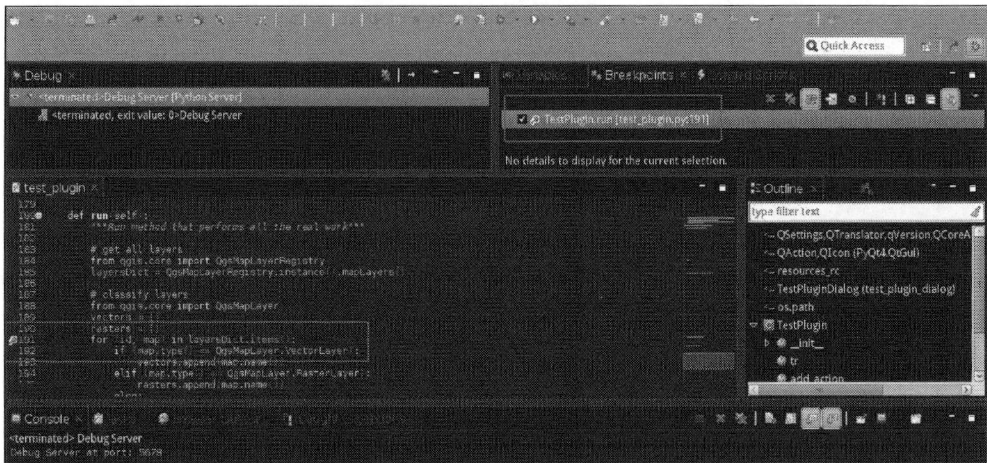

The line where the breakpoint is added is marked with the red box on the left, and a new breakpoint will be listed in the **Breakpoints** list, as marked by the red box on the upper-right corner.

Debugging in action

Now it's time to test the debug session. Let's start the PyDev debug server and connect to it, as described previously.

In QGIS, run `TestPlugin`; QGIS will now freeze because it's starting to execute the `run()` method of the `test_plugin.py` code and a breakpoint is encountered. So, the control is passed to the PyDev debugger; the Aptana Debug perspective will appear similar to this:

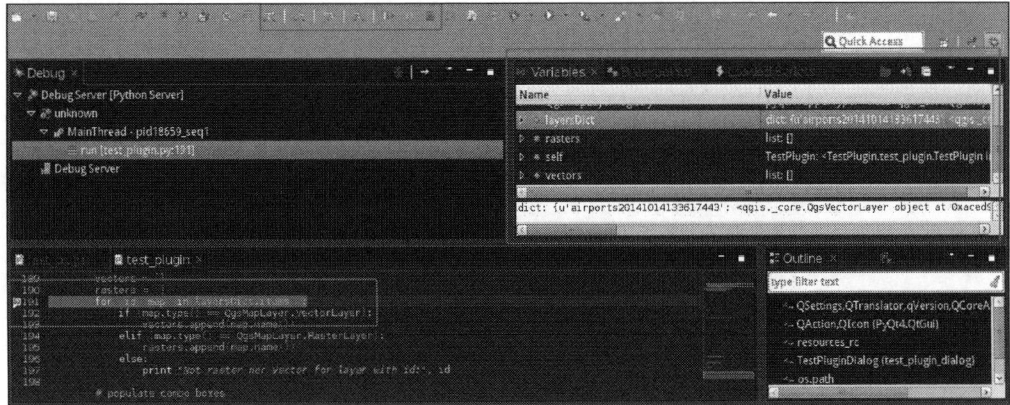

Here, the red box on the left shows where the code is stopped, adding an arrow to the previous green bullet. The **Variables** Aptana section, marked with the red box on the right, displays variables used in the code and their values.

There are buttons, marked in the preceding screenshot by the upper-red box, to run statements in a step-by-step way, to enter in a function or continue with an execution.

A detailed description of how to work with the PyDev Debug perspective is out of the scope of this chapter, but it's possible to find more documentation on PyDev at `http://pydev.org/manual_adv_debugger.html`.

Summary

In this chapter, we approached three important topics on developing plugins. First, how to get help to solve programming problems; second, how to create a basic plugin as a template to develop more complex plugins; and finally, how to debug it. These topics demonstrate basic skills to manage plugin development that can become complex during their design and development.

The chapter focused on creating a basic infrastructure to easily solve problems that could be found during the development of a working plugin.

In the next chapter, we will explore the PyQGIS programming in depth and learn to manage raster, vector, algorithm, and QGIS interface interactions. These skills will be useful to add specific business functions to QGIS to solve practical processing problems.

10
PyQGIS Scripting

This chapter is focused on a specific use case or user. QGIS can be used in many different ways, and the GIS user is an eclectic user who has many different ways to interact with data and QGIS instruments. The main focus of this chapter is a user who has an algorithm and wants to integrate it with QGIS.

An algorithm can be an external program, such as a water-modeling tool, or a processing toolbox's set of instructions.

It's possible to interact with QGIS in many different ways, from experimenting with PyQGIS in the Python console to creating plugins that control events generated by QGIS. This chapter will give you an overview on the following topics:

- Learning Python
- Loading rasters by code
- Loading vectors by code from files or database
- Describing vector structure and how to browse and edit features
- Using Processing Toolbox algorithms by code and executing your custom algorithm
- Calling external algorithms
- Interacting with canvas events to draw or pick values from a raster or vector

Where to learn Python basics

This chapter is not intended to give you an introduction to Python programming. There are a lot of free online resources and MOOC (`http://en.wikipedia.org/wiki/Massive_open_online_course`) courses on the web.

The main resources can be obtained directly from the Python homepage at `https://www.python.org/about/gettingstarted/`, where there is a big collection of guides and free books and tutorials.

Tabs or spaces, make your choice!

During programming in Python, it's important to give special attention to edit code with correct indentation. Avoid mixing spaces and tabs because it can generate errors that can be difficult to understand, especially for someone who is a beginner at Python programming.

Loading layers

Loading layers in QGIS involves different steps, which are as follows:

1. Load the layer. This step creates a variable with the layer information and related data.
2. Register the layer in QGIS so that it can be used by other QGIS tools.

Loading a layer means loading a reference to the layer and its metadata. The layer is not necessarily loaded in memory, but is usually fetched only when data is accessed to be processed or visualized.

Loading and registering a layer are separate steps. A layer can be loaded, processed, and modified before it is visualized, or it can be loaded as temporary data for an algorithm. In this case, it's not necessary that the QGIS framework would be aware of the layer.

The `iface` object has shortcuts to load raster and vector layers in a single step instead of loading and registering them via separated steps.

Every layer type is managed by a provider manager. QGIS has some internal implemented providers, but most of them are external libraries. The list of available providers depends on the QGIS installation. This list can be obtained by typing the following code snippet in the QGIS Python console:

```
>>> QgsProviderRegistry.instance().providerList()
[u'WFS', u'delimitedtext', u'gdal', u'gpx', u'grass',
u'grassraster', u'memory', u'mssql', u'ogr', u'ows', u'postgres',
u'spatialite', u'wcs', u'wms']
```

The preceding result shows a Python list of strings that have to be used when a PyQGIS command needs the provider parameter.

Managing rasters

Like most free software projects, the QGIS community doesn't want to reinvent the wheel if it's not strictly necessary. For this reason, most raster formats that are managed by QGIS can be loaded, thanks to the GDAL library that is documented at `http://gdal.org/`.

To code the loading of our first raster named `landcover.img` that is available in the `qgis_sample_data` folder, execute the following code snippet in the QGIS Python console by adapting the path to `landcover.img` based on your operating system and data location:

```
myRaster =
QgsRasterLayer("/qgis_sample_data/raster/landcover.img")
```

In this way, the layer is loaded and referred to with the `myRaster` variable. If we want the layer to be visible in the legend with the name `MyFirstRaster`, we need to modify the preceding code snippet by adding a second parameter, as follows:

```
myRaster =
QgsRasterLayer("/qgis_sample_data/raster/landcover.img",
"MyFirstRaster")
```

Two things should be noted: the first is that loading a raster layer is usually not necessary to specify the raster provider because it is GDAL by default. The second is that loading a layer is not the same as visualizing it in QGIS; a layer reference is loaded in memory to be processed and it is eventually visualized.

One of the basic actions after loading a layer, raster or vector, is to ensure that it has been loaded correctly. To verify this, execute the following code:

```
myRaster.isValid()
```

It should return `True` if the layer has been loaded correctly. The following snippet does some recovery actions in case loading fails:

```
if not myRaster.isValid():
    <do something if loading failed>
```

Exploring QgsRasterLayer

The `myRaster` variable is an instance of the `QgsRasterLayer` class. This means that all methods of the raster are documented at `http://qgis.org/api/classQgsRasterLayer.html`. This class is a specialization of the generic `QgsMapLayer` class.

Remember that API documentation refers to C++ APIs, but not all methods are visible to Python. If you want to have all the methods available in Python, use the Python `help` command by typing the `help(QgsRasterLayer)` command in the Python console.

For example, we can get some raster information by calling the methods, as follows:

```
print myRaster.height(), '-', myRaster.width()
```

The preceding code will produce the following output:

```
5046337 - 5374023
```

To get the extent of the layer, it is necessary to use the `extent()` method of the `QgsMapLayer` class; so, execute the following code:

```
print myRaster.extent()
```

This will generate a strange result that is similar to the following output:

```
<qgis._core.QgsRectangle object at 0xaa55dd0>
```

This shows that the result of the `extent()` method is a `QgsRectangle` instance where it is possible to call all the methods belonging to `QgsRectangle`. For example, the bounding box coordinates can be printed with the following code snippet:

```
ext = myRaster.extent()
print ext.xMinimum(), ext.yMinimum(), '-', ext.xMaximum(),
ext.yMaximum()
```

This will produce the following result:

```
-7117600.0 1367760.0 - 4897040.0 7809680.0
```

Visualizing the layer

Finally, we can visualize the raster using the centralized QGIS layer manager called `QgsMapLayerRegistry`. This class is like the hub where we can manage layer loading and unloading. It's useful to read the list of its methods in the QGIS API documentation.

`QgsMapLayerRegistry` is a singleton class. This means that it can't be instantiated multiple times like `QgsRasterLayer`. For example, we can have different loaded raster layers and each one is an instance of the `QgsRasterLayer` class, but it's not possible to have different `QgsMapLayerRegistry` instances. This is because it is blocked by code and it's possible to get only the unique instance using the `instance()` method.

Finally, to visualize the layer, we have to execute the following code:

```
QgsMapLayerRegistry.instance().addMapLayer(myRaster)
```

This will produce an output similar to the following:

```
<qgis._core.QgsRasterLayer object at 0x955f3b0>
```

Another way to load it is by using a method similar to the one shown in the following code:

```
QgsMapLayerRegistry.instance().addMapLayers( [ myRaster ] )
```

This gives a similar result as before, but with two more brackets because it returns a list:

```
[<qgis._core.QgsRasterLayer object at 0x955fc20>]
```

The latter `addMapLayers` method differs from `addMapLayer` because it accepts a list of layers, mixing rasters, and vectors. Layers will be displayed at the same time by following the list order.

After the image is loaded, QGIS will appear as shown in the following screenshot:

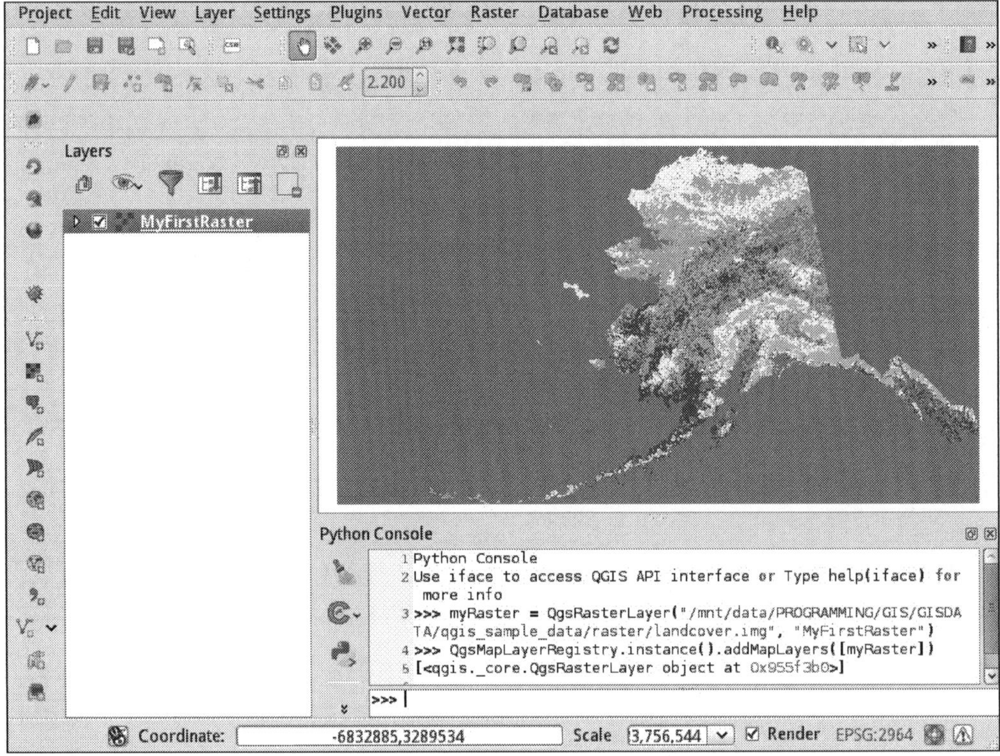

The preceding screenshot displays the image loaded in QGIS with a default false-color rendering palette.

Managing vector files

Similar to the raster layer in the previous section, most of the vector formats managed by QGIS are supported by the OGR library, a part of the GDAL library. OGR is documented at the same link of the GDAL library. All vector formats managed by OGR are listed at `http://www.gdal.org/ogr_formats.html`.

To read vector data, it's always necessary to specify the provider because it can be provided by different sources.

To code the loading of our first shapefile named `alaska.shp` that is available in `qgis_sample_data`, execute the following code snippet in the QGIS Python console:

```
myVector =
QgsVectorLayer("/qgis_sample_data/shapfiles/alaska.shp",
"MyFirstVector", "ogr")
```

This way the layer is loaded and referred by the `myVector` variable. After adding the layer to `QgsMapLayerRegistry`, it will be visualized in the legend with the name `MyFirstVector`. In the `QgsVectorLayer` constructor call, is possible to find a third string parameter, `ogr`, that specifies to use the OGR library to load the `alaska.shp` file.

As usual, we will check whether the loaded layer is valid using the following code:

```
myVector.isValid()
```

Managing database vectors

If vector data is hosted in a spatial database, it can be loaded by specifying the location and connection information using the `QgsDataSourceURI` class. A URI (short form for Uniform Resource Identifier) is how a resource can be identified on a network like the World Wide Web.

The following code snippet shows how to fill the URI with the necessary information to connect to a remote spatial database as PostGIS:

```
uri = QgsDataSourceURI()
uri.setConnection("localhost", "5432", "myDb", "myUserName",
"myPassword")
uri.setDataSource("public", "myTable", "the_geom", "myWhere")
print uri.uri()
```

The first line creates an instance of `QgsDataSourceURI` that is filled with other information in the next lines.

The `setConnection` method accepts the IP or the symbolic name of the database engine, the connection port, the database name, the username, and the password. If the password is set to `None`, QGIS will ask you for the password for connecting to database.

The `setDataSource` parameter refers to the schema name, the table name, and the geometry column where the geometry is archived. Finally, an optional where string could be set to directly filter data, in this case, `myWhere`.

> You can load a query without having it as a table. Just write your query, instead of the table name, and place round brackets around it. For example, the previous `setDataSource` method will become `uri.setDataSource("public", "( <here your query> )", "the_geom", "myWhere")`.

The last line shows you the URI string that will be used to point to the vector data. It will be a string similar to the following one:

```
dbname='myDb' host=localhost port=5432 user='myUserName'
password='myPassword' table="public"."myTable" (the_geom)
sql=myWhere
```

An alternative way is to create the URI string manually, rather than populating the `QgsDataSourceURI` class, but it's generally more readable and less error-prone to write the previous code than a complex string.

If the database is on a SpatiaLite file, it's necessary to substitute the `setConnection` method with the following code:

```
uri = QgsDataSourceURI()
uri.setDatabase("/path/to/myDb.sqlite")
uri.setDataSource("", "myTable", "the_geom", "myWhere")
print uri.uri()
```

This generates the following URI string:

```
dbname='/path/to/myDb.sqlite' table="myTable" (the_geom)
sql=myWhere
```

After the URI string is created, we can use it to create a new vector layer with the following code:

```
myVector = QgsVectorLayer(uri.uri(), "myVector", "postgres")
```

The third string parameter specifies the data provider, which in the case of vector data that is hosted on a SpatiaLite database would have the value as `spatialite`.

As usual, to visualize the vector, we have to use the following code:

```
if myVector.isValid():
  QgsMapLayerRegistry.instance().addMapLayer(myVector)
```

The preceding code visualizes the vector only if it has been correctly loaded. Failures can happen for reasons such as errors in parameter settings, a restriction of the vector provider, or a limitation by the database server. For example, a PostgreSQL database can be configured that would allow access to a vector table only for a specific group of users.

Vector structure

The `QgsVectorLayer` class is more complex that its raster equivalent. To describe it, we will first approach basic layer parameters and then we will explore how the vector is organized. We will explore some classes that are involved in the vector structure that represent rows and headers.

The basic vector methods

We will explore the vector class working on a real vector; we will load `alaska.shp` in the `myVector` variable.

This variable is an instance of the `QgsVectorLayer` class. This means that all methods of the vector are documented at `http://qgis.org/api/classQgsVectorLayer.html`. As for rasters, this class is a specialization of the generic `QgsMapLayer` class.

To get the extent of the layer, it's necessary to use the `extent()` method of the `QgsMapLayer` class:

```
print myVector.extent().toString()
```

Executing the preceding code will generate the following result:

```
-7115212.9837922714650631,1368239.6063178631011397 :
4895579.8114661639556289,7805331.2230994049459696
```

This shows the corner coordinates in the format `xmin,ymin: xmax,ymax`.

To know how many records or features contain the vector, use the following code:

```
myVector.featurecout()
```

This will produce the result of `653L` records.

In the result, `L` means that it is a Python long integer, which is an integer limited only by the available memory.

As we saw earlier, vectors can be sourced from different providers, each one with its proper capabilities and limitations. To discover the capability of `myVector`, use the following method:

```
myVector.capabilitiesString()
```

This will give the following result:

```
u'Add Features, Delete Features, Change Attribute Values, Add
Attributes, Delete Attributes, Create Spatial Index, Fast Access
to Features at ID, Change Geometries, Simplify Geometries with
topological validation'
```

A Unicode string describes all the possible actions available on the vector.

Describing the vector structure

Compared to rasters, vectors are more complex. A vector involves a set of classes that are used to represent every piece of the vector, from the header to the single attribute.

We can think of a vector as a table with rows and columns, and one header that describes each column of the table. Each row has its own geometry and attributes that is archived in the columns of the row. Each vector could contain only a geometry type. For example, it can be composed of only points, lines, polygons, or collections of these geometry types.

The structure of the classes involved in a vector table is shown in the following picture:

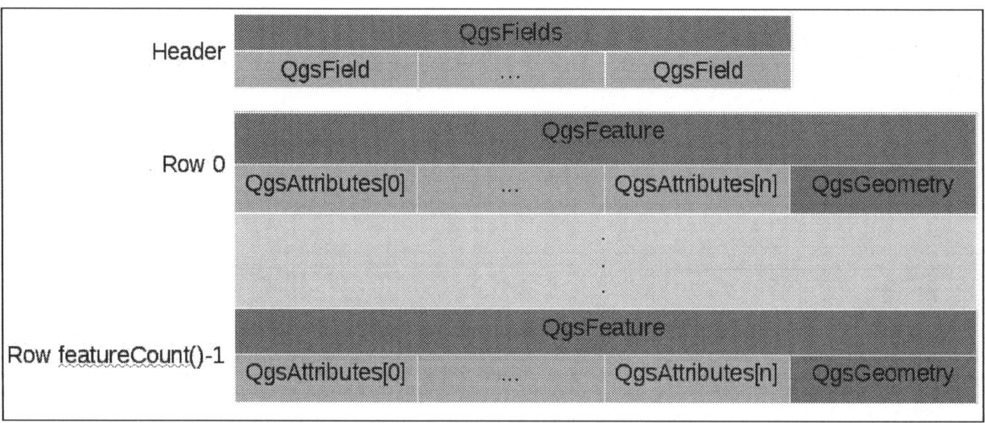

A description of these classes is the subject of the following paragraphs.

Describing the header

The container of the header information is the `QgsFields` class that contains methods to point to every column description. A column description is abstracted by the `QgsField` class.

To get the header container for `myVector`, we use the following code:

```
header = myVector.pendingFields()
```

Here, `header` will store a `QgsFields` instance. The `pendingFields()` method is named pending because it always refers to the current state of the vector. This is also the case for editing the vector, and adding or removing columns.

We can use `QgsFields` methods to add or remove columns, get the column index by name with `indexFromName`, or get a specific field using its index with the following code:

```
field_0 = header[0]
```

Usually, it is more useful to manage all the column data as a list. For this reason, there is a specific method; for example, to iterate on all column fields use this snippet:

```
for column in header.toList():
  <do something with the variable "column" that is a QgsField>
```

Each `QgsField` has its methods to obtain the column name with `name()`, get its `type()` and `typeName()` methods, and also get its `precision()` method if it is numeric.

In the following code, we can explore the characteristics of the header of `myVector`:

```
header = myVector.pendingFields()
print "How many columns?", header.count()
print "does the column 4 exist?", header.exists(4)
print "does the column named 'value' exist?", header.
indexFromName('value')
print "Column 0 has name", header[0].name()
for column in header.toList():
  print "name", column.name()
  print "type", column.typeName()
  print "precision", column.precision()
```

This will produce the following output:

```
How many columns? 3
does the column 4 exist? False
does the column named 'value' exist? -1
Column 0 has name cat
name cat
type Real
precision 0
name NAME
type String
precision 0
name AREA_MI
type Real
precision 15
```

Describing the rows

Each row of `myVector` is a `QgsFeature` instance. The feature contains all attribute values and a geometry. There are also as many values as `QgsField` in the header.

Each feature has its own unique ID that is useful to retrieve the feature directly. For example, to retrieve the feature with ID `3`, we use the following code:

```
features = myVector.getFeatures( QgsFeatureRequest( 3 ) )
feature = features.next()
```

The preceding code could appear overcomplicated to retrieve a single feature; in the next section, we will show you the reason for this complexity by explaining the role of the `QgsFeatureRequest` class to retrieve features.

With the feature, we can retrieve all the attributes and the geometry of the feature using the following code:

```
print feature.attributes()
geom = feature.geometry()
print geom
```

This will produce something similar to the following result:

```
[4.0, u'Alaska', 0.322511]
<qgis._core.QgsGeometry object at 0x99f0050>
```

This shows an array of values we get from the `attributes()` call and an instance of a `QgsGeometry` result of the `geometry()` method that is saved in the `geom` variable.

Exploring QgsGeometry

The `QgsGeometry` class is a complex and powerful class that can be used for a lot of geometry operations, and most of them are based on the capability of the underlying GEOS library.

GEOS means Geometry Engine - Open Source. It is an extensively used library to manage geometry entities. You can find more information about this at `http://trac.osgeo.org/geos/`.

It's difficult to describe the richness of this class and all the available methods; for this reason, it's best to read the API documentation. Here, we will give you only a brief introduction to some of the useful and commonly used methods.

It's possible to have the `length()` and `area()` methods of the geometry, when these values have sense depending on geometry `type()`. For the `geom`, get in the previous paragraph the following code:

```
print "Is this a Polygon?", geom.type() == QGis.Polygon
print "it's length is", geom.length()
print "it's area measure", geom.area()
print "Is it multipart?", geom.isMultipart()
```

This will generate the following output:

```
Is this a Polygon? True
it's length is 19143.8757902
it's area measure 8991047.15902
Is it multipart? False
```

The area and length unit depend on the `myVector` CRS and can be obtained with the following code:

```
myVector.crs().mapUnits()
```

This returns `0` for `QGis.Meters`, `1` for `QGis.Feet`, or `2` for `QGis.Degrees`.

Other interesting methods of the `QgsGeometry` class are related with spatial operators such as `intersects`, `contains`, `disjoint`, `touches`, `overlaps`, `simplify`, and so on.

Useful methods can be found to export geometry as a **Well-Know Text (WKT)** string or to GeoJSON with `exportToWkt` and `exportToGeoJSON`.

There are a bunch of static methods that can be used to create geometry from a WKT or QGIS primitives such as `QgsPoint`, `QgsPolygon`, and so on. A static method is a method that can be called without an instance variable. For example, to create geometry from a point that is expressed as a WKT, we can use the following code:

```
myPoint = QgsGeometry.fromWkt('POINT(  -195935.165    7663900.585
)')
```

Notice that the `QgsGeometry` class name is used to call the `fromWkt` method. This is because `fromWkt` is a static method.

In the same way, it's possible to create `myPoint` from `QgsPoint` with the following code:

```
newPoint = QgsPoint( -195935.165, 7663900.585)
myPoint = QgsGeometry.fromPoint( newPoint )
```

The two ways that we just described are equivalent and generate `QgsGeometry` in the `myPoint` variable.

Iterating over features

Now, it's time to discover how to get all the features or a subset of them. The main way to iterate over all features or records of `myVector` is by using the following code that shows the ID of each feature:

```
for feature in myVector.getFeatures():
    feature.id()
```

This will print a list of all the 653 record IDs as shown here:

```
0L
1L
...[cut]...
652L
```

It's not always necessary to parse all records to get a subset of them. In this case, we have to set the `QgsFeatureRequest` class parameters to instruct `getFeatures` and then retrieve only a subset of records; in some cases, we must also retrieve a subset of columns.

The following code will get only a subset of features and columns:

```
rect = QgsRectangle(  1223070.695,  2293653.357 , 9046974.211,
4184988.662)

myVector.setSubsetString(' "AREA_MI" > 1000 ')
request =  QgsFeatureRequest()
request.setSubsetOfAttributes([0, 2])
request.setFilterRect( rect )

for index, feature in enumerate( myVector.getFeatures( request )
):
    print "The record %d has ID %d" % ( index, feature.id() )
```

This will produce the following list of only eight records:

```
The record 0 has ID 223
The record 1 has ID 593
The record 2 has ID 596
The record 3 has ID 599
The record 4 has ID 626
The record 5 has ID 627
The record 6 has ID 630
The record 7 has ID 636
```

In the preceding code, the first line creates a `QgsRectangle` method that is used in the `setFilterRect()` method to get only features that are within the rectangle. Then, only the values of columns 0 and 2 are fetched, setting the filter with `setSubsetOfAttributes`.

It should be noted that the QgsFeatureRequest class has the setFilterExpression method that is useful to select only features that are bigger than 1000, but it can't be used in the upper case. The QgsFeatureRequest code forces to exclusively use a spatial filter or an expression filter. For this reason, to filter at the same time by expression and by bound box, it's necessary to set the expression at a layer level with the setSubsetString method.

The `enumerate` statement is a Python instruction to get something that can enumerate and return pairs of elements with the first element as the index and the second as the enumerated element.

Describing the iterators

The preceding code uses the PyQGIS `getFeatures` statement that doesn't return features directly but instead returns an iterator. In fact, executing the code `myVector.getFeatures()` produces an output similar to the following one:

```
<qgis._core.QgsFeatureIterator object at 0xd023c20>
```

An iterator is a Python object that gets the record every time it is asked to get one; in our case, the `for` statement requests a record after every iteration.

The iterator works like a proxy: it doesn't load all the features in memory, but gets them only when it is necessary. In this way, it is possible to manage big vectors without memory limitations.

Editing features

After being able to parse all the features, it's necessary to learn how to modify them to satisfy our processing needs. Features can be modified in two ways:

- Using the data providers of the vector
- Using the methods of `QgsVectorLayer`

The difference that exists between these two ways is the ability to interact with some editing features of the QGIS framework.

Updating canvas and symbology

We will now modify the Alaska shapefile in the following subsections. If we modify some geometry of the legend classification, it will be necessary to refresh the canvas and/or layer symbology. The canvas can be refreshed with the following command:

```
iface.mapCanvas().refresh()
```

The symbology of a modified `QgsVectorLayer` instance saved in the `myVector` variable can be updated with the following code:

```
iface.legendInterface().refreshLayerSymbology(myVector)
```

Editing through QgsVectorDataProvider

Each `QgsMapLayer`, as a `QgsVectorLayer` instance, has its own data provider that can be obtained with the `dataProvider()` method. This is shown in the following code snippet that is executed in the Python console:

```
myVector =
QgsVectorLayer("/qgis_sample_data/shapfiles/alaska.shp",
"MyFirstVector", "ogr")
QgsMapLayerRegistry.instance().addMapLayers([myVector])
myDataProvider = myVector.dataProvider()
print myDataProvider
```

This will print something similar to <qgis._core.QgsVectorDataProvider object at 0xaabdc20> on the Python console. This is the instance of the `QgsVectorDataProvider` class.

The data provider will directly access the stored data, avoiding any control by QGIS. This means that no undo and redo options will be available and no events related to the editing actions will be triggered.

The code snippets that follow describe how to interact with vector data directly using the data provider. These code samples will modify the Alaska shapefile set of files, so it's better to have a copy of the original files to restore them after you apply the following examples.

Some of the following examples will work directly on features of `myVector`. We can get a feature directly using the `QgsFeatureRequest`. For example, to get the feature with ID `599`, we can use the following code snippet:

```
features = myVector.getFeatures( QgsFeatureRequest(599) )
myFeature = features.next()
```

The feature 599 is the biggest polygon available in the Alaska shapefile. Remember that `getFeatures` returns an iterator and not the feature directly, so it's necessary to use `next()` to get it.

The `next()` method could generate a `StopIteration` exception when the iterator arrives at the end of the features' list; for example, when the `getFeatures` result is empty. In our case, we don't care about this exception because we are sure that the feature with ID 599 exists.

Changing a feature's geometry

After getting feature 599, we can change its geometry. We'll substitute its current geometry with its bounding box. The code snippet to do this is as follows:

```
oldGeom = myFeature.geometry()
bbox = oldGeom.boundingBox()
newGeom = QgsGeometry.fromRect( bbox )
newGeomMap = { myFeature.id() : newGeom  }
myDataProvider.changeGeometryValues( newGeomMap )
```

After we refresh the canvas, the shapefile will appear as in the following screenshot:

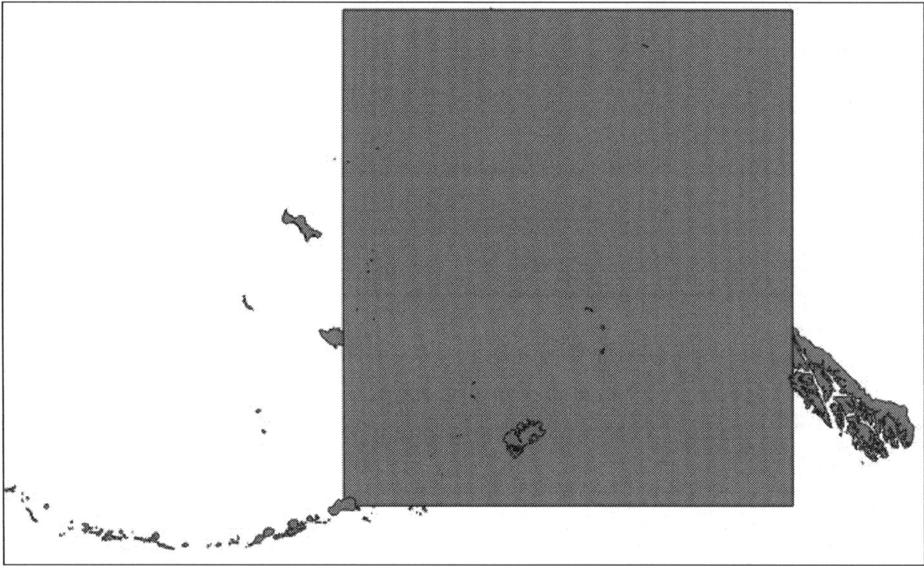

The `changeGeometryValues()` method accepts a `QgsGeometryMap` object. This is the Python dictionary that contains the ID of the feature to change as a key and the new geometry as a value.

Changing a feature's attributes

After getting feature 599, we can change its attributes in a way similar to how we changed the geometry of the feature in the previous subsection.

In this case, the map is a `QgsChangedAttributesMap` class that will be a Python dictionary. This is composed of a key, the ID of the feature to change, and another dictionary as a value. This last dictionary will have the index of the column to change as the key and the new value that has to be set as the value. For example, the following code snippet will change the area value to 0 for column 2 of feature 599:

```
columnIndex = myVector.pendingFields().fieldNameIndex( "AREA_MI" )
newColumnValueMap = { columnIndex : 0  }
newAttributesValuesMap = { myFeature.id() : newColumnValueMap  }
myDataProvider.changeAttributeValues( newAttributesValuesMap )
```

You can check whether the value of the parameter has changed by navigating to **View | Identity Features**.

If you want to change more than one attribute, you just have to add more key/value pairs in the `newColumnValueMap` dictionary, using the following syntax:

```
newColumnValueMap = { columnIndex1:newValue1, …,
columnIndexN:newValueN}
```

Deleting a feature

A feature can be deleted by pointing at it with its ID. The ID of the feature can be obtained with the `id()` method of the `QgsFeature` class. The following snippet will remove feature 599:

```
myDataProvider.deleteFeatures([599])
```

After you refresh the canvas, `myVector` will be shown as in the following screenshot:

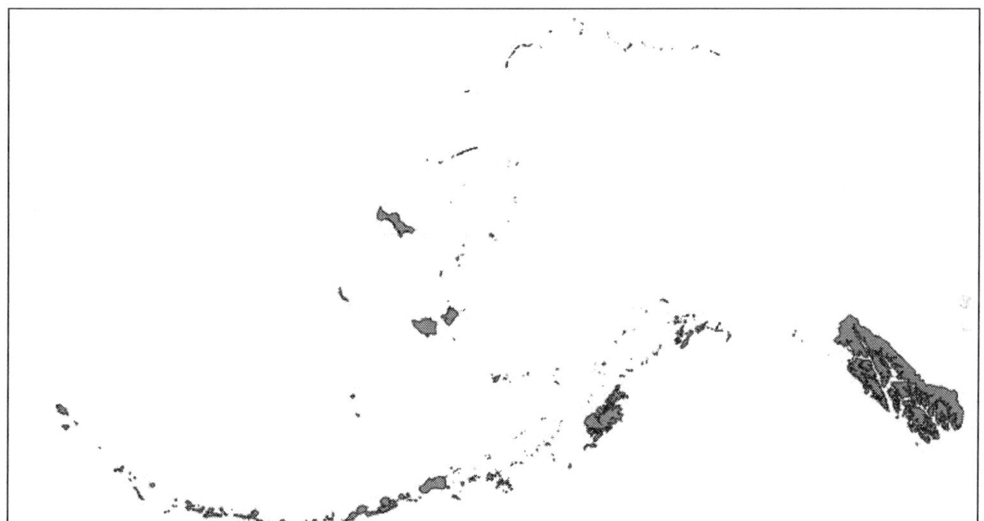

Adding a feature

After we reload the original Alaska shapefile, we will again get the feature 599 that we will use as the base to create a new feature. The geometry of this new feature will be set as the bounding box of feature 599; this is done using the following code:

```
# get data provider
myDataProvider = myVector.dataProvider()
# get feature with id 599
features = myVector.getFeatures( QgsFeatureRequest(599) )
myFeature = features.next()
# create geometry from its bounding box
bbox = myFeature.geometry().boundingBox()
newGeom = QgsGeometry.fromRect( bbox )
# create a new feature
newFeature = QgsFeature()
# set the fields of the feature as from myVector
# this step only sets the column characteristic of the feature
# not its values
newFeature.setFields( myVector.pendingFields() )
# set attributes values
newAttributes = [1000, "Alaska", 2]
newFeature.setAttributes( newAttributes )
# set the geometry of the feature
newFeature.setGeometry( newGeom )
# add new feature in myVector using provider
myDataProvider.addFeatures( [newFeature] )
```

The preceding code is explained in the inline comments and it adds a new feature. The new feature can be checked by opening the attribute table and selecting the last record. This will produce an interface that is similar to the following screenshot:

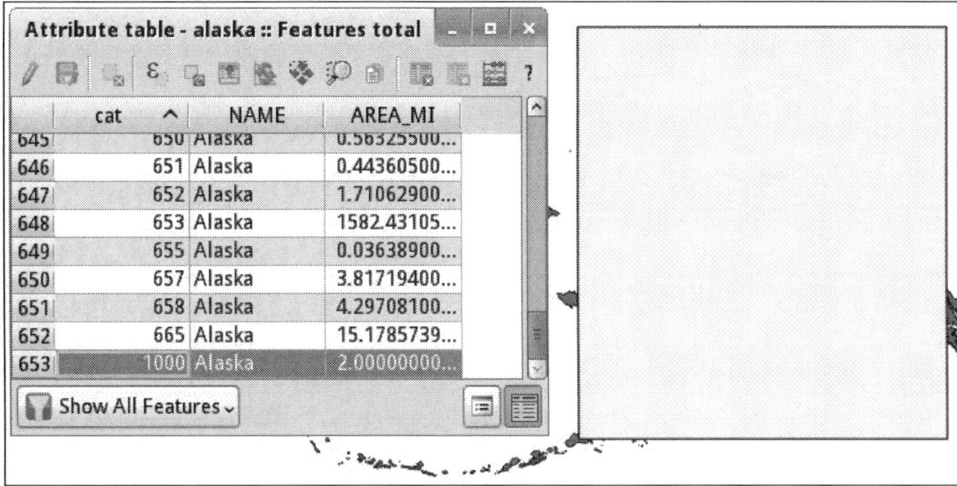

When you select the last record in the attribute table, it will be highlighted.

Editing using QgsVectorLayer

Editing using `QgsVectorLayer` gives you much more power to interact with the QGIS interface and to control the editing flow.

The `QgsVectorLayer` methods to modify the attributes or geometry of a feature are slightly different than the method used in `QgsVectorDataProvider`, but the main characteristic is that all these methods work only if the layer is in the editing mode, otherwise they return `False` to notify failure.

An editing session on the `myVector` vector follows the steps described in the following pseudocode:

```
myVector.startEditing()
< do vector modifications saved in myVector.editBuffer() >
if <all ok>:
      myVector.commitChanges()
else:
      myVector.rollback()
```

Each step generates events that can be cached if they are useful for our processing scopes. The list of generated events can be read in the `QgsVectorLayer` documentation. For example, `startEditing()` will generate the `editingStarted()` event, adding a feature will generate the `featureAdded()` event, committing changes will emit the `beforeCommitChanges()` event before applying changes, and then the `editingStopped()` event will be generated.

A useful exercise for you is to create a simple script to connect all these events to print commands. This is a good way to learn the event sequence that is generated during vector editing.

For example, the following code snippet in the editing console will print a message every time someone starts to edit the vector layer, `myVector`:

```
def printMessage():
    print "Editing is Started"

myVector.editingStarted.connect( printMessage )
```

In the last line, we instruct Python to call the `printMessage` function every time the `editingStarted` event is emitted by `myVector`. In this case, the `printMessage` function is usually known as a callback or a listener.

Discovering the QgsVectorLayerEditBuffer class

It's possible to have a fine-grained control of the editing session managing event of the `QgsVectorLayerEditBuffer` class that stores all modifications of the layer. It's also possible to access the buffer using the vector layer with the following code:

```
myEditBuffer = myVector.editBuffer()
```

A detailed description of this class is outside the scope of this chapter, but it's strongly suggested to explore it to discover all the PyQGIS editing opportunities such as setting the attribute of a new feature based on some parameters of the nearest geometry of another layer.

Changing a feature's geometry

After we have reloaded the original Alaska shapefile and got feature 599, we can change its geometry. We'll substitute the current geometry with its bounding box, and the code snippet to do this is as follows:

```
oldGeom = myFeature.geometry()
bbox = oldGeom.boundingBox()
newGeom = QgsGeometry.fromRect( bbox )
myVector.startEditing()
myVector.changeGeometry( myFeature.id(), newGeom )
myVector.commitChanges()
```

In this case, it's not necessary to refresh the canvas because a canvas refresh is triggered by events generated during a commit. After the commit, the interface will appear similar to the image shown in the *Adding a feature* section.

In the preceding code, you can see that the changing geometry has a different API using the data provider. In this case, we can change a feature each time.

Changing a feature's attributes

After we get feature 599, we can change its attributes in a way similar to how we changed the geometry of the feature in the previous section. The following snippet will change the area value to 0 for column 2 of feature 599;

```
columnIndex = myVector.pendingFields().fieldNameIndex( "AREA_MI" )
myVector.startEditing()
myVector.changeAttributeValue( myFeature.id(), columnIndex, 0 )
myVector.commitChanges()
```

You can check whether the value of the parameter has been changed by navigating to **View | Identity Features**.

In the preceding code, notice that the changing attribute has a different API using the data provider. In this case, we can change features one at a time.

Adding and removing a feature

Since the procedure is really similar to those applied using the data provider, you can test these actions by removing and adding features inside an editing session.

Running processing toolbox algorithms

QGIS's versatility is due mainly to two reasons. The first is the ability to customize it by adding functions, thanks to its plugin structure. The second is the power of the processing toolbox that can connect different backend algorithms such as GRASS GIS, SAGA, GDAL/OGR, Orfeo Toolbox, OSM Overpass, and many more with dedicated providers.

In this way, for example, we can access all GRASS processing algorithms by using QGIS as the project and presentation manager. Another important ability of the processing toolbox is that it can be used to join together all the backend algorithms, allowing you to connect the best algorithms. For example, we can connect GRASS as a producer for another algorithm that is better developed in another backend such as SAGA. Here, QGIS processing becomes the place where you can add your specific algorithm in a more complex and integrated workflow.

This section is focused on how to code the execution of algorithms that are already available in the processing toolbox. The main points to learn are as follows:

- Looking for a processing toolbox algorithm
- Discovering parameters accepted by the algorithm
- Running the algorithm

In the following sections, we will be using the processing commands after we have imported the processing module with the following code:

```
import processing
```

If the processing module is not imported, every processing command will generate an error such as the following one:

```
Traceback (most recent call last):
  File "<input>", line 1, in <module>
NameError: name 'processing' is not defined
```

Looking for an algorithm

The processing toolbox contains a huge list of algorithms that can be searched for using keywords. Similar to how we can look for an algorithm in the processing toolbox GUI, it's possible to search for an algorithm using the PyQGIS commands.

For example, to look for commands to convert something, we can execute the following command at the Python console:

```
import processing
processing.alglist("convert")
```

This will generate some output lines, and among them, we will find the command that we are looking for:

```
Convert format----------------------------------------
>gdalogr:ogr2ogr
```

If it's not the previous command, it can be this (depending on the processing toolbox version):

```
Convert format----------------------------------------
>gdalogr:convertformat
```

If the version of the processing toolbox is greater than 2.2, substitute the `gdalogr:ogr2ogr` string with `gdalogr:convertformat`. To find out the version of the processing toolbox, look for it in the QGIS plugin manager.

This string is composed of two parts; `Convert format` is the command as shown in the processing toolbox GUI and `gdalogr:ogr2ogr` is the command recognized by the processing commander. This means that in our PyQGIS script, we can refer to the algorithm with the name `gdalogr:ogr2ogr`. In this case, the `ogr2ogr` algorithm belongs to the `gdalogr` backend. The `alglist` method looks for only the left part. Notice that the `alglist` method will also show custom scripts. This means that a custom script or model will be accessible in the PyQGIS interface of the processing toolbox.

Getting algorithm information

Every processing algorithm has its own GUI with input and output parameters. You may wonder about the parameters, their names, and the values that may be used in the same algorithm using PyQGIS scripts? To discover these elements, we will use the `alghelp` processing command.

This command accepts the command name that is used internally by `processing` as a parameter; for example the `gdalogr:ogr2ogr` string that we saw in the previous paragraph. We can get help for this command by using the following code:

```
import processing
processing.alghelp("gdalogr:ogr2ogr")
```

The preceding code snippet will produce the following output that would depend on the installed version of GDAL/OGR;

```
processing.alghelp("gdalogr:ogr2ogr")
ALGORITHM: Convert format
  INPUT_LAYER <ParameterVector>
  DEST_FORMAT <ParameterSelection>
  DEST_DSCO <ParameterString>
  OUTPUT_LAYER <OutputVector>


DEST_FORMAT(Destination Format)
  0 - ESRI Shapefile
  1 - GeoJSON
  2 -  GeoRSS
```

```
3 - SQLite
...[cut]...
16 - S-57 Base file
17 - Keyhole Markup Language
```

As you can see, these are the same parameters that were accepted in the algorithm GUI. There is also the list of format-accepted values.

Running algorithms from the console

Running a processing algorithm can be done by using the `runalg` method or the `runandload` method. The first one generates the output without visualizing it and is useful when you want to generate temporary data. The second method loads and visualizes the output layer in QGIS.

The parameters accepted in this method are the processing command name strings followed by all the parameters, depending on the command used.

We will perform an exercise and convert the `alaska.shp` shapefile that is available in `qgis_sample_data/shapefiles` into the SpatiaLite format. This format is a very powerful SQLite spatial database that creates a self-contained spatial database in a single file. The SQLite format is referred to with the value `3` as specified in the algorithm help shown before.

To export algorithms into this format, we'll follow these steps:

- Load the Alaska shapefile in QGIS
- Run the `convert` algorithms
- Load the result in QGIS

Assuming that the `alaska.shp` shapefile has been loaded in QGIS, we will run the algorithm based on the parameters shown in the previous section; this is done using the following snippet:

```
processing.runalg("gdalogr:ogr2ogr", "alaska", 3, None,
"F:/temp/alaska")
```

In the preceding code, it should be noted that the fourth parameter is `None` instead of an empty string, but for the processing toolbox both are equivalent. The fifth parameter is the output file name, but it could be set to `None`. In this case, the output will be generated in a temporary file.

The return value of `runalg` is a dictionary with a key and the output name as specified in the `alghelp`, and the value of the key is the reference of the filename generated by the algorithm. In the preceding example, the output dictionary is something like the `{'OUTPUT_LAYER': 'F:/temp/alaska.sqlite'}` dictionary.

The last step is displaying the layer. This can be done in two ways: by loading a vector layer as usual or by running the algorithm with the `runandload` method as specified earlier. In this case, the following code will generate and load a new layer:

```
processing.runandload("gdalogr:ogr2ogr", "alaska", 3, None,
"F:/temp/alaska")
```

This is shown in the following screenshot:

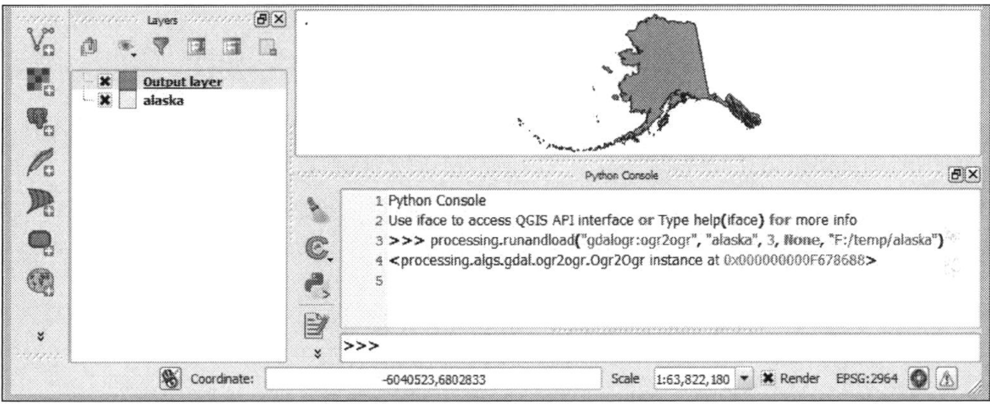

The new layer will be called **Output layer**, which is the beautified name of the parameter in the dictionary returned by `runalg`.

Running your own processing script

Running a custom processing script is not much different from running a generic processing command. We only need to find out how the custom script is addressed by the toolbox.

To discover all this information, we will create and run a simple processing script.

Creating a test processing toolbox script

We will start by opening the processing toolbox by navigating to **Processing** | **Toolbox**. Next, navigate to **Scripts** | **Tools** | **Create new script** in the toolbox. These actions will open a new interface where we can paste the following code snippet:

```
import time
for index in range(100):
    progress.setPercentage(index)
    print index
    time.sleep(0.1)
```

We will save it with the name `emptyloop`. The code is shown in the following screenshot:

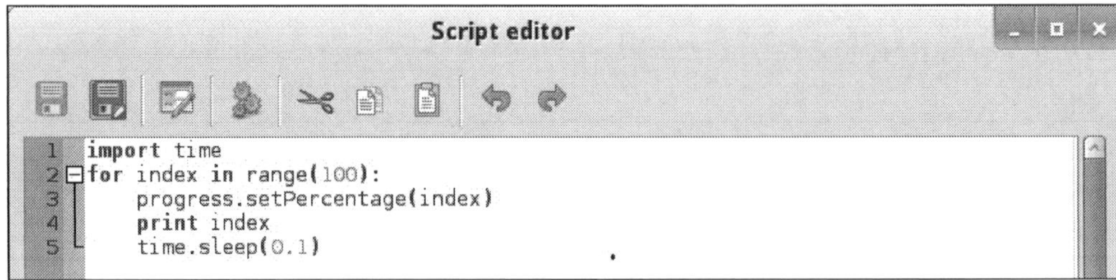

The default directory where processing will look for user scripts is `<your home dir>/.qgis2/processing/scripts/`.

So, our file script will be available with the name `<your home dir>/.qgis2/processing/scripts/emptyloop.py`.

The preceding script will count from 0 to 99. In addition, the algorithm will set the progress bar and write the step number in the Python console. The last instruction will wait for 0.1 seconds before running a loop again.

Looking at the custom script

Now, run the following processing command:

```
processing.alglist("empty")
```

This will generate the following output:

```
emptyloop------------------------------------------
>script:emptyloop
```

This shows that the processing toolbox knows our custom script with the name `script:emptyloop`.

Running the script

We can run the custom script as usual in the Python console with the following command:

```
processing.runalg("script:emptyloop")
```

This will increment the progress bar and will print progress in the console, as shown in the following screenshot:

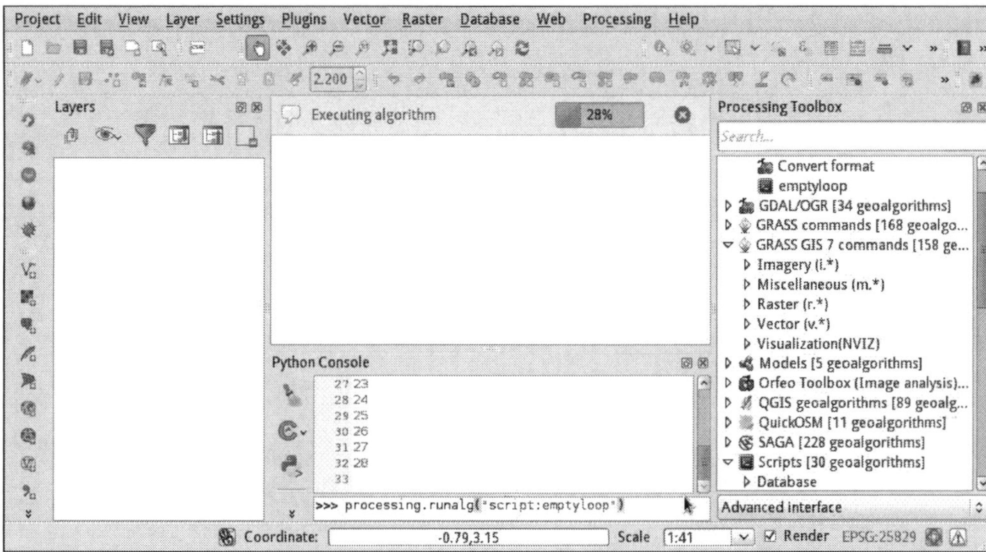

In this case, the progress bar will be opened in `QgsMessageBar` in the QGIS canvas because the algorithm is executed from the Python console.

Running an external algorithm or command

Often there are a bunch of legacy programs or scripts for which there are no resources to port them into another language or framework. Thanks to Python and PyQGIS, it's simple to integrate your existing programs into QGIS.

Running a simple command

We can run an external command in different ways, but we will explore how to do it with the processing toolbox that supports the progress bar, which is often useful to log algorithm steps.

To execute an external command, we will follow these steps:

1. Create a processing toolbox script called `runping`.
2. Code the script.
3. Test the script.

Step one is similar to that described in the *Creating a test processing toolbox script* section.

The code of the script is in the following code snippet:

```
import subprocess
import time

proc = subprocess.Popen(
    ["ping", "-c", "10", "localhost"],
    stdout=subprocess.PIPE,
    stdin=subprocess.PIPE,
    stderr=subprocess.PIPE)

counter = 0
for line in iter(proc.stdout.readline, ''):
    print line
    progress.setPercentage(counter)
    counter += 10
```

The preceding code runs the `ping` command to `localhost` and stops after `10` pings.

> In case of Windows OS, replace `["ping", "-c", "10", "localhost"]` with `["ping", "-n", "10", "localhost"]`.

There are different ways to run a system command in Python. The preceding method, using the `subprocess` module, allows for a non-blocking run and interaction with the program using the `stdin` pipe.

After creating a subprocess.Popen pipe, the code snippet starts a for loop to read the standard output of the stdout program printing the messages in the console.

> If your command is stuck in the QGIS interface, try to wrap it in a Python script and run the wrapper with ["python", "-i", "<your command wrapper>"] where your command wrapper could be simply a one-line code like import os; os.system("<your command>").

Run the runping script in the processing toolbox GUI by double-clicking on it. Its execution will produce the following screenshot:

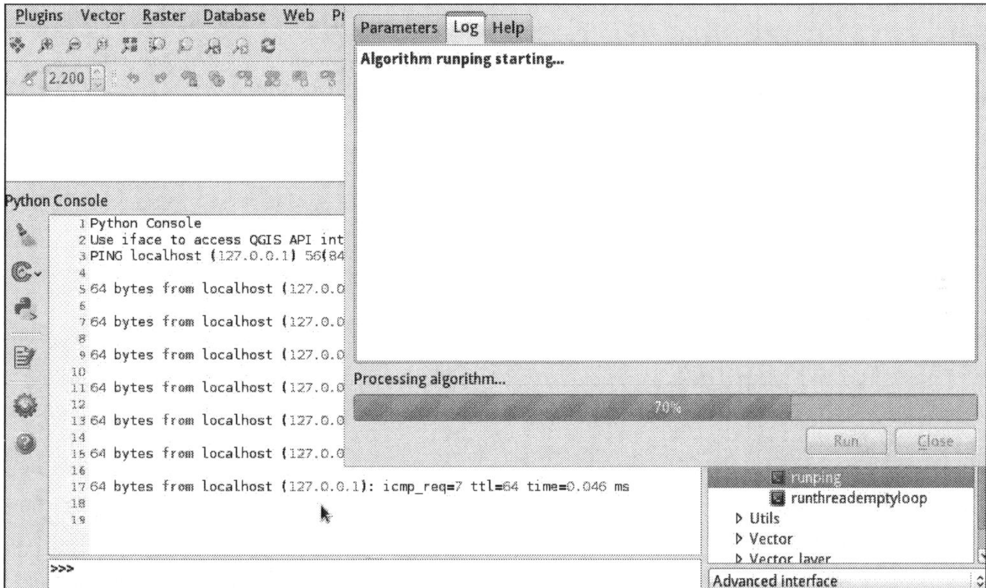

This shows progress in the progress bar of the processing toolbox and the output of the command in the Python console.

Interacting with the map canvas

A plugin will commonly interact with the map canvas to get some useful information. This information could be, for example, point coordinates or features identified by these coordinates. We can use them to draw geometry entities like points, lines, or polygons.

Getting the map canvas

The `QgsMapCanvas` class is the class that represents a QGIS canvas. There can be different canvas instances, but the main canvas instance can be referenced with the following code snippet:

```
mapCanvas = iface.mapCanvas()
```

The `QgsMapCanvas` class generates some useful events to support location-based plugins. For example, `xyCoordinates()` sends point locations based on canvas coordinates and the `keyPressed()` event allows us to know which mouse button has been clicked on the canvas.

Explaining Map Tools

The most powerful method to interact with a map canvas class is to set one of the predefined Map Tools or create a custom one that is derived from the predefined Map Tools classes.

In this chapter, we will not create custom Map Tools using inheritance and overloading, which are two basic concepts of the object-oriented programming paradigm. The following paragraphs are focused on using Map Tools that already exist and customizing them without deriving classes and overloading methods.

The base class for Map Tools is `QgsMapTool`, which has a set of specializations that can be useful for most of the user interaction with the canvas. These derived tools are listed as follows;

- `QgsMapToolEmitPoint`: This is focused on intercepting point clicks on canvas and returning the map coordinates
- `QgsMapToolIdentify`: This is focused on getting layer values at specified point-clicked coordinates
- `QgsMapToolIdentifyFeature`: This is similar to the previous tool, but results also reference the pointed features
- `QgsMapToolPan:` This is focused on managing panning and its events
- `QgsMapToolTouch:` This is focused on managing touch events on the canvas
- `QgsMapToolZoom:` This is focused on managing zoom events

Setting the current Map Tool

For each map canvas, only one map tool runs at a time. When it's necessary to set a Map Tool, it's good practice to get the previous one, and set it back again at the end of use of the new Map Tool. The following code snippet shows you how to get an old Map Tool, set a new one, and restore the previous one:

```
# import the map tool to use
from qgis.gui import QgsMapToolZoom
# get previous map tool and print it
oldMapTool = iface.mapCanvas().mapTool()
print "Previous map tool is a", oldMapTool
# create a zoom map tool pointing to the current canvas
# the boolean parameter is False to zoom in and True to zoom out
newMapTool = QgsMapToolZoom( iface.mapCanvas(), False)
# set the current map tool and print it
iface.mapCanvas().setMapTool( newMapTool )
print "Current map tool is a", iface.mapCanvas().mapTool()
#
# here is your code
#
# set the previous map tool and print it
iface.mapCanvas().setMapTool( oldMapTool )
print "Current map tool is a ", iface.mapCanvas().mapTool()
```

The preceding code will generate an output that is similar to the following console lines:

```
Previous map tool is a  <qgis._gui.QgsMapToolPan object at
0x7fe4a0e2e4d0>
Current map tool is a  <qgis._gui.QgsMapToolZoom object at
0x7fe4a13a04d0>
Current map tool is a  <qgis._gui.QgsMapToolPan object at
0x7fe4a0e2e4d0>
```

You will notice that changing the current Map Tool with `setMapTool()` will also change the cursor icon.

Getting point-click values

In this paragraph, we will create a code that will be useful to get point-click coordinates and print them in the console. We will use the `QgsMapToolEmitPoint` Map Tool, but the structure of the following code can be applied to other available Map Tools as well.

We will write all the code in the Python console, but it can be used in a custom plugin; for example, to create a GUI interface to trace mouse movement or to plot a polygon that is based on clicked points.

We will use the following steps for getting the clicked points:

1. Save the previous Map Tool.
2. Create a `QgsMapToolEmitPoint` Map Tool.
3. Create an event handler for the map canvas to trace mouse movement.
4. Register the event above the event handler to the `xyCoordinate` event.
5. Create an event handler for the Map Tool to trace clicked points by setting the following conditions:
    - If the left button clicked, then print coordinates
    - If the right button clicked, then restore the previous Map Tool
6. Register the event handler to the click event generated by the Map Tool.
7. Activate the new `QgsMapToolEmitPoint` Map Tool.

These steps are coded in the next paragraphs.

Getting the current Map Tool

To return to the current Map Tool after setting the new one, we need to save it in a variable that can be used later. We can get the current Map Tool by using the following code snippet:

```
previousMapTool = iface.mapCanvas().mapTool()
```

Creating a new Map Tool

We can create the Map Tool with this simple code snippet:

```
from qgis.gui import QgsMapToolEmitPoint
myMapTool =  QgsMapToolEmitPoint( iface.mapCanvas() )
```

You will notice that each Map Tool constructor needs a parameter that is the canvas on which it will operate.

Creating a map canvas event handler

An event handler is useful to execute actions that are based on user interaction with the canvas. First, we will create the handler that prints coordinates based on mouse movements on the canvas.

The event handler will receive the parameters passed by the event to which it is attached. The event handler will be attached to the `QgsMapCanvas` event, `xyCoordinates( QgsPoint )`, and it can be coded using the following code snippet:

```
def showCoordinates( currentPos ):
    print  "move coordinate %d - %d" % ( currentPos .x(),
currentPos.y() )
```

After creating the handler, we have to attach it to the canvas event with the following code:

```
iface.mapCanvas().xyCoordinates.connect( showCoordinates )
```

If you want to remove the handler, use the following code:

```
iface.mapCanvas().xyCoordinates.disconnect( showCoordinates )
```

Ensure that you write the function name as `showCoordinates` because if you don't pass any parameters to the `disconnect` call, then all handlers attached to the `xyCoordinates` event will be removed.

Creating a Map Tool event handler

An event handler will be attached to the `QgsMapToolEmitPoint` event, `canvasClicked( QgsPoint, Qt.MouseButton)`, and then it can be coded using the following code snippet:

```
# import the Qt module that contain mouse button definitions like
Qt.LeftButton or  Qt.RightButton used later
from PyQt4.QtCore import Qt
# create handler
def manageClick( currentPos, clickedButton ):
    if  clickedButton == Qt.LeftButton:
        print  "Clicked on %d - %d" % ( currentPos .x(),
currentPos.y() )
    if  clickedButton == Qt.RightButton:
        # reset to the previous mapTool
        iface.mapCanvas().setMapTool( previousMapTool )
        # clean remove myMapTool and relative handlers
        myMapTool.deleteLater()
```

After creating the handler, we have to attach it to the Map Tool event using the following code:

```
myMapTool.canvasClicked.connect( manageClick )
```

Setting up the new Map Tool

Now it's the time to activate the new Map Tool to pass canvas control to its event handlers. This can be done with the following code:

```
iface.mapCanvas().setMapTool( myMapTool )
```

After executing the preceding command, the new Map Tool will be activated and it will print coordinates in the console as shown in the following screenshot:

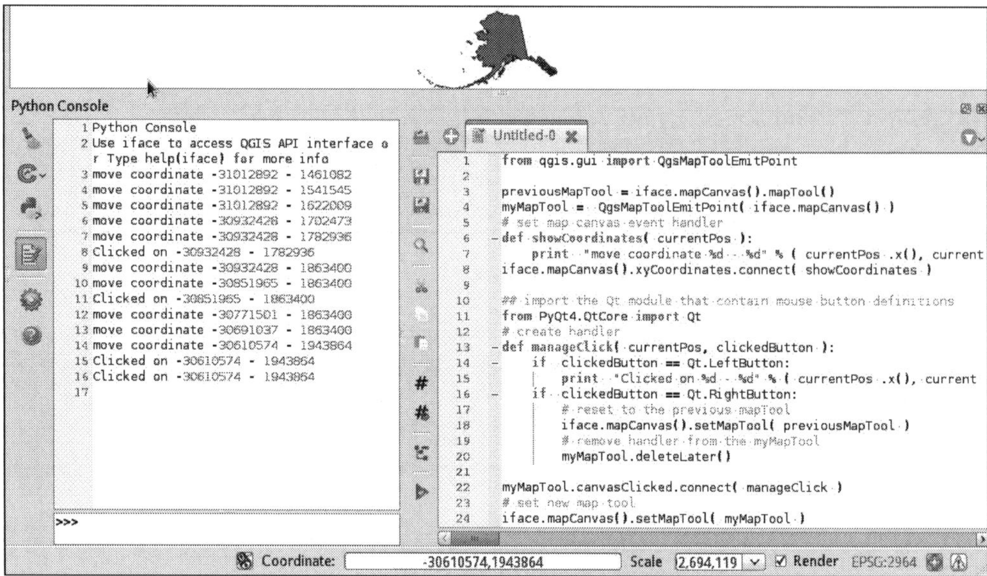

Right-click on the canvas to return to the previous Map Tool, but you still need to remove the canvas event handler. As explained in the previous paragraph, removing the `xyCoordinates` handler is done by executing the following code:

```
iface.mapCanvas().xyCoordinates.disconnect( showCoordinates )
```

Using point-click values

The previous paragraph explained how to get a point-click coordinate. This coordinate can be used to get the correspondent value in a raster layer or to get the underlying feature of a vector layer.

To identify a feature for a vector layer, it's better to use the dedicated Map Tool `QgsMapToolIdentifyFeature` directly, but for a raster layer that has point coordinates, we can use the `QgsRasterDataProvider.identify()` method to get raster values at a specified point.

By loading and selecting the `landcover` raster from `qgis_sample_data/raster`, we can modify the `manageClick` method of the previous example in the following way:

```
def manageClick( currentPos, clickedButton ):
    if  clickedButton == Qt.LeftButton:
        provider = iface.activeLayer().dataProvider()
        result = provider.identify( currentPos, QgsRaster.
IdentifyFormatValue )
        if result.isValid():
            print "Value at %d - %d" % ( currentPos.x(),
currentPos.y() )
            print result.results()
    if  clickedButton == Qt.RightButton:
        # reset to the previous mapTool
        iface.mapCanvas().setMapTool( previousMapTool )
        # clean remove myMapTool and relative handlers
        myMapTool.deleteLater()
```

Running the code of the previous paragraph with the `manageClick` function will generate an output similar to the following screenshot:

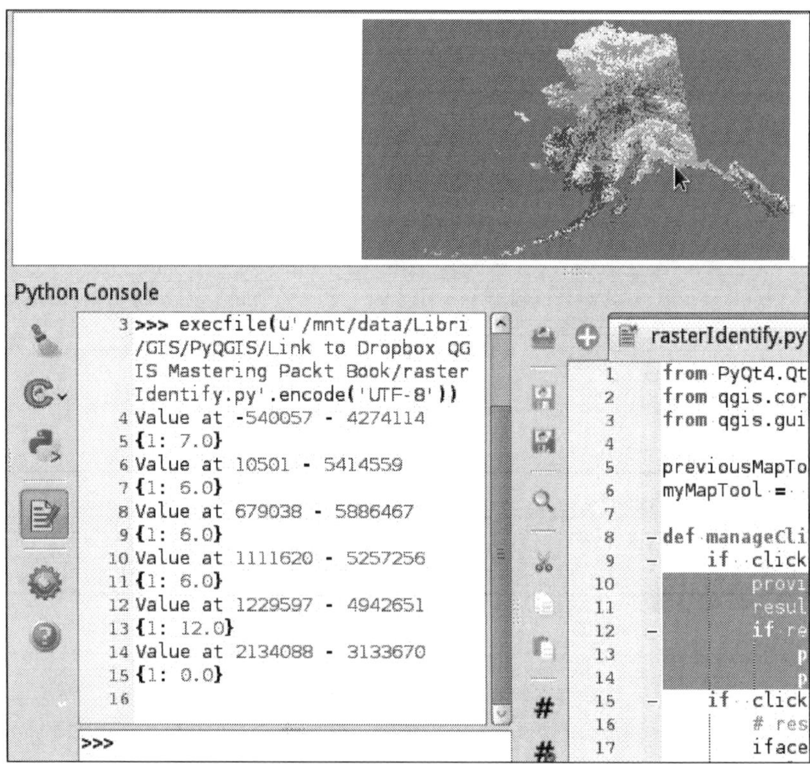

The result of the `identify()` call is a `QgsRasterIdentifyResult` object that contains all the information of the result. In this case, the return of `results()` is a Python dictionary with the band number as the key and the raster value in the clicked point as the value.

Exploring the QgsRubberBand class

A rubber band is the graphical canvas item that can be used to draw geometry elements on the canvas, for example, points, lines, or polygons. It is generally used in combination with a customized Map Tool to get click coordinates that are used to add or move points of the rubber band object.

The following code snippet will upgrade the previous example, to get canvas-click coordinates, to draw a polygon in the canvas:

```
from PyQt4.QtCore import Qt
from PyQt4.QtGui import QColor
from qgis.core import QGis
from qgis.gui import QgsMapToolEmitPoint, QgsRubberBand

previousMapTool = iface.mapCanvas().mapTool()
myMapTool =  QgsMapToolEmitPoint( iface.mapCanvas() )

# create the polygon rubber band associated to the current canvas
myRubberBand = QgsRubberBand( iface.mapCanvas(), QGis.Polygon )
# set rubber band style
color = QColor("red")
color.setAlpha(50)
myRubberBand.setColor(color)

def showCoordinates( currentPos ):
    if myRubberBand and myRubberBand.numberOfVertices():
        myRubberBand.removeLastPoint()
        myRubberBand.addPoint( currentPos )

iface.mapCanvas().xyCoordinates.connect( showCoordinates )

def manageClick( currentPos, clickedButton ):
    if clickedButton == Qt.LeftButton:
        myRubberBand.addPoint( currentPos )
    # terminate rubber band editing session
    if clickedButton == Qt.RightButton:
        # remove showCoordinates map canvas callback
        iface.mapCanvas().xyCoordinates.disconnect( showCoordinates )
        # reset to the previous mapTool
        iface.mapCanvas().setMapTool( previousMapTool )
        # clean remove myMapTool and relative handlers
        myMapTool.deleteLater()
        # remove the rubber band from the canvas
        iface.mapCanvas().scene().removeItem(myRubberBand)

myMapTool.canvasClicked.connect( manageClick )

iface.mapCanvas().setMapTool( myMapTool )
```

Executing the preceding code and clicking on the canvas with the left mouse button will produce results similar to the following screenshot:

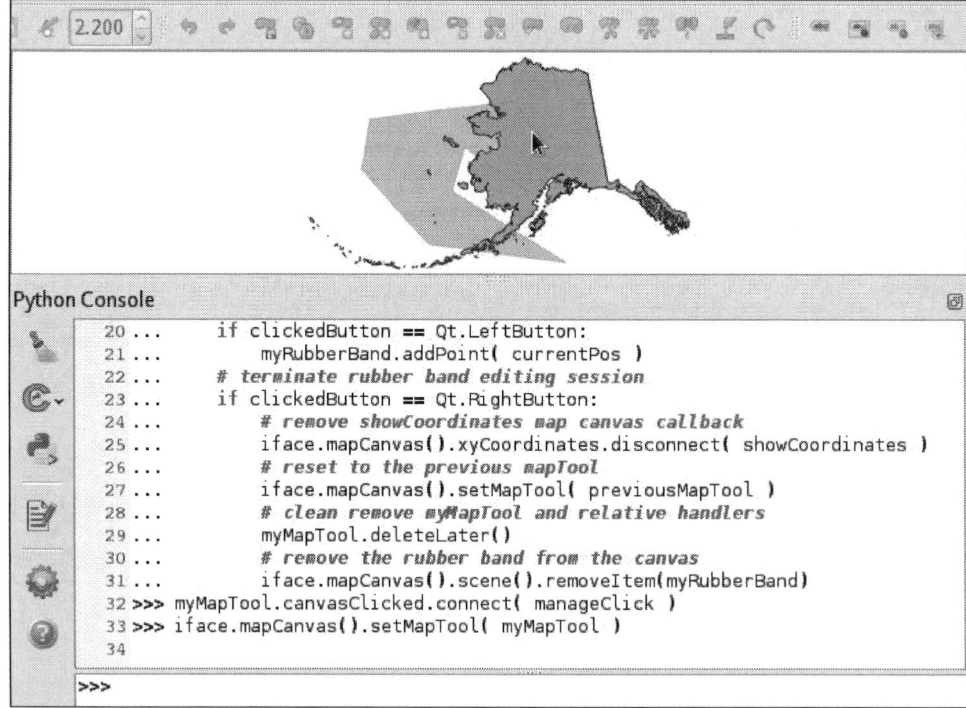

The image in the preceding screenshot has the `alaska.shp` layer as base map to show the evidence of the transparency of the drawn rubber band.

Summary

This chapter offered you a simplified way to interact with QGIS and it is more oriented towards a GIS analyst than a GIS programmer or a computer scientist. The chapter is also oriented to GIS companies that are interested in reusing code that is already developed but was probably developed for GIS platforms that are not free.

This chapter gives basic knowledge on how to interact with QGIS using the PyQGIS programming language.

We saw how to programmatically load different kinds of layers, from raster to vector. We also explained vectors and how to manage different kinds of vector resources, from filesystems to remote database connections. We also explored the vector structure in more detail and you learned how to browse and edit its records. Different kinds of editing workflows were proposed in the chapter so that you can interact with the QGIS framework in a better manner.

You learned how to launch processing toolbox algorithms and user-developed processing toolbox scripts to enhance QGIS with new functionalities. You also learned how to launch external commands or scripts to offer a way to integrate already developed code, and thereby reduce developing and testing costs.

Lastly, we explored the QGIS map canvas and how to interact with that using Map Tools. We obtained canvas coordinates and created new Map Tools to draw canvas objects. This will give you the basic skills needed to create new plugins that interact with layers displayed in the QGIS canvas.

Index

A

B

C

D

E

F

G

H

I

K

L

M

O

P

Q

R

U

V

W

Thank you for buying
Mastering QGIS

About Packt Publishing

Packt, pronounced 'packed', published its first book, *Mastering phpMyAdmin for Effective MySQL Management*, in April 2004, and subsequently continued to specialize in publishing highly focused books on specific technologies and solutions.

Our books and publications share the experiences of your fellow IT professionals in adapting and customizing today's systems, applications, and frameworks. Our solution-based books give you the knowledge and power to customize the software and technologies you're using to get the job done. Packt books are more specific and less general than the IT books you have seen in the past. Our unique business model allows us to bring you more focused information, giving you more of what you need to know, and less of what you don't.

Packt is a modern yet unique publishing company that focuses on producing quality, cutting-edge books for communities of developers, administrators, and newbies alike. For more information, please visit our website at `www.packtpub.com`.

About Packt Open Source

In 2010, Packt launched two new brands, Packt Open Source and Packt Enterprise, in order to continue its focus on specialization. This book is part of the Packt Open Source brand, home to books published on software built around open source licenses, and offering information to anybody from advanced developers to budding web designers. The Open Source brand also runs Packt's Open Source Royalty Scheme, by which Packt gives a royalty to each open source project about whose software a book is sold.

Writing for Packt

We welcome all inquiries from people who are interested in authoring. Book proposals should be sent to `author@packtpub.com`. If your book idea is still at an early stage and you would like to discuss it first before writing a formal book proposal, then please contact us; one of our commissioning editors will get in touch with you.

We're not just looking for published authors; if you have strong technical skills but no writing experience, our experienced editors can help you develop a writing career, or simply get some additional reward for your expertise.

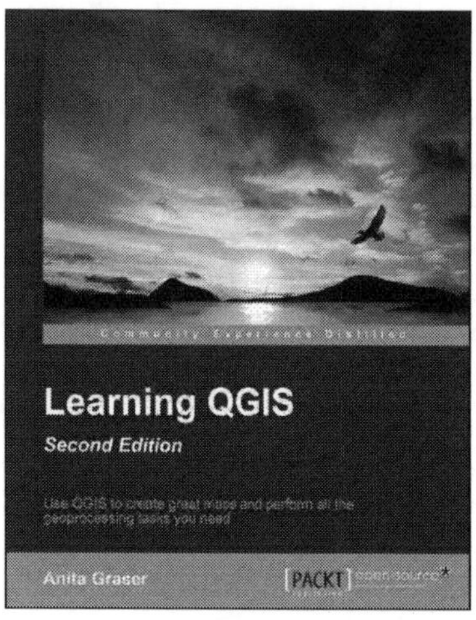

Learning QGIS

Second Edition

ISBN: 978-1-78439-203-1 Paperback: 150 pages

Use QGIS to create great maps and perform all the geoprocessing tasks you need

1. Load, visualize, and edit vector and raster data.
2. Create professional maps and applications to present geospatial data.
3. A concise guide, packed with detailed real-world examples to get you started with QGIS.

Building Mapping Applications with QGIS

ISBN: 978-1-78398-466-4 Paperback: 264 pages

Create your own sophisticated applications to analyze and display geospatial information using QGIS and Python

1. Make use of the geospatial capabilities of QGIS within your Python programs.
2. Build complete standalone mapping applications based on QGIS and Python.
3. Use QGIS as a Python geospatial development environment.

Please check **www.PacktPub.com** for information on our titles

PostGIS Cookbook

ISBN: 978-1-84951-866-6 Paperback: 484 pages

Over 80 task-based recipes to store, organize, manipulate, and analyze spatial data in a PostGIS database

1. Integrate PostGIS with web frameworks and implement OGC standards such as WMS and WFS using MapServer and GeoServer.
2. Convert 2D and 3D vector data, raster data, and routing data into usable forms.
3. Visualize data from the PostGIS database using a desktop GIS program such as QGIS and OpenJUMP.

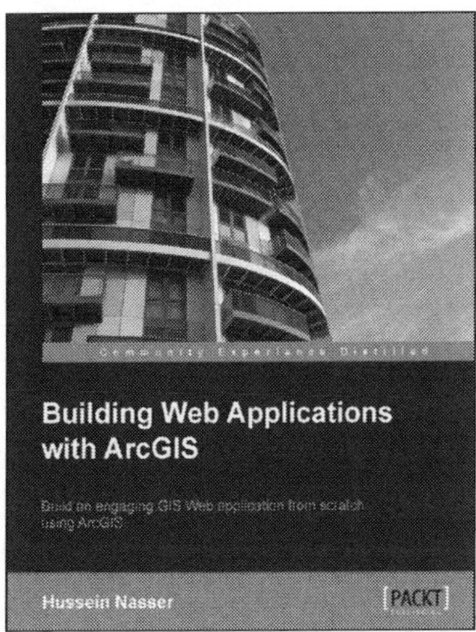

Building Web Applications with ArcGIS

ISBN: 978-1-78355-295-5 Paperback: 138 pages

Build an engaging GIS Web application from scratch using ArcGIS

1. Learn how to design, build, and run high performance and interactive applications with the help of ArcGIS.
2. Incorporate ArcGIS for Server services to allow end users to visualize, query, and edit GIS data using the ArcGIS JavaScript APIs.
3. Step-by-step tutorial that teaches you how to design and customize a GIS web application from scratch.

37991974R00235

Made in the USA
San Bernardino, CA
28 August 2016